BEGINNER'S
BENGALI (BANGLA)
with Audio CD

BEGINNER'S BENGALI (BANGLA)
with Audio CD

Hanne-Ruth Thompson

Hippocrene Books, Inc.
New York

For information, address:
HIPPOCRENE BOOKS, INC.
171 Madison Ave.
New York, NY 10016
www.hippocrenebooks.com

Library of Congress Cataloging-in-Publication Data

Names: Thompson, Hanne-Ruth, author.
Title: Beginner's Bengali (Bangla), with audio cd / by Hanne-Ruth Thompson.
Description: New York : Hippocrene Books, Inc., [2017] | Includes index.
Identifiers: LCCN 2016037208| ISBN 9780781813525 (pbk./with audio CD) |
  ISBN 0781813522 (pbk./with audio CD)
Subjects: LCSH: Bengali language--Textbooks for foreign speakers--English. |
  Bengali language--Spoken Bengali. | Bengali language--Self-instruction. |
  Bengali lanugage--Sound recordings for English speakers.
Classification: LCC PK1657 .T48 2017 | DDC 491.4/482421--dc23
LC record available at https://lccn.loc.gov/2016037208

Printed in the United States of America.

CONTENTS

ACKNOWLEDGEMENTS

Most of this book was written in Freetown, Sierra Leone, where my husband was working for the Department of International Development for three years from 2012 to 2015. Almost as soon as we got to Freetown, I was lucky in finding a keen beginner Bangla learner, Imran Shahryar, to teach and to test out some ideas on. We established a monthly Bangla Adda with Bengali friends working in Sierra Leone. Apart from Imran, I am particularly grateful to Dr. Hashina Begum, Shumon Sengupta, Afrina Karim, Helal Uddin, Nasir Uddin Khan, and Sudipto Mukerjee for their warmth and support. Of course, the influences on this book go back a lot further than just these last three years in Sierra Leone. My Bangladeshi family in Kashipur, Dr. Monsur Musa of Dhaka University, Professor Probal Dasgupta at the ISI in Kolkata, Dr. Mina Dan, and my PhD supervisor, colleague, and friend Dr. William Radice have all given me invaluable encouragement over the years. I am grateful to my wonderful recording artists Sahana, Sunny, Richie, and Bulbul in London, and Bappy and Prince in Dhaka.

BENGALI/BANGLA, BENGAL AND BANGLADESH

Bengali/Bangla is the language of Bangladesh and of the Indian states of Paschim Banga (formerly West Bengal), Tripura, and South Assam. (Paschim Banga is pronounced pôshcim bɔnggô.) With a total of almost 200 million speakers, it is the seventh most-spoken language in the world. Bengali/Bangla has a long history and a rich literature of a thousand years and is a direct descendant of Sanskrit, a sister language to Hindi/Urdu, Telugu, Nepali, Marathi, and other Indian languages. It has its own script, distinct from Devanagari which is used for Sanskrit, Hindi, and Nepali.

In 1947, the new-born independent India was split into two: the predominantly Hindu India and the Muslim country of Pakistan. The Eastern part of Bengal (now Bangladesh) was mainly Muslim and became a province of Pakistan with the whole of India separating it from the rest of the country and from the seat of the central government in Karachi. Unlike the other provinces of Pakistan, East Pakistan was very densely populated and more than half of the total Pakistani population was Bengali. In the attempt to establish some kind of national unity, the government declared Urdu to be the only state language of Pakistan; but this situation soon became unbearable to the East Pakistani Bengalis. While they had at first welcomed the idea of a Muslim country, they became more and more aware of their Bengali identity and numerous movements and protests took place to get Bangla recognized as a state language of Pakistan. At a Dhaka University rally on 21 February 1952, five students were shot dead by the police. They were instantly regarded as national martyrs and a Shahid Minar (martyrs' monument) was built in their memory and 21 February was made a national holiday and observed as Language Movement Day in Bangladesh. It took another four years before Bangla was recognized as a state language but the Bengalis continued to feel sidelined by the government. Decades of protests and struggle against the Pakistani government led to a nine-month-long brutal civil war in 1971. On 16 December 1971 Bangladesh became an independent country.

The Bangla language also, of course, continues to be spoken in Paschim Banga, and in the nearly seventy years since the two halves of the former province of Bengal were divided, some differences have developed in the way the language is spoken. For instance: the preposition *after* is পরে pɔre in Bangladesh, বাদে bade in Paschim Banga; an *orphan* is এতিম etim in Bangladesh, অনাথ ɔnath in Paschim Banga; *water* is পানি pani in Bangladesh, জল jɔl in Paschim Banga; *vegetables* are সবজি sôbji in Bangladesh, আনাজ anaj in Paschim Banga. However, these differences are not (yet?) significant enough to justify the question "Which Bangla?" This book may have a slight bias towards Bangladesh, simply because that is where the author learned her Bangla, but what is being taught in this book is the Standard Bangla language which is spoken in Dhaka as well as in Kolkata. In the glossary at the end of the book, variations in vocabulary are indicated by BD for Bangladesh, PB for Paschim Banga.

The name 'Bengali' for the language was established during the time of British Rule in India (1858 to 1947) and has been widely used in the West. It is seen by some Bengali linguists as a colonial name and they, followed by many Western linguists, have changed to using the name 'Bangla' for the language and 'Bengali' for the people. This is the practice adopted in this book. At the moment we still use Bengali (Bangla) in the titles of our books but in twenty years time it will probably be Bangla (Bengali).

LEARNING BANGLA: SOME GUIDELINES

You have decided to learn Bangla and with that decision you have made an excellent choice. Bangla is a rich and beautiful language that will give you access to a fascinating new world, colorful new impressions (think of those sarees!), deliciously spiced food, sounds so sweet that just listening to them will make you tingle, breathtakingly gorgeous landscapes full of vast rivers and endless rice-fields, and people who are no doubt among the most warm-hearted and hospitable in the world.

Anyone seriously interested in learning a new language ought to spend some time in the homeland of that language and find people with whom to practice. No book can be a substitute for real communication. But books offer two particular features that can be an invaluable support to your language learning: they can slow things down to a manageable pace and they build up the language gradually, systematically and from close up. They introduce you to the components and functions of the languages and show you how to practice and eventually master them. Unlike in a real communicative situation, you are in charge with a book, you set the pace and determine what and how much you want to learn—a book will never rush you.

Learning a new language takes you out of your comfort zone. This book will help you to step out of that comfort zone calmly and confidently. The book takes you, step by step, through the main areas and processes of the Bangla language in a graded and systematic way. Bangla is not as difficult to learn as you might expect. The initial challenge of learning a new script can be an enjoyable and rewarding journey of discovery. Unit 1 deals with the sounds and the script of Bangla: it sets them out comprehensively and clearly. This Unit should be considered a reference chapter as you will want to return to it again and again during your learning progress. From Unit 2 onward you will be introduced to the main grammatical categories and procedures of the language.

Some students have an instinctive dislike of grammar and grammatical terms. (Why bother to learn what a participle is when you could be learning **real** language instead?) But think about it: if you were training to become a chef, you would want to know what your ingredients and the different cooking processes were called, because only by naming things do we really get to know and understand them. The instinctive acquisition of language that we all went through as children is no longer available to us as adults and we need to replace it with a conscious awareness of what goes on in a language. Learning about grammar gives us the equipment to master a new language well. In learning a language (as in cooking) you want to be able to be creative, make your own sentences (dishes), make sense of the whole thing and express yourself. In order to do this, you need to understand how it works and what the ingredients do. There is nothing more deadening and disheartening in language learning than ready-made phrases learned parrot-fashion without really understanding them. Learning a language is about empowerment and confidence building. In this book you will be given the ingredients, the tools, and the processes to take control of your own learning. (*A glossary of grammar terms is given on page xv.*)

The Bangla words you will be learning here constitute the raw ingredients for you to work with. It is sensible to build up a good routine with your vocabulary learning right from the start. Learning your words in groups (animals, colors, parts of the body, numbers, fruit, etc.) or in contexts will help you to remember them better. Make flashcards for yourself or keep a vocabulary notebook or both, and remember that a few words frequently (say five or ten every day) is a lot more effective than long lists of words all in one go. Each Unit contains a list of new words in the order they appear in the dialogue or narrative. Learn these words in batches or pick out the ones that are most relevant to you to learn first. Learning vocabulary is not a one-time activity: it needs constant revision and, if at all possible, practical application, e.g. try to integrate your newly-learned Bangla vocabulary into your everyday life, even if it is just putting up little post-it notes with the Bangla words for household or food items on your fridge. Take your Bangla with you wherever you are—don't limit it to a separate language-learning slot which doesn't interact with your real life. The more real-life situations you can bring Bangla into, the easier it will be for you to learn.

Listening to spoken Bangla is of crucial importance to your learning process. This book is accompanied by recordings of all the dialogues and the narratives as well as the alphabet and numbers to one hundred. This has the advantage that you can listen and read at the same time. But apart from this, there is a whole world of Bangla sounds available on the Internet—songs, movies, dialogues, recitations, etc. It is worth checking this out and setting aside a little time for just listening: it does not matter if you don't understand everything at first, but surrounding yourself with the sounds of Bangla is a great way to adjust your ear and get into 'the zone.'

GLOSSES

The gloss is a paraphrased translation of the Bangla words. A gloss is given in Units 2 to 5 in addition to the transliteration and translation of the dialogues and narratives. The gloss can help you to understand the composition and components (morphemes) of words. Bangla nouns have case endings and indicators for plural and definiteness all combined into one word. Bangla verbs have person and tense indicators. A translation of these individual lexical items usually requires more than one word in English. In order to show that we are referring to one lexical item in Bangla, the English words in the gloss are written together and separated by full stops, for instance বাড়িতে baṛite at.home; ছেলেটিকে cheleṭike to.the.boy; তুমি বলবে tumi bôlbe you you.will.say. The layout of the glosses underneath the Bangla and transliteration should make it easy for you to see what the glosses refer to. They are not meant to be read as an ongoing sentence but provide information on each individual word.

An example of a Bangla sentence with transliteration, gloss, and translation:

Bangla:	আমরা বাংলায়ও	টেবিল বলি।	
Transliteration:	amra baṃlaŷo	ṭebil	bôli
Gloss:	we	in.Bangla.also	table	we say
Translation:	*We also say table in Bangla.*		

GRAMMAR TERMS
for Beginner Learners of Bangla

Many of us don't know very much about language structure in general until we start learning a foreign language. Building up language awareness helps us to recognize patterns, not only in the language we are learning, but also in our own language. This awareness helps us to ask relevant questions and speed up our learning processes considerably. It is therefore worth investing some time and effort in familiarizing yourself with the terminology. This list is intended as a reference for you when you need it. There is little point in learning these terms by heart as long as you have no context for them, but when you get to the actual language structures, you will quickly realize that grammar and grammatical terminology actually give us the tools we need and, more often than not, provide a short-cut to successful language learning.

ACTIVE: a type of sentence that has a nominative subject and agreement between the subject and the verb

ADJECTIVE: a word that describes or modifies nouns: *the **awful** truth, a **beautiful** mind*

ADVERB: a word that is used to modify verbs, adjectives, or sentences, e.g., *slowly, very, quite*; when there is more than one word involved we call them adverbials or adverb clauses, e.g., *very soon, at 12 o'clock*

AGREEMENT: a formal concord between subject and verb; 1st-person pronouns take 1st-person verb endings; 3rd-person nouns take 3rd-person verb endings.

ANIMATE: Bangla makes a distinction between animate and inanimate nouns in, for instance, the formation of the plural.

ARTICLE: a class of words that qualify nouns. In English we have definite and indefinite articles: ***the** Wizard of Oz* (definite), ***an** American in Paris* (indefinite). Instead of articles, Bangla has a small number of classifiers that distinguish between singular and plural and between definite and indefinite noun phrases.

ASPECT: a grammatical category of the verb that expresses a type of temporal activity: e.g., progressive (continuous) *the birds are singing*; perfective *the prophet has spoken*

ASPIRATION: the property of consonants that are pronounced with a puff of air; aspirated consonants in Bangla are: খ kh, ঘ gh, ছ ch, ঝ jh, ঠ ṭh, ঢ ḍh, থ th, ধ dh, ফ ph, ভ bh

ATTRIBUTIVE: adjectives that occur as modifiers within a noun phrase, describing the noun: *the **blue** car, the **proud** parents*

CASE: a category of nouns and pronouns, marked by case endings, to show a grammatical relationship. In English, pronouns have some case distinctions, e.g., *he, his, him*; but nouns only distinguish the genitive, *the girl's*. Bangla has four cases for nouns and pronouns: nominative, genitive, objective, and locative.

CAUSATIVE: verbs expressing a causal relationship, e.g., in English the verb *lie* has a causative *lay = cause to lie*

CLASSIFIER: noun attachments which determine properties like singular and plural, definiteness and indefiniteness; টা ṭa, টি ṭi, জন jɔn, খানা khana, গুলো gulo are classifiers in Bangla

CLAUSE: a group of words containing a subject and predicate and functioning as part of a complex or compound sentence: ***the tiger who came to tea*** is a clause

COMPLEMENT: the predicate in equational (copulative) sentences

COMPOUND: two words of the same class used together to express one meaning; e.g., in English, ***sitting room, water dispenser*** are compound nouns; e.g., in Bangla, ভুলে যাওয়া bhule yaoŷa *forget*, খেয়ে ফেলা kheŷe phæla *eat up* are compound verbs.

COMPOUND MAKER: one of a small number of verbs that can combine with the perfective participle of other verbs to form a compound verb

COMPOUND VERB: a type of verb in Bangla that combines a perfective participle with a compound maker to express one meaning

CONCESSIVE: in apparent contradiction to the main argument, expressing: *in spite of, although*

CONDITIONAL: expressing a condition: *if you come*

CONDITIONAL PARTICIPLE: the non-finite verb form in Bangla which ends in –le: করলে kôrle, গেলে gele, হলে hôle

CONJUGATION: the systematic change of verb forms to express tense, person, degree of politeness

CONJUNCT: consonant cluster

CONJUNCTION: connecting words, e.g., *and, but, although, because*

CONJUNCT VERB: a type of verb in Bangla that consists of a noun or adjective plus a common verb

CONSONANT: a sound that is produced by closing part of the vocal tract, as opposed to a vowel (*see* VOWEL)

COPULA: a type of verb that serves to connect two equal parts of a sentence, e.g., *the day **is** done, nothing **seems** right, if I **were** a rich man* (*see* EQUATIONAL)

COUNT NOUN: a noun that can form a plural and, in the singular, can be used with the indefinite article (e.g. *books, a book; ideas, an idea*)—contrasts with mass (or non-count) nouns: water, flour, happiness. Bangla classifiers such as টা ṭa, টি ṭi and গুলো gulo occur with count nouns.

DEFINITE: In English, definite noun phrases are formed with *the* before the noun; in Bangla they are formed with টা ṭa, টি ṭi, খানা khana, গুলো gulo, or গুলি guli after the noun.

DEMONSTRATIVE: pointing words like এ e *this* and ও o *that*

DIRECT OBJECT: the part of the sentence that is the goal of the verbal action, e.g., *to kill a mockingbird, tie a yellow ribbon*

EQUATIONAL: the type of sentence that has a copula (a word used to link subject and predicate), e.g., *how green was my valley*

EXPERIENCER: a human being involved in an event. In many Bangla sentences this experiencer is not the grammatical subject of the sentence. Experiencer contrasts with the subject in impersonal sentences.

EXTENDED VERB: a type of verb in Bangla that has a two-syllable verb stem and a verbal noun ending in নো no: e.g., পাঠা-নো paṭha-no *send* and বানা-নো banano *prepare*

FAMILIAR: form of address, in many languages distinct from a polite or honorific form

FINITE: verb forms that contain endings for person and tense – most sentences contain a finite verb form (*see* NON-FINITE)

GENITIVE: a noun case, can express possession (***Jenny's** skirt*) or association (***Gulliver's** travels*)

HONORIFIC: polite form of address (*see* POLITE; FAMILIAR)

IMPERATIVE: an order-giving mode: ***meet me** in St Louis!, **don't look** now!*

IMPERFECTIVE PARTICIPLE: the non-finite verb form in Bangla that ends in –te: করতে kôrte, যেতে yete, হতে hôte

IMPERSONAL: a type of sentence that does not have a 'doing' subject, e.g., *it makes sense*

INDEFINITE: in English, indefinite noun phrases are formed with *a* before the noun; in Bangla they are formed with একটা ækṭa, একটি ekṭi, etc. before the noun.

INDIRECT OBJECT: the part of the sentence for or towards whom the action is performed; in the sentence *I gave you my heart* we have a direct object, *my heart,* and an indirect object, *you.*

INFINITIVE: a non-finite verb form. In English, the base form of a verb or used with *to*, e.g., *you can't **take** it with you* or *nowhere **to hide**, an affair **to remember***

INTERROGATIVE: relating to questions

LOCATIVE: a case of the noun, used, for instance, to express location or direction

MEASURE WORD: words that indicate a measure of some kind, such as distance, stretch of time, weight, volume. The classifier টা ṭa is not used with measure words.

MODAL: anything that goes beyond a mere stating or questioning of facts, such as suggestions, commands, suppositions, promises, or threats, counts as a modal feature

MODIFIER: all the words in a noun phrase that are not the noun itself

MORPHOLOGY: the branch of grammar that studies the structure (or composition) of words

NOMINATIVE: the base form of nouns and pronouns (*see* CASE)

NON-FINITE: verb forms that are not conjugated and do not stand alone in a sentence (*see* FINITE). Each Bangla verb has four non-finite verb forms: verbal noun, imperfective participle (IP), perfective participle (PP), and conditional participle (CP).

NOUN: naming words like *book, potato, moon, Eric, disaster*

NOUN PHRASE: a noun together with its modifiers

OBJECT: the sentence part towards which the action of the verb is directed: *I asked **him**, he denied **his statement**.* (*See also* DIRECT OBJECT; INDIRECT OBJECT)

OBJECT(IVE) CASE: a case of the noun used to indicate direct and indirect objects. In Bangla, the object case ending –কে –ke is added to animate objects and sometimes to inanimate objects.

PARTICIPLE: a non-finite verb form that functions as a clause or an adjective: ***towering** inferno, **gone** with the wind*

PARTICLE: a grammatical term that is used for non-essential, short, indeclinable words

PASSIVE: derived from active structures: *he built the house: the house was built (by him)*

PERFECTIVE PARTICIPLE: the non-finite verb form in Bangla that ends in –e, e.g., করে kôre *having done*, গিয়ে giŷe *having gone*

PHONEME: the smallest sound unit in language that makes a difference in meaning

PHONOLOGY: the study of the sound systems of languages

PHRASE: a group of two or more grammatically related words that form a sense unit expressing a thought. A phrase goes with a single part of speech such as a noun, a verb, an adverb, or a pre/postposition: ***under** the tree* is a prepositional phrase; *the older **students*** is a noun phrase.

PLURAL: more than one

POLITE: respectful form of address (many languages, including Bangla, distinguish between a familiar and a polite form)

POSSESSIVE: expresses belonging

POSTPOSITION: has the same function as a preposition, but comes **after** the noun phrase; a language has either prepositions or postpositions: English has prepositions; Bangla has postpositions.

PREDICATE: the part of a sentence that is not the SUBJECT. The subject and predicate together form a sentence. A predicate can consist of a verb, with or without OBJECTS, or of a COMPLEMENT.

PREDICATIVE: adjectives are often used as compliments in a sentence: *the children were **asleep**, the climb is **dangerous***; predicative adjectives contrast with ATTRIBUTIVE adjectives.

PREPOSITION: a word that positions a noun, e.g., ***in, against, for, beyond***; prepositions form prepositional phrases: ***on** the waterfront, **within** our lifetime, **under** the influence (Bangla does not use prepositions; see POSTPOSITION)*

PRO-DROP: omission of nominative and sometimes objective pronouns where their reference can be inferred from the context

PROGRESSIVE: an aspect expressing an ongoing or repeated process: *they were talking, he was knocking*

PRONOUN: a word that takes the place of a previously mentioned noun, e.g., *John was angry, but **he** didn't know why. **I, you, we, us** are also pronouns.*

QUANTIFIER: words that specify an amount: অনেক ɔnek *much,* সব sɔb *all,* কিছু kichu *some*

REFLEXIVE: referring back to itself, e.g., *he is washing **himself**, they are proud of **themselves***

RELATIVE: a kind of pronoun relating to something already mentioned; e.g., *the man **who** knew too much*

ROOT: the basic unit that carries the meaning of a word, e.g., from the Latin root "flux" *flow* we have English words like *fluent, influence, fluctuate, fluid*

SEMANTICS: the study of meaning of language

SENTENCE: a grammatically self-contained unit of speech or writing

SINGULAR: one

STEM: the base form (usually of a verb) to which endings are added

SUBORDINATE CLAUSE: dependent clause; a sentence that cannot stand on its own, e.g., **why we fight*

SUBJECT: the noun, pronoun, or noun phrase in the sentence that is usually in the nominative case and that has agreement with the finite verb. Bangla also has genitive experiencer subjects without verb agreement.

SYNTAX: sentence structure

TENSE: expression of time in verbs; the most basic tenses are past, present, future

VERB: word class (doing or action words) *ride, consider, forget, destroy*

VERB ENDING: added to the stem of the verb for use in sentences, e.g., *walk: we walk**ed** home, he was walk**ing** away*

VERBAL NOUN: a non-finite verb form that is used as a noun: করা kɔra *doing,* যাওয়া yaoŷa *going,* হওয়া hɔoŷa *being.*

VOWEL: a sound that has no audible constriction, e.g., vowels *a, e, i, o, u,* as opposed to consonants

WORD CLASS: a group of words that share the same syntactic features

ZERO VERB: the copula in simple present equational sentences in Bangla

---

* indicates that an example is ungrammatical

ABBREVIATIONS

(for verb class abbreviations see below)

adj.	adjective
adv.	adverb
B	Bangladesh
CL	classifier
CP	conditional participle
cvb.	compound verb
conj.	conjunction
emp.	emphasizer
excl.	exclamation
expr.	expressing
f.	female
fam.	familiar
fut.	future
GEN.	genitive
H.	Hindu
hon.	honorific
imp.	imperative
IP.	imperfective participle (*formerly*: infinitive)
LOC.	locative
m.	male
Musl.	Muslim
num.	numeral
ord.	ordinary
PB	Paschim Banga (West Bengal)
per.	person (grammatical)
p.c.	past continuous
p.hab.	past habitual
phr.	phrase
pl.	plural
pp.	postposition
PP.	perfective participle
p.perf.	past perfect
p.s.	past simple
pr.	pronoun
pr.c.	present continuous
pr.perf.	present perfect
pr.s.	present simple
qu.	question word
rel.	relative (pronoun)
sg.	singular
vb.	verb
vn.	verbal noun

Verb classes abbreviations

Verb conjugation is determined by the stem formation of the verb. Bangla verbs have the following stem formations:

Class 1:

CVC = consonant – vowel – consonant, e.g., বল- bɔl–

VC = vowel – consonant, e.g., ওঠ oṭh–

Class 2:

CaC = consonant – a – consonant, e.g., থাক- thak

aC = a – consonant, e.g., আস- as–

Class 3:

CV or Ca = consonant – vowel or consonant – a, e.g., দে- de- or যা- ya–

Class 4:

CVCa or CaCa = consonant – vowel (incl. a) – consonant – a, e.g., ঘুমা- ghuma or লাগা- laga

UNIT 1
SOUNDS AND SCRIPT

This chapter sets out all you need to know about Bangla sounds and the Bangla script in a systematic and progressive order, so that you can come back to it for reference at any time. Learning the script will take time, practice, and lots of revision.

There is, on the whole, a good match between spelling and pronunciation in Bangla, so learning the script and the sounds together works well.

1. The Script: An Overview

The Bangla alphabet is divided into vowels and consonants, with a few other symbols in between the two groups. The Bangla script has some similarities with Hindi (Devanagari): there is only one set of letters, i.e., the distinction between lower case and upper case letters is absent. The letters hang from a top line rather than standing on a bottom line (as they do in English). The top line is usually written first but note that there are some letters without the top line.

আনারস *pineapple*   আ না র স
                        a na rɔ s

Even if you do not intend to produce hand-written documents in Bangla, it is a good idea, as well as an enjoyable experience, to practice writing the letters. Practicing individual letters and making them into words will add a tangible, physical dimension to your learning and will make it much easier for you to recognize the letters in Bangla sentences. As you are beginning to write Bangla letters, it is useful to know that the hand movement goes in the opposite direction from when you are writing English letters:

English (from bottom left to top right):   Bangla (from bottom right to top left):

eeeeeee   ɘɘɘɘɘɘɘ

Vowels and vowel signs

All vowels in Bangla, except for the first inherent vowel অ ɔ/ô have two symbols; one for the full vowel written at the beginning of words or syllables and a vowel sign that is attached to consonants. These vowel signs occur before, after, underneath, or around the consonant, but wherever the vowel sign is attached, it is always pronounced after the consonant. This means that a consonant–vowel combination forms a syllable. Where no vowel sign is written, the inherent vowel is usually pronounced, e.g., কলা banana is pronounced kɔla. From a linguistic viewpoint, this type of writing system where vowels are attached to consonants and there is an (unwritten) inherent vowel is called an abugida or a syllabic alphabet.

This is shown in Chart 1. Examples are given for each letter.

CHART 1: Bangla vowels and vowel signs

This chart gives the following information:

Col. 1: full vowel
Col. 2: vowel sign that is attached to consonants
Col. 3: transliteration of the Bangla letter *(see below for explanation of transliteration)*
Col. 4: position of each vowel in combinations with consonants
Col. 5: demonstration of each vowel with the consonant ক k

1	2	3	4	5
অ	- inherent	ɔ/ô	no vowel sign is written	ক– kɔ
আ	া	a	after the consonant	কা ka
ই	ি	i	before the consonant	কি ki
ঈ	ী	ī	after the consonant	কী kī
উ	ু	u	underneath the consonant	কু ku
ঊ	ূ	ū	underneath the consonant	কূ kū
å	ৃ	ṙ	underneath the consonant	কৃ kṙ
এ	ে , ৈ	e, æ	before the consonant	কে ke
ঐ	ৈ , ৈ	oi	before the consonant	কৈ koi
ও	ে ... া	o	around the consonant	কো ko
ঔ	ে ... ৗ	ou	around the consonant	কৌ kou

When two vowels follow one another, the second vowel is written as the full vowel:
কেউ = keu *someone,* দাও = dao *give,* তাই = tai *so, therefore*
(see also: Adjacent Consonants, page 33).

Consonants
Chart 2 shows the sounds and symbols of the Bangla consonants. This chart is arranged by the articulation and positioning of the consonants in the mouth for those of you who like to know the logic behind the alphabetical arrangement. It is not essential for you to know all the terminology in order to learn the letters. Note that this chart gives the sounds (i.e., the pronunciation) NOT a transliteration, of the Bangla letters. The transliteration is given in Alphabetical Order List (page 4).

CHART 2: Consonants
Positioning of Bangla consonants in the mouth (with pronunciation)

front of the mouth _ _ _ _ _ _ _ _ back of the mouth

	labial	dental	retroflex (cerebral)	palatal	velar	post-velar
plosives (stops)						
voiceless						
unaspirated	p পূ	t তৎ	ṭ ট	c চ	k ক	
aspirated	ph ফ	th থ	ṭh ঠ	ch ছ	kh খ	
voiced						
unaspirated	b ব	d দ	ḍ ড	j জয	g গ	
aspirated	bh ভ	dh ধ	ḍh ঢ	jh ঝ	gh ঘ	
nasals	m ম	n ন	n ণ	ñ এঃ	ng ংঙ	
flaps		r র	ṛ ড়, ṛh ঢ়			
lateral		l ল				
spirants		sh স	sh ষ	sh শ		h হ

R01

Bangla Alphabetical Order with transliteration
(*read across and then down*)

This one is important! If at all possible, make an enlarged photocopy of this list and keep it with you when you are beginning to read Bangla to remind you of how each letter is pronounced.

Vowels (with vowels signs)

অ - ɔ, ô   আ া a   ই ি i   ঈ ী ī

উ ু u   ঊ ূ ū   ঋ ৃ ṙ (ri)   এ েে e, æ

ঐ ৈ oi   ও ে cons ৗ o   ঔ ে cons ৗ ou

য় ŷ (semivowel) pronounced y or w

Other symbols

ং ṃ (ng)   ঃ ḥ   ँ ~ (nasal)

Consonants

ক k	খ kh	গ g	ঘ gh	ঙ ṅ
চ c	ছ ch	জ j	ঝ jh	ঞ ñ
ট ṭ	ঠ ṭh	ড ḍ ড় ṛ	ঢ ḍh ঢ় ṛh	ণ ṇ
ত t ৎ t̲	থ th	দ d	ধ dh	ন n
প p	ফ ph	ব b	ভ bh	ম m
য, য় y	র r	ল l		
শ ś	ষ ṣ	স s	হ h	

Numbers

১ 1   ২ 2   ৩ 3   ৪ 4   ৫ 5   ৬ 6   ৭ 7   ৮ 8   ৯ 9   ০ 0

Note that the Bangla 3 ৩ looks like the letter ত t without the line (matra) at the top; the Bangla 4 (৪) looks like a Roman 8; and the Bangla 7 (৭) looks like a Roman 9.

2. Transliteration and Pronunciation

In order to help you read and write in Bangla script as quickly and easily as possible, a Roman transliteration is given in the first few chapters of this book. The transliteration provides a specific symbol for each Bangla letter so that it reflects the spelling of Bangla words precisely. For আমি we can write ami, for তুমি tumi, and so on. Because Bangla has more letters than English, we need some additional symbols to distinguish the letters from one another. Below are the particular features that distinguish Bangla sounds and writing from English. Sections 2.1 and 2.2 refer to the relationship between sound and script, 2.3 and 2.4 to some particular sound features, and 2.5 to a script issue.

2.1 Script and sound

Consonants
Bangla consonants are very consistent in their pronunciation. This means that the spellings represent the sounds reliably.

Vowels
The pronunciation of Bangla vowels, on the other hand, has moved on from the traditional spellings. There are two symbols for i and two symbols for u that traditionally are called short ই i and উ u and long ঈ ī and উ ū respectively. The sounds these letters produce, however, can be either long or short, depending on where they occur in words. The letter এ e produces either a closed e (as in the French *née*) or an æ (as in *glad*). These variations are explained below.

   Don't spend too much time on learning the transliterations. They are only meant to be a temporary helping hand at the beginning until you can move on to using the Bangla script independently. For Units 2, 3, and 4, the transliteration is given along with the Bengali texts and, where necessary, a guide to the pronunciation is also given. Section 4 below follows the same principle: the transliteration is given first; the pronunciation follows in brackets.

Bangla vowels consist of pure sounds, which means they stay in one place in the mouth and do not move around as some English vowel sounds do. All vowels, except for ঋ ri, which is really a consonant and vowel combined, and ও o, which is always long, can be pronounced long or short. Both ঐ oi and ঔ ou are diphthongs (combinations consisting of two vowels) and are always pronounced long. For the remaining vowels, long pronunciations are particularly common in one-syllable words. Long vowels have a colon (:) added after them in the pronunciation guide. Examples are given below.

The inherent vowel

The first vowel of the Bangla alphabet অ pronounced ɔ (as in British English *hot*) or long o is an inherent vowel, i.e., a kind of default vowel that steps in where no other vowel is written. The Bangla word for *hot* for instance is গরম g + r + m, consisting of three consonants only. The inherent vowel is pronounced after each of these consonants, so the word comes out as gɔrôm. The inherent vowel is often not pronounced at the end of words that end in a single consonant, so even though the sequence গরম could be pronounced gɔ–rô–mô, in practice the final inherent vowel is usually dropped. (See "Conjuncts" below for other exceptions.)

2.2 Conjuncts

In order to stop the inherent vowel from being pronounced between consonants, Bangla has an extensive set of consonant clusters (conjuncts) where two (or more) consonants are written and pronounced together. For example, if we want to write the word ɔntôr *interior* in Bangla, the ন n and the ত t form a conjunct to prevent the word from being pronounced ɔnɔtôr. The conjunct for ন n + ত t looks like this ন্ত nt, with the ন n sitting on top of the ত t so the Bangla word is অন্তর. In many conjuncts the combined consonants are easily recognized, but there are also quite a few conjuncts that look quite different from their components, e.g., the combination of ক k and ত t comes out as ক্ত kt as in রক্ত rɔktô *blood*. (Common conjuncts for each consonant are given in the description of each letter starting on page 12.)

2.3 Voice and aspiration

Bangla distingishes voiced and voiceless stops as English does: t, k, and p are voiceless (hard); d, g, and b are their voiced (soft) counterparts. In addition to this, Bangla also distinguishes between aspirated (with extra air, i.e., with a following h) and non-aspirated (with no air) stops. This distinction will need careful listening and a bit of practice: k ≠ kh, g ≠ gh, t ≠ th, d ≠ dh, b ≠ bh. English stops are somewhere in-between the two but they are not systematically distinguished. For instance, the initial k in *king* has a lot more aspiration than the medial k in *asking*. You can practice the aspirated sounds by starting with two syllables, e.g. bɔhɔ, and then gradually phasing out the vowel between the two consonants, so that you finish with a nice aspirated bh, the first sound in the word ভাল bhalô *good*. Practicing the non-aspirated stops is a bit more tricky for speakers of English as we tend to link voiceless sounds with aspiration and voiced sounds with no aspiration. On the whole, Bangla non-aspirated sounds are softer than their English equivalents. An awareness, right from the beginning, that aspiration and voicedness are separate entities in Bangla will help you to develop your powers of differentiation.

2.4 Dental and retroflex stops

Bangla has two different sets of t, th, d, and dh. One set is dental, pronounced with the tongue touching the back of the teeth—this is the way Italians pronounce their t and d. The other set is retroflex, with the tongue curled back and the underside of the tongue touching the roof of the mouth (the palate). These stops are also called palatal. They are closer to English stops than the dental ones but are articulated further back in the mouth and produce a slightly hollow sound. For the transliteration of the retroflex set ট, ঠ, ড, and ঢ we use a dot underneath the English letters: ট = ṭ, ঠ = ṭh, ড = ḍ, ঢ = ḍh.

2.5 Sibilants

Bangla has three different letters s (usually pronounced sh) and even though they are pronounced the same, we need to be able to distinguish them so that we can match them to the correct Bangla letter in writing: শ = ś, ষ = ṣ, and স = s.

3. Bangla Letters, Symbols and Sounds

Abbreviations: B = Bangla, T = transliteration, P = pronunciation

NOTE: The letter number in the first column refers to the list of descriptions of letters in Section 4 below (pages 12-32) where you can get more information about each individual letter and its pronunciation and use.

Vowels and vowel signs (overview)

Letter no.	B	T	P	B, P, translation
1	অ –	ɔ/ô	ɔ	বলা bɔla *speak*
			ɔ	অনেক ɔnek *many*
			o	ছবি chôbi *picture*
			o	অতীত ôtīt *past*
2	আ া	a	a	রান্না ranna *cooking*
			a:	আম a:m *mango*
3	ই ি	i	i	জিনিস jinis *thing*
			i:	ইতি iti *end*
4	ঈ ী	ī	i	দীর্ঘ dīrghô (dirgho) *long*
			i:	ঈদ ī:d (i:d) *Eid*

Letter no.	B	T	P	B, P, translation
5	উ ়ু	u	u	মুক্তি mukti *freedom*
			u:	দুধ du:dh *milk*
6	ঊ ়ু	ū	u	মূল্য mūlyô (mullo) *value*
			u:	দূর dūr (du:r) *distance*
7	ঋ ়	ṙ	ri	তৃপ্ত tṙptô (tripto) *satisfied*
8	এ ে	e	e	সে ~~kena buy~~
			æ	দেখা dekha (dækha) *see*
9	ঐ ৈ	oi	oi	তৈরি toiri *ready*
10	ও, ো	o	o	লোক lok *person*
11	ঔ, ৌ	ou	ou	পৌনে poune *three quarters*

Consonants (overview)

12	ক	k	k	কলা kɔla *banana*
13	খ	kh	kh	খেলা khæla *play*
14	গ	g	g	গলা gɔla *voice*
15	ঘ	gh	gh	ঘর ghɔr *building*
16	ঙ	ṅ	ng	ভাঙা bhaṅa *broken*
17	চ	c	c	চাবি cabi *key*
18	ছ	ch	ch	ছবি chôbi *picture*
19	জ	j	j	জাল jal *net*
20	ঝ	jh	jh	ঝাল jhal *spicy*
21	ঞ	ñ	n	চঞ্চল cɔñcɔl (cɔncɔl) *mobile*
				বিজ্ঞান bijñan (biggan) *science*

Letter no.	B	T	P	B, P, translation
22	ট	ṭ	ṭ	টাকা ṭaka *taka*
23	ঠ	ṭh	ṭh	ঠেলা ṭhæla *push*
24	ড	ḍ	ḍ	ডাল ḍal *lentils*
25	ড়	ṛ	ṛ	আড়াই aṛai *two and a half*
26	ঢ	ḍh	ḍh	ঢালা ḍhala *pour*
27	ঢ়	ṛh	ṛh	গাঢ় gaṛho *dense*
28	ণ	ṇ	n	কারণ karoṇ *reason*
29	ত	t	t	তুমি tumi *you*
30	ৎ	t	t	সৎ sɔt̪ (sɔ:t) *honest*
31	থ	th	th	থামা thama *stop*
32	দ	d	d	দল dɔl *group*
33	ধ	dh	dh	ধান dhan *paddy*
34	ন	n	n	না na *not*
35	প	p	p	পাল pal *sail*
36	ফ	ph	ph	ফল phɔl *fruit*
37	ব	b	b	বাবা baba *father*
38	ভ	bh	bh	ভুল bhu:l *mistake*
39	ম	m	m	মামা mama *uncle*
40	য	y	j	যদি jodi *if*
41	য্	y		æ as a vowel: ব্যথা bytha (bætha) *pain* or doubling a consonant: জন্য jônyô (jônnô) *for*
42	য়	ŷ	y, w	মেয়ে meye *girl* হাওয়া haowa *weather*
43	র	r	r	রাগ ra:g *anger*
44	ল	l	l	লাল la:l *red*

Letter no.	B	T	P	B, P, translation
45	শ	ś	sh, s	শাক sha:k *spinach*
46	ষ	ṣ	sh	ষোল sholo *sixteen*
47	স	s	sh, s	সাপ sha:p *snake*
48	হ	h	h	হাত ha:t *hand*

Other symbols

49	ং	ṃ	ng	মাংস maṃsô (mangsho) *meat*
50	ঃ	ḥ	'	দুঃখ duḥkhô (du'kho) *sadness*
51	ঁ	~	nasal	কাঁচা kãca *raw*
52	(a) ৹ v bophola *(see below)*			স্বামী svamī (shami) *husband*
	(b) ৹ m mophola *(see below)*			পদ্মা pɔdma (pɔdda) *Padma (River)*

Similar letters by shape

This chart brings together the letters that are similar in shape and can cause confusion. Note that it does not contain all the letters. It is just a way of placing similar letters side by side to help you recognize the distinctions between them.

distinctive,
easy to remember   ল l   ন n   শ ś (sh)   দ d   ঢ় ŷ jophola   ঙ ṅ (ng)   ং ṃ (ng)

ত and similar shapes   ত t   অ ɔ/ô   আ a

ব and similar shapes   ব b   র r   ক k   ধ dh   ঝ jh   রু ru

এ and similar shapes   এ e/æ   ঐ oi   ত্র tr   ক্র kr   ক্রু tru

য and similar shapes   য y   য় ŷ   ষ ṣ (sh)   ফ ph

থ and similar shapes   থ th   খ kh   ঘ gh   ঋ ṛ (ri)

চ and similar shapes   চ c   ছ ch   ঢ ḍh   ট ṭ

ড and similar shapes   ড ḍ   উ u   ড় ṛ   ভ bh

Pairs easy to confuse:

ম m — স s (sh)	প p — গ g
হ h — ই i	ঙ ṅg (ngg) — ঈ ī
এ e/æ — ত্র tr	ও o — ট্ট tt
য y (j) — ষ ṣ (sh)	ড ḍ — ভ bh

Note: Try to find a Bengali Script Tutor on the Internet that demonstrates the formation of the letters.

Frequency chart

In order to help you organize your learning in a sensible way, here is a chart with the most frequently used vowels and consonants. These are the ones you ought to learn first. It is a good idea to memorize a word for each letter and to practice writing the letters and the words. Once you are familiar with these letters, you will have a solid basis to work from. (*The numbers given in parentheses with each letter correspond to the other alphabet charts in this section and to the detailed descriptions in Section 4 below.*)

frequent vowels					
অ ɔ/ô (1)	আ, া a (2)	ই, ি i (3)	উ, ু u (5)	এ, ে e/æ (8)	ও, ে ...ী o (10)
glide, semi-vowel য় ŷ (৪২)		jophola ্য y (41)		nasal £ ~ (51)	

frequent consonants					
ক k (12)	খ kh (13)	গ g (14)	ঙ ṅ (ng) (16)	চ c (17)	ছ ch (18)
জ j (19)	ঝ jh (20)	ট ṭ (22)	ত t (29)	থ th (31)	দ d (32)
ন n (34)	প p (35)	ব b (37)	ভ bh (38)	ম m (39)	য y (j) (40)
র r (43)	ল l (44)	শ ś (sh) (45)	স s (sh) (47)	হ h (48)	

frequent conjuncts					
ক্ষ kṣ (kh/kkh)	ঙ্গ ṅg (ngg)	ন্ত nt	প্র pr	ত্র tr	স্ত st

frequent consonant-vowel combinations
রু ru   ন্তু ntu

4. Sounds and script of individual letters

The following section gives details and examples for each individual letter and includes the vowel signs (*see page 2*) of each letter and the common conjuncts (*see page 6*) with each consonant. A list of conjuncts is also given separately in Appendix 6 (*page 338*) and the pronunciation of individual words is given, where necessary, in brackets after the transliteration.

There is more information here than you will be able to take in in one reading, so take your time, concentrate on the letters you want to learn first (*see the Frequency Chart above*) and be prepared to come back to the other ones at a later stage. But be sure to read about the vowels (1 thru 11) first so you understand the placement of the vowels in the script before, under, and after the consonants.

Note: The symbols ◌ং ṃ, ◌ঃ ḥ, and ◌ঁ ~ that come between the vowels and the consonants in the alphabet are given as entry numbers 49, 50, and 51 at the end of this section.

• •

1. অ – ɔ/ô (*the inherent vowel*)

The inherent vowel is pronounced either open ɔ as in English *on,* বলা bɔla *hot,* or closed ô as in Italian pronunciation of *Roma*: ছবি chôbi. These pronunciations are indicated in the transliteration and in the glossary at the end of the book.

The inherent vowel in Bangla has no separate vowel sign and is only written (as a full vowel অ) at the beginning of words, e.g., অনেক ɔnek *many,* অন্তর ɔntôr *inside*. It is usually pronounced between consonants where no other vowel is written, e.g., সব *all* is pronounced shɔb, গরম *hot* is pronounced gɔrôm, বন্ধ *closed* is pronounced bɔndhô.

Note that the ô pronunciation of the inherent vowel is the same as that of the letter ও o (#10). We give a separate symbol for it so you can work out the spelling of the Bangla word, e.g.: বন bôn *forest,* বোন bon *sister*. The pronunciation of these two words is identical.

অ at the beginning of words:

অমর ɔmôr *immortal*	অলস ɔlôs (ɔlôsh) *lazy*	অনেক ɔnek *many*
অসুখ ɔśukh *illness*	অতীত ôtīt *past*	অতিথি ôtithi *guest*

The inherent vowel (unwritten) in the middle and end of words:

শহর śɔhôr (shɔhôr) *town*	কলম kɔlôm *pen*	খবর khɔbôr *news*
মত mɔtô *like*	গত gɔtô *last*	কত kɔtô *how much*

• •

2. আ া a

This vowel is pronounced short as in English *samba* or long as in *llama*.

The vowel sign (a-kar) for আ is া and is written *after* the consonant it occurs with:
ক k + আ a = কা ka

আ occurs at the beginning, in the middle, and at the end of words.

at the beginning:

আম a:m *mango*	আকাশ akaś *sky*	আলমারি almari *cupboard*
আনা ana *bring*	আমার amar *my*	আগুন agun *fire*

in the middle and at the end of words:

বাগান bagan *garden*	মাথা matha *head*	কাগজ kagoj *paper*
হাত ha:t *hand*	বাবা baba *father*	মামা mama *maternal uncle*

. . . .

3. ই ি i *or* i:

The Bangla name for this letter is হ্রস্ব ই hrɔssho i (*short i*) but it can be pronounced short as in the English *tin* (i) or long as in *teen* (i:).

short: কিশমিশ kiśmiś (kismis) *raisin*   কিছু kichu *something*
long: কি ki: *what*   শিয়াল śi:yal (shi:yal) *fox*

The vowel sign (hrɔssho i-kar) for ই is ি and is written *before* the consonant it occurs with: ক k + ই i becomes কি ki *what*. You can see by the shape of this letter where it should be positioned — it bends protectively over its consonant.

Occurs at the beginning:

ইঞ্জিন iñjin *engine*	ইট i:ṭ *brick*
ইতিহাস i:tihas *history*	ইত্যাদি ityadi (ittadi) *etcetera*

and in the middle and at the end of words:

আমি ami *I*	চিঠি ciṭhi *letter*	বিল bi:l *floodplane*
তিমি ti:mi *whale*	দিন di:n *day*	মিনিট miniṭ *minute*
হাতি hati *elephant*	চাবি cabi *key*	খালি khali *empty*

. . . .

4. ঈ ী ī *or* ī:

The Bangla name for this letter is দীর্ঘ ঈ dirgho i (*long i*) but, like ই (#3), it can be pronounced short as in the English *tin* (ī) or long as in English *teen* (ī:).

short: দীর্ঘ dīrgho *long*   ভীতি bhīti *fear*
long: নীল nīl (ni:l) *blue*   সীমা sīma (shi:ma) *border*

The vowel sign (dirgho i-kar) for ঈ is ী and is written *after* the consonant it occurs with: ক k + ঈ ী = কী kī (ki:). Again you can see the protective leaning!

Occurs at the beginning, in the middle, and at the end of words:

ঈগল īgôl (i:gol) *eagle*   ঈশ্বর īśvôr (isshor) *God*
দীপ dīp (di:p) *lamp*   শীত śīt (shi:t) *cold*
নদী nôdī *river*   ছাত্রী chatri *student (f.)*

. . . .

5. উ ু u *or* u:

This letter is called হ্রস্ব উ hrɔssho u (*short u*) in Bangla but it can be pronounced short as in English *put* (u) or long as in English *due* (u:).

short: মুক্তি mukti *freedom*   সুন্দর sundôr (shundor) *beautiful*
long: কুমির ku:mir *crocodile*   উট u:ṭ *camel*

The vowel sign (u-kar) for উ is ু and is written *underneath* the consonant it occurs with: ক k + উ u = কু ku.

It occurs at the beginning, in the middle, and at the end of words:

উকুন ukun *louse*   উনি uni *he, she* (hon.)   উঠান uṭhan *courtyard*
চুল cu:l *hair*   খুব khu:b *very*   নুন nu:n *salt*
চুমু cumu *kiss*   দুপুর dupur *midday*   পুকুর pukur *lake*
বালু balu *sand*   জাদু jadu *magic*   ঝাড়ু jhaṛu *broom*

When র r (#43) combines with উ, the combination is written with the vowel sign *beside* the consonant as রু = ru as in রুটি ruṭi *bread*.

There are special symbols for the following combinations with উ u, although the regular forms for some of these combinations are also in use, e.g.:

গ g + উ u = গু gu   শ ś + উ u = শু śu   হ h + উ u = হু hu

গ g + উ u = গ্ঌ or গু gu as in গুহা / গুহা guha *cave*
ত t + র r + উ u = ত্রু tru as in শত্রু śôtru [shotru] *enemy*
ন n + ত t + উ u = ন্তু ntu as in কিন্তু kintu *but*
শ ś + উ u = শু or শু śu as in শুক্রবার / শুক্রবার śukrôbar [shukrobar] *Friday*
স s + ত t + উ u = স্তু stu as in প্রস্তুত prôstut *ready*
হ h + উ u = হু or হু hu as in হুকুম / হুকুম hukum *order, command*

. . . .

6. ঊ ূ ū *or* ū:

ঊ is called দীর্ঘ উ dirgho u (*long ū*) in Bangla but can be pronounced either short as in English *put* (ū) or long as in English *due* (ū:).

short: মূল্য mūllô *value*   শূন্য śūnyô (shunno) *zero*
long: দূর dūr (du:r) *distance* ভূমি bhūmi *land*

The vowel sign (dirgho u-kar) for উ is ু and is written *underneath* the consonant it occurs with: ক k + উ ū = কূ kū.

This vowel is rare at the beginning and at the end of words but occurs in the middle of words. It is a lot less common than উ u (#5).

শূকর śūkôr (shukor) *pig*	নূপুর nūpur *ankle-bells*
সূর্য sūryô (shurjo) *sun*	পূর্ব pūrbô *east*

When উ combines with র r (#43), the combination is written as রূ rū, as in রূপ rūp (ru:p) *form*.

• •

7. ঋ ৃ ṙ (ri)

ঋ ṙ (pronounced *ri* as in ***Rio***, except with a rolled *r*) counts as a vowel in the Bangla alphabet for historical reasons and because it has both a full symbol and a sign that attaches to consonants. It is, however, always pronounced as the consonant-vowel combination *ri*.

The vowel sign (ri-kar) for ঋ is ৃ and is written *underneath* the consonant it occurs with: ক k + ঋ ṙ = কৃ kṙ.

There are only two words in common use starting with ঋ ṙ. They are:

ঋতু ṙtu (ritu) *season*	ঋণ ṙṇ (rin) *debt*

ঋ ṙ occurs in the middle of Sanskrit-derived words such as the following:

পৃথিবী pṙthibī (prithibi) *world*	কৃষক kṙṣôk (krishok) *farmer*
বৃষ্টি bṙṣṭi (brishṭi) *rain*	স্মৃতি smṙti (sriti) *memory*
তৃপ্ত tṙptô (tripto) *satisfied*	প্রকৃতি prôkṙti (prokriti) *nature*
বৃহস্পতিবার bṙhôspôtibar (brihôshpôtibar) *Thursday*	

• •

8. এ ে ে e, æ

This vowel has two distinct pronunciations: closed e as in French *chez* and open æ as in English *cat*.

closed: কে ke (ke:) *who*	সে se (she:) *he, she*	এখানে ekhane *here*
open: এক æk *one*	কেন kæno *why*	এখন ækhôn *now*

The vowel sign (e-kar) for এ is ে (or ে at the beginning of words) and is written *before* the consonant it occurs with: য j + এ e: = যে je: *that*

Occurs at the beginning, in the middle, and at the end of words:

একা æka *alone*	এলাকা elaka *area*	এখানে ekhane *here*
দেশ desh *country*	ভেড়া bhæṛa *sheep*	পেয়ারা peyara *guava*
মেঝে mejhe *floor*	মেয়ে meye *girl*	ছেলে chele *boy*

9. ঐ ৈ ৈ oi

ঐ oi is a diphthong (a vowel sequence) combining the sounds of long o and i, pronounced oi.

The vowel sign (oi-kar) for ঐ is ৈ (or ৈ at the beginning of words) and is written *before* the consonant it occurs with: ক k + ঐ oi = কৈ koi.

ঐ is rare at the beginning of words and not very frequent in the middle and at the end of words.

তৈরি toiri *ready*	দৈনিক doinik *daily*	সৈনিক shoinik *soldier*

হৈচৈ hoicoi *fuss*: this word is also spelled হইচই hoicoi which shows that ঐ oi and the inherent vowel followed by ই i (#3) produce the same sound.

10. ও ে (consonant) া o

ও o is pronounced as a long closed o sound as in the Italian pronunciation of *Roma.*

The vowel sign (o-kar) for ও consists of two strokes, the ে (ে) for এ and the া for আ. Written *around* the consonant, these two symbols together produce a long o sound: ক k + ও o = কো ko

Occurs at the beginning, in the middle, and at the end of words:

ওড়না orṇa *shawl*	ওজন ojôn *weight*	ওষুধ osudh *medicine*
ছোট choṭô *small*	দোকান dokan *shop*	মোজা moja *socks*
আলো alo *light*	পুরানো purano *old*	বোঝানো bojhano *explain*

11. ঔ ে (consonant) ৗ ou

ঔ ou is another diphthong consisting of long o and u, pronounced ou.

The vowel sign (ou-kar) for ঔ consists of two strokes, the ে (ে) for এ before the consonant and ৗ after the consonant. Written *around* the consonant, these two symbols together produce an ou sound: ক k + ঔ ou = কৌ kou.

Occurs in the middle and at the end of words:

পৌনে poune *three quarters*	নৌকা nouka *boat*	বৌ bou *wife*
মৌমাছি moumachi *bee*	দৌড়ানো douṛano *run*	সৌন্দর্য soundoryo *beauty*

12. ক k

ক k is a soft k pronounced as in English *asking*.

It occurs at the beginning, in the middle, and at the end of words:

কলম kɔlôm *pen*	কুকুর kukur *dog*	কান kan *ear*
কচ্ছপ kɔcchôp *turtle*	কিছু kichu *something*	কোন kon *which*
আকাশ akaś (akash) *sky*	উকিল ukil *lawyer*	পাকা paka *ripe*
বুক buk *breast*	লোক lok *person*	তালাক talak *divorce*

ক occurs in the following conjuncts:

ক k + ক k = ক্ক kk   ধাক্কা dhakka *push*   মক্কা mɔkka *maize*
ক k + ত t = ক্ত kt   মুক্তি mukti *freedom*   রক্ত rɔkto *blood*
ক k + র r = ক্র kr   আক্রমণ akrômôṇ *attack*   ক্রিয়া kriya *work*
ক k + স s = ক্স ks *(pronounced ksh)* বাক্স baksô (baksho) *box*
ক k + ষ ṣ = ক্ষ kṣ *(pronounced kh at the beginning and kkh in the middle of words)*
         ক্ষতি kṣôti (khôti) *harm*   ক্ষমা kṣôma (khôma) *forgiveness*
         অক্ষর ôkṣôr (ôkkhôr) *syllable*   দক্ষিণ dôkṣiṇ (dôkkhin) *south*

13. খ kh

খ kh is an aspirated sound, pronounced as in English *king*.

It occurs at the beginning, in the middle, and at the end of words:

খবর khɔbor *news*	খরগোশ khɔrgoś (khɔrgosh) *rabbit*	খাতা khata *notebook*
মাখন makhon *butter*	পাখা pakha *fan*	
অসুখ ɔshukh *illness*	তারিখ tarikh *date*	

14. গ g

গ g is a voiced, unaspirated sound, pronounced as in English *get*.

It occurs at the beginning, in the middle, and at the end of words:

গাছ gach *tree*	গরু gôru *cow*	গলা gɔla *throat*
আগুন agun *fire*	বাগান bagan *garden*	জাগা jaga *wake up*
ভাগ bhag *part*	দাগ dag *mark*	যুগ jug *era*

গ occurs in the following conjuncts:

গ g + ধ dh = গ্ধ gdh   মুগ্ধ mugdho *enchanted*
গ g + র r = গ্র gr   গ্রাম gram *village*

গ also occurs in the following consonant-vowel combination:

গ g + উ u = গু gu   গুরুত্ব gurutto *importance*

. . . .

15. ঘ gh

ঘ gh is a voiced, aspirated sound, pronounced as in English *doghouse*.

It occurs at the beginning, in the middle, and at the end of words:

ঘোড়া ghoṛa *horse*	ঘড়ি ghôṛi *clock*	ঘুম ghum *sleep*
ঘুঘু ghughu *dove*	ঘাস gha:s *grass*	ঘর ghɔr *building*
আঘাত aghat *blow*	মেঘ megh *cloud*	বাঘ ba:gh *tiger*

. . . .

16. ঙ ṅ

ঙ ṅ is a nasal. Its Bangla name is উঁয়ো ũwo and it is pronounced ng like in English *king* or ngg.

ঙ does not occur at the beginning of words. It has an allophone (a letter that is pronounced the same), #49 ং ṃ, which steps in when no vowel follows the consonant. *(See more on this under #49.)*

আঙুর aṅur (anggur) *grape*	আঙুল aṅul (anggul) *finger*
ভাঙা bhaṅa (bhangga) *broken*	বাঙালি baṅali (banggali) *Bengali*

ঙ forms conjuncts with ক k and গ g:

ঙ ṅ + ক k = ঙ্ক ṅk	অঙ্ক ɔṅkô *maths*
ঙ ṅ + গ g = ঙ্গ ṅg	ইঙ্গিত iṅgit (inggit) *sign*

. . . .

17. চ c

চ c is an unvoiced, unaspirated sound, pronounced as in English *pitcher* with very little aspiration.

চ occurs at the beginning, in the middle, and at the end of words:

চাবি cabi *key*	চিঠি ciṭhi *letter*	চোখ cokh *eyes*
চাঁদ cãd *moon*	চামচ camoc *spoon*	চেনা cena *know, recognize*
আচার acar *pickle*	কাঁচা kãca *raw*	বিচার bicar *judgement*
নাচ na:c *dance*	কাচ ka:c *glass*	মরিচ moric *chili*

চ occurs as the first letter in the following conjuncts:

চ c + চ c = চ্চ cc	বাচ্চা bacca *child*
চ c + ছ ch = চ্ছ cch	ইচ্ছা iccha *wish*

. . . .

18. ছ ch

ছ ch is an unvoiced, aspirated sound pronounced as in English *chin* with aspiration.

It occurs at the beginning, in the middle, and at the end of words:

ছাগল chagôl *goat*	ছবি chôbi *picture*	ছাতি chati *umbrella*
ছেলে chele *boy*	ছুরি churi *knife*	ছোট choṭô *small*
বছর bɔchôr *year*	মাছ mach *fish*	গাছ gach *tree*

• •

19. জ j

জ j is a voiced, unaspirated sound as in English *hedge* with no aspiration.

It is called বর্গীয় জ bôrgīŷô jɔ to distinguish it from য y (#40) which is pronounced the same.

জ occurs at the beginning, in the middle, and at the end of words:

জমি jômi *land*	জল jɔl *water*	জুতা juta *shoes*
জানালা janala *window*	জায়গা jaŷga *place*	জাহাজ jahaj *ship*
গাজর gajor *carrot*	গুজব gujôb *gossip*	দরজা dɔrja *door*
লেজ lej *tail*	আওয়াজ aoyaj *sound*	কাগজ kagôj *paper*

জ occurs in the following conjuncts:

জ j + জ j = জ্জ jj	লজ্জা lɔjja *shame*
জ j + ঞ ñ = জ্ঞ jñ	জিজ্ঞাসা jijñasa (jiggasha) *question*
জ j + ব (v = bophola)* = জ্ব jv	জ্বালানো jvalano (jalano) *irritate*
জ j + জ j + ব (v = bophola)* = জ্জ্ব jjv	উজ্জ্বল ujjvôl (ujjol) *bright*

(*ব is not pronounced; *See more on* ্ব bophola *at #53 below.*)

• •

20. ঝ jh

ঝ jh is a voiced, aspirated sound, pronounced as in English *hedgehog*.

It occurs at the beginning, in the middle, and at the end of words:

ঝড় jhɔṛ *storm*	ঝাড়ু jharu *broom*	ঝগড়া jhɔgra *quarrel*
ঝামেলা jhamela *hassle*	ঝুড়ি jhuṛi *basket*	ঝিনুক jhinuk *oyster*
বোঝা bojha *understand*	মেঝে mejhe *floor*	মাঝ majh *middle*

• •

21. ঞ ñ

ঞ ñ is a nasal. It is called ইঁয়ো ĩyo and occurs only in conjuncts with other letters. (This means you do not need to practice writing this letter!)

জ j + ঞ ñ = জ্ঞ jñ, pronounced g at the beginning and gg in the middle of words.
   (This conjunct was already given under #19.)
ঞ ñ + চ c = ঞ্চ ñc, pronounced nc: অঞ্চল ɔñcɔl *area*   মঞ্চ mɔñcô *stage*
ঞ ñ + জ j = ঞ্জ ñj pronounced nj: গেঞ্জি geñji *vest*   ইঞ্জিন iñjin *engine*

. . . .

22. ট ṭ

ট ṭ is an unvoiced, unaspirated retroflex stop, pronounced as in English *hut* but with the tongue a bit further back in the mouth. The best way to practice this letter (and the following five) is to curl your tongue back and touch the hard ridge on the top of your gum with the underside of your tongue. This should produce a slightly hollow sound. ট ṭ, ঠ ṭh (#23), ড ḍ (#24), and ঢ ḍh (#26) are called retroflex (turned back) for this reason.

ট occurs at the beginning, in the middle, and at the end of words:

টাকা ṭaka *money*	টিকিট ṭikiṭ *ticket*	টুপি ṭupi *hat*
নাটক naṭok *drama*	রুটি ruṭi *bread*	মাটি maṭi *earth*
পেট peṭ *stomach*	মোট moṭ *total*	পাট paṭ *jute*

When ট is doubled, it is written ট্ট:

ট ṭ + ট ṭ = ট্ট ṭṭ   ঠাট্টা ṭhaṭṭa *joke*   চট্টগ্রাম cɔṭṭôgram *Chittagong*

. . . .

23. ঠ ṭh

ঠ ṭh is an unvoiced, aspirated retroflex stop, pronounced as in English *tin* but with strong aspiration. (*See pronunciation of hollow sound under #22.*)

It occurs at the beginning, in the middle, and at the end of words:

ঠিক ṭhik *correct*	ঠকা ṭhɔka *cheat*	ঠিকানা ṭhikana *address*
পিঠা piṭha *cake*	লাঠি laṭhi *stick*	পাঠানো paṭhano *send*
হঠাৎ hɔṭhat *suddenly*	মাঠ maṭh *field*	পিঠ pi:ṭh *back*

. . . .

24. ড ḍ

ড ḍ is a voiced, unaspirated retroflex stop, pronounced as in English *mad* but with the tongue further back in the mouth. (*See explanation under #22.*) This letter is not very common.

ড occurs at the beginning of words, in conjuncts with ণ ṇ (#28), and in foreign words:

ডাল ḍal *lentils*   ডানা ḍana *wing*   ডিম ḍim *egg*   ডাক ḍak *call*

foreign words:
পাউডার pauḍar *powder*   ডাক্তার ḍaktar *doctor*   ডজন ḍɔjon *dozen*

When ড ḍ is doubled, it is written ড্ড ḍḍ:

ড ḍ + ড ḍ = ড্ড ḍḍ   আড্ডা aḍḍa *social get-together*

· ·

25. ড় ṛ

ড় ṛ does not count as a separate letter but is considered an offshoot of ড ḍ (#24). It is a voiced unaspirated retroflex flap.

ড় never occurs at the beginning of words, only in the middle and at the end of words.

In order to distinguish it from র r (#43), ড় ṛ can be referred to as ডয়ে বিন্দু ড় ḍɔye bindu rɔ, i.e., a ড ḍɔ with a dot.

বিড়াল biṛal *cat*   বাড়ি baṛi *home*   ভেড়া bhæṛa *sheep*
গাড়ি gaṛi *car* ·   চামড়া camṛa *skin*   ঝগড়া jhɔgṛa *fight*
কাপড় kapoṛ *cloth*   গুড় guṛ *molasses*   পাহাড় pahaṛ *mountain*

· ·

26. ঢ ḍh

ঢ ḍh is a voiced, aspirated retroflex stop, pronounced as in English *madhouse* but with the tongue further back in the mouth. (*See pronunciation explanation with #22.*)

ঢ occurs infrequently and only at the beginning of words:

ঢাকা ḍhaka *Dhaka*   ঢেউ ḍheu *wave*
ঢোকা ḍhoka *enter*   ঢেঁড়স ḍhẽṛosh *lady's finger /okra*

· ·

27. ঢ় ṛh

ঢ় ṛh does not count as a separate letter but is considered an offshoot of ঢ ḍh (#26). It is a voiced, aspirated retroflex trilled flap.

ঢ় is extremely rare and does not occur at the beginning of words:

গাঢ় gaṛho *deep-colored*   আষাঢ় ashaṛh *Ashar month*

· ·

28. ণ ṇ

ণ ṇ is a nasal. It is called মূর্ধন্য ণ murdhonyo ṇɔ and is pronounced the same as ন n (#34) as in English **nun**.

ণ is not very common and never occurs at the beginning of a word. It occurs exclusively in words derived from Sanskrit:

গ্রহণ grôhoṇ *acceptance*	দারুণ daruṇ *very*	হরিণ hôriṇ *deer*
প্রাণ praṇ *life*	ভীষণ bhīṣôṇ *extremely*	প্রমাণ prômaṇ *proof*

ণ forms conjuncts with the retroflex stops ট ṭ (#22), ঠ ṭh (#23), and ড ḍ (#24):

ণ ṇ + ট ṭ = ণ্ট ṇṭ	ঘণ্টা ghɔnṭa *hour*
ণ ṇ + ঠ ṭh = ণ্ঠ ṇṭh	কণ্ঠ kɔnṭho *throat*
ণ ṇ + ড ḍ = ণ্ড ṇḍ	ঠাণ্ডা ṭhanḍa *cold*

. . . .

29. ত t

ত t is an unvoiced, unaspirated dental stop. Dental sounds are produced with the tongue touching the back of the teeth. The pronunciation of ত t is similar to the pronunciation of the t in Italian words like *tanto*.

ত occurs at the beginning, in the middle, and at the end of words:

তুমি tumi *you*	তেল tel *oil*	তিন ti:n *three*
নতুন notun *new*	বাতাস batash *wind*	বালতি balti *bucket*
ভাত bhat *rice*	রাত rat *night*	হাত hat *hand*

ত occurs as the first letter in the following conjuncts:

ত t + ত t = ত্ত tt	উত্তর uttor *north*
ত t + ব (v = bophola)* = ত্ব tv	দূরত্ব dūrôtvô (durotto*) *distance*
ত t + ত t + ব (v = bophola)* = ত্ত্ব ttv	সত্ত্বেও sɔttveo (shɔtteo*) *despite*
ত t + র r = ত্র tr	মাত্র matro *only*
ত t + ম m** = ত্ম tm	আত্মা atma (atta) *soul*

*The ্ব (bophola) doubles the ত sound (see #53).
**The ্ম (mophola) doubles the ত sound (see #53).

. . . .

30. ৎ ṭ

ৎ ṭ does not count as a separate consonant but is considered a variant of ত t (#29). It is called খণ্ড ৎ khɔṇḍo tɔ *(shortened t)* and is pronounced the same as ত t. It is not common and occurs only at the end of syllables and words. It is never followed by a vowel.

Common words with ৎ t̠:

উৎসব utshɔb *ceremony*   চমৎকার cɔmot̠kar *excellent*
চিৎকার cit̠kar *shouting*   হঠাৎ hɔt̠hat̠ *suddenly*
জগৎ jɔgot̠ *world*   বিদ্যুৎ bidyut̠ (biddut) *electricity*

The close relationship between ৎ and ত is seen in the fact that ৎ changes to ত when case endings are added to a word ending in ৎ :

জগৎ jɔgot *world*   but   জগতে jɔgote *in the world*

· ·

31. থ th

থ th is an unvoiced, aspirated dental stop as in English *hothouse* but with the tongue directly behind the teeth.

It occurs at the beginning, in the middle, and at the end of words:

থলি tholi *bag*   থানা thana *police station*
থালা thala *plate*   কথা kɔtha *word*
পাথর pathor *stone*   মাথা matha *head*
মিথ্যা mithya (mittha) *lie*   পথ pɔth *path, way*

· ·

32. দ d

দ d is a voiced, unaspirated dental stop as in English **did** but with the tongue directly behind the teeth.

It occurs at the beginning, in the middle, and at the end of words:

দাঁত dãt *tooth*   দড়ি dori *rope*
দুধ dudh *milk*   দেশ desh *country*
দোকান dokan *shop*   দিন di:n *day*
পরদা pɔrda *curtain*   বাদাম badam *peanut*
মদ mɔd *alcohol*   মসজিদ moshjid *mosque*

দ d occurs in the following conjuncts:

দ d + দ d = দ্দ dd   উদ্দেশ্য uddeśyo (uddessho) *purpose*
দ d + ধ dh = দ্ধ ddh   বুদ্ধি buddhi *wisdom*
দ d + ব v = দ্ব dv   দ্বিতীয় dvitīŷô (ditiyo) *second (bophola not pronounced; see #53)*
দ d + ব b = দ্ব db   উদ্বিগ্ন udbigno *worried (bophola pronounced; see #53)*
দ d + ভ bh = দ্ভ dbh   অদ্ভুত ɔdbhut *strange*

· ·

33. ধ dh

ধ dh is a voiced, aspirated dental stop as in English *madhouse* but with the soft dental sound formation.

It occurs at the beginning, in the middle, and at the end of words:

ধান dhan *paddy*	ধোয়া dhoŷa *wash*	ধর্ম dhɔrmô *religion*
শুধু śudhu (shudhu) *only*	আধ adh *half*	শোধ śodh (shodh) *repayment*
অপরাধ ɔpôradh *crime*	ওষুধ oṣudh (osudh) *medicine*	কাঁধ kãdh *shoulder*

• •

34. ন n

ন n is a nasal, pronounced as in English *nut*.

It occurs at the beginning, in the middle, and at the end of words:

না na *not*	নদী nodi *river*	নারিকেল narikel *coconut*
নৌকা nouka *boat*	নীল nil *blue*	অনেক ɔnek *many*
কেন kæno *why*	স্নান snan *bath*	বিমান biman *plane*

ন occurs in conjuncts with dental stops:

ন n + ত t = ন্ত nt	শান্তি santi *peace*
ন n + থ th = ন্থ nth	গ্রন্থ grontho *book*
ন n + দ d = ন্দ nd	মন্দ mɔndo *bad*
ন n + ধ dh = ন্ধ ndh	অন্ধ ɔndho *blind*
ন n + ন n = ন্ন nn	ভিন্ন bhinno *different*

ন also occurs in conjuncts with three letter combinations:

ন n + ত t + র r = ন্ত্র ntr	মন্ত্রী montri *minister*
ন n + দ d + র r = ন্দ্র ndr	তন্দ্রা tɔndra *sleep*
ন n + ত t + উ u = ন্তু ntu	কিন্তু kintu *but*

In foreign words ন can combine with retroflex stops, i.e., ট ṭ and ড ḍ:

প্যান্ট pæṇṭ *trousers*   আন্ডারগ্রাউন্ড anḍargrauṇḍ *underground*

• •

35. প p

প p is an unvoiced, unaspirated bilabial stop as in English *mop* without aspiration.

It occurs at the beginning, in the middle, and at the end of words:

পা pa *foot*	পেট peṭ *stomach*	পাখি pakhi *bird*	পেঁয়াজ pẽyaj *onion*

কপাল kɔpal *forehead, luck*   উপকার upôkar *favor, benefit*   খারাপ kharap *bad*
সাপ sha:p *snake*   আলাপ alap *conversation*   চুপ cup *quiet*

প p appears in the following conjuncts:

প p + ত t = প্ত pt   সপ্তাহ shɔptaho *week*
প p + প p = প্প pp   খাপ্পা khappa *angry*
প p + র r = প্র pr   প্রথম prothom *first*
প p + ল l = প্ল pl   প্লাবন plabon *flood*

· ·

36. ফ ph

ফ ph is an unvoiced, aspirated bilabial fricative, pronounced like the *f* in English *full*.
Alternative pronunciations are *pf* or an aspirated *ph* as in English *haphazard*.

It occurs at the beginning, in the middle, and at the end of words:

ফুল phul *flower*   ফিতা phita *ribbon*   ফেরি pheri *ferry*
কফি kophi *coffee*   তুফান tuphan *typhoon*   মাফ maph *forgiveness*
বরফ bɔroph *ice, snow*   লাফ laph *jump*   গোঁফ gõph *moustache*

· ·

37. ব b

ব b is a voiced, unaspirated bilabial stop as in English *bin*.

It occurs at the beginning, in the middle, and at the end of words:

বছর bɔchor *year*   বাতাস batash *wind*   বিছানা bichana *bed*
বাঘ bagh *tiger*   বন bôn *forest*   বানর banôr *monkey*
রবিবার rôbibar *Sunday*   লবণ lɔbôn *salt*   সবজি sôbji *vegetables*
সবুজ sôbuj *green*   সাবান saban *soap*   সব sɔb *all*

ব b occurs in the following conjuncts:

ব b + দ d = ব্দ bd   শব্দ śɔbdô (shɔbdo) *word*
ব b + ধ dh = ব্ধ bdh   লুব্ধ lubdhô *enticing*
ব b + ব b = ব্ব bb   আব্বা abba *father*

ব v also occurs as a doubling or silent bophola (*see #53*):

স্বামী svamī (shami) *husband*   বিশ্বাস biśvas (bisshash) *belief*

· ·

38. ভ bh

ভ bh is a voiced, aspirated bilabial stop as in English *dab hand*.

It occurs at the beginning, in the middle, and at the end of words:

ভাই bhai *brother*   ভাল bhalo *good*   ভিজা bhija *wet*
উভয় ubhɔŷ *both*   গভীর gobhir *deep*   লাভ la:bh *profit*

. . . .

39. ম m

ম m is a bilabial nasal, pronounced like the *m* in English ***mom***.

It occurs at the beginning, in the middle, and at the end of words:

মধু modhu *honey*   মশা mɔsha *mosquito*   মাছ ma:ch *fish*
মানুষ manush *person*   মা ma: *mother*   মুখ mukh *face*
আম a:m *mango*   আরাম aram *rest*   একদম ækdɔm *altogether*

ম m occurs in the following conjuncts:

ম m + প p = ম্প mp   কম্প kɔmpo *tremor*
ম m + ব b = ম্ব mb   কম্বল kɔmbol *blanket*
ম m + ভ bh = ম্ভ mbh   আরম্ভ arɔmbho *beginning*
ম m + ম m = ম্ম mm   সম্মান sɔmman *respect*

ম m also occurs as a doubling or silent mophola (*see #53*):

আত্মীয় attiyo *relative*   স্মৃতি sriti *memory*

. . . .

40. য y

য y is a voiced, unaspirated palatal fricative, pronounced the same as জ j (#19), as in English *hedge* with no aspiration. It is called অন্তঃস্থ য ɔntɔshtho jɔ.

It occurs at the beginning and in the middle of words:

যাওয়া yaowa *go*   যুক্তি yukti *reason*   যাত্রা yatra *journey*
যদি yodi *if*   মর্যাদা mɔryada *dignity*   পর্যন্ত poryonto *until*

য y does not appear in conjuncts (except with reph, *see #52*) but it has an additional symbol ্য called the jophola (*see #41*).

. . . .

41. ্য y (jophola)

This symbol is called the **jophola**. The jophola is historically a variant of য y (#40) but for learners of Bangla it is easier to treat it as a separate letter. It has four distinct uses and three different pronunciations. It never occurs at the beginning of words and some linguists think of it as the second component of a conjunct (uses c and d only).

  (a) It can act as a vowel on its own and is usually pronounced æ (or e when it precedes a high vowel, such as i or u): ব্যস্ত bystô (bæsto) *busy,* ব্যক্তি bykti (bekti) *person*
  (b) It can act as a vowel æ in conjunction with া a-kar (#2). The jophala always precedes the া a-kar: ব্যাপার byapar (bæpar) *matter,* হ্যাঁ hyæঁ (hæঁ) *yes*
  (c) It can appear after consonants and has the effect of doubling the consonant it follows: শূন্য śūnyô (shunno) *zero,* বিদ্যা bidya (bidda) *learning*
  (d) It can follow conjuncts without any effect on the pronunciation: সন্ধ্যা sɔndhya (shɔndha) *evening,* স্বাস্থ্য svasthyô (shastho) *health*

- -

42. য় ŷ

য় ŷ does not count as a separate letter but is a variant of য y (#40). য় is a semivowel or glide that occurs between vowels and is pronounced either *y* as in *layer,* *w* as in *away,* or at the end of syllables as e. When য় appears right after a consonant, as in ভয় bhɔe *fear,* the inherent vowel is pronounced before য়. Its name is অন্তঃস্থ য় ɔntɔshtho ɔ.

য় never occurs at the beginning of words or syllables:

মেয়ে meŷe *girl*	বয়স bɔŷôs (bɔyôsh) *age*
আয়না aŷna *mirror*	জায়গা jaŷga *place*
হাওয়া haoŷa (haowa) *wind*	কুয়াশা kuŷaśa (kuwasha) *fog*
উপায় upaŷ (upae) *way*	চেয়ার ceŷar *chair*

(*More information on য় is given in Section 5 of Unit 1: Vowel sequences, page 33.*)

- -

43. র r

র r is a dental flap, pronounced similar to the Italian *r* in *Roma.* In order to distinguish it from ড় ṛ (#25) it is also sometimes referred to as বয়ে শূন্য র bɔe shunno rɔ (bɔ *with a dot*).

র occurs at the beginning, in the middle, and at the end of words:

রসুন roshun *garlic*	রাস্তা rasta *road*	রিকশা riksha *rickshaw*
গরম gɔrom *hot*	চেহারা cehara *appearance*	কুকুর kukur *dog*
খবর khɔbor *news*	চাকর cakor *servant*	ঘর ghɔr *room*

র r has two special symbols for combining with other consonants. These are explained under #52.

র r has a special symbol for combining with উ u (#5): রু = ru. Common words with রু ru are: রুটি ruṭi *bread,* গরু gôru *cow,* গুরু guru *teacher.*

র r has a special symbol for combining with ঊ ū (#6): রূ = rū. Common words for রূ rū are: রূপ rūp *shape,* রূপা rūpa *silver.*

• •

44. ল l

ল l is a dental lateral, pronounced as in English *lot.* Take care to pronounce this sound at the front of the mouth, not at the back as in English *well.*

It occurs at the beginning, in the middle, and at the end of words:

লাল la:l *red*	লাঠি laṭhi *stick*	লোক lok *person*
এলাকা elaka *area*	আলনা alna *rack*	বেলা bæla *hour*
আলাদা alada *separate*	চুল cu:l *hair*	উকিল ukil *lawyer*

ল l forms the following conjuncts:

ল l + ট ṭ = ল্ট lṭ	উল্টা ulṭa *opposite*
ল l + প p = ল্প lp	কল্পনা kɔlpona *imagination*
ল l + ল l = ল্ল ll	উল্লাস ullash *delight*

• •

45. শ ś

শ ś is a sibilant (or spirant) pronounced like the *sh* in English *shine.* It is called তালব্য শ talobbo shɔ to distinguish it from ষ ṣ (#46) and স s (#47) which are both pronounced the same.

শান্তি śanti (shanti) *peace*	শুকনা śukna (shukna) *dry*
আশা aśa (asha) *hope*	মুশকিল muśkil (mushkil) *problem*
হতাশা hɔtaśa (hɔtasha) *despair*	বেশ beś (besh) *quite*

শ ś occurs in the following conjuncts (note that in some of these conjuncts শ is pronounced s):

শ ś + চ c = শ্চ śc (shc)	নিশ্চয় niścɔŷ (nishcɔy) *of course*
শ ś + র r = শ্র śr	শ্রেষ্ঠ śreṣṭô (sreshṭo) *best*
শ ś + ল l = শ্ল śl (shl)	শ্লিষ্ট śliṣṭô (shlishṭo) *joined*

• •

46. ষ ṣ

ষ ṣ is a sibilant (or spirant) pronounced like the *sh* in English *shine.* It is called মূর্ধন্য ষ murdhonno shɔ to distinguish it from শ ś (#45) and স s (#47) which are both pronounced the same. ষ is much rarer than the other two sibilants and there are very few words that start with ষ.

ষোল ṣolô (sholo) *sixteen*   ষাট ṣaṭ (shat) *sixty*
ভাষা bhaṣa (bhasha) *language*   সরিষা sôriṣa (shorisha) *mustard*
কৃষি kṛṣi (krishi) *agriculture*   মানুষ manuṣ (manush) *person*
দোষ doṣ (dosh) *fault*   শেষ śeṣ (shesh) *end*

ষ occurs in the following conjuncts:

ষ ṣ + ক k = ষ্ক ṣk   পরিষ্কার pôriṣkar (porishkar) *clean*
ষ ṣ + ট ṭ = ষ্ট ṣṭ   চেষ্টা ceṣṭa (ceshta) *attempt*
ষ ṣ + ঠ ṭh = ষ্ঠ ṣṭh   ঘনিষ্ঠ ghôniṣṭhô (ghonishto) *close*
ষ ṣ + ণ ṇ = ষ্ণ ṣṇ   উষ্ণ uṣṇô (ushno) *warm*

. . . .

47. স s

স s is a sibilant (or spirant), pronounced like the *sh* in English *shine*. In some conjuncts it is pronounced like the *s* in *sun*. It is called দন্ত্য স dɔntyo shɔ to distinguish it from শ ś (#45) and ষ ṣ (#46) which are both pronounced the same.

স is by far the most common of the sibilants. It occurs at the beginning, in the middle, and at the end of words:

সবজি sôbji *vegetable*   সাগর sagor *sea*   সাদা sada *white*
ফসল phɔsôl *harvest*   জলসা jɔlsa *concert*   পিসি pisi *paternal aunt*
মাস mas *month*   ফুসফুস phusphus *lungs*   ইতিহাস itihas *history*

স occurs in the following conjuncts, where it is often pronounced s:

স s + ক k = স্ক sk (shk)   পুরস্কার purôskar (puroshkar) *prize*
স s + ত t = স্ত st   রাস্তা rasta *road*
স s + ত t + উ u = স্তু stu   প্রস্তুত prôstut *ready*
স s + ত t + র r = স্ত্র str   স্ত্রী stri *wife*
স s + থ th = স্থ sth   ব্যবস্থা bybôstha (bæbostha) *arrangement*
স s + ন n = স্ন sn   স্নান snan *bath*
স s + ৄ v (bophola)* = স্ব sv   স্বপ্ন svɔpnô (shɔpno) *dream*
স s + ম m (mophola)* = স্ম sm   স্মরণ smɔrôṇ (shɔron) *memory*

More on the bophola and mophola under #53.

. . . .

48. হ h

হ h, the last consonant of the Bangla alphabet, is an aspirate and is pronounced as the *h* in English *hot*.

It occurs at the beginning, in the middle, and at the end of words. When it occurs at the end of a word, the inherent vowel o (#1) is always pronounced:

হাত hat *hand*	হেমন্ত hemonto *autumn*	হলুদ holud *yellow*
লোহা loha *iron*	চেহারা cehara *appearance*	সিংহ shingho *lion*

হ occurs in the following conjuncts:

হ h + ন n = হ্ন hn	চিহ্ন cihnô (cinho) *sign*
হ h + ম m = হ্ম hm	ব্রাহ্ম brahmô *Brahman*
হ h + ্য jophola = হ্য	সহ্য sɔhyô (shɔjjho) *endurance*

There is a special conjunct when হ combines with ঋ ṙ (ri):

হ h + ঋ ṙ = হৃ hṙ	হৃদয় hṙdɔŷ (ridɔy) *heart*

• •

49. ং ṃ

ং ṃ is called অনুস্বর onusvor or অনুস্বার ônusvar. It is a variant of and pronounced the same as ঙ ṅ (#16): either ng or ngg. While ঙ ṅ can be followed by vowels as in ভাঙা bhaṅa (bhangga) *broken* and গোঙানো goṅano (gonggano), ং ṃ only occurs at the end of words and syllables without a following inherent vowel. In the alphabetical order it comes right after the vowels.

Neither ঙ ṅ nor ং ṃ occur at the beginning of words:

রং rɔng *color*	ব্যাং bæng *frog*
মাংস mangsho *meat*	আংটি angṭi *ring*

A good pair of words to help you remember the difference between the two symbols is বাঙালি baṅali (banggali) for the Bengali people and বাংলা baṃla (bangla) for the Bangla language.

• •

50. ঃ ḥ

This letter has become quite rare but you will still find it in some older texts. It is called বিসর্গ bisɔrgô and occurs after vowels, at the end of a word, or before the onset of a new syllable. Its effect on the pronunciation of words is slight: it produces a tiny hesitation, almost a breath, and a shortening of the vowel it follows.

দুঃখ duḥkhô (dukho) *sorrow, grief*	নিঃশ্বাস niḥśvas (nisshash) *breath*
বাঃ baḥ *wow!*	

• •

51. ঁ ~ (nasal)

This is চন্দ্র-বিন্দু côndrô-bindu, the sign for a nasal sound. It is pronounced in the vowel but written over the consonant (or the full vowel), not the vowel sign.

চাঁদ cãd *moon*   হাঁটা hãṭa *walk*   সিঁড়ি sĩṛi *stairs*   খোঁজা khõja *search*

The nasal can occur with all Bangla vowels but it is more common with আ া a (#2) than with any other vowel. Particularly in Bangladesh, nasal vowels in spoken language are sometimes pronounced with an n, so কাঁদ না kãdô na *don't cry* will sound like kando na. The minimal nasal distinction between ordinary (এর er, ওর or) and honorific genitive pronouns (এঁর ẽr, ওঁর õr) is avoided by using এনার enar and উনার unar for the honorific pronouns instead. Nasals are however an essential part of the language as they distinguish meanings:

with nasal

গাঁ gã *village*
কাঁদা kãda *weep*
কাঁচা kãca *unripe, green*

without nasal

গা ga *body*
কাদা kada *mud, clay*
কাচা kaca *wash*

. . . .

52. ́ reph   ্ৰ rophola

Conjuncts with র r (#43) are very common and very regular. When র r *precedes* another consonant, it is placed as an oblique line above that consonant, e.g., র্দ = rd. This applies to *all* combinations with র r as the first element of a conjunct. The oblique line is called the *reph* (রেফ). Examples are:

গর্ত gɔrtô *hole*   ধর্ম dhɔrmô *religion*   পূর্ব pūrbô *east*   চর্চা cɔrca *practice*

When র r *follows* another consonant, it is placed as a wavy line ্ৰ underneath that consonant, e.g., দ্র = dr. This line is called the *rophola* (রফলা). This applies to all combinations except to those with ক k and ত t: ক k + র r is ক্র kr and ত t + র r is ত্র tr. Both these conjuncts are very common, so it is worth remembering them. Examples with the rophola are:

প্রথম prothom *first*   গ্রাম gram *village*   ভদ্র bhɔdrô *gentle*   ভ্রমণ bhrômôṇ *travel*

There are two common words in Bangla containing both a reph and a rophola. One is প্রার্থনা prarthôna *prayer* and the other is আর্দ্র ardrô *humid, moist* where the two র combine with the same letter.

. . . .

53. ব্ bophola ম্ mophola

These two symbols, derived from ব b (#37) and ম m (#39) respectively, can be attached to other consonants and fulfill the same function: in the middle of words they double the consonant they are attached to, much like the য jophola (#41), but when they occur with the first consonant of a word they make no difference to the pronunciation at all. However, you still need to remember the spellings of these words. If a non-English speaker heard the word *knife*, he would need to be told that the written word starts with a *k*, not an *n*. This is a spelling convention that has historical roots, and the situation with ব্ bophola and ম্ mophola is exactly the same. The ব্ bophola is more common than the ম্ mophola, but in fact there are only a handful of words with either one of these symbols in the language. The best way to deal with them is to memorize some common words:

Silent bophola at the beginning of words:

স্বামী svamī (shami) *husband*   স্বপ্ন svɔpnô (shɔpnô) *dream*
স্বর্গ svɔrgô (shɔrgo) *heaven*   স্বাভাবিক svabhabik (shabhabik) *ordinary*
স্বস্তি svôsti (shôsti) *comfort*   স্বাধীন svadhīn (shadhin) *independent*
স্বাস্থ্য svasthyô (shasthô) *health*   স্বাদ svad (shad) *taste*
জ্বর jvɔr (jɔr) *fever*   দ্বিতীয় dvitīŷô (ditiyô) *second*

Bophola with doubling effect in the middle of words:

বিশ্বাস biśvas (bisshash) *belief*   নিঃশ্বাস niḥśvas (nisshash) *breath*
বিশ্ব biśvô (bisshô) *world*   উজ্জ্বল ujjvôl (ujjol) *bright*

Silent bophola following a conjunct:

সান্ত্বনা santvôna (shantona) *consolation*

Silent mophola at the beginning of words:

স্মরণ smɔrôṇ (shɔron) *memory, recollection*   স্মৃতি smṙti (sriti) *memory*

Mophola with doubling effect in the middle of words:

আত্মীয় atmīŷô (attiyo) *relative*   ছদ্ম chɔdmô (chɔddo) *disguised*
পদ্ম pɔdmô (pɔddo) *lotus*

• •

You now have all the raw material, all the building blocks that make up Bangla words. The following two sections discuss some specific rules for putting words together.

5. Notes on word and sentence formation

Vowel Sequences

Each consonant in Bengali can only support one vowel. When two vowels follow one another, the second vowel is written either as a full vowel or as a vowel sign linked by য়.

- Full vowel following a full vowel or a vowel sign:

  ভাই bhai *brother*   শিউলি śiuli (shiuli) *flower*   সুই sui *needle*
  লাউ lau *bottle-gourd*   আইন ain *law, regulation*   উই ui *termite*

  When a full vowel appears to follow a consonant directly, the inherent vowel is present and needs to be pronounced:

  দই dôi *yogurt*   বউ bôu *wife*   সই sôi *signature*

- য় is a glide that always follows a vowel and can support a vowel. It is transliterated as ŷ.

  য় is pronounced y after আ a, এ e, ই i, and অ ɔ:

  মায়া maŷa *sympathy*   মেয়ে meŷe *girl*   দিয়ে diŷe *with*
  আয়োজন aŷojɔn *preparation*   নিয়ম niŷôm *system*   শিয়াল śiŷal (shiyal) *fox*

  য় is pronounced w between ও o and আ a; উ u and আ a; উ u and ও o:

  খাওয়া khaoŷa (khaowa) *eat*   জুয়া juŷa (juwa) *gambling*
  শূয়োর shuŷor (shuor) *pig*

  When য় appears to follow a consonant directly, the inherent vowel is present and needs to be pronounced:

  দয়া dɔŷa *kindness*   বয়স bɔŷôs *age*   গয়না gɔŷna *jewelry*

  য় can occur at the end of a syllable (without a following vowel), in 3rd person verb forms: সে শোয় se śoŷ *he lies down,* সে দেয় se dæŷ *she gives,* তা হয় ta hɔŷ *it happens,* but also in many nouns: সময় sɔmɔŷ *time,* ভয় bhɔŷ *fear,* আয় aŷ *income.*

Adjacent Consonants

The general rule is that two adjacent consonants have either the inherent vowel between them or should be combined into a conjunct, but there are also a number of cases where two consonants stand next to one another without forming a conjunct and without the inherent vowel between them. An explanation for inherent vowels is given in Appendix 1 (*page 322*).

Punctuation

At the end of sentences, Bangla uses a । (দাঁড়ি dãɽi) in the place of a full stop. Commas, question marks, and exclamation marks are used as in English.

Exercises: Unit 1

Exercise 1:1a

Read, copy, and write the Bangla or the transliteration in the empty box and memorize the words.

মা		mother
	pa:	foot
	ga:	body
মামা		maternal uncle
মাল		goods
	mala	necklace
লাল		red
	kal	time
গাল		cheek
	cal	rice (uncooked)
দল		group
কল		machine
	phɔl	fruit
	cɔla	go, move
কলা		banana
	gɔla	throat, voice
তলা		storey, floor
	bɔla	say, speak

মশা		mosquito
	śɔsa	cucumber
	kɔṣa	tight
দশা		phase, stage
	rat	night
ভাত		rice (cooked)
	sat	seven
হাত		hand
	katha	notebook
কান		ear
	ṭa:n	pull
গান		song
	dha:n	rice (paddy)
থানা		police station
	da:m	price
নাম		name
	a:m	mango
খাম		envelope
	tama	copper
থামা		stop
নামা		get down

	ar	more
	kar	whose
তার		his, her
	bar	time
	tara	star; they
মারা		hit, beat
	kara	who (pl.)
সারা		all
হারা		be defeated
চিনি		sugar
	kini	I buy
	tini	he, she (hon.)
	timi	whale
চিঠি		letter
দুপুর		midday
	nupur	ankle-bells
পুকুর		pond, lake
	kukur	dog
সকাল		morning
	bikal	afternoon

Exercise 1:1b
Write the following words in Bangla:
(Note: This exercise uses only the letters given in the frequency chart on page 11.
Remember where the vowel signs go!)

• *with* আ া a (#2) *and* ই ি i (#3):

gan *song* _____	mali *gardener* _____
bagan *garden* _____	lipi *letter* _____
ma *mother* _____	nak *nose* _____
mal *luggage* _____	kan *ear* _____
lal *red* _____	cãd *moon* _____
am *mango* _____	kaṭa *cut* _____
ami *I* _____	hãṭa *walk* _____
amar *my* _____	asa *come* _____
amra *we* _____	miniṭ *minute* _____
rat *night* _____	bikal *afternoon* _____
din *day* _____	mas *month* _____

• *with the inherent vowel (#1; not written):*
  (Remember that in the transliteration both ɔ and ô represent the inherent vowel.)

kɔla *banana* _____	kɔlôm *pen* _____
gɔla *throat* _____	śɔhôr *town* _____
gɔrôm *hot* _____	bɔchôr *year* _____
khɔbôr *news* _____	ɔnek *much* _____
sɔkôl *all* _____	ɔlôs *lazy* _____
nɔrôm *soft* _____	

• *with* উ ু u

kukur *dog* _____	agun *fire* _____
pukur *pond, lake* _____	guli *marble* _____
dupur *midday* _____	mukh *face* _____
khub *very* _____	cul *hair* _____
ukil *lawyer* _____	

• *with* এ ে e

chele *boy* _____   bela *hour* _____

elomelo *disarray* _____   theke *from* _____

mæla *fair* _____   gele *if you go* _____

mejhe *floor* _____

Exercise 1:2

Copy the consonants and fill in the missing vowel signs in the right place. (The transliteration gives the complete words.)

i	দ র	deri	*late*	
ii	গ ল	gôli	*lane, alley*	
iii	চ ম	cumu	*kiss*	
iv	ম ঝ	mejhe	*floor*	
v	চ ব	cabi	*key*	
vi	প র	pari	*I can*	
vii	ব ল	balu	*sand*	
viii	ভ ল	bhalô	*good*	
ix	চ ক	caka	*tire*	
x	শ ন	śuni	*I hear*	
xi	ছ ল	chele	*boy, son*	
xii	খ র প	kharap	*bad*	
xiii	চ ম চ	camôc	*spoon*	
xiv	ক গ জ	kagôj	*paper*	
xv	ন ত ন	nôtun	*new*	
xvi	গ ল প *1	golapī	*pink*	
xvii	ক ম ল	kɔmla	*orange*	
xviii	ব ম ন	biman	*airplane*	

xix	মন ষ	manuṣ	*human being*	
xx	প র ষ *²	puruṣ	*man*	

*¹ Remember that the vowel sign for o is written around the consonant. Check the vowel chart (*page 3*) if necessary.

*² Remember the special conjunct of র + উ = রু.

Exercise 1:3a

Write the Bangla word. The following ten words contain vowel sequences and the য় ŷ glide (#42). Remember that when two vowels follow one another directly (without the glide) the second vowel is always a full vowel, e.g.:

ন + ই + উ becomes নিউ niu *new*

i	ক	keu	*someone*	
ii	দ	dui	*two*	
iii	খ	khai	*I eat*	
iv	দ	dôi	*yogurt*	
v	ব য়	biŷe	*wedding, marriage*	
vi	ম য়	meŷe	*girl*	
vii	প য় *³	paoŷa	*get*	
viii	ধ য়	dhoŷa	*wash*	
ix	দ য় ল *³	deoŷal	*wall*	
xx	শ য় ল	śiŷal	*fox, jackal*	

*³ Note that the glide য় ŷ can follow a full vowel to create a three-vowel sequence.

Exercise 1:3b

Read the following and write the transliteration:

(i) মায়ের *mother's* _____

(ii) দুই *two* _____

(iii) পাওয়া *get, receive* _____

(iv) খেয়াল *care* _____

(v) জয় *victory* _____

(vi) রেওয়াজ *custom* _____

(vii) নিউ *new* _____

(viii) খাই *I eat* _____

(ix) কাউকে *to someone* _____

(x) হয়ে *through* _____

(xi) রেহাই *aquittal* _____

(xii) ইউরোপ *Europe* _____

Exercise 1:3c
Write in Bangla script (vowel sequences and glide য):

(i) śoŷa *lie down* _____   (vi) deoŷal *wall* _____

(ii) upaŷ *way, means* _____   (vii) meŷad *time limit* _____

(iii) dayī *responsible* _____   (viii) hɔoŷa *be, become* _____

(iv) kriŷa *work* _____   (ix) raŷ *judgement, verdict* _____

(v) rui *trout* _____   (x) śɔŷtan *devil* _____

Exercise 1:3d
Write in Bangla script (full vowels – vowel signs):

(i) unun *oven* _____   (vii) ora *they* _____

(ii) amar *my* _____   (viii) nouka *boat* _____

(iii) ini *he, she* _____   (ix) itihas *history* _____

(iv) ɔmɔr *immortal* _____   (x) upôkar *favor* _____

(v) elebele *incoherent* _____

(vi) tôiri *ready* (ô + i = তৈ / find the equivalent vowel sign) _____

Note: The following two exercises deal with conjuncts. Before you tackle them, make sure that you feel confident about what you have learned so far — there is nothing wrong with going through this chapter multiple times.

Exercise 1:4a
The following ten words contain conjunct letters.

i	ছা_____	chatrô	student
ii	শি_____	śôkti	strength
iii	সে_____	sɔnge	with
iv	_____িম	gram	village

v	বি____াস	biśvas	*belief*
vi	শাি____	śanti	*peace*
vii	শু____বার	śukrôbar	*Friday*
viii	আ____াজ	andaj	*guess*
ix	মিি____	miṣṭi	*sweet*
x	আে____	aste	*slow*

Exercise 1:4b

Conjuncts: fill in the gaps. If you are feeling confident, try to write the transliterated words in Bangla.

i	ন	+	ন	=		unnôti *development*	
ii	স	+	ত	=		rasta *road*	
iii		+	ত	=	ন্ত	ɔntôr *interior*	
iv	ঙ	+		=	ঙ্গ	sɔṅge *with*	
v	ত	+		=	ত্ত	uttôr *north, answer*	
vi	ন	+	দ	=		sundôr *beautiful*	
vii	ক	+		=	ক্ষ	ôkṣôr *letter*	
viii		+	এ৹	=	জ্ঞ	bijñan *science*	
ix	দ	+	ধ	=		buddhi *wisdom*	
x	ম	+	প	=		kɔmpô *tremor*	

Exercise 1:5

Reph and Rophola: Fill in the blanks and see if you can write the transliterated words in Bangla.

i	প	+	র	=		prôti *each*	
ii		+	র	=	গ্র	gram *village*	
iii	র	+	ম	=		dhɔrmô *religion*	

iv		+	র	=	ত্র	matrô *only*	
v		+	ক	=	র্ক	tɔrkô *argument*	
vi	র	+	শ	=		adôrśô *ideal*	
vii	ব	+	র	=		brij *bridge*	
viii	র	+		=	র্য	pôryôntô *until*	
ix	র	+		=	র্ত	muhūrtô *moment*	
x	ভ	+	র	=		bhrômôṇ *travel*	

UNIT 2

Dialogue: এটা কি? ও কে? (প্রথম অংশ)
What's this? Who is he? (Part 1)
Transliteration and glosses for dialogue
Vocabulary: Dialogue
Grammar 1: Sentence construction
Exercises

A few notes on using the dialogues

The first dialogue in this book is in two parts, divided between this and Unit 3. You should take your time to go through the dialogue carefully, thoroughly, and more than once. The transliteration and literal translation (the gloss) are given below the Bangla. The gloss is not a translation but a word by word equivalent and helps you to understand the structure of the Bangla sentence. In some cases, particularly with case endings on nouns and verb forms, one Bangla item is equivalent to two or more words in English. In these cases the English words are written together, divided by a period. The abbreviations for the glosses are given just before Unit One. The more you pick up early on, the smoother your learning process. Listen to the dialogue at least twice on the CD before looking at the script, then read along with the spoken dialogue. Don't worry if you can't keep up at first — you can repeat this process as many times as you like. Then try to read the Bangla on its own without the CD — keep your alphabet chart handy. Always read out loud to practice your sounds and keep your vowels level and clear. Your reading will be very slow at the beginning while you are still working out the letters but the sentences are short. Once you have worked out the individual words, read the whole sentence again, picking up the speed a little bit and paying attention to the intonation and emphasis.

R03

Dialogue

এটা কি? ও কে? (প্রথম অংশ)

দুজন ছেলে ছবি দেখছে। একজন ছেলে আমেরিকান, অন্যজন বাঙালি।

সুব্রত: এই যে দেখ আমার ছবির বই। এতে অনেক জিনিস আছে। আমি তোমাকে সেগুলোর বাংলা নাম বলব।

মাইক: আচ্ছা। আমারও কয়েকটা ছবি আছে। আমার পরিবারের। আমি তোমাকে তাদের নাম বলব। এটা বাংলায় কি? আমরা ইংরেজিতে টেবিল বলি।

সুব্রত: আমরা বাংলায়ও টেবিল বলি কারণ এটা বিদেশি জিনিস। এগুলো কি জান?

মাইক: না, বাংলায় আমি এগুলো জানি না। তুমি বল।

সুব্রত: এগুলো আমার পড়ার টেবিলের জিনিস: বই, খাতা, কলম, পেনসিল, কমপিউটার, বাতি।

মাইক: পেনসিল, কমপিউটার তো ইংরেজিতেও একই – সহজ !

• •

Transliteration and glosses for dialogue

এটা	কি?	ও	কে?
eṭa	ki?	o	ke?
this	what	he	who

দুজন	ছেলে	ছবি	দেখছে।	একজন	ছেলে	আমেরিকান,	অন্যজন	বাঙালি।
dujon	chele	chôbi	dekhche.	ækjɔn	chele	amerikan,	ɔnyôjɔn	baṅali.
two	boy	picture	see	one	boy	American	other.one	Bengali.

সুব্রত:

এই	যে	দেখ	আমার	ছবির	বই।	এতে	অনেক	জিনিস	আছে।
ei	ye	dækhô	amar	chôbir	bôi.	ete	ɔnek	jinis	ache.
this	that	see	my	of.picture	book.	in.this	many	thing	is.present.

Subroto:

আমি	তোমাকে	সেগুলোর	বাংলা	নাম	বলব।
ami	tomake	segulor	baṁla	nam	bôlbô.
I	you	of.those	Bangla	name	I.will.say.

মাইক:

আচ্ছা।	আমারও	কয়েকটা	ছবি	আছে।	আমার	পরিবারের।
maik:	accha	amaro	kɔyekṭa	chôbi	ache.	amar	pôribarer.
Mike:	OK.	of me.also	a.few	picture	is.present.	my	of.family.

What's this? Who is he? (Part One)

Two boys are looking at pictures. One boy is Bengali, the other one American.

Subroto: *Here, have a look at my picture book. There are lots of things here. I'll tell you their Bangla names.*

Mike: *OK. I also have a few pictures. Of my family. I'll tell you their names. What's this in Bangla? In English we call it a table.*

Subroto: *In Bangla we also say tebil because it is a foreign thing. Do you know what these are?*

Mike: *No, I don't know them in Bangla. You tell me.*

Subroto: *These are the things on my study desk: books, notebooks, pens, pencils, a computer and a lamp.*

Mike: *Pencil and computer are also the same in English — easy!*

• •

আমি তোমাকে তাদের নাম বলব। এটা বাংলায় কি? আমরা ইংরেজিতে টেবিল বলি।
ami tomake tader nam bôlbô. eṭa baṁlaŷ ki? amra iṁrejite ṭebil bôli.
I   to.you   their   name I.will.say. this in.Bangla what we   in.English table we.say.

সুব্রত: আমরা বাংলায়ও   টেবিল বলি   কারণ এটা বিদেশি জিনিস। এগুলো কি   জান?
subrôtô: amra baṁlaŷo   ṭebil bôli   karôṇ eṭa bideśi jinis. egulo ki   janô?
Subroto: we   in.Bangla.also table   we.say reason this foreign thing   these what you.know?

মাইক: না, বাংলায়   আমি এগুলো জানি না। তুমি   বল।
maik: na baṁlaŷ   ami egulo jani na. tumi   bôlô.
Mike: no in.Bangla I   I.know not. you   you.say.

সুব্রত: এগুলো আমার পড়ার   টেবিলের জিনিস: বই,   খাতা,   কলম,   পেনসিল,
subrôtô: egulo amar pôṛar   ṭebiler jinis: bôi, khata, kɔlôm, pensil,
Subroto: these my   of.reading of.table thing: book, notebook, pen,   pencil,

কমপিউটার,   বাতি।
kɔmpiuṭar, bati.
computer,   lamp.

মাইক: পেনসিল, কমপিউটার তো ইংরেজিতেও   একই - সহজ!
maik: pensil, kɔmpiuṭar to iṁrejiteo   æki — sɔhôj!
Mike: pencil,   computer   even in.English.also same — easy!

Vocabulary: Dialogue
(Words are given in order of occurrence in the dialogue.)

সুব্রত subrôtô Subroto *(m.)*
মাইক maik Mike *(m.)*

———————————

এটা ¹ eṭa *n.* this *(thing)*
কি ki: *pr.* what
ও o *n./pr.* that (person), he, she
কে ke *pr.* who *(sg.)*
কারা kara *pr.* who *(pl.)*
প্রথম prôthôm *adj.* first
অংশ ɔṃśô *n.* part
দুজন dujon *num.* two (people)
ছেলে chele *n.* boy
ছবি chôbi *n.* picture
দেখা dækha *vb.* see
একজন ækjɔn *num.* one (person)
আমেরিকান amerikan *n./adj.* American
অন্যজন ɔnyôjɔn *n.* another (person)
বাঙালি baṅali *n./adj.* Bengali
এই যে ei ye *phr.* look here
আমার amar *pr.* my
বই bôi *n.* book
এতে ete *pr.* in this
অনেক ɔnek *adj.* much, many
জিনিস jinis *n.* thing
আছে ache *vb.* exists, is present

আমি ami *pr.* I
তোমাকে tomake *pr.* to you
তাদের tader *pr.* their
বাংলা baṃla *n.* Bangla
নাম nam *n.* name
বলা bɔla *vb.* say, speak, tell
আচ্ছা accha *phr.* OK
ও o *adv.* also
কয়েক kɔŷek *num.* a few
পরিবার pôribar *n.* family
আমরা amra *pr.* we
ইংরেজি iṃreji *adj.* English
কারণ karôṇ *n./conj.* reason, because
বিদেশি bideśi *adj.* foreign
এগুলো egulo *pr.* these
জানা jana *vb.* know
পড়া pɔṛa *vb.* read
খাতা khata *n.* notebook
কলম kɔlôm *n.* pen
পেনসিল pensil *n.* pencil
কম্পিউটার kɔmpiuṭar *n.* computer
বাতি bati *n.* lamp
তো ² to *adv.* but
একই eki *adj.* same
সহজ sɔhôj *adj.* easy

Vocabulary notes

1. টা ṭa is a very important attachment to Bangla nouns. It can make an adjective into a noun এ *this* → এটা *this (one)*; it is almost always attached to numbers and quantifiers কয়েকটা kɔŷekṭa *a few*; it forms the indefinite article with এক *æk one*: একটা অফিসে ækṭa ôphise *in an office*; and it can be attached to nouns to make them definite: নামটা namṭa *the name.* গুলো gulo is the plural equivalent of টা ṭa: এটা eṭa *this (one)*, এগুলো egulo *these ones.* We call these attachments classifiers. They will be properly introduced in Unit 5 (page 81).

2. তো to is an emphasizer. It is very commonly used but almost impossible to translate. One meaning of তো implies that the speaker expects the listener to be already aware of what he (the speaker) is saying. It implies: it's obvious, isn't it? But তো has other nuances as well – look out for it as you read more Bangla. Translating তো as *but* is a compromise. In practicing these two words, remember the difference in pronunciation between ত t (dental) and ট ṭ (palatal, with the underside of the tongue touching the roof of the mouth.)

Grammar 1: Sentence construction

The word order in English is subject – verb – object (*I look at the picture*), whereas in Bangla the verb follows the object. This means that the verb is often the last word in a sentence:

তারা ছবি   দেখছে।
tara chôbi dekhche.
they picture look.at
They are looking at pictures.

Bangla has four basic patterns for simple sentences. The first three of these can be found in the dialogue in this Unit (the fourth sentence pattern, impersonal structures, is introduced and discussed in Unit 10).

Dynamic sentences have an active subject and a *doing* verb with an ending that agrees with the subject. Depending on the particular verbs, these sentences can contain direct and/or indirect objects. Here are some example sentences from the dialogue:

subject	indirect object	direct object	verb
দুজন ছেলে		ছবি	দেখছে।
dujɔn chele		chôbi	dekhche
two boys		picture	look.at

Two boys are looking at pictures.

আমি	তোমাকে	তাদের নাম	বলব।
ami	tomake	tader nam	bôlbô
I	you	their name	will.say

I will tell you their names.

তুমি			বল।
tumi			bôlô
you			say

You say (it).

Equational sentences of the type *Today is Monday* or *He is my father* have a subject and a complement. In Bangla these sentences have no verb form, i.e., they have a **zero verb** in the present tense. We call this absence of a verb form the zero verb because the verb forms appear in other tenses and also in negative contexts:

আমি বাঙালি।	আমি বাঙালি নই।
ami baṅali.	ami baṅali nôi.
I Bengali	I Bengali not
I am Bengali	*I am not Bengali.*

The remaining negative verb forms are given in Unit 6. Here are some sentences from the dialogue:

subject	complement		subject	complement
একজন ছেলে	আমেরিকান।		এটা	বিদেশি জিনিস।
ækjɔn chele	amerikan		eṭa	bideśi jinis.
one boy	American		this	foreign thing
One boy is American.			*This is a foreign thing.*	
অন্যজন	বাঙালি।		এগুলো	কি?
ɔnyôjɔn	baṅali		egulo	ki?
other.person	Bangali		these	what?
The other one is Bengali.			*What are these?*	

Existential sentences with the incomplete verb আছ- ach- express location and possession. আছ- means *be present, exist,* i.e., আমি আছি ami achi means *I am here* or *I exist.* But আছ- ach- is also used to express possession. Instead of saying *I have a brother* in Bangla we say *My brother exists.* The negative of আছ- ach- is always নেই nei which expresses absence.

এতে অনেক জিনিস আছে।
ete ɔnek jinis ache
in this many thing it.exists
There are many things in here.

আমারও কয়েকটা ছবি আছে।
amaro kɔŷekṭa chôbi ache
of.me.also a.few picture it.exists
I also have a few pictures.

আমার পড়ার টেবিল আছে।
amar pɔṛar ṭebil ache
of.me reading table it.exists
I have a desk.

The negative of this last sentence would be:

আমার পড়ার টেবিল নেই।
amar pɔṛar ṭebil nei
of.me reading table is.absent.
I don't have a desk.

Exercises: Unit 2

Exercise 2:1: Grammar practice

Copy the sentences below (good for your handwriting development!) and mark each sentence by its sentence pattern: (a) for dynamic sentences, (b) for equational (zero verb) sentences, and (c) for existential sentences. Existential sentences contain either আছে *is present, exists* or its negative নেই *is absent, does not exist.* Again, this is a one-off exercise and once you have developed an awareness of the underlying principle, you won't need to concern yourself with the grammatical terminology anymore but will quickly build up your competence in Bangla. Translate the sentences if you find it helpful.

(i) এতে অনেক জিনিস আছে।
     ete ɔnek jinis ache

(ii) আমরা টেবিল বলি।
      amra ṭebil bôli

(iii) আমারও কয়েকটা ছবি   আছে।
       amaro kɔŷekṭa chôbi ache

(iv) এটা বিদেশি জিনিস।
      æṭa bideśi jinis

(v) আমি তোমাকে তাদের নাম বলব।
     ami tomake tader nam bôlbô

Exercise 2:2: Script practice

Write the following words in Bangla. Remember the positioning of the vowel signs.

(i)   kɔŷekṭa *a few*   _____

(ii)   egulo *these*   _____

(iii) tomake *to you*   _____

(iv)   ete *in this*   _____

(v)   jinis *thing*   _____

(vi)   baṃlaŷ *in Bangla*   _____

(vii) ɔnek *many* _____

(viii) kɔlôm *pen* _____

(ix) chôbi *picture* _____

(x)   kɔmpiuṭar *computer* _____

UNIT 3

R04
Dialogue

এটা কি? ও কে? (দ্বিতীয় অংশ)

মাইক: এইবার আমার পালা। এই যে আমার ছবিগুলো দেখ।

সুব্রত: উনি কি তোমার বাবা?

মাইক: হ্যাঁ, উনি আমার বাবা। ওঁর নাম লুইস। উনি একজন সাংবাদিক। আর ইনি আমার মা। এঁর নাম সিলভিয়া। ইনি একটী অফিসে কাজ করেন।

সুব্রত: আর ওরা কারা? তোমার বোন?

মাইক: হ্যাঁ, ওরা আমার ছোট তিন বোন: স্যালি, এলি আর ডলি।

সুব্রত: বাঃ ! ডলি নামটা আমাদের এখানে ও আছে। তোমার কি ভাই নেই?

মাইক: না, আমার ভাই নেই। আমি একমাত্র ছেলে। তোমার আর কয়েকটা ছবি দেখি?

সুব্রত: ঠিক আছে। এই যে দেখ, গ্রামের ছবি। এখানে আছে বাড়ি, উঠান, মাঠ, নদী, পুকুর, ছোট রাস্তা, মহিষ গাড়ি, ঠেলাগাড়ি, সাইকেল, গরু, কুকুর, ছাগল আর হাঁস। আর এটা কি জান?

মাইক: হ্যাঁ, তা আমি জানি। এটা রিকশা। মহিষ তো খুব বড়।

সুব্রত: হ্যাঁ, ওরা অনেক বড় আর তাদের অনেক শক্তি আছে।

মাইক: আচ্ছা, আজকে মনে হয় আর কিছু শিখব না: রাস্তা, পুকুর, নদী, মাঠ, বাড়ি, বই, খাতা, কলম ... । চল, আমরা ফুটবল খেলি।

• •

Transliteration and glosses for dialogue

মাইক:	এইবার	আমার	পালা।	এই যে	আমার	ছবিগুলো	দেখ।
maik:	eibar	amar	pala.	ei ye	amar	chôbigulo	dækhō.
Mike:	this time	my	turn.	this that	my	pictures	look.

সুব্রত:	উনি	কি	তোমার	বাবা?
subrôtô:	uni	ki	tomar	baba?
Subroto:	he	what	your	father?

মাইক:	হ্যাঁ,	উনি	আমার	বাবা।	ওঁর	নাম	লুইস।	উনি	একজন	সাংবাদিক।
maik:	hæ,	uni	amar	baba.	ōr	nam	luis.	uni	ækjɔn	saṁbadik (sangbadik).
Mike:	yes,	he	my	father.	his	name	Louis.	he	one	journalist.

	আর	ইনি	আমার	মা।	এঁর	নাম	সিলভিয়া।	ইনি	একটা	অফিসে	কাজ	করেন।
	ar	ini	amar	ma.	ēr	nam	silbhia.	ini	ækṭa	ôphise	kaj	kɔren.
	and	she	my	mother.	her	name	Sylvia.	she	one	in.office	work	she.does.

সুব্রত:	আর	ওরা	কারা?	তোমার	বোন?
subrôtô:	ar	ora	kara?	tomar	bon?
Subroto:	and	they	who?	your	sister?

What's this? Who is he? *(Part Two)*

Mike: Now it's my turn. Here, have a look at my pictures.

Subroto: Is that your father?

Mike: Yes, that is my father. His name is Louis. He is a journalist. And this is my mother. Her name is Sylvia. She works in an office.

Subroto: And who are they? Your sisters?

Mike: Yes, they are my three little sisters: Sally, Ellie and Dolly.

Subroto: Wow! We also have the name Dolly here. You don't have any brothers?

Mike: No, I don't have any brothers. Let's look at a few more of your pictures.

Subroto: OK, look at this one, a picture of a village. Here we have a house, a courtyard, fields, a river, a lake, a small road, a buffalo cart, a pushcart, a cycle, cows, a dog, goats, and ducks. And do you know what this is?

Mike: Yes, I do know this one: it's a rickshaw. Buffalos are very big, aren't they?

Subroto: Yes, they are very big and very strong.

Mike: Well, I don't think I am going to learn anything more today: road, lake, river, field, home, book, notebook, pen ... Let's go and play football.

• •

মাইক: হ্যাঁ, ওরা আমার ছোট তিন বোন: স্যালি, এলি আর ডলি।
maik: hæ̃ ora amar chôṭô tin bon: syali, eli ar ḍôli.
Mike: yes, they my small three sister: Sally, Ellie and Dolly.

সুব্রত: বাঃ ! ডলি নামটা আমাদের এখানেও আছে। তোমার কি ভাই নেই?
subrôtô: bah! ḍôli namṭa amader ekhaneo ache. tomar ki bhai nei?
Subroto: wow! Dolly name our here.also it.exists. your what brother does.not.exist?

মাইক: না, আমার ভাই নেই। তোমার আর কয়েকটা ছবি দেখি?
maik: na, amar bhai nei. tomar ar kɔŷekṭa chôbi dekhi?
Mike: no, my brother does.not exist. your more a few picture I see?

সুব্রত: ঠিক আছে। এই যে দেখ, গ্রামের ছবি। এখানে আছে বাড়ি, উঠান, মাঠ,
subrôtô: ṭhik ache. ei ye dekho gramer chôbi. ekhane ache baṛi, uṭhan, maṭh,
Subroto: right it.exists. this that you.see of.village picture here it.exists home, courtyard, field,

নদী, পুকুর, ছোট রাস্তা, মহিষ গাড়ি, ঠেলাগাড়ি, সাইকেল, গরু,
nôdī, pukur, chôṭô rasta, môhiṣ gaṛi, ṭhelagaṛi, saikel, gôru,
river, lake, small road, buffalo car, push car, cycle, cow,

কুকুর, ছাগল আর হাঁস। আর এটা কি জান?
kukur, chagôl ar hãs. ar eṭa ki janô?
dog,   goat   and duck. and this what you.know?

মাইক: হ্যাঁ, তা আমি জানি। এটা রিকশা। মহিষ তো খুব বড়।
maik: hæ̃, ta ami jani. eṭa rikśa. môhiṣ to khub bɔrô.
Mike: yes, that I I.know this rickshaw. buffalo even very big.

সুব্রত: হ্যাঁ, ওরা অনেক বড় আর তাদের অনেক শক্তি আছে।
subrôtô: hæ̃, ora ɔnek bɔrô ar tader ɔnek śôkti ache.
Subroto: yes, they much big and of.them much strength it.exists

মাইক: আচ্ছা, আজকে মনে হয় আর কিছু শিখব না: রাস্তা, পুকুর, নদী,
maik: accha, ajke mône hɔŷ ar kichu śikhbô na: rasta, pukur, nôdī,
Mike: OK,   today in.mind it.is more something I.will.learn not: road, pond,   river,

মাঠ, বাড়ি, বই, খাতা, কলম ... চল, আমরা ফুটবল খেলি।
maṭh, baṛi, bôi, khata, kɔlôm ... cɔlô, amra phuṭbɔl kheli.
field, home, book, notebook, pen ...   you.go, we   football we.play

Vocabulary: Dialogue

লুইস luis Louis
সিলভিয়া silbhiẏa Sylvia
স্যালি syali Sally
এলি eli Elly
ডলি ḍɔli Dolly

——————————

দ্বিতীয় dvitīŷô *adj.* second
এইবার eibar *adv.* this time
পালা pala *n.* turn
উনি uni *pr.* he, she *(hon.)*
ইনি ini *pr.* he, she *(hon.)*
তোমার tomar *pr.* your *(fam., sg.)*
বাবা baba *n.* father
হ্যাঁ hæ̃ *phr.* yes
তাঁর tãr *pr.* his, her *(hon.)*
সাংবাদিক sambadik *n.* journalist
আর ar *conj.* and, more
মা ma *n.* mother
একটা ækṭa *num.* a, one
অফিস ɔphis *n.* office
কাজ kaj *n.* work
করা kɔra *vb.* do
ওরা ora *pr.* they
বোন bon *n.* sister
ছোট choṭô *adj.* small
তিন tin *num.* three
বাঃ baḥ *phr.* wow!
আমাদের amader *pr.* our
এখানে ekhane *adv.* here
ভাই bhai *n.* brother

নেই nei *vb.* is absent, does not exist
না na *phr./adv.* no, not
একমাত্র elmatrô *adj.* only
ঠিক আছে ṭhi:k ache *phr.* OK
গ্রাম gram *n.* village
বাড়ি[1] baṛi *n.* (village) home
উঠান uṭhan *n.* yard
মাঠ maṭh *n.* field
নদী nôdī *n.* river
পুকুর pukur *n.* pond, lake
রাস্তা rasta *n.* road
মহিষ môhiṣ *n.* buffalo
গাড়ি gaṛi *n.* car, cart, vehicle
ঠেলাগাড়ি ṭhælagaṛi *n.* pushcart
সাইকেল saikel *n.* bicycle
গরু gôru *n.* cow
কুকুর kukur *n.* dog
ছাগল chagôl *n.* goat
হাঁস hãs *n.* duck
তা ta *pr.* it, that
রিকশা rikśa *n.* rickshaw
খুব khub *adv.* very
বড় bɔrô *adj.* big
শক্তি śôkti *n.* strength
আজকে ajke *adv.* today
মনে হয়[2] mône hɔŷ *phr.* I think
শেখা śekha *vb.* learn
চলা cɔla *vb.* move, go
ফুটবল phuṭbɔl *n.* football (soccer)
খেলা khæla *vb.* play

Vocabulary notes

1. The word বাড়ি baṛi means *home*. Many people have a village home (গ্রামের বাড়ি gramer baṛi) where they grew up and where parents, siblings, or other relatives still live. Town houses, particularly rented ones, are called বাসা basa in Bangladesh, though in Kolkata many people call their (own) town houses বাড়ি baṛi too. A গ্রামের বাড়ি gramer baṛi usually consists of a few buildings (ঘর ghɔr): the house proper, kitchen, cowshed, etc., built around a courtyard (উঠান uṭhan). When you ask people where they come from (আপনার বাড়ি কোথায়? apnar baṛi kothaŷ?) they are likely to give you the name of their village, though in a town context and if you are planning on visiting them, they may also give you their address in town.

2. মনে হয় mône hɔŷ literally means *it is in the mind*. It is a common phrase to refer to personal impressions, ideas, and thoughts. In a story instead of a dialogue we would say মাইকের মনে হয় যে সে আর শিখবে না। maiker mône hɔŷ ye se ar śikhbe na *Mike thinks that he won't learn any more.* We can say আমার মনে হয় amar mône hɔŷ *I think, it occurs to me* or তোমার কি মনে হয়? tomar ki mône hɔŷ? *What do you think?* but in many cases, when the reference is clear, the personal pronouns are left out. (More about মনে mône at the end of Unit 4.)

Grammar 2: কি as a question marker

The inanimate pronoun কি ki means *what*: এটা কি? eṭa ki? *What is this?*; এটা বাংলায় কি? eṭa baṁlaŷ (banglay) ki? *What is this in Bangla?*

কি can also be used as a question marker for yes-no questions. The difference between the two meanings is entirely in the stress: তুমি কি খাবে? tumi <u>ki</u> khabe (stressed) means *What will you have (to eat/drink)?* The answer would be something like আমি চা খাব। ami ca khabô. *I will have some tea.* The same sentence with an unstressed কি ki: তুমি কি খাবে? tumi ki <u>khabe</u>? means *Will you eat?* The answer would be either, for yes: হ্যাঁ, আমি খাব। hyæ̃, ami khabô. *Yes, I will eat.*; or for no: না, আমি খাব না। na, ami khabô na. *No, I won't eat.* The words for *yes* and *no* in Bangla are হ্যাঁ hæ̃ *yes* and না na *no, not*.

In our dialogue we have the sentence তোমার কি ভাই নেই? tomar ki bhai nei? *Don't you have any brothers?* কি ki in this sentence is unstressed and simply indicates that a question is being asked. In spoken language this question marker কি ki is often left out, so that the only difference between a statement and a question is the rising tone of voice for questions.

Grammar 3: Pronouns

English pronouns *(I, you, we, they)* take different case endings according to their roles in a sentence: we use *he* for the nominative case (the subject of the sentence): *He is going out, he is asleep, he works at home.* We use *his* when we talk about things that belong to him or his characteristics: *his new computer, his bad temper, his family.* This is the genitive case. We use *him* when he is the object of the verb (objective case): *I saw him, she will wait for him, we admire him.* Apart from case we distinguish persons: 1st person *I*, 2nd person *you*, 3rd person *he, she*; gender: *he* versus *she*; and we distinguish singular *I, he* from plural *we, they*. The same distinctions are made in Bangla but there are the following exceptions and additional features:

- **gender:** Bangla does not distinguish gender in its pronouns: সে can mean *he, she* and, occasionally, *it.*
- **singular-plural:** Bangla distinguishes singular and plural in the 1st person: আমি *I* vs আমরা *we*; the 3rd person: সে, তিনি *he* vs তারা, তাঁরা *they*, and it also has separate forms for plural *you*: তুমি *you* and আপনি *you* are singular, তোমরা *you* and আপনারা *you* are plural.
- **respect:** Bangla distinguishes between familiar তুমি and honorific আপনি forms of address in the 2nd person. আপনি *you* is used with strangers, between work colleagues, and with respected persons. তুমি *you* is used between friends, within the family, and to children. Bangla also distinguishes between ordinary and honorific in the 3rd person, when talking about people. In general তিনি, উনি are used when talking about (adult) strangers or respected people. সে, এ, ও are used to refer to people who are on the same social level as the speaker and about children. You will get a feeling for these distinctions when you start communicating in Bangla.
- **distance:** In the 3rd person we specify the proximity or distance to the speaker. সে, তিনি are the unmarked (U = unmarked) forms (i.e. the person talked about may not be physically present), এ, ইনি are used about people nearby (N = near) *this person here*, and

ও, উনি refer to someone further away (F = far) *that person over there*. In actual language use, these distinctions are much more flexible and it will be quite sufficient for you to memorize সে, তার, তাকে or ও, ওর, ওকে for a start. The near forms are the least used.

Personal pronouns

Singular	Nominative	Genitive	Objective
1st per.	আমি ami *I*	আমার amar *my*	আমাকে amake *me*
2nd per. *(fam.)*	তুমি tumi *you*	তোমার tomar *your*	তোমাকে tomake *(to) you*
2nd per. *(hon.)*	আপনি apni *you*	আপনার apnar *your*	আপনাকে apnake *(to) you*
3rd per. *(ord.)*	(U) সে se *he, she*	তার tar *his, her*	তাকে take *to him, her*
	(N) এ e *he, she*	এর er *his, her*	একে eke *to him, her*
	(F) ও o *he, she*	ওর or *his, her*	ওকে oke *to him, her*
3rd per. *(hon.)*	(U) তিনি tini *he, she*	তাঁর tãr *his, her*	তাঁকে tãke *to him, her*
	(N) ইনি ini *he, she*	এঁর ẽr *his, her* এনার enar *his, her*	এঁকে ẽke *to him, her* এনাকে enake *to him, her*
	(F) উনি uni *he, she*	ওঁর õr *his, her* উনার unar *his, her*	ওঁকে õke *to him, her* উনাকে unake *to him, her*
Plural			
1st per.	আমরা amra *we*	আমাদের amader *our*	আমাদের amader *us*
2nd per. *(fam.)*	তোমরা tomra *you*	তোমাদের tomader *your*	তোমাদের tomader *you*
2nd per. *(hon.)*	আপনারা *you*	আপনাদের apnader *your*	আপনাদের apnader *you*
3rd per. *(ord.)*	(U) তারা tara *they*	তাদের tader *their*	তাদের tader *them*
	(N) এরা era *they*	এদের eder *their*	এদের eder *them*
	(F) ওরা ora *they*	ওদের oder *their*	ওদের oder *them*
3rd per. *(hon.)*	(U) তাঁরা tãra *they*	তাঁদের tãder *their*	তাঁদের tãder *them*
	(N) এঁরা ẽra *they* এনারা enara *they*	এঁদের ẽder *their* এনাদের enader *their*	এঁদের ẽder *them* এনাদের enader *them*
	(F) ওঁরা õra *they* উনারা unara *they*	ওঁদের õder *their* উনাদের unader *their*	ওঁদের õder *them* উনাদের unader *them*

Inanimate pronouns

No distinction is made between nominative and objective inanimates.

	Nominative/Objective	**Genitive (possessive)**	**Locative** (in or through)
sg.	তা ta *it* (U)	তার tar *its*	তাতে tate *in it*
	সেটা seṭa *it, that one* (U)	সেটার seṭar *its*	সেটাতে seṭate *in it*
	এটা eṭa *this one* (N)	এটার eṭar *this one's*	এটাতে eṭate *in this*
	ওটা oṭa *that one* (F)	ওটার oṭar *that one's*	ওটাতে oṭate *in that*
pl.	সেগুলা segulo *they*	সেগুলোর segulor *their*	সেগুলোতে segulote *in them*
	এগুলো egulo *these ones*	এগুলোর egulor *of these ones*	এগুলোতে egulote *in these*
	ওগুলো ogulo *those ones*	ওগুলোর ogulor *of those ones*	ওগুলোতে ogulote *in those*
qu.	কি ki *what*	কিসের kiser *of what*	কিসে kise *in what, how*

When pronouns are used as adjectives before nouns, the classifiers টা and গুলো are attached to the nouns:

সেটা আমার কলম। seṭa amar kɔlôm. *This (thing) is my pen.*
but
আমার সে কলমটা amar se kɔlômṭa *this pen of mine*

(*More on classifiers in Unit 5, page 87.*)

Question pronouns

sg.	কে ke *who*	কার kar *whose*	কাকে kake *(to) whom*
pl.	কারা kara *who*	কাদের kader *whose*	কাদের kader *(to) whom*
inanimate	কি ki *what*	কিসের kiser *of what*	কি ki *what*

Don't be discouraged when you look at the chart above – it contains more forms than you need to memorize at present, but having the whole chart should help you to discover the regularities in the system. Do you notice that all plural nominative forms end in রা -ra and all genitive forms (singular and plural) in র -r? If you also notice that genitive and objective plural forms are always identical, ending in –দের der, you have already reduced your workload.

Grammar practice 3:1

Go back to the dialogue and pick out all the pronouns you can find in the Bangla. Write down the phrases they occur in and match them up with the pronouns in the chart.

Here as an example is a sentence from Unit 2:

আমি তোমাকে তাদের বাংলা নাম বলব।
I will tell you their Bangla names.

আমি	1st per. singular, nominative: *I*
তোমাকে	2nd per. singular, familiar, objective: *to you*
তাদের	3rd per. plural, familiar, genitive: *their*

Once you have done an exercise like this, you will quickly begin to recognize the Bangla pronouns directly and manage without the terminology!

Idiomatic Expressions

Some idiomatic phrases are worth learning as a whole so we will introduce some in a few of the chapters.

like and dislike:

আমার তা ভাল লাগে।
amar ta bhalô lage.
of me that good it attaches
I like it.

আমাদের কলা ভাল লাগে না।
amader kɔla bhalô lage na.
of us banana good it attaches not
We don't like bananas.

তোমার কেমন লাগে?
tomar kæmôn lage?
of you how it attaches
How do you like (it)?

(See more about the verb লাগা laga *be attached* and its uses in Unit 7, page 119.)

Exercises: Unit 3

Note: The sooner you get used to dealing with the Bangla script, the better, but it may help you to add the transliteration for the following exercises just to break up the learning process into smaller components.

Exercise 3:1
Match the Bangla pronouns in the first column with their English equivalents in the second column by connecting them with a line:

(i)	আমার	*we*
(ii)	কারা	*your*
(iii)	ওরা	*who (sg.)*
(iv)	তোমার	*their*
(v)	উনি	*you (object)*
(vi)	তুমি	*who (pl.)*
(vii)	তোমাকে	*my*
(viii)	আমরা	*you*
(ix)	কে	*he (hon.)*
(x)	তাদের	*they*

Exercise 3:2
Yes-No questions: change the statements into questions by inserting কি ki *(straight after the subject, i.e. the first noun or pronoun in the sentence) and by changing the pronouns as required:*

Example: আমার বাবার নাম লুইস।   →   তোমার বাবার নাম কি লুইস?
My father's name is Louis. →   *Is your father's name Louis?*

(i) এটা আমার কলম। *This is my pen.*

(ii) আমার বাবা সাংবাদিক। *My father is a journalist.*

(iii) আমার তিনটি ছোট বোন আছে। *I have three little sisters.*

(iv) মহিষ খুব বড়। *Water buffaloes are very big.*

(v) আমার কয়েকটা ছবি আছে। *I have a few pictures.*

(vi) এগুলো আমার পড়ার টেবিলের জিনিস। *These are the things on my desk.*

(vii) উনার নাম সিলভিয়া। *Her name is Sylvia.*

(viii) এটা একটা গ্রামের ছবি। *This is a picture of a village.*

(ix) তাদের অনেক শক্তি আছে। *They are very strong.*

(x) এইবার তোমার পালা। *Now it's your turn.*

Exercise 3:3

Find the pronouns in the grid (words run horizontally or vertically only):

আমি, আমার, আমরা, আমাদের, তুমি, তোমার, উনি, ওরা, তাদের, কারা

গা	লি	তো	কু	পি	উ
এক	আ	মার	অন	ভা	নি
কো	থাক	হে	তা	দের	সা
আ	শো	টি	যে	ঠো	উন
মা	মূ	তু	মি	সু	ই
দের	নীল	বন	থে	ও	রা
যা	কা	রা	আম	ভুল	প্র
ছি	হয়	ত	রা	আ	মি

Exercise 3:4

Translate the following sentences into English (you will need to have worked through the grammar and the vocabulary before doing this translation exercise):

(i)   এটা খুব বড়। æṭa khub bɔṛô

(ii)   এটা কি তোমার ছবি? æṭa ki tomar chôbi

(iii) আমি জানি না। ami jani na

(iv)   সে আমার বোন। se amar bon

(v)   তার নাম কি? tar nam ki

(vi)   আমার ভাই নেই। amar bhai nei

(vii) তোমার বোন ছোট। tomar bon choṭô

(viii) তার বাবার নাম লুইস। tar babar nam luis

(ix)   আমার মা একটা অফিসে কাজ করেন। amar ma ækṭa ôphise kaj kɔren

(x)   সে তাদের একমাত্র ছেলে। se tader ækmatrô chele

Exercise 3:5
Translate the following sentences into Bangla:

(i)   My three sisters are very small.

(ii)   He is my brother.

(iii)   This is a river.

(iv)   I have a few things.

(v)   There are many pens here.

(vi)   We say this in English.

(vii)   I don't have a sister.

(viii)   There is a lake here.

(ix)   Who are they?

(x)   What is your name?

UNIT 4

Dialogue: সাঈদা কোথায়? *Where is Saida?*
Transliteration and glosses for dialogue
Vocabulary: Dialogue
Grammar 4: Question words
Narrative: বিমলের বাড়ি *Bimol's village home*
Transliteration and glosses for narrative
Vocabulary: Narrative
Grammar 5: Case
Additional Vocabulary
Numbers to fifteen
Points on the compass
Days of the week
মন môn *heart, mind*
Exercises

Dialogue

সাঈদা কোথায়?

একজন মহিলা আর একটি ছেলে কথা বলছে।

রহিম:	সাঈদা কোথায়? অনেক দিন তো তাকে দেখিনি।
আমিনা বেগম:	সাঈদা চলে গেছে।
রহিম:	মানে কি? কোথায় গেছে?
আমিনা বেগম:	সে রাজশাহীতে আছে।
রহিম:	তাই নাকি? আমি তা জানতাম না। কবে গেছে?
আমিনা বেগম:	মোট তিন সপ্তাহ হল।
রহিম:	কি করে গেছে?
আমিনা বেগম:	ট্রেনে।
রহিম:	কেন? ওখানে কি করে?
আমিনা বেগম:	সে ওখানে নার্সিং শিখতে গেছে।
রহিম:	কতদিন থাকবে?
আমিনা বেগম:	তার ঠিক নেই, কিন্তু আমরা আশা করছি দুই বছর থাকবে।
রহিম:	অনেক দিন তো। ওখানে কার কাছে থাকে?
আমিনা বেগম:	সে তার চাচার বাড়িতে থাকে।
রহিম:	কেমন লাগছে তার?
আমিনা বেগম:	ভালই লাগছে তবে ছোট বোনের কথা তো মনে পড়ে।
রহিম:	আপনারা কি তার সঙ্গে মাঝে মাঝে টেলিফোনে কথা বলেন?
আমিনা বেগম:	হ্যাঁ, প্রায় রোজই ফোন করি।
রহিম:	দিনে কখন টেলিফোন করেন?
আমিনা বেগম:	সাধারণত আমরা রাত আটটায় কথা বলি।
রহিম:	আজকের রাতে আমাকে সাঈদার সঙ্গে একটু কথা বলতে দেবেন?
আমিনা বেগম:	নিশ্চয় ! তুমি আটটার সময় এসে কথা বলতে পারবে।
রহিম:	আচ্ছা, আসব তাহলে।

Where is Saida?

A woman and a boy are speaking.

Rohim:	*Where is Saida? I haven't seen her for a long time.*
Amina Begum:	*Saida has left.*
Rohim:	*What do you mean? Where has she gone?*
Amina Begum:	*She is in Rajshahi.*
Rohim:	*Is that so? I didn't know. When did she go?*
Amina Begum:	*About three weeks ago.*
Rohim:	*How did she get there?*
Amina Begum:	*By train.*
Rohim:	*Why? What is she doing there?*
Amina Begum:	*She is training as a nurse.*
Rohim:	*How long will she stay there?*
Amina Begum:	*We are not sure yet but we hope for two years.*
Rohim:	*That's a long time! Who is she staying with?*
Amina Begum:	*She is staying at her uncle's house.*
Rohim:	*How does she like it?*
Amina Begum:	*She likes it fine but she is missing her little sister.*
Rohim:	*Do you sometimes talk to her on the phone?*
Amina Begum:	*Yes, we phone almost every day.*
Rohim:	*At what time do you phone her?*
Amina Begum:	*Usually we phone around 8 o'clock at night.*
Rohim:	*Would you allow me to talk to her briefly tonight?*
Amina Begum:	*Yes, of course. If you come at 8 tonight, you'll be able to talk to her.*
Rohim:	*OK, I'll be here.*

Transliteration and glosses for dialogue

সাঈদা কোথায়?
saīda   kothaŷ
Saida   where?

একজন মহিলা আর একটি ছেলে কথা বলছে।
ækjɔn môhila ar ekṭi chele kɔtha bôlche.
one.CL woman and one boy   word is.speaking

রহিম: সাঈদা কোথায়? অনেক দিন তো তাকে দেখিনি।
rôhim: saīda kothaŷ? ɔnek din to take dekhini.
Rohim: Saida where? many day EMP her I.have.not.seen

আমিনা বেগম: সাঈদা চলে   গেছে।
amina begôm: saīda côle   gæche.
Amina Begum: Saida having.moved has.gone

রহিম: মানে কি? কোথায় গেছে?
rôhim: mane ki   kothaŷ gæche?
Rohim: meaning what where has.gone

আমিনা বেগম: সে রাজশাহীতে আছে।
amina begôm: se rajśahīte ache.
Amina Begum: she in.Rajshahi she.is

রহিম: তাই   নাকি? আমি তা জানতাম না। কবে গেছে?
rôhim: tai   naki? ami ta jantam na kɔbe gæche?
Rohim: that.EMP not.what I   that I.knew not when has.gone

আমিনা বেগম: মোট তিন সপ্তাহ   হল।
amina begôm: moṭ tin sɔptahô hôlô.
Amina Begum: all.in.all three week it.was

রহিম: কি করে গেছে?
rôhim: ki kôre gæche?
Rohim: what do.PP has.gone

আমিনা বেগম: ট্রেনে।
amina begôm: ṭrene.
Amina Begum: on.train

রহিম: কেন? ওখানে কি করে?
rôhim: kænô? okhane ki kɔre?
Rohim: why   there what she.does

আমিনা বেগম: সে ওখানে নার্সিং   শিখতে গেছে।
amina begôm: se okhane narsing śikhte gæche.
Amina Begum: she there nursing to.learn she.has.gone

রহিম:	কতদিন থাকবে?	
rôhim:	kɔtodi:n thakbe?	
Rohim:	how.much.day she.will.stay	

আমিনা বেগম: তার ঠিক নেই, কিন্তু আমরা আশা করছি দুই বছর থাকবে।
amina begôm: tar ṭhik nei kintu amra aśa kôrchi dui bɔchôr thakbe.
Amina Begum: of.that fixed is.absent but we hope are.doing two year she.will.stay

রহিম: অনেক দিন তো। ওখানে কার কাছে থাকে?
rôhim: ɔnek di:n to okhane kar kache thake?
Rohim: much day EMP there whose with she.stays

আমিনা বেগম: সে তার চাচার বাড়িতে থাকে।
amina begôm: se tar cacar baṛite thake.
Amina Begum: she her uncle's in.house she.stays

রহিম: কেমন লাগছে তার?
rôhim: kæmôn lagche tar?
Rohim: how it.is.feeling her

আমিনা বেগম: ভালই লাগছে তবে ছোট বোনের কথা তো মনে পড়ে।
amina begôm: bhalôi lagche tɔbe chotô boner kɔtha to mône pɔre.
Amina Begum: good.EMP it.is.feeling but little of.sister word EMP in.mind it.falls

রহিম: আপনারা কি তার সঙ্গে মাঝে মাঝে টেলিফোনে কথা বলেন?
rôhim: apnara ki tar sɔṅge majhe majhe ṭeliphone kɔtha bɔlen?
Rohim: you.pl what her with sometimes on.telephone word you.speak

আমিনা বেগম: হ্যাঁ, প্রায় রোজই ফোন করি।
amina begôm: hyæ̃, praŷ roji phon kôri.
Amina Begum: yes, almost daily.EMP phone we.do

রহিম: দিনে কখন টেলিফোন করেন?
rôhim: dine kɔkhôn ṭeliphon kɔren?
Rohim: day.LOC when telephone you.do

আমিনা বেগম: সাধারণত আমরা রাত আটটায় কথা বলি।
amina begôm: sadharônôtô amra rat aṭṭaŷ kɔtha bôli.
Amina Begum usually we night at.eight word we.speak

রহিম: আজকের রাতে আমাকে তার সঙ্গে একটু কথা বলতে দেবেন?
rôhim: ajker rate amake tar sɔṅge ekṭu kɔtha bôlte deben?
Rohim: of.today at.night to.me her with a.bit word to.speak you.will.give

আমিনা বেগম: নিশ্চয় ! তুমি আটটার সময় এসে কথা বলতে পারবে।
amina begôm: niścɔŷ! tumi aṭṭar sômôŷ ese kɔtha bôlte parbe.
Amina Begum: of.course you of.eight time having.come word to.speak you.will.be.able

রহিম: আচ্ছা, আসব তাহলে।
rôhim: accha, asbô tahôle.
Rohim: OK I.will.come in.that.case

Vocabulary: Dialogue

সাঈদা saīda Saida *(f.)*
রহিম rôhim Rohim *(m.)*
আমিনা বেগম amina begôm Amina Begum *(f.)*
রাজশাহী rajśahī Rajshahi *(town)*

_____

কোথায় kothaŷ *qu.* where
মহিলা môhila *n.* woman
তাকে take *pr.* him, her
চলে যাওয়া côle yaoŷa *vb.* go away
মানে mane *n.* meaning
কবে kɔbe *qu.* when
মোট moṭ *adv.* in total
তিন tin *num.* three
সপ্তাহ sɔptahô *n.* week
কি করে ki kôre *qu.* how, by what transport
ট্রেন ṭren *n.* train
ওখানে okhane *adv.* there
নার্সিং narsiṁ (narsing) *n.* nursing
শেখা śekha *vb.* learn
কতদিন kɔtôdin *qu.* for how long
তার ঠিক নেই tar ṭhik nei *phr.* it is uncertain

বছর bɔchôr *n.* year
কার সঙ্গে kar sɔṅge *qu.* with whom
চাচা caca *n.* father's younger brother
লাগা laga *vb.* here: like
তবে tɔbe *conj.* but
বোন bon *n.* sister
মনে পড়া mône pɔra *vb.* miss (someone)
আপনারা apnara *pr.* you *(pl.)*
মাঝে মাঝে majhe majhe *adv.* sometimes
টেলিফোন ṭeliphon *n.* telephone
রোজ roj *adv.* daily
কখন kɔkhôn *qu.* when
সাধারণত sadharôṇôtô *adv.* usually
রাত rat *n.* night
আটটায় aṭṭaŷ *adv.* at eight o'clock
আজকে ajke *adv.* today
একটু ekṭu *adj.* a little bit
দেওয়া deoŷa *vb.* give, here: allow
নিশ্চয় niścɔŷ (nishcɔŷ) *adv.* of course
আটটার সময় aṭṭar sômôŷ *adv.* at eight o'clock
এসে → আসা asa *vb.* come

Grammar 4: Question words

The following question words appear in the dialogue between Rohim and Mrs. Begum. All question words in Bangla begin with ক k. You have already been introduced to the question pronouns কে ke *who* and কি ki *what* in Unit 2.

কোথায় kothaŷ *where?*
মানে কি mane ki *what is the meaning?*
কি করে ki kôre *how?, having done what?* (sometimes asks about mode of transport)
কেন kænô *why?*
কত kɔtô *how much?*
কতদিন kɔtôdi:n *how long?*, literally *how many days?* (দিন = *day*)
কত দূর kɔtô dūr *how far?*, literally *how much distance?*

For counting individual items the word কয়টা kɔŷṭa is used:

> তার বাগানে কয়টা আমগাছ আছে?
> *How many mango trees are there in his garden?*

কার সঙ্গে kar sɔṅge *with whom?*

কার is the genitive of কে *who* and সঙ্গে (pronounced shɔngge) is a postposition meaning *with*. We will look at postpositions in Unit 5, but for now just remember that সঙ্গে means *with* and that the noun or pronoun before সঙ্গে needs to be in the genitive case (*see Grammar 5 on case, page 74*).

কেমন kæmôn *how?*

কেমন লাগে kæmôn lage or কেমন লাগছে kæmôn lagche is a very common phrase meaning *How do you (does he/she) like?*

কবে kɔbe *when?*   কখন kɔkhôn *when?*

কবে kɔbe and কখন kɔkhôn both mean *when*, but কখন usually refers to a shorter time frame than কবে, usually within a day. কবে asks for points in time in the context of years or months, কখন asks for the time of day.

কোন kon *which?*

Common combinations with কোন are কোন সময় *at what time?*; কোন জায়গা *at what place?, where?*; কোন দিকে *which way?*. In the dialogue, instead of দিনে কখন টেলিফোন করেন? Rohim could have asked দিনে কোন সময় টেলিফোন করেন? *At what time of the day do you phone?*

Narrative

Note: *From now on each unit contains a short narrative passage for practice, to help you build up your vocabulary, to give you a little cultural background, and to see language structures in context. Have your alphabet and your conjunct charts at hand to help you work out the words. Once you have done this you can check the transliteration and the vocabulary. Then listen to the recording with the narrative in front of you to make sure you get the pronunciation right.*

. . . .

বিমলের বাড়ি

কলকাতার উত্তর দিকে একটা গ্রাম আছে। গ্রামের নাম ছাপড়া। ছাপড়া কলকাতা থেকে বেশি দূর নয়, মাত্র তিন ঘণ্টার পথ। এই গ্রামে বিমল নামে একজন লোকের বাড়ি আছে। বিমলের বাড়িতে তার বউ ও দুটি ছেলেমেয়ে আছে। বউয়ের নাম বিন্দুবাসিনি। ছেলের নাম ফটিক, মেয়ের নাম শালিনি। ছেলেটি বড়। তার বয়স প্রায় দশ বছর। শালিনির বয়স মাত্র দেড় বছর। বিমলের বাড়ি গ্রামের একেবারে দক্ষিণ দিকে। বাড়ির মাঝখানে উঠান। উঠানের এক পাশে একখানা কুঁড়ে ঘর। কুঁড়ে ঘরখানার দেওয়াল বাঁশ আর মাটির। চাল খড়ের। ঘরের সামনে বারান্দা। বারান্দার ডান দিকে রান্নাঘর। উঠানের অন্য পাশে গোয়াল। বিমলের একটা ছোট বাগানও আছে। ফলগাছের মধ্যে চার–পাঁচটা পেঁপে গাছ, অনেকগুলো কলা গাছ আর একটা আম গাছ। আমগাছটার আম তেমন মিষ্টি নয়। বাড়ির সামনে রাস্তা। পিছনে মাঠ। বাঁ দিকে আরও কিছু বাড়ি। ডান দিকে একটু দূরে ছোট একটা পুকুর।

Bimol's village home

North of Kolkata there is a village called Chapra. Chapra is not very far away from Kolkata, only about three hours journey. A man named Bimol has a house in this village. His wife and two children live in this house. His wife's name is Bindubashini, his son's name Photik and his daughter's name Shalini. The son is older. He is almost ten years old, Shalini is only one-and-a-half. Bimol's house is at the extreme south end of the village. In the middle of the homestead is a courtyard. To one side of the courtyard is a thatched hut. The walls of the hut are made from bamboo and mud. The roof is made from straw. At the front of the house is a verandah. To the right of the verandah is the kitchen. At the other side of the verandah is the cowshed. Bimol also has a small garden. Among the fruit trees are four or five papaya trees, many banana plants, and one mango tree. The mangoes on the mango tree are not particularly sweet. There is a road in front of the house, a field at the back. To the left there are a few more houses, to the right, some distance away, is a little lake.

Transliteration and glosses for narrative

বিমলের   বাড়ি
bimɔler   baṛi
of.Bimol   home

কলকাতার   উত্তর   দিকে   একটা   গ্রাম   আছে। গ্রামের   নাম   ছাপড়া।
kôlkatar   uttôr   dike   ækṭa   gram   ache. gramer   nam   chapṛa.
of.Kolkata   north   direction.LOC   one.CL   village   exists   of.village   name   Chapra

ছাপড়া   কলকাতা   থেকে   বেশি   দূর   নয়, মাত্র   তিন   ঘণ্টার   পথ।
chapṛa   kôlkata   theke   beśi   dūr   nɔŷ, matrô   tin   ghɔnṭar   pɔth.
Chapra   Kolkata   from   much   distance   is.not   only   three   of.hour   way

এই   গ্রামে   বিমল   নামে   একজন   লোকের   বাড়ি   আছে।
ei   grame   bimɔl   name   ækjɔn   loker   baṛi   ache.
this   in.village   bimol   name.LOC   one.CL   of.person   home   exists

বিমলের   বাড়িতে   তার   বউ   ও   দুটি   ছেলেমেয়ে   আছে।
bimɔler   baṛite   tar   bôu   o   duṭi   chelemeŷe   ache.
of.Bimol   home.LOC   his   wife   and   two.CL   children   exists

বউয়ের   নাম   বিন্দুবাসিনি। ছেলের   নাম   ফটিক,   মেয়ের   নাম   শালিনি।
bôuŷer   nam   bindubasini. cheler   nam   phôṭik,   meŷer   nam   śalini.
of.wife   name   Bindubashini   of.son   name   Photik   of.daughter   name   Shalini

ছেলেটি   বড়। তার   বয়স   প্রায়   দশ   বছর।   শালিনির   বয়স   মাত্র   দেড়   বছর।
cheleṭi   bɔṛô. tar   bɔŷôs   praŷ   dɔś   bɔchôr.   śalinir   bɔŷôs   matrô   deṛ   bɔchôr.
son.CL   big   his   age   almost   ten   year   of Shalini   age   only   one.and.a.half   year

বিমলের   বাড়ি   গ্রামের   একেবারে   দক্ষিণ   দিকে।   বাড়ির   মাঝখানে   উঠান।
bimɔler   baṛi   gramer   ækebare   dôkṣin   dike.   baṛir   majhkhane   uṭhan.
of Bimol   home   of village   totally   south   direction.LOC   of home   middle.LOC   courtyard

উঠানের   এক   পাশে   একখানা   কুঁড়ে   ঘর।
uṭhaner   æk   paśe   ækkhana   kūṛe   ghɔr.
of courtyard   one   side   one.CL   thatched   room

কুঁড়ে   ঘরখানার   দেওয়াল   বাঁশ   আর   মাটির। চাল   খড়ের।
kūṛe   ghɔrkhanar   deoŷal   bāś   ar   maṭir. cal   khɔrer.
thatched   room.CL.GEN   wall   bamboo   and   of soil   roof   of straw

ঘরের   সামনে   বারান্দা। বারান্দার   ডান   দিকে   রান্নাঘর।
ghɔrer   samne   baranda. barandar   ḍan   dike   rannaghɔr.
of room   in front   verandah   of verandah   right   direction.LOC   kitchen

উঠানের   অন্য   পাশে   গোয়াল।
uṭhaner   ɔnyô   paśe   goŷal.
of courtyard   other   side.LOC   cowshed

বিমলের   একটা   ছোট   বাগানও   আছে।
bimɔler   ækṭa   choṭô   bagano   ache.
of Bimol   one.CL   small   garden also   exists

ফলগাছের   মধ্যে   চার–পাঁচটা   পেঁপে   গাছ,   অনেকগুলো   কলা   গাছ   আর একটা   আম
phɔlgacher   môdhye   car–pãcṭa   pẽpe   gach,   ɔnekgulo   kɔla   gach   ar   ækṭa   am
of fruit-tree   among   four five.CL   papaya   tree   many.CL   banana tree   and   one.CL   mango
গাছ।
gach.
tree

আমগাছটার   আম   তেমন   মিষ্টি   নয়।
amgachṭar   am   tæmôn   miṣṭi   nɔŷ.
of mango tree   mango   so   sweet   is not

বাড়ির   সামনে   রাস্তা।   পিছনে   মাঠ।
baṛir   samne   rasta.   pichone   maṭh.
of home   front.LOC   road   behind   field

বাঁ   দিকে   আরও   কিছু   বাড়ি।   ডান   দিকে   একটু   দূরে   ছোট   একটা   পুকুর।
bã   dike   aro   kichu   baṛi.   ḍan   dike   ekṭu   dūre   choṭô   ækṭa   pukur.
left   direction   more   some   house   right   direction   a little   distance.LOC   small   one.CL   lake

. . . .

Remember the conjuncts:

ত্ত tt = ত t + ত t	উত্তর uttôr *north*
গ্র gr = গ g + র r	গ্রাম gram *village*
ত্র tr = ত t + র r	মাত্র matrô *only*
ন্দ nd = ন n + দ d	বারান্দা baranda *verandah*, বিন্দুবাসিনি bindubasini *name (f)*
প্র pr = প p + র r	প্রায় praŷ *almost*
ক্ষ kṣ = ক k + ষ ṣ	(pronounced kkh or kh) দক্ষিণ dôkṣiṇ (dokkhin) *south*
ন্ন = ন n + ন n	রান্না ranna *cooking*, রান্নাঘর rannaghɔr *kitchen*
ষ্ট = ষ ṣ + ট ṭ	মিষ্টি miṣṭi (mishṭi) *sweet*
স্ত = স s + ত t	রাস্তা rasta *road*

Vocabulary: Narrative

কলকাতা kôlkata Kolkata *(town)*
ছাপড়া chapṛa Chapra *(village)*
বিমল bimɔl Bimol *(m.)*
বিন্দুবাসিনি bindubasini Bindubashini *(f.)*
ফাটিক phaṭik Phatik *(m.)*
শালিনি śalini Shalini *(f.)*

উত্তর uttôr *n.* north
দিক dik *n.* direction
বেশি beśi *adj.* much, too much
দূর dūr *n.* distance
মাত্র matrô *adv.* only
ঘণ্টা ghɔṇṭa *n.* hour
পথ pɔth *n.* way, road
লোক lok *n.* person, man
বউ bou *n.* wife
ছেলেমেয়ে chelemeŷe *n.* children
বয়স bɔŷôs (bɔyosh) *n.* age
দশ dɔś (dɔsh) *num.* ten
দেড় deṛ *num.* one and a half
একেবারে ækebare *adv.* completely, totally
দক্ষিণ dôkṣiṇ (dokkhin) *n.* south
মাঝখানে majhkhane *pp.* in the middle of
কুঁড়ে ঘর kūṛe ghɔr *n.* thatched hut
দেওয়াল deoŷal (deowal) *n.* wall

বাঁশ bãś *n.* bamboo
মাটি maṭi *n.* earth, soil
চাল cal (chal) *n.* roof
খড় khɔṛ *n.* straw
ঘর ghɔr *n.* house, room
সামনে samne (shamne) *pp.* in front of
বারান্দা baranda *n.* verandah
ডান ḍan *adj.* right *(opposite of left)*
রান্নাঘর rannaghɔr *n.* kitchen
অন্য ɔnyô *adj.* other
পাশে paśe *pp.* alongside, on the side
গোয়াল goŷal (gowal) *n.* cowshed
বাগান bagan *n.* garden
গাছ gach *n.* tree
ফলগাছ phɔlgach *n.* fruit tree
মধ্যে môdhye *pp.* among
পাঁচ pãc *num.* five
পেঁপে pẽpe *n.* papaya, pawpaw
কলা kɔla *n.* banana
আম a:m *n.* mango
তেমন tæmôn *adv.* so, so much
মিষ্টি miṣṭi *adj.* sweet
সামনে samne *pp.* in front of
পিছনে pichône, পেছনে pechône *pp.* behind
বাঁ দিকে bã dike *pp.* to the left
ডান দিকে ḍan dike *pp.* to the right

Grammar 5: Case

If you compare the nouns in the narrative passage with the vocabulary list, you will see that many nouns change their shape: in sentence (1) we have গ্রাম *village,* in sentence (2) গ্রামের নাম *the name of the village.* A couple of sentences later we have গ্রামে *in the village.* The difference is noun cases. Case specifies the role of a particular noun or pronoun within a sentence—it adds to the meaning of a noun or pronoun, i.e., the equipment it needs to function in a sentence. There are four cases in Bangla, each with its own set of case endings: nominative, genitive, objective, and locative. The objective case ending is rare for inanimate objects, the locative is rarely used with human beings.

Nominative Case

The nominative is the unmarked case that has no case ending and is used for the subjects of sentences. Nominative nouns and pronouns often appear at the beginning of sentences.

বৃষ্টি পড়ছে।	*Rain is falling.*
সাঈদা রাজশাহীতে আছে।	*Saida is in Rajshahi.*
ছেলেটি বড়।	*The boy is older.*
আমি ভাল আছি।	*I am well.*

Genitive Case

The genitive ending is added to nouns that modify other nouns. Genitive nouns by themselves often act as experiencer subjects in existential and impersonal structures (Unit 10). Postpositions (discussed in Unit 5), such as উপরে *above,* সামনে *in front of,* সঙ্গে *with,* কাছে *near,* usually follow genitive nouns or pronouns.

তিন ঘণ্টার পথ	*three hours' journey*
তার বউয়ের নাম	*his wife's name*
আমগাছটার আম	*the mangoes on the mango tree* (lit: *the mango tree's mangoes*)
বাড়ির সামনে	*in front of the house*

The case ending for the genitive is –র –r after vowels and –এর –er after consonants:

Nominative	Genitive *(of)*
বাবা *father*	বাবার *father's*
বাড়ি *home*	বাড়ির *of the home*
ছেলে *boy, son*	ছেলের *the boy's*
মেয়ে *girl, daughter*	মেয়ের *the girl's*
গ্রাম *village*	গ্রামের *of the village*
শহর *town*	শহরের *of the town*
লোক *person*	লোকের *of the person*
খড় *straw*	খড়ের *of the straw*

One-syllable nouns ending in a vowel often take এর –er or –য়ের –ŷer endings:

ভাই *brother*	ভাইয়ের *brother's*
মা *mother*	মায়ের *mother's*

Nouns ending in the inherent vowel drop the অ ô and add –এর –er:

কষ্ট kɔṣṭô *trouble*	কষ্টের kɔṣṭer *of the trouble*
তর্ক tɔrkô *argument*	তর্কের tɔrker *of the argument*

Objective Case

The objective case ending is used to mark animate (living) objects. With inanimate objects (things) the case ending is usually dropped. In our dialogue Rohim says: অনেক দিন তাকে দেখিনি। *I haven't seen her for a long time (many days).* তাকে is an object pronoun here, but we could just as well use the girl's name with an object ending: অনেক দিন সাঈদাকে দেখিনি। *I haven't seen Saida for a long time.* This is how the object case is used.

The objective ending is –কে –ke.

Nominative	Objective
বাবা *father*	বাবাকে
মা *mother*	মাকে
লোক *person*	লোককে
মানুষ *human being*	মানুষকে

Here are two example sentences:

আমি তার বাবাকে চিনি।	আমিনা বেগম রহিমকে আসতে বলেছে।
I know his father.	*Amina Begum told Rohim to come.*

Locative Case

The locative marks physical or abstract positions, directions, and processes and corresponds to English prepositions such as *on, in, by, at.*

Nominative	Locative
নদী *river*	নদীতে *on the river*
সকাল *morning*	সকালে *in the morning*
মন *mind*	মনে *in the mind*
হাত *hand*	হাতে *by hand, with the hand*

The locative endings are –এ –e for nouns ending in a consonant, and –তে –te for nouns ending in vowels:

Nominative	Locative
পুকুর *lake*	পুকুরে *in the lake*
দূর *distance*	দূরে *in the distance*
গ্রাম *village*	গ্রামে *in the village*

ঘর *building, room*   ঘরে *in the building*
বাড়ি *home*   বাড়িতে *at home*
শুরু *beginning*   শুরুতে *in the beginning*
বালু *sand*   বালুতে *in the sand*

Nouns ending in a (া) can add য় y rather than –তে –te:

ঢাকা *Dhaka*   ঢাকায় *in Dhaka*
কলকাতা *Kolkata*   কলকাতায় *in Kolkata*
মাথা *head*   মাথায় *in/on the head*

Nouns ending in the inherent vowel drop the অ ô and add এ e:

পূর্ব *east*   পূর্বে *in the east*
মুহূর্ত muhūrtô *moment*   মুহূর্তে muhūrte *in/at the moment*

Additional Vocabulary

Numbers to fifteen
Numbers in Bangla are not as simple and repetitive as numbers in English, so it is a good idea to start learning them early on.

1	১	এক æk		11	১১	এগারো ægaro
2	২	দুই dui		12	১২	বারো baro
3	৩	তিন tin		13	১৩	তেরো tæro
4	৪	চার car		14	১৪	চৌদ্দো couddo
5	৫	পাঁচ pãc		15	১৫	পনেরো pɔnero
6	৬	ছয় chɔŷ				
7	৭	সাত sat				
8	৮	আট aṭ				
9	৯	নয় nɔŷ				
10	১০	দশ dɔś				

Listen to the CD (R02) and recite the numbers out loud to practice your pronunciation. Can you hear the difference between চ and ছ in চার *four* and ছয় *six*? Practice the difference between dental (tongue behind teeth) ত in সাত *seven* and retroflex (tongue curled back) ট in আট *eight*.

In addition to the full numbers, Bangla also has separate terms for *one and a half* (দেড় deṛ) and *two and a half* (আড়াই aṛai). They are used, as the other numbers, for stretches of time: দেড় বছর *one and a half years*; distances: আড়াই মাইল *two and a half miles*: weights: দেড় কেজি *one and a half kilos*; and time on the clock: আড়াইটা বাজে *half past two*. (Time on the clock is explained further in Unit 8, page 145.)

A complete list of numbers is given in Appendix 9. Numbers have to be learned individually up to 100—when and how you learn them is up to you. Listening to the recording over and over can be very helpful in fixing the sequence of numbers in your ear and in your mind.

Points on the compass
উত্তর uttôr *north*	দক্ষিণ dôkṣiṇ (dokkhin) *south*
পূর্ব pūrbô / পুব pub *east*	পশ্চিম pôścim (poshcim) *west*

These can take case endings or combine with দিকে to give directions:

উত্তরদিকে গেলে...	*When you go northward ...*
পূর্বদিকের রাস্তা	*the Eastern road*
পশ্চিমের দেশে	*in Western countries*
দক্ষিণে একটা ছোট গ্রাম আছে।	*There is a small village to the south.*

Note: Bengalis on the whole, but perhaps particularly rural people, are much more aware of the points on the compass than Western city dwellers tend to be: they name their rooms or huts দক্ষিণের ঘর *South room*, পশ্চিমের জমি *the Western field*.

Days of the week

রবিবার rôbibar *Sunday*

সোমবার sombar *Monday*

মঙ্গলবার mɔṅgôlbar (mɔnggolbar) *Tuesday*

বুধবার budhbar *Wednesday*

বৃহস্পতিবার br̊hôspôtibar (brihoshpotibar) *Thursday* (stress on 3rd syllable)

শুক্রবার śukrôbar *Friday*

শনিবার śônibar *Saturday*

মন môn *heart, mind*

In our dialogue we have the phrase মনে পড়া (lit: *fall in the mind*) to express the concept of missing someone. মন is the part of a human being that is concerned with moods, emotions, memory, inclination, thought, concentration, and will. *Heart* is often a more suitable translation for মন than *mind*. Here are some common phrases using মন:

মনে করা *think, consider*

তুমি কি মনে কর? *What do you think?*

মনে হওয়া *occur (in the mind), think*

তার মনে হয়েছে *it occurred to him*

মনে আছ–/ থাকা *be aware of, remember*

তার কথা আমার মনে আছে। *I remember him.*

মনে থাকবে তো? *You will remember, won't you?*

মনে রাখা *keep in mind, remember*

এসব মনে রাখতে পারব না। *I won't be able to remember all this.*

মনে পড়া *miss*

তার কথা আমার মনে পড়ে। *I miss him.*

মন দেওয়া *give one's mind = concentrate*

কাজে মন দিতে হবে। *You have to concentrate on your work.*

মন খারাপ *sad, depressed*

তার আজ খুব মন খারাপ। *He is very low today.*

মন কেমন করা *feel out of sorts*

মনের মানুষ *mind's person = kindred spirit, soulmate*

মন ছোট *petty, small-minded*

মনের কথা *words of the heart = feelings, secrets*

মনের মিল *agreement, good understanding*

Exercises: Unit 4

Exercise 4:1
Translate the questions into English (but do not answer the questions):

(i) বিমলের মেয়ের নাম কি?

(ii) ছাপড়া কলকাতা থেকে কত দূর?

(iii) বিমলের বাড়ি কোথায়?

(iv) তারা কোন সময় টেলিফোন করে?

(v) সাঈদা কার বাড়িতে আছে?

(vi) সাঈদার মায়ের নাম কি?

(vii) রহিম কে?

(viii) বিমলের বাগানের আম কেমন?

(ix) বাগানে কয়টা পেঁপে গাছ আছে?

(x) রহিন কখন তাদের বাড়িতে আসবে?

Exercise 4:2
Answer the questions in Bangla (all the answers can be found in the narrative though not necessarily in the same order). Please answer in full sentences.

(i) বিমলের বাগানে কয়টা আম গাছ আছে? bimɔler bagane kɔŷṭa am gach ache?

(ii) বিমলের ছেলের নাম কি? bimɔler cheler nam ki?

(iii) শালিনির বয়স কত? śalinir bɔŷôs kɔtô?

(iv) ঘরের সামনে কি আছে? ghɔrer samne ki ache?

(v) বিমলের গ্রামের নাম কি? bimɔler gramer nam ki?

(vi) পেঁপেঁ গাছের ফল কি? pẽpẽ gacher phɔl ki?

(vii) বিমলের আমগাছটার আমগুলো কি খুব মিষ্টি? bimɔler amgachṭar amgulo ki khub miṣṭi?

(viii) বিমলের বাড়িতে কে কে আছে? bimɔler baṛite ke ke ache?

(ix) বাড়ির মাঝখানে কি? baṛir majhkhane ki?

(x) রান্নাঘরটা কোথায়? rannaghɔrṭa kothaŷ?

Exercise 4:3

Connect the nouns by putting a genitive ending on the first noun and translate the phrase:

(i)   মা   বাগান   _____

(ii)   বিমল   বাড়ি   _____

(iii) ঘর   দেওয়াল   _____

(iv)   উঠান   পাশে   _____

(v)   মেয়ে   নাম   _____

(vi)   বাগান   গাছ   _____

(vii) গাছ   ফল   _____

(viii) গ্রাম   দক্ষিণে   _____

(ix)   ছেলে   বয়স   _____

(x)   চাচা   বাড়িতে   _____

Exercise 4:4

Match the Bangla words in the first column with their English translations in the second column by connecting them with a line:

গাছ	*garden*
কলম	*river*
গ্রাম	*day*
আম	*verandah*
বাগান	*fruit*
বাড়ি	*village*
ছবি	*night*
নদী	*tree*
ফল	*courtyard*
পুকুর	*mango*
রাত	*house*
রাস্তা	*pen*
দিন	*picture*
বারান্দা	*road*
উঠান	*lake*

UNIT 5

Dialogue

চিড়িয়াখানায়

দুইজন বন্ধু কথা বলছে:

সোহেল: তোমার বাবা কি গতকাল অফিসে গিয়েছেন?

সুজন: হ্যাঁ, তাঁর এই সময়ে অনেক কাজ থাকে। সে জন্যে ছুটির দিনেও কাজ করতে হয়।

সোহেল: আর তুমি গতকাল কি করেছ?

সুজন: আমি বাবার হয়ে ছোট বোনদের চিড়িয়াখানায় নিয়ে গিয়েছিলাম। অনেক ফুর্তি হয়েছে।

সোহেল: তোমার কয়জন বোন? তোমার মা কি যাননি?

সুজন: চারজন। ছোট দুজন হচ্ছে জমজ। আর মাকে দিদিমার সঙ্গে থাকতে হয়েছে।

সোহেল: আগে জানালে আমিও তোমার সঙ্গে যেতাম। সাহায্য করতাম।

সুজন: আসলে কোনও সমস্যা হয়নি। মেয়েদের সব পশু দেখতে এমন ভাল লেগেছে, আমাকে কোনও কষ্ট দেয়নি।

সোহেল: কি কি পশু সবচেয়ে ভাল লেগেছে?

সুজন: জিরাফ, হাতি, বানর, কুমির, সব ভাল লেগেছে। শুধু সাপটা দেখে একটু ভয় পেয়ে গেছে।

সোহেল: মজা তো। আর একবার গেলে আমাকেও নিয়ে যাবে, কেমন? চিড়িয়াখানায় আমার খুবই ভাল লাগে। আমার একটা প্রিয় জায়গা।

সুজন: এত ভাল লাগে কেন? কোনও বিশেষ কারণ আছে?

সোহেল: হ্যাঁ, তা তো আছে। ওখানে শহরের মধ্যে সবচেয়ে ভাল আইসক্রিম পাওয়া যায়।

সুজন: তাই নাকি? আমি তা জানতাম না। তাহলে তোমাকে নিয়ে গেলে তুমি আমাদের সবাইকে আইসক্রিম খাওয়াবে?

সোহেল: আচ্ছা, ঠিক আছে, খাওয়াব। তোমাদের সঙ্গে গেলে খুশি হব।

At the zoo

Two friends are talking:

Sohel: *Did your father go to the office yesterday?*

Sujon: *Yes, he has a lot of work at the moment. That's why he has to work even on holidays.*

Sohel: *And you, what were you doing yesterday?*

Sujon: *I stood in for my father and took my younger sisters to the zoo. We had a lot of fun.*

Sohel: *How many sisters do you have? Didn't your mother go?*

Sujon: *I have four sisters. The two little ones are twins. My mother had to stay with my grandmother.*

Sohel: *If you had told me, I would have come with you to help.*

Sujon: *Actually there were no problems at all. The girls loved looking at all the animals so much that they didn't give me any grief.*

Sohel: *What animals did they like best?*

Sujon: *Giraffes, elephants, monkeys, crocodiles, they liked them all. Only seeing the snake frightened them a bit.*

Sohel: *Sounds like fun! Next time you go, take me with you too. I really like the zoo. It's one of my favorite places.*

Sujon: *Why do you like it so much? Is there a special reason?*

Sohel: *Yes, there is. You can get the best ice cream in town there.*

Sujon: *Really? I didn't know that. In that case if we take you with us, will you treat us all to an ice cream?*

Sohel: *Sure, fine, I'll treat you. I'll be very happy to go with you.*

Transliteration and glosses for dialogue

চিড়িয়াখানায়
ciṛiŷakhanaŷ
at zoo

দুইজন	বন্ধু	কথা	বলছে
duijɔn	bôndhu	kɔtha	bôlche
two	friend	word	they are speaking

সোহেল: তোমার বাবা কি গতকাল অফিসে গিয়েছেন?
Sohel: tomar baba ki gɔtôkal ôphise giŷechen?
Sohel: your father what yesterday to.office he.has.gone

সুজন: হ্যাঁ, তাঁর এই সময়ে অনেক কাজ থাকে।
Sujɔn: hyæ̃, tãr ei sômôŷe ɔnek kaj thake.
Sujon: yes, of.him this time much work it.stays

সে জন্যে ছুটির দিনেও কাজ করতে হয়।
se jônye chuṭir dineo kaj kôrte hɔŷ.
that for of.holiday on.day.also work to.do it.is

সোহেল: আর তুমি গতকাল কি করেছ?
Sohel: ar tumi gɔtôkal ki kôrechô?
Sohel: and you yesterday what you.have.done

সুজন: আমি বাবার হয়ে ছোট বোনদের চিড়িয়াখানায় নিয়ে গিয়েছিলাম।
Sujɔn: ami babar hôŷe chotô bonder ciṛiŷakhanaŷ niŷe giŷechilam.
Sujon: I of.father having.become small of.sisters to.zoo having.taken I had gone

অনেক ফুর্তি হয়েছে।
ɔnek phurti hôŷeche.
much fun it.has.been

সোহেল: তোমার কয়জন বোন? তোমার মা কি যাননি?
Sohel: tomar kɔŷjɔn bon? tomar ma ki yanni?
Sohel: your how.many sister your mother what she.did.not.go

সুজন: চারজন। ছোট দুজন হচ্ছে জমজ।
Sujɔn: carjɔn. chotô dujɔn hôcche jɔmôj.
Sujon: four.person small two.person be twin

আর মাকে দিদিমার সঙ্গে থাকতে হয়েছে।
ar make didimar sɔṅge thakte hôŷeche.
and to.mother of.grandmother with to.stay it.has.become

সোহেল: আগে জানালে আমিও তোমার সঙ্গে যেতাম। সাহায্য করতাম।
Sohel: age janale amio tomar sɔṅge yetam. sahayyô kôrtam.
Sohel: before if.informing I.also of.you with I.would.go help I.would.do

সুজন: আসলে কোনও সমস্যা   হয়নি।
Sujɔn: asôle   kono sɔmôsya hɔyni.
Sujon: actually any   problem   did.not.happen

মেয়েদের সব পশু দেখতে এমন ভাল লেগেছে,   আমাকে কোনও কষ্ট   দেয়নি।
meŷeder sɔb pôśu dekhte æmôn bhalô legeche   amake kono kɔṣṭô dæŷni.
of.the.girls all animal to.see such good it.has.touched to.me any trouble did.not.give

সোহেল: কি কি পশু সবচেয়ে ভাল   লেগেছে?
Sohel: ki   ki   pôśu sɔbceŷe bhalô legeche?
Sohel: what what animal most   good   it.has.touched

সুজন: জিরাফ, হাতি,   বানর, কুমির,   সব ভাল   লেগেছে।
Sujɔn: jiraf   hati   banôr kumir   sɔb bhalô legeche.
Sujon: giraffe elephant monkey crocodile all good it.has.touched

শুধু   সাপটাকে   দেখে   একটু ভয়   পেয়ে   গেছে।
śudhu saptake   dekhe   ektu bhɔɔ̂ŷ peŷe   gæche.
only   to.the.snake having.seen a.bit fear having.got has gone

সোহেল: মজা তো। আর একবার গেলে আমাকেও নিয়ে   যাবে,   কেমন?
Sohel: mɔja to. ar   ækbar gele amakeo niŷe   yabe,   kæmôn?
Sohel: fun   EMP more one.time if.going me.also having.taken you.will.go how

চিড়িয়াখানায়   আমার খুবই   ভাল লাগে।   আমার একটা প্রিয়   জায়গা।
ciṛiŷakhanaŷ amar khubi   bhalô lage.   amar ækṭa priŷô jaŷga.
at.zoo   of.me very.EMP good it.touches of me one.CL favorite place

সুজন: এত   ভাল লাগে কেন? কোনও বিশেষ কারণ আছে?
Sujɔn: ætô bhalô lage kænô? kono biśeṣ karôn ache?
Sujon: so.much good it.touches why   any   special reason there.is

সোহেল: হ্যাঁ, তা তো আছে। ওখানে   শহরের   মধ্যে   সবচেয়ে ভাল আইসক্রিম পাওয়া যায়।
Sohel: hyæ̃ ta   to ache. okhane śɔhôrer môdhye sɔbceŷe bhalô aiskrim paoŷa yaŷ.
Sohel: yes that EMP there.is there   of.town within   all.than good ice-cream getting it.goes

সুজন: তাই   নাকি? আমি তা জানতাম না।
Sujɔn: tai   naki? ami ta jantam na.
Sujon: that.EMP not.what? I   that I.knew not

তাহলে   তোমাকে   নিয়ে   গেলে তুমি   আমাদের সবাইকে আইসক্রিম খাওয়াবে?
tahôle   tomake niŷe   gele tumi amader sɔbaike aiskrim khaoŷabe?
that.if.being you   having taken if going you us   to.all ice-cream you.will.feed

সোহেল: আচ্ছা, ঠিক আছে, খাওয়াব।   তোমাদের সঙ্গে গেলে খুশি   হব।
Sohel: accha ṭhik ache, khaoŷabô.   tomader sɔ̇nge gele khuśi hɔbô.
Sohel: OK   right it.is I.will.feed of.you.PL with if.going happy I.will.be

Vocabulary: Dialogue

বন্ধু bôndhu *n.* friend

কথা kɔtha *n.* word, fact

কথা বলা kɔtha bɔla *vb.* talk

গতকাল gɔtôkal *adv.* yesterday

এই ei *adj.* this

সে জন্যে se jɔnye *conj.* for that reason

ছুটি chuṭi *n.* holiday

দিন di:n *n.* day

হয়ে hôŷe *pp.* in place of

চিড়িয়াখানা ciṛiŷakhana *n.* zoo

নেওয়া neoŷa *vb.* take

যাওয়া yaoŷa *vb.* go

নিয়ে যাওয়া niŷe yaoŷa *vb.* take along

জমজ jɔmôj *n.* twins

দিদিমা didima *n.* maternal grandmother

জানানো janano *vb.* inform, let know

সাহায্য sahayyô *n.* help

আসলে asôle *adv.* actually

কোনও kono *adj.* any

সমস্যা sɔmôsya *n.* problem

মেয়ে meŷe *n.* girl

সব sɔb *adj.* all

পশু pôśu *n.* animal

এমন æmôn *adv.* such, so

ভাল লাগা bhalô laga *vb.* like

কষ্ট kɔṣṭô *n.* trouble, hardship

সবচেয়ে sɔbceŷe *pp.* than all

হাতি hati *n.* elephant

বানর banôr *n.* monkey

কুমির kumir *n.* crocodile

সাপ sap *n.* snake

ভয় bhɔŷ *n.* fear

ভয় পাওয়া bhɔŷ paoŷa *vb.* be scared/afraid

মজা mɔja *n.* fun

তো to *emp.* (added to the end of words as an emphasizer)

আর ar *adv.* more

একবার ækbar *adv.* once, one time

ই i *emp.* (is added to the end of words as an emphasizer)

প্রিয় priŷô *adj.* favorite, well-liked

জায়গা jaŷga *n.* place

এত æto *adv.* so much

কেন kæno *qu.* why

বিশেষ biśeṣ *adj.* special

কারণ karôṇ *n.* reason

শহর śɔhôr *n.* town

আইসক্রিম aiskrim *n.* ice cream

পাওয়া যায় paoŷa yaŷ *vb.* is available

তাই নাকি tai naki *phr.* is that so?

সবাই sɔbai *n.* everybody

খাওয়ানো khaoŷano *vb.* feed, give to eat

ঠিক আছে ṭhik ache *phr.* OK, alright

Grammar 6: Bangla classifiers

If you haven't yet had a look through the grammar terms at the beginning of the book (page xv), do so before you read through this section to make sure that you understand the terms used. There is quite a lot of new information in this section but also exercises to practice your new skills.

In Unit 4 we looked at case—an important component of nouns. Now we will look at classifiers: they do the work English articles do, providing definite or indefinite, singular or plural distinctions, but they also have a number of other uses. The main classifier in Bangla is টা ṭa. Classifiers are attachments (suffixes)—they never occur on their own. When they are attached to nouns they come before the case ending.

> আমগাছ-টা-র আম
> a:mgachṭar a:m
> *the mangoes on the mango tree* (lit: *the mango tree's mangoes*)

Bangla classifiers divide into singular and plural as follows:

> singular: -টা ṭa   -টি ṭi   -জন jɔn   -খানা khana
> plural: -গুলো gulo   -গুলি guli   (-রা ra)

Each noun phrase contains only ONE classifier.

· ·

টা ṭa

টা can be considered the default classifier in Bangla. Although টা is by itself a singular classifier, it also combines with numbers and quantifiers (words that specify an amount).

Definite noun phrases
টা is added to a noun to make it definite:

> নাম *name*   নামটা *the name*   ছেলে *boy*   ছেলেটা *the boy*

টা is used mainly with inanimate nouns but can, somewhat less respectfully, follow non-honorific human nouns. Honorifc nouns don't usually take a classifier at all. *The king* is simply রাজা.

Indefinite noun phrases
টা is added to এক *one*, preceding the noun, to make a noun indefinite:

> গাছ *tree*   একটা গাছ *a tree*   লোক *person*   একটা লোক *a person*

Numbers, quantifiers, and measure words
টা is added to numbers with count nouns*:

> চারটা টেবিল *four tables*   তিনটা গাড়ি *three cars*

টা can be added to quantifiers with nouns and adjectives:

কয়েকটা ছবি   *a few pictures*

টা is dropped when numbers and quantifiers precede a measure word:

দুই বছর *two years*   অনেক দিন *many days*   তিন ঘণ্টা *three hours*

The same principle of dropping টা with measure words applies to distances:

পাঁচ মাইল *five miles*

---

*count noun: a noun that can form a plural and, in the singular, can be used with the indefinite article (e.g. *books, a book; ideas, an idea*); contrasts with mass (or non-count nouns) like *water, flour, weather*

Demonstratives, possessives, descriptives

Adding টা to demonstrative, possessive, and descriptive adjectives makes them into nouns.

demonstrative:	এটা *this (thing)*	ওটা *that (thing)*	সেটা *that (thing)*
possessive:	তোমারটা *your one*		
descriptive:	বড়টা *the big one*		

This, together with the fact that each noun phrase has only one classifier means that in order to say *this book* or *my car* টা comes **after** the noun: এই বই-টা *this book*, আমার গাড়ি-টা *my car*.

Here is the contrast in the positioning of টা within the noun phrase:

numbers, quantifiers		vs	demonstrative, possessive, descriptive	
তিনটা টেবিল	*three tables*	but	এই টেবিলটা	*this table*
কয়েক-টা কলম	*a few pens*	but	লাল কলমটা	*the red pen*
কিছুটা জমি	*some land*	but	আমাদের জমিটা	*our land*

Time reference

টা is always added to numbers for time references. To say *at 10 o'clock*, the locative ending য় is added to টা.

দশটায় *at ten o'clock*
সকাল পাঁচটায় *at five o'clock in the morning*

[There is more on telling time in Unit 8.]

• •

টি ṭi

টি can do all the same things as টা but it is not used for time reference. Traditionally, টি is said to have a less neutral, more affectionate overtone than টা. This is generally true in the context of human beings: we are more likely to have লোকটা *the man* and মেয়েটি *the girl* than the other way round. However, there are many factual contexts where টা and টি are used interchangeably without any emotional content. The following are some examples using টি. The টি in the first two examples is split off with a hyphen just to show the structure, but in normal writing টা and টি are always attached to the noun or adjective.

definite:	দিন-টি	*the day*
indefinite:	এক-টি ছেলে	*a boy*
numbers:	দুটি ছেলেমেয়ে	*two children*
quantifiers:	কয়েকটি গ্রাম	*a few villages*
possessives:	তোমার কুকুরটি	*your dog*
demonstratives:	এই ছবিটি	*this picture*
descriptives:	ছোটটা	*the little one*

· ·

জন jɔn

জন is used with human beings only and rarely follows a noun. It does not have the definite singular properties of টা or টি. জন comes into its own with numbers and quantifiers preceding nouns. It makes adjectives into animate nouns:

indefinite:	একজন লোক	*a man/person*
numbers:	দুজন ছেলে	*two boys*
quantifiers:	কয়জন বোন	*how many sisters*
adjectives:	অন্যজন	*the other person*

· ·

খানা khana (খানি khani)

খানা is not as common as টা and টি but it is useful to be able to recognize it. খানা is used for physical, inanimate objects or for objectifying living things: একটা মাছ can refer to live fish, একখানা মাছ means fish on the plate. In Narrative 1 in Unit 4 we had the sentences:

উঠানের এক পাশে <u>একখানা</u> কুঁড়ে ঘর। কুঁড়ে ঘরখানার দেওয়াল বাঁশ আর মাটির।
On one side of the courtyard is a thatched hut. The wall of the hut is made from bamboo and earth.

Some examples with খানা, খানি:

definite:	ঘরখানা	*the building*
indefinite:	একখানা ঘর	*a building*
numbers:	চারখানা বই	*four books*
quantifiers:	অনেকখানি আশা	*a lot of hope*

· ·

গুলো gulo   গুলি guli   (occasionally) গুলা gula

These are **plural classifiers**. They are used mainly with inanimate nouns but can also be used with non-honorific humans. They add definiteness as well as plurality. They are added to nouns, demonstratives, possessives, quantifiers, and other adjectives. গুলো and গুলি are never added to numbers. গুলি, similar to টি, can indicate sympathy or smallness. Indefinite plurals in Bangla are done without classifiers: গাড়ি = *cars*.

indefinite singular:	একটা বাগান *a garden*
definite singular:	বাগানটা *the garden*
indefinite plural:	বাগান *gardens*
definite plural:	বাগানগুলো *the gardens*

Case endings are added AFTER the classifiers:

definite plurals:	ছেলেগুলি *the boys*
demonstratives:	এগুলি *these ones* ওগুলো *those ones*
quantifiers:	অনেকগুলো কলা গাছ *many banana trees*
possessives:	আমারগুলো *my ones*
descriptives:	বড়গুলি *the big ones*

• •

–রা ra   –এরা era

–রা is added to animate nouns as a nominative plural ending and is therefore not a classifier but a case ending. It can be added to demonstratives এ *this* and ও *that* to form animate plurals: এরা *these people,* ওরা *those people.* Instead of the expected *সে-রা (parallel to এরা) we have তারা. রা is never added to quantifiers or possessive pronouns but it can turn descriptive adjectives into people: বড়-রা *adults,* গরিব-রা *the poor.* In the genitive and object case –রা changes to –দের. There is no locative case.

–রা follows vowels:

মেয়েরা *(the) girls*	ছেলেরা *(the) boys*
মহিলারা *(the) women*	মামারা *(the) uncles*

এরা follows consonants:

মানুষেরা *people*	লোকেরা *people*

–দের genitives/objectives:

মেয়েদের *of/to the girls*	লোকদের *of/to the people*

R08
Narrative

Note: this is the first narrative without transliteration. Keep the alphabet and conjuncts charts at hand.

আমার পরিবার

আমার নাম পল্লবী। আমার বয়স যোলো। আমি বাংলাদেশের ছোট একটা গ্রামে থাকি। গ্রামের নাম বনপাড়া। আমার পরিবারে আছে অনেক মানুষ, মা-বাবা, দাদা, দিদি, পিসি, ঠাকুরমা। বাংলাদেশ মুসলমানের দেশ কিন্তু আমরা খ্রিস্টান। সে জন্যে আমরা আপা, চাচা, ফুফু না বলে দিদি, কাকা ও পিসি বলি। বড় ভাইকে আমরা দাদা বলি। আমার দাদার নাম অরুণ। সে সামনের মাস থেকে ঢাকায় একটা কলেজে পড়বে। তার বয়স উনিস। আমার দিদির নাম উমা। তার বয়স সাতাইস। সে তার স্বামীর সঙ্গে ঢাকায় থাকে। তাদের তিনটি বাচ্চা আছে, দুটা ছেলে, একটি মেয়ে। মেয়েটি খুব ছোট, তার এক বছর বয়স এখনও হয় নি। ছেলেদের বয়স পাঁচ আর তিন, তাদের নাম প্রদীপ আর বিপ্লব। উমাদির স্বামী চন্দন তার অফিসের কাজ নিয়ে প্রায়ই আমেরিকায় যায়। তখন উমাদি বাচ্চাদের নিয়ে বাড়িতে আসে, আমরা সবাই খুব খুশি হয়ে যাই। প্রদীপ খুব দুষ্টু, খুব চালাক আর বিপ্লব খুব কথা বলে। সব কিছু নিয়ে প্রশ্ন করে। সে আমাকে অনেক ভালবাসে, প্রায় সব সময় শুধু আমার কাছে থাকতে চায়। আর এক বছর পরে প্রদীপকে ইস্কুলে যেতে হবে। তখন ওরা আর বেশি আসতে পারবে না, কিন্তু আমি হয়তো ঢাকায় গিয়ে আমার লেখাপড়া শেষ করে দেব।

My family

My name is Pollobi. I am sixteen. I live in a small village in Bangladesh. The village is called Bonpara. There are a lot of people in my family: my parents, my older brother, my sister, my aunt, and my grandmother. Bangladesh is a Muslim country but we are Christians. That's why we don't say Apa, Chacha, Phuphu but Didi, Kaka, and Pishi. We call an older brother Dada. My Dada's name is Orun. He will be studying in a college in Dhaka from next month. He is nineteen. My sister is called Uma. She is twenty-seven. She lives in Dhaka with her husband. They have three children, two boys and a girl. The girl is very young, she is not even one year old yet. The boys are five and three and their names are Prodip and Biplob. Uma's husband Chondon often goes to America for his work. Then Uma comes to the village with the children and we are all very happy. Prodip is quite naughty and clever and Biplob talks a lot. He asks about everything. He loves me very much and wants to spend almost all the time with me. From next year Prodip will have to go to school, so they won't be able to come so often anymore. But maybe I will go to Dhaka to finish my studying.

Vocabulary: Narrative

ষোলো ṣolo *num.* sixteen
বাংলাদেশ bam̐ladeś *name* Bangladesh
থাকা thaka *vb.* live, stay
মা–বাবা ma–baba *n.* parents
দাদা dada *n.* older brother *(H.)*
দিদি didi *n.* older sister *(H.)*
পিসি pisi *n.* aunt: father's sister *(H.)*
ঠাকুরমা ṭhakurma *n.* grandmother: father's
   mother *(H.)*
মুসলমান musôlman *n.* Muslim
দেশ deś *n.* country
খ্রিস্টান khrisṭan *n.* Christian
আপা apa *n.* older sister *(Musl.)*
চাচা caca *n.* uncle: father's younger brother
   (Musl.)
ফুফু phuphu *n.* aunt: father's sister *(Musl.)*
কাকা kaka *n.* uncle: father's younger
   brother *(H.)*
বড় ভাই bɔṛô bhai *n.* older brother *(Musl.)*
অরুণ orūṇ *name* Orun *(m.)*
সামনে মাস samne mas *phr.* next month
ঢাকা ḍhaka *name* Dhaka *(capital of
   Bangladesh)*
কলেজ kɔlej *n.* college
উনিশ uniś *num.* nineteen
উমা uma *name* Uma *(f.)*

সাতাশ sataś or সাতাই sataiś *num.* twenty-
   seven
বাচ্চা bacca *n.* child
এখনও ækhônô *adv.* yet, still
নিয়ে niŷe *pp.* with, about
তখন tɔkhôn *adv.* then
সবাই sɔbai *n.* everybody
খুশি khuśi *adj.* happy
দুষ্টু dusṭu *adj.* naughty
চালাক calak *adj.* clever
কথা বলা kɔtha bɔla *vb.* talk
প্রশ্ন prôśnô *n.* question
প্রশ্ন করা prôśnô kɔra *vb.* ask question
অনেক ɔnek *adj./adv.* much
ভালবাসা bhalôbasa or ভালোবাসা bhalobasa
   vb. love
সব সময় sɔb sômôŷ *n.* always
কাছে kache *pp.* near
সামনে samne *adj.* here: next
ইস্কুল iskul *n.* school
পারা para *vb.* be able to
হয়তো hɔŷto *adv.* perhaps
গিয়ে → যাওয়া yaoŷa *vb.* go
লেখাপড়া lekhapɔṛa *n.* studying, education
শেষ করা śeṣ kɔra *vb.* finish

Grammar 7: Postpositions

Bangla postpositions are equivalent to English prepositions. They appear **after** the nouns and pronouns they accompany. Many Bangla postpositions are nouns and require the preceding noun to be in the genitive. Other postpositions are derived from verbs and don't require a preceding genitive. The chart below gives the common Bangla postpositions with their case use and examples.

Temporal

আগে age *before* (gen.)   শুক্রবারের আগে *before Friday*
পরে pɔre *after* (gen.)   খাবারের পরে *after the meal*
থেকে theke *from* (nom.)   আজ থেকে *from today*
পর্যন্ত pôryôntô *until* (nom.)   বুধবার পর্যন্ত *until Wednesday*
মধ্যে môdhye *within* (gen.)   তিন ঘণ্টার মধ্যে *within three hour*
ধরে dhôre *during, for* (nom.)   তিন মাস ধরে *for three months*

Spatial

উপরে upôre *above, on* (gen.)   রাস্তার উপরে *on the road*
নিচে nice *under, underneath* (gen.)   ঠেলাগাড়ির নিচে *under the hand-cart*
বাইরে baire *outside of, beyond* (gen.)   শহরের বাইরে *outside the town*
ভিতরে bhitore *in, inside of* (gen.)   গ্রামের ভিতরে *inside the village*
    আমার ভিতরে *in my heart*
সামনে samne *in front of* (gen.)   বাড়ির সামনে *in front of the house*
পিছনে pichone *behind* (gen.)   ঘরের পিছনে *behind the building*
পাশে paśe *alongside, next to* (gen.)   উঠানের এক পাশে *on one side of the courtyard*
কাছে kache *close to, near, with* (gen.)   ছাপড়ার কাছে *close to Chapra*
    তার চাচার কাছে *with her uncle*
মাঝখানে majhkhane *in the middle of* (gen.)   বাড়ির মাঝখানে *in the middle of the homestead*
মধ্যে môdhye *among, by, within* (gen.)   ফলগাছের মধ্যে *among the fruit trees*
দিকে dike *towards* (gen.)   কলকাতার দিকে *towards Kolkata*
ডান দিকে ḍan dike *on the right side* (gen.)   টেবিলের ডান দিকে *to the right side of the table*
বাঁ দিকে bã dike *on the left side* (gen.)   গাছের বাঁ দিকে *on the left side of the tree*
থেকে theke *from* (nom.)   ঢাকা থেকে *from Dhaka*

Circumstantial

জন্য jɔnyô jɔnye *for* (gen.)   তাদের জন্যে *for them*
          fixed phrase: সেজন্য *for that reason*
সঙ্গে sɔṅge *with* (gen.)   তার স্বামীর সঙ্গে *with her husband*
মত mɔtô *like* (gen.)   আমাদের মত মানুষ *people like us*
ছাড়া chaṛa *without, except* (all cases)   তুমি ছাড়া *without you*
    ছুটিতে ছাড়া *except in the holidays*
নিয়ে diŷe *about* (nom., obj. with humans)   সব কিছু নিয়ে *about everything*
    তাকে নিয়ে *about him*
দিয়ে diŷe *through, with* (instr.) (nom.)   জানালা দিয়ে *through the window*
পরিবর্তে pôribôrte *instead* (gen.)   টাকার পরিবর্তে *instead of money*
কাছ থেকে kach theke *from (a person)* (gen.)   বাবার কাছ থেকে *from father*

সত্ত্বেও sɔttveo (sɔtteo) *despite* (nom.)   বৃষ্টি হওয়া সত্ত্বেও *despite the rain*
চেয়ে ceŷe *than* (gen.)   তোমার চেয়ে বড় *older than you*
হয়ে hôŷe *in place of* (gen.); *via* (nom.)   বাবার হয়ে *in father's place*

Other Uses for Postpositions

Double postpositions

Since many postpositions are nouns in the locative case, they can revert back to their nominal status and be followed by another postposition. We have already seen কাছ থেকে *from (a person)* and there are also combinations like আগের মত *as before* and উপর দিয়ে *along the top* (e.g., রাস্তার উপর দিয়ে *along the top of the road*).

Postpositions as adverbs

Many postpositions can also be used as adverbs. Postpositions occur within noun phrases; adverbs are more independent:

postposition: এই মাসের পরে *after this month*
adverb: এক মাস পরে *one month later*

postposition: তিনটার আগে *before three o'clock*,
adverb: তিন দিন আগে *three days ago*

postposition: তার পিছনে *behind him*
adverb: সে পিছনে বসবে। *He will sit at the back*

postposition: টেবিলের উপরে *on top of the table*
adverb: তারা উপরে থাকে। *They live upstairs*.

Grammar 8: Obligation

There is a special structure in Bangla to express obligation or *have to* meanings. In our dialogue we have two examples:

ছুটির দিনেও কাজ করতে হয়।
Work must be done even on holidays.

মাকে দিদিমার সঙ্গে থাকতে হয়েছে।
Mother had to stay with grandmother.

This is a modal structure and will properly be introduced in Unit 10 where we discuss the uses of non-finite verb forms. করতে and থাকতে are (non-finite) imperfective participles. The obligation structure uses these imperfective participles in combination with a 3rd person verb form of হওয়া *be, become*. The subject of the sentence is usually in the objective case, sometimes in the genitive case. You don't need to actively learn this structure yet at this stage but it is useful to be able to recognize it. Keep a look-out for it in the dialogue in Unit 7 between the two neighbors. Here are some more examples:

তাকে তাদের আইসক্রিম খাওয়াতে হবে।
He will have to feed them ice cream.

প্রদীপকে ইস্কুলে যেতে হবে।
Prodip will have to go to school.

আমাকে সার্টটা ফেরত দিতে হবে।
I have to return the shirt.

তোমাকে তার সঙ্গে কথা বলতে হয়েছে।
You had to talk to him.

Additional Vocabulary

In the dialogue about the zoo, you learned some animal names. In the narrative on 'My family' quite a few family relationship words came up. Here are some more lexical items in these categories. A complete list of family relationships, i.e., kinship terms is given in Appendix 7.

Animals

animal পশু pôśu, জীবজন্তু jībjôntu
bird পাখি pakhi
buffalo মহিষ môhiṣ
butterfly প্রজাপতি prôjapôti
cat বেড়াল beṛal, বিড়াল biṛal
chicken মুরগি murgi
cow গরু gôru
crocodile কুমির kumir
dog কুকুর kukur
donkey গাধা gadha
elephant হাতি hati
fish মাছ ma:ch
fly মাছি machi
frog ব্যাং byaṃ (bæng)
goat ছাগল chagôl
horse ঘোড়া ghoṛa
insect পোকা poka
lion সিংহ siṁhô
monkey বানর banôr
mosquito মশা mɔśa
mouse ইঁদুর ĩdur
pig শূকর śūkôr
sheep, lamb ভেড়া bhæṛa
snake সাপ sa:p
spider মাকড়সা makôṛsa
tiger বাঘ ba:gh

People

brother *(older)* দাদা dada
brother *(younger)* ভাই bhai
child বাচ্চা bacca, শিশু śiśu
daughter মেয়ে meye
father বাবা baba, অব্বা abba
friend *(m.)* বন্ধু bôndhu; *(f.)* বান্ধবী bandhôbī
girl মেয়ে meŷe
human being মানুষ manuṣ
husband স্বামী svamī (shami)
man পুরুষ puruṣ
mother মা ma, অম্মা amma
parents মা-বাবা ma–baba
people, person লোক lok
sister *(older)* দিদি didi, আপা apa
sister *(younger)* বোন bon
son ছেলে chele
student ছাত্র chatrô *(m.)*, ছাত্রী chatrī *(f.)*
wife স্ত্রী stri, বউ bôu
woman মহিলা môhila

Exercises: Unit 5

Exercise 5:1 Noun phrases

These phrases include the use of case endings and classifiers. Practicing phrases like these will build up your confidence in speaking and writing.

Translate into English:

(i)   আমার কলমগুলো   _____

(ii)   মেয়েটি   _____

(iii)   তার বউয়ের নাম   _____

(iv)   একটা ছোট বাগান   _____

(v)   অনেকগুলো কলা গাছ   _____

(vi)   আমার ছোট বোন   _____

(vii)   দুটা রিকশা   _____

(viii) এই বড় রাস্তাটা   _____

(ix)   কুকুর   _____

(x)   বইগুলি   _____

Translate into Bangla:

(xi)   *many girls*   _____

(xii)   *one year*   _____

(xiii) *in his garden*   _____

(xiv)   *in his mother's garden*   _____

(xv)   *the snakes*   _____

(xvi)   *how many sisters*   _____

(xvii) *a journalist*   _____

(xviii) *your brothers*   _____

(xix)   *three days*   _____

(xx)   *this village* (use টা)   _____

Exercise 5:2 Additional practice টা, টি, etc. (for self-correction)

For more practice and to build up your confidence, the following noun phrases have been picked out from the dialogues and narratives in the previous Units for translation:

Unit 2   দুজন ছেলে, কয়েকটা ছবি, এগুলো, একটা অফিসে (note the locative ending!), নামটা

_____

Unit 3   একজন মহিলা, একটি ছেলে, অনেক দিন, তিন সপ্তাহ, দুই বছর, আজ রাতে (locative!), তিন ঘণ্টার পথ

_____

Unit 4   এই সময়ে (locative!), অনেক কাজ, ছুটির দিনে (locative), ছোট দুজন, কোনও সমস্যা, সাপটা, সব পশু, আমার একটা প্রিয় জায়গা, তার তিনটি বাচ্চা

_____

Exercise 5:3 Postpositions
Translate the phrases, paying attention to the Bangla case endings.

Note: Remember that you can use the locative ending on the noun instead of a postposition in phrases that contain the English prepositions *in, at, on*: *on the table* can be টেবিলের উপরে or simply টেবিলে; *in the village* either গ্রামের মধ্যে or গ্রামে.

(i)   তোমার জন্যে   _____

(ii)   বাড়ির সামনে   _____

(iii)   আমার কলমের মত   _____

(iv)   বারান্দার ডান দিকে   _____

(v)   তার ছোট বোনদের সঙ্গে   _____

(vi)   কলকাতা থেকে   _____

(vii)   ফলগাছের মধ্যে   _____

(viii) দিনের মাঝখানে   _____

(ix)   কার কাছে   _____

(x)   শহরের মধ্যে   _____

(xi) তিন বছর আগে _____

(xii) সামনের মাস থেকে _____

(xiii) রাত পর্যন্ত _____

(xiv) উঠানের বাইরে _____

(xv) উত্তর দিকে _____

(xvi) *near the house* _____

(xvii) *underneath the table* _____

(xviii) *inside the train* _____

(xix) *until yesterday* _____

(xx) *from then on* _____

(xxi) *behind the village* _____

(xxii) *with your father* _____

(xxiii) *like my (older) brother* _____

(xxiv) *before the night* _____

(xxv) *towards the town* _____

(xxvi) *in the West* _____

(xxvii) *after Monday* _____

(xxviii) *until Saturday* _____

(xxix) *from morning to night* _____
   (use থেকে and পর্যন্ত, no case endings)

(xxx) *to the East* _____

UNIT 6
VERBS

Grammar 9: Bangla verbs complete
Verb stems – Vowel mutation
Verb endings
Conjugation patterns
Non-finite verb forms
Imperatives
Grammar 10: Making sentences
Additional Vocabulary
Essential verbs
Verbs *say, tell, talk, speak*
Exercises

Grammar 9: Bangla verbs complete

We have seen a number of verbs and verb forms already and you have probably noticed that verb endings change from person to person (e.g., আমি জানি ami jani *I know* and তুমি জান tumi jano *you know*) in the conversation between Subroto and Mike in Units 2 and 3. In this chapter we are taking a very close look at verbs and all their components, so that by the end of the chapter you have all the information you need to understand the system. Providing the correct verb forms yourself will take a bit longer and needs quite a lot of practice. Luckily, in Bangla the verb usually comes at the end of sentences so you have a bit of time to work out the verb ending before you get there. Read the following sections very carefully: there is a lot of new information here that had to be set out step by step with exercises interspersed throughout, but by the end of the unit you will have all the building blocks you need to start using Bangla verbs confidently.

Verb stems – Vowel mutation

Each Bangla verb form consists of a stem and an ending. The stem is the first part of the verb, i.e., the part we are left with when verb endings are dropped, for example from লিখতে likhte we get লিখ- likh-, from লেখা lekha we get লেখ- lekh-. Bangla verb stems mutate between two adjacent vowels according to the following patterns:

	back					front		low		high
high:	i					u		e	→	i
mid-high:		e			o			æ	→	e
mid-low:			æ	ɔ				o	→	u
low:				a				ɔ	→	o

This is a bit like the change in English verbs from simple present *sing* to simple past *sang, come* to *came, get* to *got, find* to *found*, except these count as irregular verbs in English and need to be learned individually. In Bangla the vowel mutation is systematic and affects all verbs, so basically there are no irregular verbs. The terms high, low, back, and front refer to the positioning of these vowels in the mouth. ই i is the highest vowel at the back of the mouth, উ u is the highest vowel at the front of the mouth. These changes do **not** apply to verbs that have an -a- in the stem or to extended verbs ending in –নো -no. The verbal noun (VN.) (low stem + a) is the verb form given in dictionaries.

এ, ৈ e – ই, ি i

Verbal forms change from low stem এ e (2nd and 3rd person present simple, verbal noun, imperative) to high stem ই i (all other verb forms).

VN. (low)	1st per. pr. s. (high)	3rd per. pr. s. (low)	
লেখা	আমি লিখি	সে লেখে	*write*
শেখা	আমি শিখি	সে শেখে	*learn*
চেনা	আমি চিনি	সে চেনে	*know, recognize*

এ æ – এ e

Verb forms change from low stem এ æ (2nd and 3rd person present simple, verbal noun, imperative) to high stem এ e (all other verb forms). **There is no change in spelling!**

VN. (low)	1st per. pr. s. (high)	3rd per. pr. s. (low)	
ফেলা phæla	আমি ফেলি pheli	সে ফেলে phæle	*throw*
দেখা dækha	আমি দেখি dekhi	সে দেখে dækhe	*see*
খেলা khæla	আমি খেলি kheli	সে খেলে khæle	*play*

ও o – ঊ u

Verb forms change from low stem ও o (2nd and 3rd person present simple, verbal noun, imperative) to high stem ঊ u (all other verb forms).

VN. (low)	1st per. pr. s. (high)	3rd per. pr. s. (low)	
খোলা	আমি খুলি	সে খোলে	*open*
বোঝা	আমি বুঝি	সে বোঝে	*understand*
ওঠা	আমি উঠি	সে ওঠে	*rise, get up*

অ ɔ – অ o

Verb forms change from low stem ɔ (short, open) (2nd and 3rd ps present simple, verbal noun, imperative) to high stem ô (long) (all other verb forms). The inherent vowel covers both these sounds, i.e., there is no change in spelling!

VN. (low)	1st per. pr. s. (high)	3rd per. pr. s. (low)	
করা kɔra	আমি করি kôri	সে করে kɔre	*do, make*
বলা bɔla	আমি বলি bôli	সে বলে bɔle	*say, speak*
বসা bɔsa	আমি বসি bôsi	সে বসে bɔse	*sit*

Verbs with আ a in the stem retain this vowel in all persons and tenses except the perfect (present and past) tenses, where the আ –a becomes an এ –e (in all persons).

VN. (a)	1st per. pr. s. (a)	1st per. pr. perf. (e/i)	
রাখা	আমি রাখি	আমি রেখেছি	*put, keep*
থাকা	আমি থাকি	আমি থেকেছি	*stay*
আসা	আমি আসি	আমি এসেছি	*come*
যাওয়া	আমি যাই	আমি গিয়েছি*	*go*

*Note: গিয়েছি from যাওয়া is irregular.

It is important to be aware of these vowel mutations, not so much because of the present simple verb forms—no one will complain if you say সে বুঝে instead of সে বোঝে for *he understands*—as the verb endings are quite distinctive enough. But if you want to look up verbs in the dictionary, you'll need to know that for চেপে for instance, you need to look up চাপা, or for ছুঁতে you have to go to ছোঁয়া and so on.

Note: A list of common verbs ordered by vowel mutation pattern is given in Appendix 4.

Verb endings

Bangla has eight tenses. Here are their English equivalents.

Verb: খেলা *to play*

present simple (pr.s.)	আমি খেলি	*I play*
present continuous (pr.c.)	আমি খেলছি	*I am playing*
present perfect (pr.perf.)	আমি খেলেছি	*I have played*
future tense (fut.)	আমি খেলব	*I will play*
past simple (p.s.)	আমি খেললাম	*I played*
past continuous (p.c.)	আমি খেলছিলাম	*I was playing*
past perfect (p.perf.)	আমি খেলেছিলাম	*I had played*
past habitual (p.habit)	আমি খেলতাম	*I would play / I used to play*

In addition to these tenses, Bangla verbs have imperatives and four non-finite verb forms:

imperative		খেল	*play!*
non-finites	VN.	খেলা	*playing*
	IP.	খেলতে	*to play*
	CP.	খেললে	*if playing*
	PP.	খেলে	*having played*

Bangla verb conjugation is very regular. It is the same for singular and plural, for example:

আমরা *we* has the same verb endings as আমি *I*

তোমরা *you* (fam., pl.) has the same endings as তুমি *you* (fam., sg.)

তারা, ওরা *they* (ord.) has the same endings as সে, ও *he, she* (ord.)

আপনারা *you* (hon., pl.) and তাঁরা *they* (hon., pl.) have the same endings as
   আপনি *you* (hon., sg.) and তিনি *he, she* (hon., pl.).

This means that all honorific forms have the same endings. For neuter তা ta *it* and all non-living things the ordinary forms (as for সে se *he, she*) are used.

As we saw at the beginning of this Unit, all conjugated verb forms consist of a stem and an ending. The stem carries the meaning of the verb; the ending marks tense and person. Verb endings can again be divided into a tense marker and a person marker. Here is an overview of the forms:

verb tense markers		verb endings			
		1st per. আমি	2nd per. fam. তুমি	3rd per. ord. সে	hon. আপনি, তিনি
fut.	ব b	–o	–e	–e	–en
pr.s.	–	–i	–o	–e	–en
pr.c.	ছ ch				
pr.perf.	এছ ech				
p.s.	ল l	–am	–e	–o	–en
p.c.	ছিল chil				
p.perf.	এছিল echil				
p. habit	ত t				

(Note: The shaded boxes present the area of difficulty in remembering verb endings correctly.)

Bangla verbs can be divided into four classes according to their stem formation:

Class 1: CVC = consonant – vowel – consonant, e.g., কর- kɔr- *do*
      VC = vowel – consonant, e.g., ওঠ- oth- *rise, get up*
Class 2: CaC = consonant – a – consonant, e.g., থাক- thak- *stay*
      aC = a – consonant, আস- as- *come*
Class 3: CV = consonant – vowel, e.g., হও- hɔo- *be, become,*
      Ca = consonant – a, e.g., যা- ya- *go*
Class 4: CVCa = consonant –vowel – consonant – a, e.g., ঘুমা- ghuma *sleep*
      CaCa = consonant – vowel (incl. a) – consonant – a, e.g., বানা- bana- *prepare*

Note on spelling: all verb endings in the inherent vowel are pronounced long and can also be written with the vowel sign of the long ও, i.e., you will find যাবো as well as যাব for 1st person future tense. On the whole this book follows the inherent vowel system.

Conjugation patterns

The charts for করা kɔra *do* (Class 1) and খাওয়া khaoŷa *eat* (Class 3) are given below. English translations for each verb form are given here, so that once you have seen and grasped the pattern, you will easily be able to provide the translations for the remaining charts yourselves. All 3rd person verb forms apply to *he, she,* and *it* as well as *they.* Note that the translations for the tenses are somewhat stylized here. In real language the present perfect, for instance, often acts as a past tense and will require a past tense translation *I did / I ate.* A more detailed discussion on tenses will be given in Unit 10.

Demonstration verb chart:
Class 1 CVC (ɔ – ô) করা kɔra *do* and Class 3 (Ca) খাওয়া khaoŷa *eat*

Tenses	আমি 1st person	তুমি 2nd per. fam.	সে 3rd per. ord.	আপনি, উনি honorific
pr.s.	করি kôri *I do*	কর kɔrô *you do*	করে kɔre *he does*	করেন kɔren *you do / he does*
	খাই *I eat*	খাও *you eat*	খায় *he eats*	খান *you eat / he eats*
pr.c.	করছি *I am doing*	করছ *you are doing*	করছে *he is doing*	করছেন *you are doing / he is doing*
	খাচ্ছি *I am eating*	খাচ্ছ *you are eating*	খাচ্ছে *he is eating*	খাচ্ছেন *you are eating / he is eating*
pr.perf.	করেছি *I have done*	করেছ *you have done*	করেছে *he has done*	করেছেন *you have done/ he has done*
	খেয়েছি *I have eaten*	খেয়েছ *you have eaten*	খেয়েছে *he has eaten*	খেয়েছেন *you have eaten / he has eaten*
fut.	করব *I will do*	করবে *you will do*	করবে *he will do*	করবেন *you will do / he will do*
	খাব *I will eat*	খাবে *you will eat*	খাবে *he will eat*	খাবেন *you will eat / he will eat*

p.s.	করলাম *I did*	করলে *you did*	করল *he did*	করলেন *you did /* *he did*
	খেলাম *I ate*	খেলে *you ate*	খেল *he ate*	খেলেন *you ate / he ate*
p.c.	করছিলাম *I was doing*	করছিলে *you were doing*	করছিল *he was doing*	করছিলেন *you were doing /* *he/she was doing*
p.perf.	খাচ্ছিলাম *I was eating*	খাচ্ছিলে *you were eat-* *ing*	খাচ্ছিল *he was eating*	খাচ্ছিলেন *you were eating /* *he was eating*
	করেছিলাম *I had done*	করেছিলে *you had done*	করেছিল *he had done*	করেছিলেন *you had done /* *he/she had done*
	খেয়েছিলাম *I had eaten*	খেয়েছিলে *you had eaten*	খেয়েছিল *he had eaten*	খেয়েছিলেন *you had eaten /* *he/she had eaten*
p.habit	করতাম *I would do*	করতে *you would do*	করত *he would do*	করতেন *you would do /* *he/she would do*
	খেতাম *I would eat*	খেতে *you would eat*	খেত *he would eat*	খেতেন *you would eat /* *he would eat*
imp.	---	কর kɔrô *do!* করিও kôrio *do!*	করুক *let him do!*	করেন kɔren *do!* করুন kôrun *do!*
	---	খাও *eat!*	খাক *let him eat!*	খান *eat!*
non-finites	VN করা *doing*	IP করতে *to do* *if doing*	CP করলে *if doing*	PP করে *having done*
	VN খাওয়া *eating*	IP খেতে *to eat*	CP খেলে *if eating*	PP খেয়ে *having eaten*

Non-finite verb forms – Introduction

Apart from the verb forms expressing person and tense, verbs also have non-finite (non-restricted) forms. They operate in combination with finite verb forms. English examples for this kind of thing are sentences like the following. The non-finite verb forms are underlined.

> *I want to stay.* (inf.)
> *She carries on talking.* (VN., gerund)
> *All the food is gone.* (past participle)

The underlined verb forms are independent of time and person and remain the same when their environment changes, e.g., *He wants to stay.* / *She carried on talking.* / *They are gone.*

English has three non-finite verb forms, the *to-* infinitive, the *-ing* form, and the past participle *(taken, gone, seen, done)*. They link up with other verbs to expand sentences. Each Bangla verb has four of these forms, a verbal noun (VN), an imperfective participle (IP), a conditional participle (CP), and a perfective participle (PP). The various uses of these forms are demonstrated from Unit 8 onward but here are the forms:

• **Verbal nouns (VN)** (equivalent to the -ing form in English) are formed by adding –a to the low stem of the verb, e.g., করা kɔra *do*, বোঝা *understand*, দেখা dækha *see*, লেখা lekha *write*, থাকা *stay*. Verbs whose stem ends in a vowel, such as হও– *be, become*, দে– *give*, যা– *go*, have a verbal noun ending of ওয়া oŷa: হওয়া, দেওয়া, যাওয়া.

Extended and causative verbs have a verbal noun ending of –ano, e.g., পাঠানো *send*, বানানো *prepare*, ঘুমানো *sleep*. The verbal noun is the verb form given in dictionaries. The verbal noun has an alternative form that adds বা ba to the high stem of the verb instead of just আ a, so instead of লেখা *write* we get লিখবা, instead of যাওয়া *go* we get যাবা, instead of পালানো *flee* we get পালাবা. This form is rarely used in the nominative but occurs in the genitive: তার যাবার আগে *before his going* = *before he goes*, তাদের পালাবার সময় *at the time of their escape*.

• **Imperfective participles (IP)** (equivalent to an infinitive *to do* in English) adds –তে –te to the high stem of the verb, e.g., করতে, বুঝতে, দেখতে, লিখতে, থাকতে

IP forms of some very common verbs:

যেতে	from যাওয়া *go*
আসতে	from আসা *come*
পেতে	from পাওয়া *get*
খেতে	from খাওয়া *eat*
চাইতে	from চাওয়া *want*
দিতে	from দেওয়া *give*
নিতে	from নেওয়া *take*
হতে	from হওয়া *be, become*

• **Conditional participles (CP)** (if/when doing) have no English equivalents but translate roughly as *if doing, when doing*. They are formed by adding –লে –le to the high stem of the verb, e.g., করলে, বুঝলে, দেখলে, লিখলে, থাকলে.

CP forms of very common verbs:

গেলে	from যাওয়া *go*
এলে / আসলে	from আসা *come*
পেলে	from পাওয়া *get*
খেলে	from খাওয়া *eat*
চাইলে	from চাওয়া *want*
দিলে	from দেওয়া *give*
নিলে	from নেওয়া *take*
হলে	from হওয়া *be, become*

• **Perfective participles (PP)** are the most commonly used non-finite verb form. They are equivalent to *having done, having gone*, etc. in English. They are formed by adding –e to the high stem of the verb, e.g., করে, বুঝে, দেখে, লিখে, থেকে.

PP forms of very common verbs:

গিয়ে	from যাওয়া *go*
এসে	from আসা *come*
পেয়ে	from পাওয়া *get*
খেয়ে	from খাওয়া *eat*
চেয়ে	from চাওয়া *want*
দিয়ে	from দেওয়া *give*
নিয়ে	from নেওয়া *take*
হয়ে	from হওয়া *be, become*

All verbs with আ –a in the stem form the past participle with এ –e, e.g., থেকে theke from থাকা thaka *stay*, এসে ese from আসা asa *come*, ভেঙে bheṅe (bhenge) from ভাঙা bhaṅa (bhanga) *break*, খেয়ে kheẏe from খাওয়া khaoẏa *eat*.

Extended verbs drop the আ –a in the stem and insert -i, e.g., ঘুমিয়ে ghumiẏe from ঘুমানো ghumano *sleep*, দেখিয়ে dekhiẏe from দেখানো dækhano *show*, জানিয়ে janiẏe from জানানো janano *inform*

The formation of non-finites is quite regular. Their uses will be discussed in detail in Unit 8 and 9. **A full set of verb charts is given in Appendix 4** (page 333).

Imperatives

The forms for 2nd person (তুমি and আপনি) imperatives are the same as the present tense forms, so from তুমি যাও *you go* we get just যাও ! *Go!*. From the honorific আপনি যান *you go* we get যান ! *Go!*. These forms are used for giving direct orders or commands. There is an alternative set of forms for more indirect imperatives. For the honorific আপনি form the e of the present simple form is changed to u: আপনি বলেন apni bɔlen *you* (hon.) *speak* to বলুন ! bôlun *Speak!*, আপনি আসেন *you come* to আসুন ! asun *Come!* These forms have often been called future imperatives, but in modern use their impact is more to do with indirectness and politeness than with tense. Where two forms are given in the verb charts in the Appendix 4, the second form is less direct and more polite.

For negative imperatives we use the future tense, not the present simple, of the verb plus না : এটা খাবে না ! *Don't eat that!*; এটা ধরবে না ! *Don't touch that!* The reason for using the future tense verb forms for negative imperatives is that না after a present simple verb form actually has an intensifying, not a negating effect, so যাও না ! means *Do go!* whereas যাবে না ! (future tense) means *Don't go!*

In addition to 2nd person imperatives, Bangla also has 3rd person imperatives that are formed by adding -uk to the high stem of Class 1 and Class 2 verbs: করুক ! *let him/her do!*; বসুক ! *Let them sit down!*; আনুক ! anuk *Let him bring!*; থাকুক thakuk *Let him stay!*. And by adding just ক to Class 3 and Class 4 verbs, whose stems end in a vowel: খাক ! *Let him eat!* from খাওয়া; নিক ! nik *Let him take!* from নেওয়া; ঘুমাক ! *Let him sleep!* from ঘুমানো. 3rd person Imperatives in the 3rd person can express hopes and wishes for someone: সে ভাল হোক ! *May he get well!* but they can also indicate a couldn't-care-less attitude: মরুক ! *Let him die!* implies *I don't care.* Keep a lookout for these imperatives when you start reading Bangla—you will quickly develop an understanding of them.

Grammar 10: Making sentences

With all the information given on verbs in Grammar 10, you are now ready to handle full sentences in Bangla. There is a systematic way of doing it. Let us consider the following two sentences to demonstrate, one quite simple, the other a bit more complex:

Sentence 1: *He will buy a pen.*
Sentence 2: *I go to the office in the morning.*

Step 1: Assemble your vocabulary:

Sentence 1: *he* = সে, *buy* = কেনা, *pen* = কলম
Sentence 2: *I* = আমি, *go* = যাওয়া, *office* = অফিস, *morning* = সকাল

Step 2: Order and adjust your components:

Sentence 1: Subject comes first, verb comes last.
The object (কলম) immediately precedes the verb.
For the indefinite *a pen* we need to add the classifier (*see page 87*):
একটা কলম.

Sentence 2: Subject comes first, verb comes last.
Of the other two elements *to the office* and *in the morning,*
the office belongs more closely to the verb and precedes it directly.
As we have **to the office** and **in** the morning both nouns need a
locative ending (*see page 75*), so we get আমি সকালে অফিসে (যাওয়া).

Step 3: Work out your verb form:

Sentence 1: According to vowel mutation (*see page 100*), in the future tense কেন
changes to কিন, the future tense verb ending for সে is –বে so you
have কিনবে.

Sentence 2: We need the first person form of যাওয়া in the present simple.
যাওয়া *go* is one of the verbs given in the Verb Charts in Appendix 4,
so we can just pick out the correct form from the chart: আমি যাই।

Step 4: Assemble your components:

Sentence 1: সে একটা কলম কিনবে।
Sentence 2: আমি সকালে অফিসে যাই।

By following this logical step-by-step method you will be able to tackle quite a lot more complex structures than the two we have here. Don't let long sentences faze you but proceed calmly and steadily from one element to the next until you have assembled all your sentence parts.

Additional Vocabulary

Essential verbs

A list of essential verbs, arranged by their vowel mutation patterns is given in Appendix 4 (page 333). You should familiarize yourself with these verbs now as they will not be given separately in subsequent units. Two slightly unusual verbs that do not fit easily into a pattern are ভালবাসা bhalôbasa *love* and মারা যাওয়া mara yaoŷa *die*. In both cases only the second element is conjugated:

> আমি তাকে ভালবেসেছিলাম। *I had loved him.*
> সে অনেক আগে মারা গেছে। *He died a long time ago.*

Verbs *say, tell, talk, speak*

The verb বলা bɔla *speak, say* is always accompanied by a direct object. That's why we say কথা বলা kɔtha bɔla (lit: *speak word*), not just বলা bɔla on its own. কথা kɔtha can be replaced by কি ki: *what*, কিছু kichu *something*, সব sɔb *everything*, or similar items, all of which function as objects to বলা bɔla.

Examples:

> বলা *say, tell*
>
> > তুমি কি বলেছ? *What did you say?*
> > সে আমাকে সব বলেছে। *She told me everything.*
> > আমি কিছু বলব না। *I won't say anything = I won't tell.*
> > সে কি বলেছে তা আমাকে বলবে না? *Won't you tell me what he said?*
>
> কথা বলা *talk, speak*
>
> > মেয়েটি কথা বলে না। *The girl doesn't speak.*
> > আস্তে আস্তে কথা বল। *Speak slowly.*
> > আমি তার সঙ্গে কথা বলব। *I will talk to him.*
> > কি কথা বলছ? *What are you talking about?*

Exercises: Unit 6

Exercise 6:1
Following the patterns for verb endings on page 102, give the following verb forms:

Example: 1st person present simple of লেখা *write* → আমি লিখি *I write*

(i) 3rd person present simple of তোলা *lift* _____

(ii) 1st person present perfect of থামা *stop* _____

(iii) 3rd person present simple of শোনা *hear, listen* _____

(iv) 1st person present perfect of পারা *be able to* _____

(v) 1st person present simple of জানা *know* _____

(vi) 1st person present simple of ঢোকা *enter* _____

(vii) 3rd person present simple of পড়া (pɔṛa) *read* (indicate the pronunciation)

   _____

(viii) 1st person present perfect of আনা *bring* _____

(ix) 1st person present simple of ঘোরা *wander around* _____

(x) 1st person present perfect of কাটা *cut* _____

Exercise 6:2
Following the patterns given on page 106, give the verbal nouns from the 1st person present simple forms:

Example: আমি শিখি *I learn*   →   শেখা *learn*

    1st person present simple   →   Verbal noun

(i) আমি চিনি *I know*   →   _____

(ii) আমি শুনি *I hear*   →   _____

(iii) আমি দেখি *I see*   →   _____

(iv) আমি আসি *I come*   →   _____

(v) আমি লিখি *I write*   →   _____

(vi) আমি পড়ি *I read*   →   _____

(vii) আমি বুঝি *I understand*   →   _____

(viii) আমি আনি *I bring*   →   _____

(ix) আমি বসি *I sit*   →   _____

(x)   আমি ফিরি *I return*   →   _____

Exercise 6:3

Give the 1st person present perfect from the 1st person present simple forms:

Example: আনি *I bring*   →   এনেছি *I have brought*

(i)   আসি *I come*   →   _____

(ii)   থাকি *I stay*   →   _____

(iii) শুনি *I hear*   →   _____

(iv)   দেখি *I see*   →   _____

(v)   করি *I do*   →   _____

(vi)   রাখি *I put*   →   _____

(vii) জানি *I know*   →   _____

(viii) পড়ি *I fall*   →   _____

(ix)   ধরি *I hold*   →   _____

(x)   কিনি *I buy*   →   _____

Exercise 6:4

Here are some sentences to practice forming Bangla sentences as shown on page 109. (Remember the way to express like and dislike in Bangla, see page 59). The vocabulary in the following sentences is kept simple to help you concentrate on the verb forms. (Note: there are dictionaries given at the end of the book, see page 279.) For all past tense sentences in this exercise, use the present perfect in Bangla.

(i)   *I have bought a pen.*

(ii)   *I have seen the film.* (film: ছবি)

(iii) *They will see the film.*

(iv)   *We will not buy these pens.*

(v)   *He will not come.*

(vi)   *Will you come?*

(vii)   *He will go to the office in the morning.*

(viii)   *I will tell you their names.*

(ix)   *They are looking at the pictures.*

(x)   *We will not go to the office.*

(xi)   *She came in the morning.*

(xii)   *He will tell you his name.*

(xiii)   *Do you like this pen?*

(xiv)   *He will buy ice cream.*

(xv)   *I have seen the boy.* (classifier and case-ending!)

(xvi)   *We saw the girl.* (classifier and case-ending!)

(xvii)   *The boy will come in the morning.*

(xviii) *She is eating ice cream.*

(xix)   *They liked the ice cream.*

(xx)   *You* (pl.) *will come to the office.*

Exercise 6:5

Insert a correct noun or pronoun to go with the verb form and translate the sentences. There is often more than one correct answer in these sentences. Remember that singular and plural pronouns have the same verb endings. The second (তুমি) and third (সে) have the same verb ending in the future tense. In impersonal structures, with আছে and also with নেই any person can be the subject of the sentence. Just make sure that your translation matches the sentence you have made.

(i)   _____ বনপাড়া যাচ্ছি।

(ii)   _____ ভাত খেয়েছেন?

(iii)   _____ চিঠি লিখবে।

(iv)   _____ এখানে নেই।

(v)   _____ আমাকে দশ টাকা দিতে পার?

(vi)   _____ কাল বিকালে আসবে?

(vii)   _____ কোথায় কাজ করে?

(viii)   _____ বাবার সঙ্গে বাজারে গিয়েছি।

(ix)   _____ তোমার ভাইকে চিনি না।

(x)   _____ গাড়ি নেই। (case!)

(xi)   _____ কলকাতায় থাকেন।

(xii)   _____ কি অফিসে যাবে না?

(xiii)   _____ তোমাকে টেলিফোন করব।

(xiv)   _____ রহিমকে সাঈদার কথা বলেছেন।

(xv)   _____ দুটি বাচ্চা আছে। (case!)

(xvi)   _____ তাকে কি বলেছ?

(xvii)   _____ খুব সকালে ওঠেন।

(xviii)   _____ মাংস খাই না।

(xix)   _____ মহিষ খুব ভাল লাগে। (case!)

(xx)   _____ আমার বন্ধু। (zero verb)

UNIT 7

Dialogue

প্রতিবেশী

মি খান: আপনার বাগানটা খুব সুন্দর। আমার খুব ভাল লাগছে।

মি চৌধুরী: তাই নাকি? এটা আমার একটা শখ। অবশ্যই বাগান করতে অনেক সময় ও পরিশ্রম লাগে। কিন্তু আমার শরীর তো আগের মত নয়। আমি আর যুবক নই। তাই সম্প্রতি একজন মালি লাগিয়েছি।

মি খান: বেশ ভাল। এবার কি কি নতুন গাছ লাগাবেন?

মি চৌধুরী: রবিবারে কুষ্টিয়া ও রংপুর থেকে কিছু নতুন ধরনের গোলাপ গাছ এনেছি।

মি খান: আপনার হাতে কি হয়েছে? ব্যান্ডেজ লাগিয়েছেন কেন?

মি চৌধুরী: আর বলবেন না। গতকাল রিকশা থেকে পড়ে গেছিলাম। হাতে লেগেছে।

মি খান: ডাক্তারকে দেখিয়েছেন তো?

মি চৌধুরী: হ্যাঁ, একটা মলম লাগিয়েছেন। কিন্তু ব্যথা লাগছে, সেটা এখনও কমেনি।

মি খান: কমবে। আপনার দোতালাটা কি ভাড়া দিচ্ছেন?

মি চৌধুরী: হ্যাঁ, গেটে একটা বিজ্ঞাপন লাগিয়ে দিয়েছি। ভাল লোক পেলে একটু বলবেন?

মি খান: আচ্ছা, চলি। একটু বাজারে যেতে হবে।

মি চৌধুরী: অনেক কেনাকাটা করবেন নাকি?

মি খান: আরে না, না। গতকাল একটা সার্ট কিনেছি, কিন্তু এখন দেখি সেটা গায়ে লাগছে না। ওটা ফেরত দেব।

মি চৌধুরী: হ্যাঁ, আপনি মোটা হয়ে যাচ্ছেন, তাই। আমাদের মত বয়সের মানুষের একটু বেশি করে নড়াচড়া করা উচিত। না হলে আমরা মোটা হয়ে যাই। আমাকে বাগানের কাজে একটু সাহায্য করতে ইচ্ছা করছে না?

মি খান: দূর ! কি বলছেন? সার্টটা বড় হয়েছে, ছোট নয়। বিদেশি সার্টের সাইজগুলো আমি ঠিক বুঝতে পারি না। প্রসঙ্গত, আমার তো মনে হয় আমি আপনার অন্তত বিশ বছরের ছোট।

Neighbors

Mr. Khan:	*Your garden is very beautiful. I like it very much.*
Mr. Choudhuri:	*Is that so? It's a hobby for me. Of course looking after a garden takes a lot of time and hard work. But my health is not what it used to be. I am not a young man anymore. That's why I have recently employed a gardener.*
Mr. Khan:	*Very good. What new plants are you going to plant?*
Mr. Choudhuri:	*On Sunday I brought some new types of rosebushes brought from Kustia and from Rongpur.*
Mr. Khan:	*What has happened to your hand? Why have you got a bandage round it?*
Mr. Choudhuri:	*Oh, don't even mention it. I fell off a rickshaw yesterday and hurt my hand.*
Mr. Khan:	*Did you show it to a doctor?*
Mr. Choudhuri:	*Yes, he has given me an ointment. But it hurts and the pain hasn't subsided yet.*
Mr. Khan:	*It will, it will. Are you renting out your first floor?*
Mr. Choudhuri:	*Yes, we've put a notice up on the gate. If you find someone suitable, will you tell me?*
Mr. Khan:	*Yes, sure. I'm off now. I have to go to the market.*
Mr. Choudhuri:	*Are you doing a lot of shopping?*
Mr. Khan:	*No, no, not at all. I bought a shirt yesterday and now I see that it doesn't fit, so I'm just going to return it.*
Mr. Choudhuri:	*Yes, you are putting on weight, that's why. People of our age ought to move around a bit more. Otherwise we put on weight. Don't you fell like helping me with my gardening a bit?*
Mr. Khan:	*Honestly, what are you saying? The shirt was too big, not too small! I don't understand these foreign shirt sizes. And, by the way, I would think that I am at least twenty years younger than you.*

Vocabulary: Dialogue

প্রতিবেশী prôtibeśi *n.* neighbor

ভাল লাগা bhalô laga *vb.* like

শখ śɔkh *n.* hobby

অবশ্যই ɔbôśyôi *adv.* of course

পরিশ্রম pôriśrôm *n.* hard work

শরীর śôrīr *n.* health, body

লাগা laga *vb.* here need

সম্প্রতি sɔmprôti *adv.* recently

মালি mali *n.* gardener

লাগানো lagano *vb.* employ, plant, put on, apply

কুষ্টিয়া kuṣṭiŷa *name* Kustia *(town)*

রংপুর rɔṃpur *name* Rangpur

থেকে theke *pp.* from

কয়েক kɔŷek *adj.* a few

ধরন dhɔrôn *n.* type, kind

গোলাপ golap *n.* rose

আনা ana *vb.* bring

হাত hat *n.* hand

কি হয়েছে? ki hôŷeche? *phr.* what has happened?

পড়ে যাওয়া pôṛe yaoŷa *cvb.* fall off, fall down

হাতে লেগেছে → হাতে লাগা hate laga *vb.* hurt one's hand

ডাক্তার ḍaktar *n.* doctor

মলম mɔlôm *n.* paste, ointment

ব্যথা bytha (bæthа) *n.* pain

কমা kɔma *vb.* reduce, decrease

দোতালা dotala *n.* second floor

ভাড়া bhaṛa *n.* rent, hire

দিচ্ছেন → দেওয়া deoŷa *vb.* give

ভাড়া দেওয়া bhaṛa deoŷa *vb.* rent out

গেট geṭ *n.* gate

বিজ্ঞাপন bijñapɔn (biggapɔn) *n.* advertisement

পেলে → পাওয়া paoŷa *vb.* get, find

বাজার bajar *n.* market

কেনাকাটা kenakaṭa *n.* shopping

আরে are *excl.* expresses contradiction

আরে না are na *excl.* not at all

সার্ট śarṭ *n.* shirt

কিনেছি → কেনা kena *vb.* buy

গা ga *n.* body

গায়ে লাগা gaŷe laga *vb.* fit

ফেরত দেওয়া pherôt deoŷa *vb.* return, give back

মোটা moṭa *adj.* overweight, fat

বেশি করে beśi kôre *adv.* much, a lot

নড়াচড়া nɔṛacɔṛa *vb.* move, move around

না হলে na hôle *conj.* otherwise

ইচ্ছা iccha *n.* wish

দূর dur *excl.* no way

সাইজ saij *n.* size

বোঝা bojha *vb.* understand

প্রসঙ্গত prôsɔṅgôtô *adv.* by the way

অন্তত ɔntôtô *adv.* at least

বিশ biś *num.* twenty

Grammar 11: Verb লাগা

লাগা is an important verb in Bangla with a variety of meanings and uses. Literally it means *be attached to, touch*, but we have already seen it together with the adjective ভাল *good* to mean *like* (page 59):

আমার সে মহিষটা খুব ভাল লাগছে। = *I like that buffalo very much.*

In combination with time and money it can mean *need, require*:

বাগান করতে অনেক সময় লাগে। = *Gardening requires a lot of time.*

In the dialogue in this unit we also have:

সার্টটা গায়ে লাগছে না। = *The shirt doesn't fit.*
আমার হাতে লেগেছে। = *I hurt my hand.*

In all these uses লাগা generates impersonal structures: the subject of the sentence is in the genitive and the verb form is always in the 3rd person. Here are some more examples:

1. *touch, hurt, affect*

তার হাতে   লেগেছে।
his   hand.LOC has.touched
(It) touched/hurt his hand.

তোমার কথা আমার মনে   লেগেছে।
your   word my   mind.LOC has.touched
Your words have hurt/touched me.

2. *need, require*

আমার আর কিছু   লাগবে   না।
my   more something will.need not
I won't need anything else.

আর কি   লাগবে?
more what will.need
What else do (you) need?

আমার একটা নতুন সার্ট লাগবে।
of.me one   new shirt will.need
I will need a new shirt.

3. *feel*

আমার ভাল লাগছে।   *I am feeling well.*

তার খুশি লাগছে।   *He is feeling happy.*

তোমার কি গরম লাগছে? *Are you feeling hot?*

4. *like*
(often with ভাল *good*)

বাগানটা আমার ভাল লেগেছে। *I liked the garden.*

তোমার এখানে কেমন লাগে? *How do you like it here?*

আমার খারাপ লাগে। *I dislike it.*

Animate objects go into the object case:

> আমার তাকে খুব ভালো লাগে। *I like him very much.*

. . . .

In addition to লাগা *be attached* we also have the verb লাগানো *apply, employ, plant* in this dialogue:

> আমি একজন মালি লাগিয়েছি।   *I have employed a gardener.*
>
> আপনি নতুন গাছ লাগাবেন।   *You will plant new trees.*
>
> উনি একটা মলম লাগিয়েছেন।   *He applied a lotion.*

The relationship between the two verbs is that of a simple verb লাগা to its causative verb লাগানো, literally *cause to be attached.* We will deal with causative and extended verbs in more detail in Unit 9.

Grammar 12: Negation

Bengali has no negative pronouns such as *nobody, no one, none, nothing* and no negative adverbials such as *never, nowhere.* This means that all negation in Bangla happens on the sentence level. In English we say *"No one will come."* In Bangla we say:

> কেউ   আসবে না।
> *someone will not come.* = *No one will come.*

(Note: The indefinite pronouns and adverbs we need to make negative sentences are explained in Grammar 13, page 123.)

Sentence negators

Bangla has four main sentence negators. Their uses and positioning in sentences are as follows:

1. না *na*

না is the universal negative particle that is placed after the finite verb and is therefore often the last word in a sentence:

affirmative	negative
ওরা কাজ করে।	ওরা কাজ করে না।
They work.	*They don't work.*
আমি তাকে চিনি।	আমি তাকে চিনি না।
I know him.	*I don't know him.*
তারা বাজারে গেল।	তারা বাজারে গেল না।
They went to the market.	*They did not go to the market.*

When answering yes–no questions in the negative, না stands independently at the beginning of the sentence and again follows the verb at the end:

সে কি তা জানে?
Does he know that?

না, সে তা জানে না।
No, he doesn't know that.

তুমি কি ছবিগুলো দেখবে?
Will you look at the pictures?

না, আমি ছবিগুলো দেখব না।
No, I won't look at the pictures.

Negative questions are answered with না *no* to confirm the question; with হ্যাঁ *yes* to contradict it.

উনি কি মাংস খান না?
Doesn't he eat meat?

না, উনি মাংস খান না।
No, he doesn't eat meat.

হ্যাঁ, উনি মাংস খান।
Yes, he eats meat.

positioning of না
When না follows the verb at the end of a sentence, the whole sentence is negated. In order to restrict the negation to specific elements, না can precede the verb. This is the case with subordinate conjunctions such as যদি *if,* যেন *so that* and with all non-finite verb forms. Examples of these will be shown in Unit 10 and 12.

. . . .

2. নেই nei

নেই is the negator for existential sentences with আছ- *be present, exist.* নেই is an incomplete verb that denotes absence and remains the same for all persons.

affirmative	**negative**
আমরা বনপাড়ায় আছি।	আমরা বনপাড়ায় নেই।
We are in Bonpara.	*We are not in Bonpara.*
তোমরা বনপাড়ায় আছ।	তোমরা বনপাড়ায় নেই।
You (fam.) *are in Bonpara.*	*You are not in Bonpara.*
তারা বনপাড়ায় আছে।	তারা বনপাড়ায় নেই।
They are in Bonpara.	*They are not in Bonpara.*
আপনারা বনপাড়ায় আছেন।	আপনারা বনপাড়ায় নেই।
You (hon.) *are in Bonpara.*	*You are not in Bonpara.*

. . . .

3. ন– nɔ (নই nôi, নও nɔo, নয় nɔŷ, নন nɔn) *is not*

Equational zero-verb sentences are negated with ন– *is not*. ন– is an incomplete verb with the following conjugation:

affirmative	**negative**
আমি খুশি। *I am happy.*	আমি খুশি নই। *I am not happy.*
তুমি খুশি। *You* (fam.) *are happy.*	তুমি খুশি নও। *You are not happy.*
সে খুশি। *He is happy.*	সে খুশি নয়। *He is not happy.*
আপনি খুশি। *You* (hon.) *are happy.*	আপনি খুশি নন। *You are not happy.*

Since the 3rd person ordinary is used for all inanimates as well as *he, she,* and *they,* the form নয় appears much more frequently than any of the other forms.

· ·

4. নি ni

All except two tenses in Bangla negate with না. Present perfect and past perfect negatives are constructed with the simple present verb forms followed by নি.

affirmative	**negative**
আমরা সাহায্য করেছি। *We helped.*	আমরা সাহায্য করিনি। *We didn't help.*

The fact that নি is used with simple present tense verb forms means that নি has tense as well as negative properties and that there is no distinction between present perfect and past perfect in the negative. Unlike না, নি never stands on its own and is often attached directly to the simple present verb form.

present perfect	আমি বইটা পড়েছি। *I have read the book.*	আমি বইটা পড়িনি। *I haven't read the book.*
past perfect	আমি বইটা পড়েছিলাম। *I had read the book.*	আমি বইটা পড়িনি। *I hadn't read the book.*

নি cannot be added to tenses other than the simple present. In some cases English translations of Bangla present perfect verb forms require a simple past tense. (There will be more on tenses in Unit 11.)

· ·

Grammar 13: Indefinites

Indefinites in English are words like *some, any, sometimes, somewhere, something, ever,* etc. In Bangla these words are derived from question words. Since Bangla has no negative lexical items, like *nothing, no one, nowhere,* indefinites are used and the whole sentence is negated.

question word	indefinite	indefinite negative
কে *who*	কেউ *someone*	কেউ না *no one*
কার *whose*	কারও *someone's*	কারও না *no one's*
কাকে *to whom*	কাউকে *to someone*	কাউকে না *to no one*
কি *what*	কিছু *some, something*	কিছু না *nothing*
কোথা *where*	কোথাও *somewhere*	কোথাও না *nowhere*
কখন *when*	কখনও *sometimes, ever*	কখনও না *never*
কোন *which*	কোনও *any*	কোনও না *not any, none*

Some simple examples:

কেউ ইংল্যান্ডে গেলে   *if anyone goes to England*
সে কারও সঙ্গে কথা বলেনি। *He didn't talk to anyone.*
আমি এখানে কাউকে চিনি না। *I don't know anyone here.*
বাঁ দিকে আরও কিছু বাড়ি।   *To the left there are some more houses.*
এটা কিছু নয়। *That's nothing.*
আমি কিছু জানি না। *I don't know anything.*
পৃথিবীর আর কোথাও এত নদী নেই।   *Nowhere else in the world are there so many rivers.*
আর কখনও এখানে আসবে না। *Don't ever come back here.*
কোনও সমস্যা হয়নি। *There were no problems.* (lit: *Any problems did not occur.*)
কোনও বিশেষ কারণ আছে? *Is there any special reason?*

There can be more than one indefinite in a sentence:

আমি কাউকে কিছু বলব না। *I won't say anything to anyone.*
তারা কখনও কোনও কাজ করেনি। *They have never done any work.*

Indefinites can combine with আর *more* or অন্য *other* to express phrases like অন্য কেউ *someone else,* আর কিছু *something more,* অন্য কোনও *any other,* etc.

আমি অন্য কারও ছবি দেখিনি। *I didn't see anyone else's pictures.*
আর কিছু লাগবে না। *(I) don't need anything more.*
তারা অন্য কোথাও গিয়েছে। *They have gone somewhere else.*
তার অন্য কোনও খাবার ভাল লাগে না।   *He doesn't like any other food.*

যে *that* (or in the case of কিছু *something,* যা *that*) preceding an indefinite increase the indefiniteness:

আমি যে কোনও জায়গায় খুশি হতে পারি।   *I can be happy anywhere at all.*
ছাগল যা কিছু খায়। *Goats eat anything at all.*
যে কোনও কিছু   *anything at all*

Narrative

গ্রামের ছুটি

আঙ্গুরী আর রেহানা কলেজের বন্ধু। তাদের কলেজের চার দিন ছুটি। আঙ্গুরী রেহানাকে তার গ্রামের বাড়িতে নিয়ে গেছে। গ্রামটা ঢাকার কাছে, একটা নদীর ধারে। সেখানে যেতে প্রায় চার ঘণ্টা লেগেছে। তিন দিন ধরে ওরা খুব মজা করেছে। নৌকায় চড়েছে। পুকুরে সাঁতার কেটেছে। জোনাকি দেখেছে সন্ধ্যাবেলায়। রাতের আকাশের তারা দেখেছে। আঙ্গুরীর মায়ের হাতের ভাল ভাল খাবার খেয়েছে। আঙ্গুরীর ছোট ভাইবোনদের সঙ্গে খেলা করেছে। আঙ্গুরীর ঠাকুরমার সঙ্গে গল্প করেছে। আঙ্গুরীর বাবার সঙ্গে মাছ ধরতে গিয়েছে।

রেহানা শহরের মেয়ে। আঙ্গুরীর বাড়িতে থাকার শেষ দিনে রেহানা আঙ্গুরীর মাকে বলেছে, 'আমার আপনাদের বাড়িতে যেমন ভাল ঘুম হয়েছে তেমন অন্য কোথাও জীবনে হয়নি। আবার আসতে পারব?' আঙ্গুরীর মা বলেছে, 'নিশ্চয় আসতে পারবে। তুমি আসলে আমরা সবাই খুব খুশি হব।'

A village holiday

Anguri and Rehana were college friends. They had four days' holiday from the college. Anguri took Rehana to her village home. The village was near Dhaka, on the bank of a river. It took them almost four hours to get there. For three days they had a lot of fun. They went on a boat ride, went swimming in the lake, watched the fire-flies in the evening and looked at the stars in the night sky. They ate the delicious food Anguri's mother cooked, they played with Anguri's younger brothers and sisters. They chatted with Anguri's grandmother and went fishing with Anguri's father.

Rehana was a city girl. On the last day of her stay in Anguri's village home, Rehana said to Anguri's mother, "I have never slept as well anywhere else as I have here at your home. May I come again?" Anguri's mother said, "Of course you can come again. We will all be very happy if you do."

Vocabulary: Narrative

আঙ্গুরা angurī *name* Anguri *(f.)*
রেহানা rehana *name* Rehana *(f.)*
কাছে kache *pp.* near
ধার dhar *n.* bank, side
ধরে dhôre *pp.* during, for *(time)*
নৌকা nouka *n.* boat
চড়া cɔra *vb.* ride
সাঁতার কাটা sătar kaṭa *vb.* swim
জোনাকি jonaki *n.* firefly
সন্ধ্যাবেলা sɔndhyabæla *n.* evening
আকাশ akaś *n.* sky

তারা tara *n.* star
খেলা করা khæla kɔra *vb.* play
মাছ mach *n.* fish
ধরা dhɔra *vb.* catch
শেষ śeṣ *n.* end
শেষ দিন śeṣ din *n.* last day
যেমন yæmôn *conj.* as
যেমন – তেমন yæmôn – tæmôn *conj.* as – as
ঘুম ghum *n.* sleep
কোথাও kothao *adv.* somewhere, anywhere
জীবন jībôn *n.* life

Grammar 14: Emphasizers ই, ও, তো

Each of these words has particular syntactic tasks and uses but can also be employed to express attitude or emphasis.

ই

ই as an emphasizer is attached to the end of words, after case endings and classifiers, and can go with almost anything. It emphasizes the word it is attached to but cannot easily be translated. We already saw two examples in the dialogue in Unit 3. When Rohim asks how Saida likes Rajshahi, her mother replies:

> ভাল-ই লাগছে তবে ছোট বোনের কথা মনে তো পড়ে।
> *She likes it very well, but she misses her little sister.*

and a bit later on she says:

> প্রায় রোজ-ই ফোন করি।   *We phone almost every day.*

ই has been split off in these two sentences for demonstration purposes only—normally it is attached directly to words.

ই is regularly used with সে, এ, and ও as pronouns or adjectives (এই ছবি *this picture,* ওই ছেলে *that boy*) without much emphasis but the emphasis can be restored with the right tone of voice.

সেই is used idiomatically on its own to say *Quite right!* or *Exactly!*

Some uses of ই are lexicalized:

তা *it*	→	তাই *so, therefore*	
এক *one*	→	একই *same*	
প্রায় *almost*	→	প্রায়ই *often*	
এমন *such*	→	এমনি (pronounced emni) *just like that*	
এখন *now*	→	এখনই *right now, at once*	

তাই নাকি? *isn't that so?* is a very common phrase added at the end of sentences for reassurance.

ই in connection with some verb forms can imply *as soon as* (see Unit 10).

• •

ও

The basic difference between ই and ও is that ই separates and ও includes. ই is a dissociative emphasizer, ও is an associative emphasizer. ও has a number of different jobs:

• ও is a pronoun in its own right:

> ও আজকে আসবে না।   *He will not come today.*

- ও is a conjunction meaning *and, also,* and sometimes *or*:

   আমিও যাব তুমিও যাবে। *You and I will go.*
   আমিও তোমার সঙ্গে যাব। *I will also go with you.*
   নাও হতে পারে *or maybe not*

- ও forms indefinite pronouns and adverbs from question words:

   কার *whose* → কারও *someone's*
   কে *who* → কেউ *someone*
   কোন *which* → কোনও *any*
   কোথা *where* → কোথাও *somewhere*

- ও changes এখন *now* to এখনও *still*:

   তারা এখন কোথায়? *Where are they now?*
   তারা এখনও আগের জায়গায়। *They are still in the same place as before.*

- Added after the conditional participle and the perfective participle, ও introduces a concessive element:

   তুমি গেলে *if you go*   তুমি গেলেও *even if you go*
   ছবিটা দেখে *having seen the film* ছবিটা দেখেও *even having seen the film*

(We will see more examples of this in Unit 10.)

. . . .

তো to

তো is probably one of the most interesting words in Bangla and it is almost impossible to translate. Here are some of its uses.

- তো on its own is used in conversation much like the English *Well?, So what?, What then?*:

   'আমার কিন্তু তাকে ভাল লাগে না।' *'But I don't like him.'*   'তো?' *'So what?'*

   তাই তো। *Quite so! Exactly!*   ঠিক তো। *Quite right!*
   তা তো বটে or তা তো অবশ্যই। *That's obvious! / Of course!*
   না তো। *Of course not!* or, with a questioning tone: *Not as far as I know.*
   'চা নেই?' *'Is there no tea?'*   'আছে তো।' *'Yes, of course there is.'*

- তো can be asking for reassurance or confirmation:

   আপনি আজ থাকবেন তো? *You will stay today, won't you?*
   ভাল আছেন তো? *You are well, aren't you?*
   তোমার তো কলা ভাল লাগে, তাই না? *You like bananas, don't you?*

- It can stand for an emphatic *but*:

আমি কিছুই বুঝি না তো ! *But I don't understand a thing!*

This sentence also shows that ই and তো can appear together in the same sentence.

- তো can reinforce an imperative:

চুপ কর তো ! *Do shut up!*

Or it can give a gentle reminder:

আমি তো সব সময় থাকি না বাড়িতে।
But I am not always at home (as you should know).

Additional Vocabulary

Time and place words
We have already seen the days of the week and the points on the compass in Unit 4 and there are some other familiar words in this list:

time সময় sɔmɔŷ

now এখন ækhôn
then তখন tɔkhôn
at first শুরুতে śurute, প্রথমে prôthôme
in the end শেষে śeṣe, অবশেষে ɔbôśeṣe
week সপ্তাহ sɔptahô
month মাস ma:s
year বছর bɔchôr
minute মিনিট miniṭ
hour ঘণ্টা ghɔnṭa
moment মুহূর্ত muhūrtô
today আজ a:j, আজকে ajke
yesterday কাল ka:l, গতকাল gɔtokal
tomorrow কাল ka:l, আগামীকাল agamīkal
day after tomorrow পরশু দিন pôrśudi:n
next আগামী agamī
last গত gɔtô
suddenly হঠাৎ hɔṭhat
gradually, slowly আস্তে আস্তে aste aste
quickly তাড়াতাড়ি taṛataṛi
still, yet এখনও æakhônô
already এরইমধ্যে erimôdhye
all day সারাদিন saradi:n
immediately সঙ্গে সঙ্গে sɔṅge sɔṅge
early সকাল সকাল sɔkal sɔkal
late দেরিতে derite
forever চিরদিন cirôdi:n

place জায়গা

direction দিক dik
left বাঁ bā
right ডান ḍan
straight সোজা soja
world পৃথিবী pṛthibī, দুনিয়া duniŷa
country দেশ deś
town শহর śɔhôr
village গ্রাম gra:m
district জেলা jela
way পথ pɔth
road রাস্তা rasta
here এখানে ekhane
there ওখানে okhane
distance দূর dūr
far দূরে ড dūre
near কাছে kache
very far অনেক দূরে ɔnek dūre
close by কাছাকাছি kachakachi
outside বাইরে baire
inside ভিতরে bhitôre
everywhere সব জায়গায় sɔb jaŷgaŷ
anywhere যে কোনও জায়গায় ye kono jaŷgaŷ

When we want to say *in the evening, on Wednesday*, or *at dawn*, we add the locative endings:

সন্ধ্যায় *in the evening*   বুধবারে *on Wednesday*   ভোরে *at dawn*

Or we use a postposition with the appropriate case ending on the noun or pronoun preceding it:

বাজারের কাছে, *near the market*

Parts of the day

day দিন di:n
dawn ভোর bhor
morning সকাল sɔkal
midday দুপুর dupur

afternoon বিকাল bikal
evening সন্ধ্যা sɔndhya
night রাত ra:t

Exercises: Unit 7

Note: There are no exercises for the emphasizers ই, ও, and তো as it will take time for you to build up confidence about them, but keep a lookout for them in the following Units, in any other reading you may do, and when you hear people talking.

Exercise 7:1
Translate the following sentences. All of them contain লাগা; the subjects of the sentences go into the genitive:

Example: *He hurt his hand.*   তার হাতে লেগেছে।

(i)   *He likes me.*

(ii)   *We need more time.*

(iii) *This takes three hours.*

(iv)   *How does he like the village?*

(v)   *How did you like the food?* (use present perfect)

(vi)   *They will need more space.*

(vii) *Are you comfortable?* (আরাম = *comfort*)

(viii) *He doesn't like his neighbor.*

(ix)   *His garden looks very beautiful.*

(x)   *He dislikes this work.*

Exercise 7:2
Change the following sentences from Unit 2 and 3 into the negative. One example is given for each type of negation, but you will need to decide which type of negation is required for each sentence. It may be helpful to translate the sentences before you negate them.

Examples:

না-negation: আমরা রোজ কথা বলি। *We talk every day.* →   আমরা রোজ কথা বলি না।

zero verb: আজ বুধবার। *Today is Wednesday.*   →   আজ বুধবার নয়।

আছে: তার গাড়ি আছে। *He has a car.*   →   তার গাড়ি নেই।

নি negation: তোমার কথা আমার মনে লেগেছে। *Your words have hurt me.*   →
তোমার কথা আমার মনে লাগেনি।

(i)   আমরা টেবিল বলি।

(ii)   আমার ভাই আছে।

(iii)   এটা বিদেশি জিনিস।

(iv)   তার নাম লুইস।

(v)   আমি একমাত্র ছেলে।

(vi)   সাঈদা চলে গেছে।

(vii)   ছোট বোনের কথা মনে পড়ে।

(viii) আমগাছটার আম মিষ্টি।

(ix)   সে তার চাচার বাড়িতে থাকে।

(x)   আমার এখানে ভাল লেগেছে।

(xi)   সে রাজশাহীতে গিয়েছে।

(xii)   উনি একটা অফিসে চাকরি করেন।

(xiii) তারা ছোট।

(xiv)   উনি তোমার বাবা।

(xv)   আমরা তাই আশা করেছি।

Exercise 7:3

Using what you learned about negation, translate the following sentences:

(i)   You are not my brother.

(ii)   I don't have a car.

(iii) I am not feeling tired. (with লাগা)

(iv) We are not American.

(v) She does not need a bandage. (with লাগা)

(vi) The car is not outside.

(vii) My hand doesn't hurt. (with লাগা)

(viii) He does not like me. (with লাগা)

(ix) She won't need anything else. (with লাগা)

(x) They are not at home.

Exercise 7:4
Translate the following sentences containing indefinites:

(i) He didn't tell me anything.

(ii) Do you have any money?

(iii) I am not going anywhere.

(iv) There aren't any banana trees in Bimol's garden.

(v) I have never seen the lake.

(vi) I put the flowers somewhere. (use present perfect, *put* = রাখা)

(vii) Nothing can be done.

(viii) He couldn't find anyone at their house. (*find* = পাওয়া)

(ix) Did you want to tell me something?

(x) Has anyone seen my sister today?

(xi) সে কারও সঙ্গে থাকে না।

(xii)   আর কখনও এই কথা বলবে না। (neg. imp.)

(xiii) তার কোনও ভাইবোন নেই।

(xiv)   সাঈদা কোথাও গিয়েছে নাকি?

(xv)   কেউ এখানে নেই।

(xvi)   আমি কিছু শুনিনি।

(xvii) আমরা কোনও গরুর মাংস খাইনি।

(xviii) তুমি কখনও ভারতে গিয়েছ? (ভারত = India)

(xix)   তাদের কোনও সবজি ভাল লাগে না।

(xx)   এখানে কোথাও একটা দোকান আছে?

Exercise 7:5
Translate the following time and place phrases:

Example: *on that day* সে দিনে

(i)   *in the afternoon* _____

(ii)   *on Friday* _____

(iii)   *at midday* _____

(iv)   *in the morning* _____

(v)   *on Monday* _____

(vi)   *inside the garden* _____

(vii)   *outside the town* _____

(viii) *on the road* _____

(ix)   *at night* _____

(x)   *this month* _____

UNIT 8

Dialogue

নিমন্ত্রণের পরে

স্বামী স্ত্রী কথা বলছেন:

স্বামী: অবশেষে চলে গেছে। লোকটা যে এত কথা বলতে পারে কে জানত।

স্ত্রী:   খাবার কেমন হয়েছে? মাংসটার খুব স্বাদ হয়েছে, তাই না?

স্বামী: কয়টা বাজে? হায়, হায়, প্রায় এগারোটা। খুব ক্লান্ত লাগছে।

স্ত্রী:   থালাগুলো কি টেবিলে রেখে যাচ্ছ? একটু সাহায্য করতে পার না?

স্বামী: আজ থাক। আর কিছু করার ইচ্ছা নেই আমার।

স্ত্রী:   দাঁড়াও ! আমি কি এসব একা করব?

স্বামী: সকালে কর। এখন কি দরকার?

স্ত্রী:   সকালে আমি আমিরাকে হাসপাতালে নিয়ে যাব, মনে আছে? তখন সময় হবে না।

স্বামী: আচ্ছা, তাহলে থাক। কালকে সন্ধ্যাবেলায় আমরা একসঙ্গে সব গুছিয়ে ঠিক করে
        রাখব।

স্ত্রী:   মাথা খারাপ ! এরইমধ্যে পিঁপড়া, মাছি, পোকা সব নষ্ট করে দেবে।

স্বামী: ওমা, এত রাগ তোমার? কথাটা কিন্তু ঠিক। রেখে গেলে সব নষ্ট হয়ে যাবে। আমার
        ঘুম ভেঙ্গে গেছে। তুমি যাও, আমি সব শেষ করে দিচ্ছি। আর কয়েকটি মিষ্টি বাকি ছিল
        নী? কোথায় ওগুলো?

স্ত্রী:   আমি রান্না ঘরে রেখে এসেছি। এক মিনিট। আমি মিষ্টি আনছি। তুমি এগুলো খেয়ে
        কাজ করতে পারবে। আর আমিও সাহায্য করব।

স্বামী: তাহালে তো তাড়াতাড়ি হয়ে যাবে। হ্যাঁ, মাংসটা খুব ভাল হয়েছে। কি দিয়ে রান্না
        করেছ?

স্ত্রী:   নারকেল দিয়ে। সে জন্য মাংসটা বেশ নরম হয়েছে। চল, কাজ করব।

After the invitation

A husband and wife are talking:

Husband: *Finally they have left. Who would have thought that the man could talk so much?*

Wife: *How was the food? The meat was very tasty, wasn't it?*

Husband: *What time is it? Oh dear, almost eleven o'clock. I am dead on my feet!*

Wife: *Are you just going to leave the plates on the table? Can't you help a little bit?*

Husband: *Leave it today. I don't feel like doing anything more.*

Wife: *Wait a minute. Am I supposed to do all this by myself?*

Husband: *Do it in the morning. There's no need right now.*

Wife: *In the morning I am taking Amira to the hospital, remember? I won't have time then.*

Husband: *OK, then leave it. Tomorrow evening we will tidy everything up together.*

Wife: *Are you crazy? By that time the ants, flies and other insects will have demolished everything.*

Husband: *Oh my goodness, are you so angry? But you are right. If we leave it, everything will be spoiled. Now I don't feel sleepy anymore. You go. I'll sort everything out. Weren't there some sweets left? Where are they?*

Wife: *I left them in the kitchen. Wait a minute, I'll get the sweets. When you've eaten them, you'll be able to work. And I'll help as well.*

Husband: *In that case, we'll get everything done quickly. Yes, the meat was delicious. What did you put in it?*

Wife: *Coconut. That makes the meat nice and tender. Come on, let's get on with it.*

Vocabulary: Dialogue

নিমন্ত্রণ nimôntrôṇ *n.* invitation

স্বামী svamī *n.* husband

স্ত্রী strī *n.* wife

অবশেষে ɔbôśeṣe *adv.* finally

খাবার khabar *n.* food

মাংস maṁso *n.* meat

স্বাদ svad *n.* taste

তাই না? tai na? *phr.* isn't that so?

কয়টা বাজে? kɔŷṭa baje *phr.* what time is it?

হায় হায় haŷ haŷ *phr. expr. of* dismay

এগারো egaro *num.* eleven

ক্লান্ত klantô *adj.* tired

থালা thala *n.* plate

টেবিল ṭebil *n.* table

রেখে যাওয়া rekhe yaoŷa *cvb.* leave behind

দাঁড়ানো dãṛano *vb.* stand, wait

এসব esɔb *n.* all this

সকাল sɔkal *n.* morning

দরকার dɔrkar *n.* need

হাসপাতাল haspatal *n.* hospital

থাক thak *vb.* stay; *in dialogue:* leave

একসঙ্গে eksɔṅge *adv.* together

গুছানো guchano *vb.* tidy up

ঠিক করা ṭhik kɔra *vb.* put straight

রাখা rakha *vb.* put, put away

মাথা matha *n.* head

খারাপ kharap *adj.* bad

মাথা খারাপ matha kharap *phr.* crazy

এরইমধ্যে erimôdhye *adv.* in the meantime, by then

পিঁপড়া pĩpṛa *n.* ant

মাছি machi *n.* fly

পোকা poka *n.* insect

নষ্ট nɔṣṭô *adj.* spoiled

নষ্ট করা nɔṣṭô kɔra *vb.* spoil, destroy

ওমা oma *excl.* My goodness!

রাগ rag *n.* anger

ঠিক ṭhik *adj.* correct, right

হয়ে যাওয়া hôŷe yaoŷa *cvb.* occur, happen, come to pass

ভেঙ্গে যাওয়া bheṅge yaoŷa *cvb.* get broken

শেষ করা śeṣ kɔra *vb.* finish

মিষ্টি miṣṭi *n.* sweets

বাকি baki *adj.* left-over

রান্না ranna *n.* cooking

রান্না ঘর ranna ghɔr *n.* kitchen

রেখে আসা rekhe asa *cvb.* leave, leave behind

মিনিট miniṭ *n.* minute

আনা ana *vb.* bring

খাওয়া khaoŷa *vb.* eat

কাজ করা kaj kɔra *vb.* work

তাড়াতাড়ি taṛataṛi *adv.* quickly

দিয়ে diŷe *pp.* with *(instr.)*

রান্না করা ranna kɔra *vb.* cook

নারকেল narkel *n.* coconut

সে জন্য se jônyô *conj.* therefore, that's why, for that reason

বেশ beś *adv.* quite

নরম nɔrôm *adj.* soft

Grammar 15: Quantifiers, amounts, আর – আরও, অনেক – বেশি

Quantifiers are adjectives that specify an amount, such as:

অনেক *much, many*	তার অনেক ভাইবোন। *He has many brothers and sisters.* আমি অনেক কাজ করেছি। *I have done a lot of work.*
কয়েক *a few*	আর কয়েকটা মিষ্টি *a few more sweets*
কিছু *some, any*	কিছু চিনি দিতে পার? *Can you give me some sugar?* আর কিছু করার ইচ্ছা নেই। *I don't feel like doing anything anymore.*
এত *so much*	সে এত কথা বলে। *He talks so much.*
একটু *a little bit*	একটু সাহায্য করতে পার না? *Can't you help a little bit?*
আরও *more*	আমি আরও মিষ্টি খাব। *I will eat more sweets.*
সব *all, everything*	আমি সব শেষ করে দিচ্ছি। *I am finishing everything off.*

We saw in the discussion on classifiers in Unit 4 that quantifiers in noun phrases take the টা and গুলো attachments away from the noun, e.g., অনেকগুলো কলা গাছ or অনেক কলা গাছ *many banana plants*, but never *অনেক কলা গাছগুলো. This distinguishes quantifiers from descriptive adjectives in their uses within a noun phrase.

Apart from adjectives we also have adverbs of degree such as:

খুব *very*	খুব ক্লান্ত লাগছে। *(I am) feeling very tired.*
অন্তত *at least*	অন্তত তিন মাস *at least three months*
প্রায় *almost*	প্রায় এগারোটা *almost eleven o'clock*
শুধু *only*	সে শুধু আমার কাছে থাকতে চায়। *He only wants to stay with me.*

The confident use of these little words will help you become a successful learner of Bangla.

. . . .

We have two pairs of words that complement one another: অনেক and বেশি meaning *much* and আর and আরও meaning *more*. অনেক and আরও ar used in affirmative sentences; আর and বেশি are used in negative sentences:

affirmative	**negative**
সে অনেক ভাত খায়।	সে বেশি ভাত খায় না।
He eats a lot of rice.	*He doesn't eat a lot of rice.*
তারা আরও টাকা দেবে।	তারা আর টাকা দেবে না।
They will give more money.	*They will not give any more money.*

However, আর, rather than আরও, is used with এক *one*: আর একটা বই *one more book* = *another book*. আর একবার *one more time* or, as we saw in our first dialogue আর কয়েকটা ছবি *a few more pictures*. আর is also used with question words:

আর কি লাগবে? *What more is needed?*

আর কে আসবে? *Who else will come?*

আর কত দূর? *how much further?*

(Note: We discuss more on আরও in the section on Comparisons in Grammar 16, page 141.)

When বেশি is used in affirmative sentences, it usually means *too much*:

সে বেশি কথা বলে। *She talks too much.*

In our gardening dialogue in Unit 7 we had the sentence আমাদের একটু বেশি করে নড়াচড়া করা উচিত which means *we ought to move around a bit more,* implying an extra effort. The following are more sentences with আর, আরও, অনেক, and বেশি from our narratives and dialogues:

আমি আর যুবক নই। *I am no longer a young man.*

আর বলবেন না। *Don't say any more.*

আর এক বছর পরে *another year later = next year*

ওরা আর বেশি আসতে পারবে না। *They won't be able to come very often anymore.*

আর একবার গেলে ... *If you go one more time ...*

বাঁ দিকে আরও কিছু বাড়ি *a few more houses on the left*

আমার সাহেবটা আরও বোকা। *My master is more stupid.*

আমার পরিবারে অনেক মানুষ আছে। *There are a lot of people in my family.*

বাগান করতে অনেক সময় লাগে। *Gardening requires a lot of time.*

সে আমাকে অনেক ভালবাসে। *He loves me a lot.*

আমি তাকে অনেক দিন দেখিনি। *I haven't seen her for a long time (many days).*

কলকাতা থেকে বেশি দূর নয়। *It's not far from Kolkata.*

ফুলের কথা বেশি কিছু জানেন না। *He doesn't know much about flowers.*

আমার অবস্থা বেশি ভাল নয়। *My situation is not very good. = I am not feeling very well.*

Narrative

বোকা চাকর

দুজন সাহেব আলোচনা করছেন কার চাকর আরও বোকা।

একজন তাঁর চাকরকে ডাক দিয়ে বললেন, 'হে, বুদ্ধু রাম, বাজারে একটা নতুন বিউইক* পাওয়া যায়। এই যে দশ টাকা দিচ্ছি – তুমি সেটা কিনে আন গা।' বুদ্ধু রাম টাকাটা পকেটে রেখে বাজারের থলি হাতে নিয়ে চলে গেল।

দ্বিতীয় সাহেব বললেন, 'এটা কিছু নয়।' তাঁর নিজের চাকরকে ডেকে বললেন, 'উল্লু চাঁদ, তুমি একটু ক্লাবে গিয়ে দেখ না আমি ওখানে আছি কিনা। ব্যাপারটা খুব জরুরি।' উল্লু চাঁদ কিছু না বলে ক্লাবের দিকে চলে গেল।

দুজন চাকরের রাস্তায় দেখা হয়। বুদ্ধু রাম বলে, 'আমার সাহেব কত বোকা তা তুমি শুনে বিশ্বাস করবে না: এই মাত্র আমাকে পাঠিয়ে দিয়েছেন একটা বিউইক কিনতে। আজ যে রবিবার, বাজার বন্ধ, তা কি ভুলে গেছেন?'

উল্লু চাঁদ উত্তর দেয়, 'আমার সাহেবটা আরও বোকা। উনি ক্লাবে আছেন কিনা তা দেখতে আমাকে ক্লাবে পাঠাচ্ছেন। ব্যাপারটা জরুরি বলেছেন কিন্তু পাশের ঘরে যে তাঁর টেলিফোন আছে, সহজে টেলিফোনে জানা যেত উনি ক্লাবে আছেন কি না তা তাঁর মনে নেই !'

---

*বিউইক = *Buick*

Stupid servants

Two gentlemen are discussing whose servant is more stupid.

One of them calls his servant and says, "Buddhu Ram, there is a new Buick available in the market. Here are ten Taka – go and buy it for me." Buddhu Ram puts the money in his pocket, picks up the shopping bag and sets off.

The second gentleman says, "That's nothing." He calls his own servant and says, "Ullu Chand, please go to the club to see whether I am there or not. This is quite urgent." Ullu Chand sets off towards the club without saying a word.

The two servants meet in the street. Buddhu Ram says, "You won't believe how stupid my master is. Just now he sends me off to the market to buy a Buick. Has he forgotten that today is Sunday and the market is closed?"

Ullu Chand replies, "My master is even more stupid. He is sending me to the club to find out whether he is there or not. He says it's urgent but he seems to have forgotten that he has a telephone in the next room and could easily find out himself whether he is at the club or not."

[Borrowed and translated from Vikram Seth's novel *A suitable boy*, p. 1302]

Vocabulary: Narrative

বোকা boka *adj.* stupid

চাকর cakôr *n.* servant

আলোচনা alocɔna *n.* discussion

আলোচনা করা alocɔna kɔra *vb.* discuss

ডাক দেওয়া ḍak deoŷa *vb.* call

বিউইক biuik *n.* Buick

গা ga *filler word used with imp.*

পকেট pɔkeṭ *n.* pocket

থলি thôli *n.* bag

নিয়ে from নেওয়া neoŷa *vb.* take

দ্বিতীয় dvitīŷô *num.* second

নিজ nij *pr.* own, self

ডাকা ḍaka *vb.* call

ক্লাব klab *n.* club

ব্যাপার byapar *n.* matter

জরুরি jôruri *adj.* urgent

বিশ্বাস biśvas *n.* belief

বিশ্বাস করা biśvas kɔra *vb.* believe

এই মাত্র ei matrô *adv.* just now

পাঠানো paṭhano *vb.* send

পাঠিয়ে দেওয়া paṭhiŷe deoŷa *vb.* send

যে ye *conj.* that

রবিবার rôbibar *n.* Sunday

বন্ধ bɔndhô *adj.* closed

ভুলে যাওয়া bhule yaoŷa *cvb.* forget

উত্তর uttôr *n.* answer, reply

উত্তর দেওয়া uttôr deoŷa *vb.* answer, reply

আরও aro *adv.* more

সহজে sɔhôje *adv.* easily

মনে আছে mône ache *vb.* remember, be aware of

মনে নেই mône nei *vb.* not remember, be unaware of

Grammar 16: Comparison

Bangla adjectives form their comparative forms with আরও *more*:

আরও ভাল *better*   আরও গরম *hotter*   আরও সুন্দর *more beautiful*

Superlative forms are formed with সবচেয়ে *than all*:

সবচেয়ে ভাল *best*   সবচেয়ে বোকা *most stupid*   সবচেয়ে সুন্দর *most beautiful*

We have already seen postpositions like চেয়ে *than* and মত *like* that can be used for comparison, as in the dialogue in Unit 7:

আমার শরীর তো আগের মত নয়।
My health is not like before. = *My health is not what it used to be.*

Comparative sentences with চেয়ে *than*

For *He is taller than I am* Bangla simply says *He than me* (genitive) *is tall*. The word for *than* is the postposition চেয়ে, which follows *me*, and, as usual in equational sentences, there is a zero verb. Note that ছোট *small* is used not only for size but also for young in age:

পল্লবী উমার   চেয়ে ছোট।
Pollobi of.Uma than small
Pollobi is younger than Uma.

আমাদের গ্রাম   তোমাদের গ্রামের   চেয়ে সুন্দর।
our   village your   of.village than beautiful
Our village is more beautiful than yours.

আমার সাহেব তোমার সাহেবের চেয়ে বোকা।
my   master your   of.master than stupid
My master is more stupid than your master.

The adjectives in these sentences can be modified by অনেক or অনেক বেশি:

তুমি তার চেয়ে অনেক ভাল রান্না করতে পার।
You can cook much better than he can.

কুমিরের চেয়ে হাতি তাদের অনেক বেশি ভাল লেগেছে।
They liked the elephants much better than the crocodiles.

This is also useful for comparing amounts and numbers:

তাদের আমাদের চেয়ে অনেক বেশি টাকা আছে।
They have much more money than we do.

তার আমার চেয়ে আরও অনেক বন্ধু আছে।
She has more friends than I do.

কম *less* is used for comparing down:

সে তোমার চেয়ে কম কথা বলে।
He talks less than you do.

মত *like* is used for equals:

তুমি তার মত বোকা নও।
You are not as stupid as he is.

Superlatives

Superlatives are formed with সবচেয়ে *than all*:

কি কি পশু সবচেয়ে ভাল লেগেছে?
Which animals did they like best?

এটা সবচেয়ে বড়।
This one is the biggest.

Grammar 17: Verbs of being

The concept of being (and having) is expressed by four verbs in Bangla, two of which we have already come across:

Zero verb *be*

The zero verb is used for equational sentences:

উনি আমার বাবা। *He is my father.*
এগুলো আমার জিনিস। *These are my things.*
আপনার বাগান খুব সুন্দর। *Your garden is very beautiful.*

Negation of these sentences is done with the incomplete verb ন-. Its forms are given in Unit 7 in Grammar 12 (page 120).

The past tense of the zero verb is the same as that of আছ-:

তার বাগান খুব সুন্দর ছিল। *His garden was very beautiful.*
চা গরম ছিল না। *The tea was not hot.*

The future tense and non-finite structures are formed with হওয়া *be, become* (see "হওয়া *be, become, happen, occur*" below):

উনি আমার শাশুড়ি হবেন। *She will be my mother-in-law.*
চা গরম হলে *if the tea is hot ...*

· · · · · · · · · · · · · · · · ·

আছ- *be present, exist*

The incomplete verb আছ- combines existential, locative, and possessive *have* meanings. Through the existence of আছ- these meanings merge together.

existential: সময় আছে। *There is time.*
locative: আমি রাস্তায় আছি। *I am on the road.*
possessive: তার কমপিউটার আছে। *He has a computer.* (lit: *His computer exists.*)

In all cases, the negation for আছ- is নেই.

In present simple contexts আছ- can be omitted when the sentence is locative in meaning:

> আমি রাস্তায়। *I am on the road.*

আছ- can also be omitted when a possessive sentence contains a numeral or a quantifier:

> তার দুইটা কমপিউটার।   *He has two computers.*
> আমার অনেক সন্দেহ।   *I have a lot of doubts.*

When these sentences are negated, নেই reappears and confirms that we are dealing with existential sentences here despite the absence of a verb.

. . . .

থাকা *stay, remain*

থাকা stands in for আছ in the future tense, in conditional sentences, and in non-finite structures:

> তার কমপিউটার থাকবে।   *He will have a computer.*
> তোমার যদি সময় থাকে   *if you have time*
> তার সন্দেহ থাকতে পারে।   *He may have doubts.* (lit: *His doubts may exist.*)

. . . .

হওয়া *be, become, happen, occur*

হওয়া is probably the most common and most versatile verb in Bangla. It is a full verb with all tenses and non-finite verb forms. It has a dynamic *growing, becoming* factor built into its meaning and is therefore used with natural processes: এখানে ধান হয়। *Rice grows here.*

We have seen it in previous dialogues:

> আমার মনে হয়   *I think.* (lit: *It grows in my mind.*)
> অনেক ফুর্তি হয়েছে।   *(We) had a lot of fun.* (lit: *Much fun occurred.*)
> কোনও সমস্যা হয়নি।   *There were no problems.*
> তোমাদের সঙ্গে গেলে খুশি হব।   *If I go with you, I will be happy.*

And in this unit we had:

> মাংসের খুব স্বাদ হয়েছে।   *The meat turned out very tasty.*
> মাংসটা বেশ নরম হয়েছে।   *The meat was quite soft.*

We can see the *becoming* element in all these sentences.

> কি হয়েছে? means *What has happened?*
> কিছু হবে না। *Nothing will happen.* (a phrase often used to imply *It doesn't matter.*)

We can see the contrast between আছে and হওয়া in the following two sentences:

তার বাচ্চা আছে।   *She has a child.* (this merely states the existence of a child)

তার বাচ্চা হয়েছে।   *She has had a baby.* (refers to the process of giving birth)

Sentences with হওয়া often have a genitive experiencer subject:

তোমার কি হয়েছে?   *What has happened to you?*

তার জ্বর হয়েছে।   *He has a fever.*

আমার কষ্ট হচ্ছে।   *I am suffering.* (lit: *My suffering occurs.*)

(Note: *We will take a closer look at these impersonal structures in Unit 10, Grammar 25, page 182.*)

Grammar 18: Reflexives and reciprocals

Reflexives

Reflexives refer back to oneself. The word নিজে (নিজের, নিজেকে, নিজেদের) means *self*; the genitive নিজের usually means *own*:

আমি নিজে বাজারে   যাই।
I   self   market.LOC   I.go
I go to the market myself.

সে নিজে আমাকে এই   কথা   বলেছে।
he self   me   this word   he.has.said
He told me this himself.

তার নিজের   গাড়ি   আছে।
his   self.GEN   car   exists
He has his own car.

There is also the word আপন *own* which is commonly used to refer to family relationships:

সে আমার আপন ভাই।   *He is my own brother.*

তাদের আপন ছেলেমেয়ে নেই।   *They have no children of their own.*

Reciprocals

Reciprocals refer to mutual interaction (between two people or two groups of people). The word পরস্পর means *one another*. The object case ending −কে is usually added.

তারা পরস্পরকে সাহায্য করে।   *They help one another.*

আমরা পরস্পরকে ভয় করি না।   *We are not afraid of one another.*

Additional Vocabulary

Telling the time

In order to tell the present time, the verb বাজা *strike, ring* is used:

এখন কয়টা বাজে। *What time is it now?* (lit: *Now how many does it strike?*)
এখন ছয়টা বাজে। *It is now six o'clock.*

The abbreviated form কষ্টা for কয়টা is common: কষ্টা বাজে? *What's the time?* For all other times we ask either কোন সময় or কয়টায় or কটার সময় *at what time?*

The numbers for the hours are always followed by টা. In West Bengal দুটো for *two o'clock,* তিনটে for *three o'clock,* চারটে for *four o'clock* is common. The locative endings are added to say *at ... o'clock.*

বারোটা *twelve o'clock*   বারোটায় *at twelve o'clock*
বারোটা দশ *ten past twelve*   বারোটা দশে *at ten past twelve*

The words used to denote *quarter to, quarter past,* and *half past* precede the numbers:

পৌনে পাঁচটা *quarter to five*   সওয়া চারটা *quarter past four*   সাড়ে দশটা *half past ten*

On their own these words mean:

পৌনে *minus one quarter*   সওয়া *plus one quarter*   সাড়ে *plus one half*

There are separate words for:

half past one দেড়টা   *half past two* আড়াইটা

For all other times the minutes after the hour are used:

বারোটা দশ *12.10 ten past twelve*   আটটা পাঁচ *8.05 five past eight*
তিনটে চল্লিশ *3.40 twenty to four*   সাতটা পঁয়ত্রিশ *7.35 thirty-five past seven*
দুইটা বিশ (দুটো কুড়ি) *2.20 two twenty*   চারটা পঁচিশ *4.25 twenty-five past four*

The following can be used for approximate time:

তিনটা বেজে গেছে। *it's just past three o'clock.*   আটটার দিকে *around eight o'clock*
একটা বাজছে। *it's almost one'clock*   তিনটার মধ্যে *by three o'clock*

To denote a stretch of time মিনিট *minute* and ঘণ্টা *hour* are used:

পনের মিনিট *fifteen minutes*   পোয়া ঘণ্টা *quarter of an hour*
আধা ঘণ্টা or আধ ঘণ্টা *half an hour*   পৌনে ঘণ্টা *three quarters of an hour*
এক ঘণ্টা *one hour*   সওয়া ঘণ্টা *five quarters of an hour*
দেড় ঘণ্টা *one and a half hours*   আড়াই ঘণ্টা *two and a half hours*
সাড়ে তিন ঘণ্টা *three and a half hours*

Exercises: Unit 8

Exercise 8:1

Translate the following sentences using আর, আরও, অনেক or বেশি :

(i)   *They don't eat a lot of meat.*

(ii)   *He does a lot of gardening.*

(iii)   *The shirt is too big.*

(iv)   *Many people were here yesterday.*

(v)   *She won't have any more tea.*†

(vi)   *I need more plates.*

(vii)   *The food was not very good.*

(viii)   *There are not a lot of people in my family.*

(ix)   *They didn't catch any more fish.*

(x)   *Can you give me more mangoes?*

---

† খাওয়া is used for eating and drinking (any kind of oral consumption).

Exercise 8:2

Fill in the blanks with one of the following words and translate the sentences:

চেয়ে = than   আরও = more   মত = like   সবচেয়ে = of all, most

(i)   আমার এখানে _____ ভাল ঘুম হয়েছে।

(ii)   গরুর মহিষের _____ শক্তি নেই।

(iii)   বিমলের বাগানে পেঁপে গাছের _____ অনেক কলা গাছ আছে।

(iv)   আপনার বাগান আমার _____ ভাল লাগে।

(v)   একটা নতুন বিউইকের দাম দশ টাকার _____ অনেক বেশি।

(vi)   বিপ্লব প্রদীপের _____ বেশি কথা বলে।

(vii) হাতি তাদের _____ ভাল লেগেছে।

(viii) আমার সাহেব _____ বোকা।

(ix)   আমাদের _____ কেউ নয়।

(x)   মি খান মি চৌধুরীর _____ বয়সে অনেক ছোট।

Exercise 8:3
Translate the following phrases:

(i)   *some more questions* _____

(ii)   *too much food* _____

(iii) *another key* _____

(iv)   *two more countries* _____

(v)   *a little bit of help* _____

(vi)   অনেক দূরে _____

(vii) কয়েক ঘণ্টা _____

(viii) আরও পরে _____

(ix)   কিছু না _____

(x)   আর কে? _____

Exercise 8:4
Translate the following comparative phrases and sentences:

(i)   *He is not like his brother.* (negate with নয়)

(ii)   *Delhi is a lot further from here.*

(iii)   *Do you have any more money?*

(iv)   *He eats more than anyone else.* (use সবার চেয়ে)

(v)   *I study less than you do.* (use কম)

(vi)   *The mango tree is the biggest tree in the garden.*

(vii)   *Rajonna* (রাজনা) *is more beautiful than her mother.*

(viii)   *Her writing is the best.*

(ix)   *We eat a lot more fruit than they do.*

(x)   *Would you like more vegetables?* (Bangla structure: *Will you take more ...*)

(xi)   তার এখানে সবচেয়ে সুন্দর ঘুম হয়েছে।

(xii)   আমার মায়ের রান্না আরও ভাল।

(xiii)   সে তোমার মত বাংলা বলতে পারে না।

(xiv)   এই জায়গার গাছগুলো আরও ছোট।

(xv)   তার আমার চেয়ে আরও অনেক ভাইবোন আছে।

(xvi)   আমি তার মত কথা বলতে পারি না।

(xvii)   তোমাকে আরও কাজ করতে হবে।

(xviii)   আমাদের গ্রামের চেয়ে অনেক সুন্দর

(xix)   হাতির চেয়ে বড় কিছু নেই।

(xx)   কারা সবচেয়ে বোকা? (Remember: কারা is the plural of কে *who*)

Exercise 8:5

Give the Bangla for the following time expressions, with locative endings where required.

(i)   quarter past one _____

(ii)   half past two _____

(iii) at 11 o'clock _____

(iv)   10 past 3 _____

(v)   four hours _____

(vi)   one and a half hours _____

(vii) 4:45 _____

(viii) at quarter to twelve _____

(ix)   twenty past eight _____

(x)   at half past one _____

UNIT 9

Dialogue

পোস্টাপিসে

কর্মচারী: সালাম ওয়ালিকুম, আপা, আপনার জন্যে কি করতে পারি?

খরিদ্দার: ওয়ালিকুম সালাম। এই দুইটা চিঠি ইটালিতে পাঠাতে হবে।

কর্মচারী: ঠিক আছে। এয়ারমেইলে পাঠাবেন?

খরিদ্দার: হ্যাঁ, অবশ্যই। এক সপ্তাহের মধ্যে পৌঁছে যাবে তো?

কর্মচারী: ঠিক বলতে পারব না। কিন্তু এক সপ্তাহের মত তো লাগবে। আর কিছু লাগবে?

খরিদ্দার: হ্যাঁ, দেশের মধ্যে পাঠানো দশটা ডাকটিকিটও দেন। আর একটা পার্সেল আছে। এটা ইংল্যান্ড যাচ্ছে।

কর্মচারী: আচ্ছা। এই যে আপনার ডাকটিকিট। পার্সেলের মধ্যে কি আছে?

খরিদ্দার: একটা শাড়ি আর দু বয়াম তেঁতুলের আচার।

কর্মচারী: তেঁতুলের আচার আপনি পোস্ট করতে পারবেন না।

খরিদ্দার: না, না, কিছু হবে না। আমি বয়ামগুলো খুব ভালভাবে বন্ধ করে দিয়েছি। আবার পলিথিনের মধ্যে রেখে দিয়েছি। শাড়িটাও কাগজের মধ্যে মোড়া আছে। বয়াম থেকে কিছু পড়বে না। ইনশা–আল্লাহ।

কর্মচারী: তার জন্য নয়, আপা। পোস্টে কোনও খাবার জিনিস পাঠানো নিষেধ।

খরিদ্দার: তাই নাকি? আমি আমার বোনকে কথা দিয়েছি এইবার আচারটা পাঠাব তার কাছে। এটা নিজের হাতে বানানো আচার। ইংল্যান্ডে এগুলো পাওয়া যায় না। এখন আমি কি করব?

কর্মচারী: কিছু করার নেই। কেউ ইংল্যান্ডে গেলে নিয়ে যেতে পারবে। কিন্তু পোস্টে এটা হবে না।

খরিদ্দার: আচ্ছা, ঠিক আছে। তাহলে সব মিলে কত টাকা হয়েছে?

কর্মচারী: আশি টাকা।

খরিদ্দার: এই যে, এক শ টাকা দিচ্ছি। আপনি আমাকে বিশ টাকা ফেরত দেন।

কর্মচারী: এই যে।

খরিদ্দার: ধন্যবাদ।

At the post office

Employee: *Good morning, madam, what can I do for you?*

Customer: *Good morning. These two letters have to be sent to Italy.*

Employee: *OK, do you want to send them by airmail?*

Customer: *Yes, of course. They will reach there within a week, won't they?*

Employee: *I can't guarantee it but it'll take about a week. Do you need anything else?*

Customer: *Yes, please give me ten inland stamps. And I have a parcel which is going to England.*

Employee: *Right, here are your stamps. What is in the parcel?*

Customer: *One saree and two jars of tamarind chutney.*

Employee: *I'm afraid you can't send the tamarind chutney in the post.*

Customer: *No, it's OK. I have sealed the jars very well and wrapped them in polythene. The saree is wrapped in paper. Nothing will spill from the jars.*

Employee: *It's not that, madam. But you are not allowed to send any food items by post.*

Customer: *Really? I promised my sister that I would send her some chutney this time. I made it myself and she can't get it in England. What am I going to do now?*

Employee: *There is nothing you can do. If someone travels to England, they can take it. But it won't go in the post.*

Customer: *Ah well, all right then. So how much is the total?*

Employee: *Eighty taka.*

Customer: *Right, here are 100 taka. Please give me twenty taka back.*

Employee: *Here you are!*

Customer: *Thank you.*

Vocabulary: Dialogue

পোস্টাপিস posṭapis *n.* post office

কর্মচারী kɔrmôcarī *n.* employee

খরিদ্দার khôriddar *n.* customer

সালাম ওয়ালিকুম salam oŷalikum *phr.*
  Muslim greeting: God be with you!

ওয়ালিকুম সালাম oŷalikum salam *phr.*
  Muslim greeting reply: God be with you!

আপা apa *n.* elder sister

ইটালি iṭali *name* Italy

চিঠি ciṭhi *n.* letter

পাঠানো paṭhano *vb.* send

এয়ারমেইল eŷarmeil *n.* airmail

পৌঁছানো põuchano *vb.* arrive

মত mɔtô *pp.* like, about

ডাকটিকিট ḍakṭikiṭ *n.* postage stamp

পার্সেল parsel *n.* parcel

শাড়ি śaṛi *n.* saree

বয়াম bɔŷam *n.* jar

তেঁতুল tẽtul *n.* tamarind

আচার acar *n.* chutney

ভালভাবে bhalôbhabe *adv.* well, thoroughly

বন্ধ করা bɔndhô kɔra *vb.* close

আবার abar *adv.* again

কাগজ kagôj *n.* paper

মোড়া mora *vb.* wrap

পড়া pɔra *vb.* fall

ইনশা-আল্লাহ inśa-allah *expr.* inshalla (God willing!)

নিষেধ niṣedh *n.* prohibition

নিজ nij *pr.* self

বানানো banano *vb.* prepare, make

ইংল্যান্ড iṁlyanḍ *name* England

সব মিলে sɔb mile *adv.* all together

এক শ æk śô *num.* one hundred

ধন্যবাদ dhɔnyôbad *expr.* thanks, thank you

Grammar 19: Perfective participles (PP) — Verbal sequences

Forms for the perfective participle (PP) are given in Unit 5. The PP is the most common non-finite verb form in Bangla. It has two distinct uses. Here we look at verbal sequences. In Grammar 21 we discuss the use of the perfective participle in compound verbs.

When two or more actions, carried out by the same subject, follow one another, all but the last verb go into the perfective participle. This means that the perfective participle describes an action or process that comes before the action of the finite verb. The finite verb can be in any tense but the action described in the perfective participle precedes it. Literally the perfective participle has the meaning *having done, having gone, having seen* etc. Let's have a look at some examples from the dialogue and the narrative in this unit:

> থালাগুলো কি টেবিলে রেখে যাচ্ছ?
> *Are you leaving the plates on the table?*
> Lit.: *Are you going, having put the plates on the table?*

The verb রাখা *put, place* is given as a perfective participle to show that the action of *putting* precedes the action of *leaving*. If we change the sentence to future or any other tense, the perfective participle stays the same: আমি থালাগুলো টেবিলে রেখে যাব। *I will leave the plates on the table.*

> একজন তাঁর চাকরকে ডাক দিয়ে বললেন, ...
> *One called his servant and said, ...*
> Lit.: *One, having called his servant, said ...*

In English these sequences are often best translated with *and* or with a *when* or *after* sentence: *He called his servant and said ...*

> বুদ্ধু রাম টাকাটা পকেটে রেখে বাজারের থলি হাতে নিয়ে চলে গেল।
> *Buddhu Ram put the money in his pocket, took the market bag and left.*
> Lit.: *Buddhu Ram, having put the money in his pocket, having taken the*
>   *market bag, left.*

As you can see we have three sequential processes here and only the last verb গেল from যাওয়া *go* is a finite verb form *he went*. (We will come back to চলে গেল in the next section.)

This kind of structure is very common and very idiomatic in Bangla, and being able to use it with confidence will be a big step up in your learning process. In many contexts the perfective participle plays the part that conjunctions or subordinate clauses play in English, so we need to adjust our translations accordingly. Negation of the perfective participle is achieved by placing না in front of it:

> উল্লু চাঁদ কিছু না বলে ক্লাবের দিকে চলে গেল।
> Lit.: *Ullu Chand, having said nothing, left in the direction of the club.*

> তুমি শুনে বিশ্বাস করবে না।
> Lit.: *You, having heard, will not believe.*

In English we can just say *You won't believe it, when you hear* or leave the *hear* out altogether: *You won't believe ...*

These few examples will, I hope, give you an impression of how this structure works. You may want to go back over the previous dialogues and narratives to see if you can find more verbal sequences with perfective participles.

Grammar 20: Compound verbs

When the perfective participle of one verb is combined with another verb, the two verbs together can form a semantic unit called a compound verb. The verbs that act as the second component in these combinations are called compound makers. Compound verbs differ from verbal sequences (two actions following one another) in meaning but in some cases the same verb combination can be either a sequence or a compound verb. Only the context can clarify the meaning. Below are two simple examples. The verb ওঠা means *rise, get up* with its perfective participle উঠে *having risen*; and থাকা means *stay, remain* with its perfective participle থেকে *having stayed*.

(1) উঠে যাওয়া

sequence:	*get up and go*	সে রিকশায় উঠে গেছে।
		He got into the rickshaw and left.
compound verb: *come off*		দাগটা উঠে গেছে।
		The stain has come off.

(2) থেকে যাওয়া

sequence:	*stay and then go*	আর একটু থেকে যান।
		Stay a little bit longer (before you leave).
compound verb: *stay*		এই দেশে থেকে যান।
		Stay in this country (forever).

Only a limited number of verbs can act as compound makers. They are:

যাওয়া *go*	আসা *come*	ওঠা *rise, get up*	পড়া *fall*
আছ- / থাকা *stay*	দেওয়া *give*	নেওয়া *take*	ফেলা *throw*
তোলা *lift*	রাখা *keep*		

Compound verbs (in Bangla as well as in other South Asian languages) are a potential and a preference of the language rather than an inventory of fixed words. Bangla just seems to find compound verbs more pleasing and more expressive than simple verbs. আমি ভুলে গেছি is much more common than আমি ভুলেছি for *I have forgotten*. You will not find compound verbs in dictionaries because the potential for compound verbs is pretty much unrestricted. Instead of বলা *speak* we can say বলে দেওয়া *say* or বলে দিয়ে যাওয়া and so on. The verbs given above have, in addition to their ordinary meaning, the potential of acting as compound makers. In these combinations the perfective participle (first component) usually carries the main meaning, while the compound maker adds some nuance to the whole. Sometimes the compound maker loses its own meaning altogether.

The compound makers one by one

যাওয়া *go*

The verb যাওয়া is by far the most common and widely used of the compound makers. It can combine with a great number of verbs, both transitive and intransitive, and has almost infinite semantic capacity. Its uses can be divided into three main categories:

- with verbs of motion to indicate motion away from the speaker
- completion of the verbal action
- continuity of the verbal action

- with verbs of motion

  In these verb combinations যাওয়া retains some of its lexical meaning and serves to direct the movement away from the speaker. Some common ones are:

চলে যাওয়া *leave, go away*	আমাদের শনিবারে চলে যেতে হবে। *We will have to leave on Saturday.*
ফিরে যাওয়া *go back, return*	তুমি কি তোমার নিজের দেশে ফিরে যাবে না? *Won't you go back to your own country?*
পালিয়ে যাওয়া *flee, escape*	কেউ এখান থেকে পালিয়ে যেতে পারবে না। *No one can escape from here.*
নেমে যাওয়া *descend, get down*	যাত্রী সব, রেলগাড়ি থেকে নেমে যান। *All passengers, please get off the train.*

- completion of verbal action

  যাওয়া in these compounds stresses the result of an action/process or indicates a change of state.

  Result: সে সকালে এসে গেছে।
  He arrived this morning stresses the result: *He is now here.*

  আমার সাইকেল ভেঙে গেছে।
  My bicycle has got broken = It is now broken.

  Change of state: তুমি পড়ে যাবে।   *You will fall.*
  বাজারের দামগুলো বেড়ে গেছে। *The prices in the market have gone up.*
  সে কখনও রেগে যায় না।   *He never gets angry.*
  ঝড়ে অনেক গাছ মরে গেল।   *In the storm many trees died.*
  কাজটা তাড়াতাড়ি হয়ে যাবে।   *The work will be done (finished) quickly.*
  গাড়িটা হঠাৎ থেমে যেত।   *The car would suddenly stop.*

- continuity of the verbal action

  With transitive verbs, যাওয়া can retain its own meaning or have no impact at all:

আমি তোমাকে নিয়ে যাব না। *I won't take you with me when I go.*
সে তার মোবাইল রেখে গেছে। *He left his mobile/cell phone behind.*
তুমি কি সব ভুলে গেছ? *Have you forgotten everything?*
সারাদিন কাজ চালিয়ে যেতে হবে। *One has to go on working all day long.*
তিনি তাঁর স্বামীকে ছেড়ে গিয়েছেন। *She has left her husband.*

. . . .

আসা *come*

Like যাওয়া, আসা combines with verbs of motion, but in the opposite direction. The movement is towards the speaker:

ফিরে আসা *come back*   নেমে আসা *come down*
চলে আসা *arrive*   ঘুরে আসা *return*

আসা can indicate gradual change, especially in the weather, time of day, etc. Examples are:

বিকালে বৃষ্টি কমে এলো। *In the afternoon the rain decreased.*
জমি এখন শুকিয়ে আসছে। *The land is drying out now.*
রাস্তাটা নির্জন হয়ে এসেছে। *The road has become deserted.*
সন্ধ্যা হয়ে আসছে। *It is evening.*

আসা is used for actions or processes that began in the distant past and continue into the present. These examples are often in the present continuous tense:

এই বাগানগুলো আমি শুরু থেকে ভালবেসে আসছি।
I have loved these gardens from the beginning.

অনেক বছর ধরে উনি এই একই খবরের কাগজ পড়ে আসছেন।
He has been reading the same newspaper for many years.

. . . .

ওঠা *rise* / পড়া *fall*

Both these verbs used as compound makers imply a change of state, colored by their original meanings, i.e., motion upwards or downwards.

with ওঠা

বেড়ে ওঠা *increase*   ভরে ওঠা *be filled up*   ফুলে ওঠা *flower, blossom*
জ্বলে ওঠা *flare up*   ভাল হয়ে ওঠা *get better*   জেগে ওঠা *wake up*

with পড়া

নেমে পড়া *get down*   ভেঙে পড়া *collapse*   ঘুমিয়ে পড়া *fall asleep*
বসে পড়া *sit down*   শুয়ে পড়া *lie down*   এসে পড়া *arrive*

These are combinations with intransitive main verbs which themselves express an upward or downward movement. In combinations with other verbs both ওঠা and পড়া imply suddenness or unexpectedness.

ওঠা can be combined with verbs expressing sounds and indicates the sudden onset of these sounds, e.g.:

হেসে ওঠা	*burst out laughing*	বলে ওঠা	*say, blurt out*
বেজে ওঠা	*ring (telephone)*	চিৎকার করে ওঠা	*shout, cry out*

পড়া combines with verbs of motion to express suddenness:

এসে পড়া	*turn up (unexpectedly)*	উঠে পড়া	*get up*
বেরিয়ে পড়া	*go out*	ঢুকে পড়া	*enter*

The compound verb হয়ে পড়া tends to have negative connotations and describes some sort of decline, i.e., the original meaning of পড়া *fall* is at least partly retained:

সে সময়ে তারা গরিব হয়ে পড়ল।
At that time they became poor.

তার অসুখের পরে ছেলেটি খুব দুর্বল হয়ে পড়েছে।
After his illness the boy became very weak.

· ·

দেওয়া *give*

দেওয়া can add finality or emphasis to an action:

বলে দেওয়া *say, tell*	তোমাকে আবারও বলে দিতে হবে?	
	Do I have to tell you again?	
রেখে দেওয়া *keep, put away*	ছুরিটা রেখে দাও !	
	Put the knife down!	
পাঠিয়ে দেওয়া *send*	আমাদের পাঠিয়ে দিলেন গ্রামের বাড়িতে।	
	He sent us to the village home.	
ছেড়ে দেওয়া *give up*	সে কফি খাওয়া ছেড়ে দিয়েছে।	
	He has given up drinking coffee.	
ফেলে দেওয়া *throw away*	পচা আমগুলো কি ফেলে দেব?	
	Shall I throw the rotten mangoes away?	
কেটে দেওয়া *cut*	তুমি দড়িটা কেটে দেবে?	
	Will you cut the rope?	

দেওয়া frequently combines with causative verbs:

পরিচয় করিয়ে দেওয়া *introduce*	তার সঙ্গে পরিচয় করিয়ে দেবে না?
	Will you not introduce me to him?

বুঝিয়ে দেওয়া *explain*	সে তোমাকে সব বুঝিয়ে দিল।
	He explained everything to you.
দেখিয়ে দেওয়া *show*	তোমার জমি আমাকে দেখিয়ে দেবে?
	Will you show me your land?
লাগিয়ে দেওয়া *plant, install*	একটা ফোন লাগিয়ে দিয়েছি।
	I have installed a telephone.
জ্বালিয়ে দেওয়া *light, ignite*	বাতিগুলো জ্বালিয়ে দাও।
	Light the lamps.
কমিয়ে দেওয়া *reduce, lower*	ভাড়াটা কমিয়ে দিচ্ছি।
	I am lowering the rent.
নামিয়ে দেওয়া *drop off*	এখানে আমাকে নামিয়ে দিতে পারেন।
	You can drop me off here.

. . . .

নেওয়া *take*

What দেওয়া *give* does for others, নেওয়া *take* does for itself. To show the contrast between the two compound makers, here are some examples with identical main verbs:

for others:

খুলে দেওয়া *open for sb*
লিখে দেওয়া *write for sb*
করে দেওয়া *do for sb*
মুছিয়ে দেওয়া *wipe for sb*

for self:

খুলে নেওয়া *open for self*
লিখে নেওয়া *write for self*
করে নেওয়া *do for self*
মুছিয়ে নেওয়া *wipe for self*

. . . .

ফেলা *throw*

ফেলা is undoubtedly one of the most interesting compound makers because it adds a variety of nuances to the main verb and renounces its own original meaning so thoroughly:

আমি তাকে সব বলে ফেলেছি।
I have (inadvertantly but irrevocably) *told him everything.*

সে তোমাকে দেখে ফেলেছে।
He has already seen you. (can imply: *You don't need to hide anymore.*)

সে মাংসটা খেয়ে ফেলেছে।
He has eaten up all the meat. (implies: *Now there is none left.*)

অপমানটা আমি মন থেকে ঝেড়ে ফেলেছি।
I have brushed away the insult from my mind. (implies: *thoroughly*)

The interpretation of these sentences depends on the context, but they show what a wide range of meanings ফেলা as a compound maker can have.

ফেলা is the only transitive compound maker that can be used with intransitive perfective participles such as কেঁদে ফেলা *burst into tears,* and হেসে ফেলা *burst out laughing.* Syntactically, these combinations are unexpected but they are very common.

- -

রাখা *keep, put*

রাখা is only partially acceptable as a compound maker. It can form close connections with other verbs, e.g., লুকিয়ে রাখা *keep hidden,* বলে রাখা *say* (the implication is that whatever needed to be said is now out in the open), খুলে রাখা *keep open*; but it retains its own meaning in these combinations.

- -

থাকা *stay, remain*   আছ *be present, exist*

These two verbs, virtually synonymous, are aspective compound makers. They add to a compound the sense of either remaining in one particular state, when the main verb is stative, e.g.:

শুয়ে থাকা *remain lying down*	বসে আছ *remain sitting*
দাঁড়িয়ে থাকা *remain standing*	চুপ করে থাকা *keep quiet*

or, with active verbs, they can convey a meaning of habitual or repetitive actions:

গেয়ে থাকা *keep singing*	কথা বলে থাকা *keep talking*
চেয়ে থাকা *keep looking*	লিখে থাকা *keep writing*

আছ- is an incomplete verb with only simple present and past tense. In all other tenses it is replaced with forms of থাকা.

রাতটা তো মানুষের জেগে থাকবার জন্য নয়।
The night is not made for people to stay awake.

তাদের উপরে রাগ করে থাকা যায় না।
It is not possible to stay angry with them.

তুমি এখনও এখানে দাঁড়িয়ে আছ কেন?
Why are you still standing here?

থাকা and আছ- as compound makers retain quite a lot of their original meanings.

(Note: *A list of common compound verbs is given in Appendix 5, page 335.*)

Narrative

মেজাজ খারাপ

অনিল সাহেবের মেজাজ খারাপ। সকাল থেকে খালি অসুবিধে। চা ঠাণ্ডা ছিল, তার মাথা ব্যথা করে, অফিসে যাওয়ার সময় তার একটা জরুরি ফাইল পড়ে গিয়ে ময়লা হয়েছে আর আজকের খবরের কাগজ দোকানে পাননি। দিনটা আস্তে আস্তে আরও খারাপ হয়ে যাচ্ছে। অফিসে একজনের সঙ্গে ঝগড়া হয়েছে, দারোয়ান আবারও বিস্কুট কিনতে ভুলে গেছে, কমপিউটারের সমস্যা, দুপুরের খাবারের কোনও স্বাদ নেই।

সন্ধ্যা বেলায় বাসায় ফিরে শুধু বিশ্রাম করবেন আজ। কিন্তু তাঁর ছোট মেয়ে প্রমী সঙ্গে সঙ্গে ডাকে 'বাবা, বাবা'! আবারও কি? একটুও শান্তি কি পাওয়া যাবে না?

তাঁর মেয়ে প্রমী কাছে এসে তাঁর হাত ধরে টান দেয়। 'বাবা, বাবা, সো, দেখ তো বাগানে কি সুন্দর জিনিস'। বাড়ির পিছনের বাগানে লাল রঙের একটা ফুল ফুটেছে। একরকম গোলাপ মনে হয়। অনিল সাহেব ফুলের কথা বেশি কিছু জানেন না। 'এই যে দেখ বাবা' প্রমী হাসিমুখে বলল 'ফুলটি আজ ফুটেছে, বাবা। তোমার মেজাজ ভাল করার উপহার'। হঠাৎ খুব লজ্জা লাগছে অনিল সাহেবের। তাঁর ছোট মেয়েটির কি বুদ্ধি!

Bad mood

Mr. Onil was in a bad mood. Nothing but problems since morning. The tea was cold; he had a headache; on the way to the office he dropped an important file and it got dirty; and he didn't manage to get today's newspaper in the shop. The day was gradually getting worse. He had an argument with someone in the office; the caretaker had forgotten to buy biscuits yet again, there were problems with the computer and the meal at lunchtime had no taste at all.

When he got back home this evening, he would just have a rest. But his little daughter Promi called him straightaway: "Daddy, Daddy!" What now? Was there no peace to be had?

His daughter took hold of his hand and pulled him, "Daddy, Daddy, come and see something beautiful in the garden!" In the garden at the back of the house a red flower had opened up. Some kind of rose probably. Mr. Onil didn't know very much about flowers. "Here, look Daddy," Promi said with a big smile. "It opened up today. It's a present to put you in a better mood!" Suddenly Mr. Onil felt ashamed. How wise his little girl was!

Vocabulary: Narrative

মেজাজ mejaj *n.* mood, temper
ঠাণ্ডা ṭhaṇḍa *adj.* cold
ব্যথা bytha (bætha) *n.* pain
ফাইল phail *n.* file
ময়লা mɔŷla *adj.* dirty
খবর khɔbôr *n.* news
খবরের কাগজ khɔbôrer kagôj *n.* newspaper
দোকান dokan *n.* shop
আস্তে আস্তে aste aste *adv.* gradually, slowly
ঝগড়া jhɔgṛa *n.* quarrel, argument
দারোয়ান daroŷan *n.* porter; guard
বিস্কুট biskuṭ *n.* biscuit
দুপুর dupur *n.* midday
বিশ্রাম biśram *n.* rest, relaxation

সঙ্গে সঙ্গে sɔṅge sɔṅge *adv.* immediately
শান্তি śanti *n.* peace
টান ṭan *n.* pull, attraction
টান দেওয়া ṭan deoŷa *vb.* pull
লাল la:l *adj.* red
রং rɔṃ *n.* color
ফুল phul *n.* flower
ফোটা phoṭa *vb.* blossom
হাসিমুখে hasimukhe *adv.* smiling, happily
উপহার upôhar *n.* present, gift
হঠাৎ hɔṭhat̪ *adv.* suddenly
লজ্জা lɔjja *n.* embarrassment
বুদ্ধি buddhi *n.* wisdom

Additional vocabulary: Around the house

bathroom স্নান ঘর snan ghɔr, গোসলখানা gosôlkhana
bed খাট khaṭ, চৌকি couki
bedding বিছানা bichana
bedroom শোবার ঘর śobar ghɔr
blanket কম্বল kɔmbôl
blouse ব্লাউজ blauj
book বই bôi
bowl বাটি baṭi
broom ঝাড়ু jhaṛu ঝাঁটা jhãṭa
bucket বালতি balti
button বোতাম botam
candle মোমবাতি mombati
cane chair মোড়া moṛa
cap টুপি ṭupi
carpet গালিচা galica
clock ঘড়ি ghôṛi
cloth কাপড় kapôṛ
clothes জামাকাপড় jamakapôṛ
comb চিরুনি ciruni
cupboard আলমারি almari

curtain পর্দা pɔrda
dining room খাবার ঘর khabar ghɔr
dish থালা thala
dhoti ধুতি dhuti
drawer দেরাজ deraj
dress *(attire)* পোষাক poṣak; *(girl's)* ফ্রক phrɔk
earring কানের ফুল kaner phul
floor মেঝে mejhe
fork কাটা চামচ kaṭa camôc
frying pan কড়াই kɔṛai
glass *(for drinking)* গেলাস gelas
glasses (eyeglasses) চশমা cɔśma
grinding stone শিল śi:l
hammer হাতুড়ি haturi
hat টুপি ṭupi
jar বয়াম bɔŷam
jewelry গয়না gɔŷna
jug জগ jɔg
kettle কেটলি keṭli
key চাবি cabi

kitchen রান্না ঘর ranna ghɔr
knife ছুরি churi
ladder মই môi
ladle হাতা hata
lamp বাতি bati
lantern হারিকেন hariken
lock তালা tala
matches দেশলাই deśôlai
mirror আয়না aŷna
necklace মালা mala, হার har
needle সূচি sūci
notebook খাতা khata
oven চুলা cula
pajamas পায়জামা paŷjama, পাজামা pajama
pan হাঁড়ি hā̃ṛi
pen কলম kɔlôm
picture ছবি chôbi
pillow বালিশ baliś
pin আলপিন alpin
plate থালা thala
pot (*cooking*) ডেকচি ḍekci
pullover গরম গেঞ্জি gɔrôm geñji
purse মানিব্যাগ manibyag
rack আলনা alna
razor ক্ষুর kṣur (khur)
ring আংটি aṃṭi (angṭi)
roof ছাদ cha:d
room ঘর ghɔr

rope দড়ি dôṛi
sandals চটি côṭi
sari/saree শাড়ি śaṛi
saucer পিরিচ piric
scarf মাফলার maphlar
scissors কাঁচি kāci, কেচি keci
shawl ওড়না oṛna
sheet চাদর cadôr
shirt সার্ট sarṭ
shoes জুতা juta, জুতো juto
sieve ছাঁকনি chākni, চালনি calni
soap সাবান saban
socks মোজা moja
spoon চামচ camôc
stairs সিঁড়ি sī̃ṛi
toilet পায়খানা paŷkhana, টয়লেট ṭɔŷleṭ
towel তোয়ালে toŷale, গামছা gamcha
trousers প্যান্ট pyanṭ
tube well নলকূপ nɔlkūp
umbrella ছাতা chata, ছাতি chati
verandah বারান্দা baranda
vest গেঞ্জি geñji
wall দেওয়াল deoŷal
watch ঘড়ি ghôṛi
water jug কলসি kôlsi
water pump কল kɔl
window জানালা janala

Grammar 21: Causative and extended verbs

Bangla has two types of verbs with a two-syllable stem ending in a and a verbal noun ending in নো no, e.g., ঘুমানো *sleep* and লাগানো *plant, employ*. Extended verbs like ঘুমানো are derived from nouns or adjectives: কামড়ানো *bite* from the noun কামড় *bite*, উলটানো *overturn* from the adjective উলটা *upside down*, ঘুমানো *sleep* from the noun ঘুম *sleep*. Causative verbs like লাগানো *cause to attach, plant* are derived from simple verbs: করানো *cause to do* from করা *do*, বোঝানো *explain* from বোঝা *understand*. Almost all simple verbs can be extended into causatives in the right context, but some are much more common than others. In the dialogue about going to the zoo in Unit 5, we had the verb খাওয়ানো *feed* from খাওয়া *eat*.

Causative verbs give us a convenient tool for making others do the work for us.

simple:	আমি চাটা আনবো।	*I will bring the tea.*
causative:	আমি চাটা আনাবো।	*I will arrange for the tea to be brought.*
simple:	আমি কাজটা করবো।	*I will do the work.*
causative:	আমি তাকে দিয়ে কাজটা করাবো।	*I will make him do the work.*

Extended and causative verbs have the same conjugation (Class 4 in the verb chart): Here are two verbs, the extended verb তাকানো *look at, gaze* and the causative verb চালানো *drive* with their verb forms. The conjugation for ঘুমানো *sleep* is given in Appendix 3.

Extended verb তাকানো *look at, gaze* from the noun তাক *aim*

tenses	আমি	তুমি	সে	আপনি, তিনি
present simple	তাকাই	তাকাও	তাকায়	তাকান
present continuous	তাকাচ্ছি	তাকাচ্ছ	তাকাচ্ছে	তাকাচ্ছেন
present perfect	তাকিয়েছি	তাকিয়েছ	তাকিয়েছে	তাকিয়েছেন
future tense	তাকাব	তাকাবে	তাকাবে	তাকাবেন
past simple	তাকালাম	তাকালে	তাকাল	তাকালেন
past continuous	তাকাচ্ছিলাম	তাকাচ্ছিলে	তাকাচ্ছিল	তাকাচ্ছিলেন
past perfect	তাকিয়েছিলাম	তাকিয়েছিলে	তাকিয়েছিল	তাকিয়েছিলেন
past habitual	তাকাতাম	তাকাতে	তাকাত	তাকাতেন
imperative	---	তাকাও	তাকাক	তাকান
VN তাকানো, IP তাকাতে, CP তাকালে, PP তাকিয়ে				

Causative verb চালানো *drive* from চলা *move*

tenses	আমি	তুমি	সে	আপনি, উনি
present simple	চালাই	চালাও	চালায়	চালান
present continuous	চালাচ্ছি	চালাচ্ছ	চালাচ্ছে	চালাচ্ছেন
present perfect	চালিয়েছি	চালিয়েছ	চালিয়েছে	চালিয়েছেন
future tense	চালাব	চালাবে	চালাবে	চালাবেন
past simple	চালালাম	চালালে	চালাল	চালালেন
past continuous	চালাচ্ছিলাম	চালাচ্ছিলে	চালাচ্ছিল	চালাচ্ছিলেন
past perfect	চালিয়েছিলাম	চালিয়েছিলে	চালিয়েছিল	চালিয়েছিলেন
past habitual	চালাতাম	চালাতে	চালাত	চালাতেন
imperative	---	চালাও	চালাক	চালান
VN চালানো, IP চালাতে, CP চালালে, PP চালিয়ে				

It is not especially important for you at this stage to know the difference between extended and causative verbs for learning them, but it is useful to know that extended verbs are fixed lexical items whereas causative verbs are a potential of the language. Here are some more causative examples:

সে নাচছে। *He is dancing.*
সে আমাকে নাচাচ্ছে। *He is causing me to dance = bossing me around.*

আমি বাংলা শিখছি। *I am learning Bangla.*
আমি তাদের বাংলা শেখাচ্ছি। *I am teaching them Bangla.*

আমি যাব না। *I won't go.*
আমি তোমাকে যাওয়াব। *I will make you go.*

ট্রেনটা থেমে গেছে। *The train has stopped.*
ও ট্রেনটা থামিয়ে দিয়েছে। *He stopped the train.*

এখানে নামব। *I will get off here.*
আমাকে এখানে নামাবেন? *Will you drop me off here?*

A particularly useful expression is সময় কাটে *time goes by* and its causative counterpart সময় কাটানো *spend time*:

আমরা এখানে বসে অনেক সময় কাটাই।
We spend a lot of time sitting here.

Common extended verbs

আটকানো *arrest*

কামড়ানো *bite*

ঘুমানো *sleep*

চেঁচানো *shout*

জুড়ানো *cool, soothe*

তাকানো *look, stare*

দাঁড়ানো *stand*

পাঠানো *send*

ফুরানো *end, finish*

বানানো *prepare*

শুকানো *dry, dry out*

উলটানো *overturn*

গুছানো *tidy up, arrange*

চিবানো *chew*

জিরানো *rest, relax*

ঠকানো *cheat*

তাড়ানো *chase away*

দৌড়ানো *run*

পালানো *flee*

বদলানো *change*

বেড়ানো *go out, visit*

সামলানো *manage*

Common causative verbs

ওঠানো *raise, lift, wake*

করানো *cause to do*

খাওয়ানো *give to eat, feed*

জমানো *collect, save*

জ্বালানো *ignite, irritate, bother*

দেখানো *show*

পড়ানো *teach, read aloud to*

বাঁচানো *save*

ভাবানো *make think*

ভরানো *fill*

লাগানো *plant, employ, apply*

শোনানো *cause to listen*

সরানো *move, shift*

কমানো *reduce, decrease*

কাটানো *spend (time)*

চালানো *lead, drive*

জানানো *inform, tell*

থামানো *make stop*

নামানো *drop off, set down*

ফেরানো *cause to return*

বাঁধানো *bind*

বোঝানো *explain*

ভেজানো *soak, make wet*

শেখানো *teach*

শোয়ানো *lay, put to bed*

হারানো *lose*

Exercises: Unit 9

Exercise 9:1

Connect the sentences with a perfective participle and translate. When the sentences are connected they need only one subject.

Example: মেয়েটি বিছানায় শুয়েছে। মেয়েটি পুরাটা বই পড়েছে।

→ মেয়েটি বিছানায় শুয়ে পুরাটা বই পড়েছে।

The girl read the whole book while lying on the bed.

(i) উনি রিকশায় উঠেছেন। উনি রিকশা থেকে পড়ে গিয়েছিলেন।

(ii) আমরা চিড়িয়াখানায় গিয়েছি। আমরা অনেক পশু দেখেছি।

(iii) সে তার সাইকেল নিয়েছে। সে অফিসে যাবে।

(iv) আমরা নাস্তা খাব। আমরা বাইরে যাব।

(v) উনি কুষ্টিয়ায় গিয়েছেন। উনি নতুন গাছ কিনেছেন।

(vi) তুমি চিঠিটা লিখবে। তুমি চিঠিটা আমার কাছে পাঠাবে।

(vii) ওরা সাপটা দেখেছে। ওরা ভয় পেয়ে গেছে।

(viii) আমি ঢাকায় যাব। আমি লেখাপড়া করব।

(ix) মেয়েটি কাছে এসেছে। সে তাঁর হাত ধরেছে। সে তাঁকে টান দিয়েছে।

(x) বাবা দেরি করেছেন। বাবা সন্ধ্যাবেলায় বাসায় ফিরে এসেছেন।

Exercise 9:2

Compound verbs: Finish the sentences with an appropriate compound maker and translate. You choose the tense.

(i)   আমার ঘুম ভেঙে _____ ।

(ii)   উনি আমাকে পাঠিয়ে _____ ।

(iii)   আমি তোমাকে নিয়ে _____ ।

(iv)   আমরা মোটা হয়ে _____ ।

(v)   সে রিকশা থেকে পড়ে _____ ।

(vi)   একটা গোলাপ ফুল ফুটে _____ ।

(vii)   দিনটা আস্তে আস্তে আরও খারাপ হয়ে _____ ।

(viii)   সে চা খাওয়া ছেড়ে _____ ।

(ix)   গতকালের ভাত ফেলে _____ ।

(x)   আমাকে এখানে নামিয়ে _____ ।

(xi)   সে তার মনের কথা লুকিয়ে _____ । (মনের কথা = *feelings*)

(xii)   সে প্রায় সারাদিন তার কম্পিউটারের সামনে বসে _____ ।

(xiii)   সে আবার ভাল হয়ে _____ ।

(xiv)   তুমি সকালে কোন সময় জেগে _____ ?

(xv)   বাচ্চাটি ঘুমিয়ে _____ ।

Exercise 9:3

Translate extended and causative verbs (all the verbs you need are given in the lists above. You just need to work out the individual verb forms).

(i)   I will let you know.

(ii)   This letter has to be sent today.

(iii)   I can't explain this to you.

(iv)   Did you show it to the doctor?

(v)   He will give us ice cream to eat.

(vi)   She prepares her own bread.

(vii)   He applied an ointment to my hand.

(viii)   I slept the whole day.

(ix)   He can't drive a car.

(x)   They arrived in the morning.

(xi)   তারা আমাকে জ্বালায়নি।

(xii)   সে আলুর দাম কমিয়ে দিয়েছে।

(xiii)   উনি আমাকে বাংলা শেখান।

(xiv)   সে অনেক কিছু হারায়।

(xv)   ওরা তাদের টাকা জমিয়ে রাখে না।

(xvi)   সে আমাদের রাস্তাটা দেখিয়েছে।

(xvii)   এখান থেকে কি করে পালাবে?

(xviii) উনি চিঠিটা পড়িয়ে দেবেন।

(xix)   আমি তাকে উঠিয়ে দেওয়ার ব্যবস্থা করছি।

(xx)   তারা নিজের বাগানে গাছ লাগায়।

REVIEW EXERCISES

Are you keeping up with learning your new words? Are you taking in all the grammatical information? How are you getting on with learning your numbers? Are you getting enough practice? This is the time to slow down a little and take a look back at what you have already learned. Below are a few mixed practice exercises to help you check your progress – you should be able to do these without looking up too many items.

Review Exercise 1. Script

Give the components, the pronunciation, and an example of the following common conjuncts:

Example: স্ত nt = ন n + ত t   শান্তি śanti *peace*

(i)   স্ত = _____

(ii)   ত্র = _____

(iii) দ্ধ = _____

(iv)   ক্ষ = _____

(v)   স্ত = _____

(vi)   জ্ঞ = _____

(vii) ঙ = _____

(viii) ষ্ঠ = _____

(ix)   স্থ = _____

(x)   র্থ = _____

Review Exercise 2. Vocabulary

Give the English translations for the following Bangla words:

স্বাদ _____   লোক _____

কেন _____   গল্প _____

কিছু _____   মাথা _____

একসঙ্গে _____   বুধবার _____

মাছ _____   পুকুর _____

জানালা _____   দূর _____

কাউকে _____   তাড়াতাড়ি _____

প্রায় _____

Give the Bangla translations for the following English words:

much _____   **only** _____

seven _____   **until** _____

day _____   **beautiful** _____

play _____   **bad** _____

meat _____   **usually** _____

garden _____   **help** _____

town _____   **green** _____

time _____

Put the words below into the correct category box on the next page. There are four words for each box:

অসুবিধা	আকাশ	আপা	আমাদের	আসা	এরা	কথা	কলম
কারা	কালো	ক্লান্ত	খবর	খুশি	গরম	গোঁফ	ঘটনা
ঘড়ি	ঘাস	ঘোড়া	চমৎকার	চাবি	চামচ	চামড়া	চালানো
চোখ	জমি	ডাল	ডিম	তা	থেকে	দাদা	দুধ
নুন	পর্যন্ত	পা	পাওয়া	পাখি	পিছনে	পিসি	বসা
বাঘ	বৃষ্টি	মামা	সবুজ	সাদা	সামনে	হলুদ	হাঁস

animals	people	colors	nature words
verbs	adjectives	postpositions	pronouns
things	abstract nouns	food	parts of the body

Review Exercise 3: Mixed grammar

Postpositions: *translate the following*:

(i) *after six o'clock* _____

(ii) *in the middle of the village* _____

(iii) *before Sunday* _____

(iv) *until morning* _____

(v) *outside the town* _____

(vi) মনের ভিতরে _____

(vii) তোমাকে ছাড়া _____

(viii) তাদের জন্যে _____

(ix) ৫টা থেকে _____

(x) পশ্চিমের দিকে _____

Pronouns: *insert a correct pronoun to go with the verb ending:*

(i) _____ রাজশাহীতে গিয়েছে।   (vi) _____ গ্রামে থাকে।

(ii) _____ রোজ টেলিফোন করি।   (vii) _____ বাইরে যাইনি।

(iii) _____ চা খাবেন?   (viii) _____ চিন্তা করেন না।

(iv) _____ ভাত খেয়েছ?   (ix) _____ জমিতে কাজ করেন।

(v) _____ ছবি দেখছে।   (x) _____ ছুটিতে যাচ্ছি।

Classifiers: *Translate the following phrases using* টা, টি, জন, গুলো *and* এই, সেই, ওই *where appropriate*:

(i) *three roads* _____   (vi) *all the books* _____

(ii) *five minutes* _____   (vii) *a few girls* _____

(iii) *the red pen* _____   (viii) *ten miles* _____

(iv) *a small child* _____   (ix) *these two rivers* _____

(v) *some rain* _____   (x) *a bit of time* _____

Verb forms: *give the imperfective participles of the following verbal nouns by inserting them into the following sentence*:

আমি _____ পারি। = *I can* _____ .

(i) কাজ করা *work*

(ii) বোঝা *understand*

(iii) আসা *come*

(iv) থাকা *stay*

(v) টাকা দেওয়া *pay*

Now give the perfective participles of the same verbs. Can you make some sentences with them?

UNIT 10

Dialogue

বাজারে

দোকানদার: কি নেবেন?

মহিলা:   আচ্ছা, একটু দেখি। টোমেটোর দাম তো অনেক। থাক। এক হালি শসা নেব
          আর একটা ফুলকপি। আলুর দাম কত?

দোকানদার: আলুর দাম পনেরো টাকা কেজি, ম্যাডাম। এগুলো খুব ভাল।

মহিলা:   বেশি ভাল নয় অবশ্যই। অনেক ছোট।

দোকানদার: ছোট তো। কিন্তু ছোটগুলোর স্বাদ বেশি।

মহিলা:   আচ্ছা, দুই কেজি দেন।

দোকানদার: তিন কেজি নিলে দাম আরও কম পড়বে। তিন কেজি দেব?

মহিলা:   দেন। গাজর আছে?

দোকানদার: গাজর আজকে নেই, ম্যাডাম। সব শেষ হয়ে গেছে। কালকে সকালে আবার
          পাওয়া যাবে।

মহিলা:   না, না, গাজর আজই খুব জরুরি দরকার। অন্য দোকানে পাওয়া যাবে না?

দোকানদার: হ্যাঁ, অবশ্যই। ওইদিকে আমার বন্ধুর দোকান আছে। তার কাছ থেকে এনে দেব?

মহিলা:   হ্যাঁ, থাকলে ছয় কেজি নেব।

দোকানদার: ছয় কেজি? তা তো অনেক। কি করবেন, ম্যাডাম, এত গাজর নিয়ে?

মহিলা:   আমি একটা বিশেষ রস বানাব। সেটা চোখের জন্য খুব উপকারী।

দোকানদার: তাই নাকি? আমি তো তা জানতাম না। আমারও খুব চোখের সমস্যা কিন্তু।

মহিলা:   আচ্ছা, তাহলে আপনি আপনার বন্ধুর দোকান থেকে গাজর এনে দিলে আমি
          কালকে আপনার জন্য ছোট এক শিশি গাজরের রস নিয়ে আসব। কেমন?

দোকানদার: খুব ভাল, ম্যাডাম। এনে দিচ্ছি – ওই বিকাশ ! তোমাদের গাজর সব এখানে
          নিয়ে এসো। এই ভদ্রমহিলা গাজর নিয়ে একটা জাদু জানেন। সেটা খেলে
          চোখের সমস্যা উঠে যায়।

মহিলা:   জাদু তো নয় সেটা।

দোকানদার: আমার কাছে জাদু, ম্যাডাম। আমি যা বুঝি না, তা আমার কাছে জাদু। এই যে,
          আপনার গাজর প্যাক করে দিয়েছি। কালকে তাহলে আসবেন আবার?

মহিলা:   হ্যাঁ, দুপুরের দিকে আসব। এই যে, আজকের টাকা দিচ্ছি। আবার কালকে দেখা
          হবে।

দোকানদার: হ্যাঁ, দেখা হবে।

At the market

Market-trader: *What would you like?*

Woman: *OK, let's have a look. The tomatoes are very expensive. Forget it. I will take four cucumbers and a cauliflower. How much are the potatoes?*

Market-trader: *Fifteen taka for a kilo, madam. They are very nice.*

Woman: *Not particularly nice, actually. They are very small.*

Market-trader: *Yes, they are small. But the small ones are more tasty.*

Woman: *OK, give me two kilos.*

Market-trader: *If you take three kilos, they will be cheaper. Shall I give you three kilos?*

Woman: *Yes, go on. Do you have any carrots?*

Market-trader: *No carrots today, I'm afraid, madam. They are all sold out. You'll be able to get some tomorrow morning.*

Woman: *No, no, I need carrots urgently today. Won't there be any at a different stall?*

Market-trader: *Yes, of course. Over there is my friend's stall. Shall I get some from him?*

Woman: *Yes. If he's got enough I want six kilos.*

Market-trader: *Six kilos? That's a lot! What will you do, madam, with so many carrots?*

Woman: *I am making a special juice. It's very beneficial for the eyes.*

Market-trader: *Is that so? I didn't know that. I am also having lots of problems with my eyes.*

Woman: *Well, in that case, get me some carrots from your friend's stall and I will bring a small bottle of carrot juice for you tomorrow. How does that sound?*

Market-trader: *Very good, madam. I'm getting them. Hey, Bikash, bring all your carrots over here. This lady here can do some magic with carrots which solves all eye problems!*

Woman: *It's not magic!*

Market-trader: *It's magic to me, madam. When I don't understand something, I think of it as magic. Here are your carrots all packed up. So you will come back tomorrow?*

Woman: *Yes, around midday. Here is your money for today. See you tomorrow.*

Market-trader: *Yes, see you.*

Vocabulary: Dialogue

দোকানদার dokandar *n.* shopkeeper

টোমেটো ṭomeṭo *n.* tomato

দাম da:m *n.* price

ম্যাডাম myaḍam *n.* madam

হালি (BD) hali *num.* group of four

শসা śɔsa *n.* cucumber

ফুলকপি phulkôpi *n.* cauliflower

আলু alu *n.* potato

পনেরো pɔnerô *num.* fifteen

টাকা ṭaka *n. taka* (currency of Bangladesh)

কেজি keji *n.* kilogram

স্বাদ svad *n.* taste

নেওয়া neoŷa *vb.* take

কম kɔm *adj./adv.* less

পড়া pɔṛa *vb.* fall

গাজর gajôr *n.* carrot

শেষ হয়ে যাওয়া śeṣ hôŷe yaoŷa *vb.* run out, come to an end, be finished

কালকে kalke *n.* tomorrow, yesterday

জরুরি jôruri *adj.* urgent

দোকান dokan *n.* shop

ওইদিকে oidike *adv.* that way

কাছ থেকে kach theke *pp.* from (a person)

ছয় chɔŷ *num.* six

রস rɔs *n.* juice

চোখ cokh *n.* eye

উপকারী upôkarī *adj.* beneficial

শিশি śiśi *n.* bottle

বিকাশ bikaś *name* Bikash *(male)*

ভদ্রমহিলা bhɔdrômôhila *n.* lady

জাদু jadu *n.* magic

যা ya *pr.* what

উঠে যাওয়া uṭhe yaoŷa *vb.* go away, vanish, disappear

প্যাক করা pyak kɔra *vb.* pack

দুপুর dupur *n.* midday

Narrative

সূর্যোদয়

গত সপ্তাহের একটা ঘটনার কথা বলতে যাচ্ছি। আমি আমার কয়েকটি বন্ধু নিয়ে অনেক আগে থেকে এক দিন সূর্যোদয় দেখতে চেয়েছিলাম। মা বলেছে যে আমাদের বাড়ির কাছের নদীর ধারে সূর্যোদয় খুব সুন্দর দেখা যায়, কিন্তু আমি তো কখনও এত সকালে ঘুম থেকে উঠিনি।

তাই গত শুক্রবারে রাত্রে আমরা সবাই আমাদের বাড়িতে ঘুমিয়ে সকাল ৫টায় ওঠার ব্যবস্থা করেছিলাম। মা আমাদের ডাক দিয়ে উঠিয়ে রাস্তাটা দেখালো। কিছু খাবার জিনিসও সঙ্গে দিল। অল্প দূরে গিয়ে নদীর পাড়ে পৌছাইলাম। তখনও অন্ধকার। আমরা বসে বসে গল্প করলাম। হঠাৎ আমাদের খুব খিদে পেয়েছে। দেখি মা কি কি দিয়েছে।

বাঃ, কি সুন্দর খাবার! মা রাতের মধ্যে কষ্ট করে আমাদের জন্যে কত কিছু বানালো। ডাল আছে, গরম আলু ভাজি, ডিম আর নিজের হাতে বানানো টাটকা রুটি –কি স্বাদ। আমরা সবাই খেতে লাগলাম। একমাত্র দুঃখের ব্যাপার: আমরা নাস্তা খেতে খেতে সূর্যোদয় আসলে দেখিনি। সব মায়ের দোষ।

Sunrise

I am going to tell you about what happened last week. Me and a few of my friends had been wanting to watch a sunrise for a long time. Mother said that you could see the sunrise very well from the riverbank close to our house, but I had never been up so early in the morning.

So last Friday night we all slept at my house and arranged to get up at 5 am. Mother called us, got us up and showed us the way. She also gave us some food to take. After only a short walk (having walked a short distance) we reached the bank of the river. It was still dark then. We sat down and chatted. Suddenly I felt very hungry and thought: Let's see what mother has given us.

Wow, what lovely food! Mother had gone to a lot of trouble during the night and prepared a real feast. There were lentils, hot fried potatoes, eggs and freshly made bread – delicious. We all started eating. The only sad thing was that while we were eating we didn't actually see the sunrise. It's all mother's fault.

Vocabulary: Narrative

সূর্যোদয় sūryodɔŷ *n.* sunrise
গত gɔtô *adj.* last
ঘটনা ghɔṭôna *n.* event
চাওয়া caoŷa *vb.* want
ওঠা oṭha *vb.* get up
গত gɔtô *adj.* last
ব্যবস্থা bybôstha *n.* arrangement
ওঠানো oṭhano *vb.* cause to wake up
দেখানো dækhano *vb.* show
অল্প ɔlpô *adj.* a little bit
তখনও tɔkhôno *adv.* still

অন্ধকার ɔndhôkar *n.* darkness
খিদে khide *n.* hunger
ডাল ḍal *n.* lentil
গরম gɔrôm *adj.* hot
টাটকা ṭaṭka *adj.* fresh
রুটি ruṭi *n.* bread
লাগা laga *vb.* start
দুঃখ duḥkhô *n.* sadness
নাস্তা nasta *n.* breakfast
দোষ doṣ *n.* fault

Grammar 22: Verbal nouns (VN)

A verbal noun can be used like any other noun. It can take case endings and classifiers. It can also act as an adjective. The verbal noun expands the meaning of a verb into other word classes. In English we have the verb, e.g. *write*, but sometimes we also want to use the noun *writing* or the adjective *written*. In order to do this in Bangla, we need the verbal noun.

Nominative verbal nouns can act as subjects in equational sentences:

আইসক্রিম <u>খাওয়া</u> খুব মজার। *Eating ice cream is a lot of fun.*

In the post office dialogue in Unit 9 we had a verbal noun subject in an impersonal structure:

কোনও খাবার জিনিস <u>পাঠানো</u> নিষেধ। *It is forbidden to send any food items.*

A genitive verbal noun can modify other nouns:

আমার <u>পড়ার</u> টেবিল   *my reading table = my desk*
<u>বসার</u> ঘর   *sitting room*
<u>ওঠার</u> ব্যবস্থা   *arrangements for getting up*
শাসন <u>করার</u> সময়   *time for punishment*

Nominative verbal nouns combine with উচিত *should, ought to* and দরকার *need*. Both of these are impersonal structures with a verbal noun subject:

তোমার আর একটু <u>থাকা</u> উচিত। *You ought to stay a bit longer.*
কথাটা মনে <u>রাখা</u> দরকার। *That needs to be remembered.*

Verbal nouns, either in the nominative or the genitive, can be followed by postpositions:

Nom: তার <u>আসা</u> পর্যন্ত   *until he comes*
        অনেক কথা <u>বলা</u> সত্ত্বেও   *despite a lot of talking*

Gen: চিঠিটা <u>লেখার</u> পরে   *after writing the letter*
        মাছ <u>ধরার</u> জন্যে   *in order to catch fish = for fishing*
        <u>ঘুমাবার</u> আগে   *before sleeping = before going to bed*

Verbal nouns can be used as adjectives before nouns:

একটা নাম <u>করা</u> বই   *a famous book*
দেশের মধ্যে <u>পাঠানো</u> ডাকটিকিট   *t en stamps to send within the country*
নিজের হাতে <u>বানানো</u> আচার   *homemade chutney*

In English we often need to use relative clause to translate these noun phrases:

তার <u>লেখা</u> বই   *the book he wrote*
নিজের চোখে <u>দেখা</u> একসিডেন্ট   *an accident I saw with my own eyes*
তোমার <u>দেওয়া</u> উপহার   *the present you gave*

Verbal nouns team up with 3rd person forms of হওয়া *be, become* and যাওয়া *go* to form impersonal passive structures, e.g.:

আমার যাওয়া হবে না *I won't be going.* (lit: *My going will not occur.*)

The structures with যাওয়া *go* express possibility. We have already had:

ওখানে সবচেয়ে ভাল আইসক্রিম <u>পাওয়া</u> যায়। *You can get the best ice cream there.*

ইংল্যান্ডে এগুলো পাওয়া যায় না। *These are not available in England.*

(Note: *Other examples will be given in Grammar 24, page 182.*)

Grammar 23: Imperfective participles (IP)

Forms for imperfective participles are given in Unit 5. We have already seen quite a few uses of imperfective participles in the previous units, particularly examples that are equivalent to English infinitives:

আমি ঠিক বুঝতে পারিনি। *I couldn't understand (it) properly.*
সূর্যোদয় দেখতে চেয়েছিলাম। *We wanted to see the sunrise.*

The imperfective participle can express purpose:

সাঈদা নার্সিং শিখতে গেছে। *Saida has gone to learn nursing.*
উনি আমাকে পাঠিয়ে দিয়েছেন একটা বিউইক কিনতে। *He has sent me to buy a Buick.*

In all these cases the imperfective participle is directly dependent on another verb:

The verb দেওয়া *give* after an imperfective participle becomes *allow*:

তার সঙ্গে একটু কথা বলতে দেবেন? *Will you allow (me) to talk with her for a bit?*

The verb লাগা *be attached* preceded by an IP (very often in simple past) expresses *start*:

আমরা খেতে লাগলাম। *We started to eat.*

The verb হওয়া *be, become* preceded by an IP expresses obligation. We have already seen this structure in Unit 5. The verb হওয়া is always in the third person, but it can be in any tense. The subject of the sentence is in the object (or occasionally in the genitive) case but it is often omitted. For instance in the following sentence, the subject আমাকে is dropped:

একটু বাজারে যেতে হবে। *(I) have to go to the market for a bit.*

Some other examples:

চিঠিটা ইটালিতে পাঠাতে হবে। *The letter has to be sent to Italy.*
মাকে দিদিমার সঙ্গে থাকতে হয়েছে। *Mother had to stay with grandmother.*
প্রদীপকে ইস্কুলে যেতে হবে। *Prodip will have to go to school.*

When the IP is doubled it expresses a parallel, ongoing action that is usually best translated into English with *while*:

আমরা নাস্তা খেতে খেতে সূর্যোদয় আসলে দেখিনি।
While we were eating breakfast, we didn't actually see the sunrise.

A more emphatic simultaneous structure has a double IP with a না in the middle and an ই at the end. This should normally be translated with *as soon as* or *just at the moment when*:

ট্রেন থেকে নামতে না নামতেই সে তার বউয়ের দেখা পেল।
(দেখা পাওয়া *catch sight of, spot, detect*)
As soon as he got off the train he spotted his wife.

Grammar 24: Impersonal structures

Here is our fourth sentence pattern. Many sentences expressing feelings, events that happen to us, possibility, or need have no nominative subjects in Bangla. We call them impersonal structures. Some may have genitive subjects but often the subject is absent. We have already come across some of these structures individually, for instance the uses of লাগা *be attached* in Unit 7. This section brings them together and gives them context. The main verbs involved in these structures are আছে *be, exist,* লাগা *be attached to,* যাওয়া *go,* and হওয়া *be, become.*

Expressing feelings, experiences, changing events

লাগা expresses need, like or dislike, or feelings:

আমার গরম লাগছে।   *I am feeling hot.*
আমার তাকে ভাল লাগে।   *I like him.*
আমাদের অনেক টাকা লাগবে।   *We will need a lot of money.*

হওয়া is used for experiences and processes:

তার অসুখ হয়েছে।   *He has become ill.*
দুধ নষ্ট হয়েছে।   *The milk has gone off.*
আমার সন্দেহ হচ্ছে।   *I am having doubts.* (সন্দেহ = *doubt*)

Expressing possibility

The verbal noun + a 3rd person form of যাওয়া (in any tense) (**note:** these sentences never have an agent [human subject], negative with না):

ভিতরে যাওয়া যায় না।   *It is not possible to go inside.*
খুব শব্দ শোনা যায়।   *A lot of noise can be heard.*
কালকে দেখা যাবে।   *(We) will see tomorrow.*

Expressing obligation

The imperfective participle + a 3rd person form of হওয়া in any tense (**note:** subject is in the object case or in the genitive, negative with না):

আমাকে এই কথা বলতে হবে। *I will have to say this.*
রোজ বাজারে যেতে হয়। *(I) have to go to the market every day.*
টাকাটা আমাকে নিতে হয়েছে। *I had to take the money.*

Expressing need

The verbal noun in the nominative or genitive + the noun দরকার (**note:** subject is in the genitive, negative with নেই, past tense with ছিল, future with হবে):

আর কি দরকার? *What else is needed?*
আমার তার সঙ্গে কথা বলা দরকার। *I need to talk to him.*
তোমার আর কিছু দরকার নেই। *You don't need anything else.*

For needing a person, that person goes into the object case:

আমার তাকে আর দরকার হবে না। *I won't need him anymore.*

Expressing *should, ought to*

The verbal noun + the adjective উচিত (**note:** subject is in the genitive, negative with নয়, past tense with ছিল, future with হবে [rare]):

আমাদের তাদের সাহায্য করা উচিত। *We ought to help them.*
তার আর কিছু বলা উচিত নয়। *He ought not to say anything more.*
তোমার এতো রাগ করা উচিত ছিল না। *You shouldn't have got so angry.*

Expressing *supposed to*

The verbal noun in the genitive + the noun কথা (**note:** subject is in the genitive, negative with নয়, past tense with ছিল, future with হবে [rare]):

আমাদের কালকে যাওয়ার কথা। *We are supposed to go tomorrow.*
তার ছুটি নেওয়ার কথা ছিল না। *He was not supposed to take a holiday.*
তোমার দেরি করার কথা নয়। *You are not supposed to be late.*

Expressing permission or prohibition

The imperfective participle + আছে or নেই (subject is in the genitive):

এখানে বিশ্রাম করতে আছে। *It is permitted to rest here.*
তার ফল খেতে নেই। *He is not allowed to eat fruit.*

Additional Vocabulary: Food, drinks, and spices

biscuit বিস্কুট biskuṭ
bread রুটি ruṭi
cheese পনির pônir
coffee কফি kôphi
egg ডিম ḍim
fish মাছ mach
honey মধু môdhu
lentil ডাল ḍal
milk দুধ dudh
oil তেল tel
rice (cooked) ভাত bhat; (uncooked) চাল
    ca:l, চাউল caul
salt লবণ lɔbôn, নুন nu:n
sugar চিনি cini
sweets মিষ্টি miṣṭi (mishṭi)
tea চা ca
water পানি pani, জল jɔl

Meats

Note: *Muslims do not eat pork; Hindus do*
    not eat beef.

beef গরুর মাংস gorur maṃsô
chicken মুর্গির মাংস murgir maṃsô
lamb খাসির মাংস khasir maṃsô
meat মাংস maṃsô (mangsho)
minced meat কিমা kima
pork শূকরের মাংস śūkôrer maṃsô

Fruits, nuts, vegetables, spices

almond কাগজি বাদাম kagôji badam
apple আপেল apel
aubergine বেগুন begun
banana কলা kɔla
bay leaf তেজপাতা tejpata
bean (broad) সীম sīm; (green) বরবটি
    bɔrbôṭi
berry জাম jam

cabbage বাঁধাকপি bādhakôpi
cardamon এলাচ elac
carrot গাজর gajôr
cauliflower ফুলকপি phulkôpi
chili মরিচ môric; green ~ কাঁচা মরিচ kãca
    môric
cinnamon দারচিনি darcini
clove লবঙ্গ lɔbôṅgô
coconut নারিকেল narikel; green ~ ডাব ḍa:b
coriander ধনিয়া dhôniŷa (BD), ধনে dhɔne
    (PB)
corn ভুট্টা bhuṭṭa
cucumber শসা śɔsa
cumin জিরা jira
custard apple আতাফল ataphɔl
date খেজুর khejur
fig ডুমুর ḍumur
fruit ফল phɔ:l
garlic রসুন rôsun
ginger আদা ada
gourd লাউ lau
guava পেয়ারা peŷara
jackfruit কাঁঠাল kãṭhal
jasmine জুঁই jũi
jujube বরই bɔroi
lady's finger (okra) ঢেঁড়স ḍhæ̃ṛôs
lemon লেবু lebu
lychee লিচু licu
maize ভুট্টা bhuṭṭa
mango আম a:m
melon ফুটি phuṭi
mint পুদিনা pudina
mustard সরিষা sôriṣa
nut বাদাম badam
nutmeg জায়ফল jaŷphɔl
okra ঢেঁড়স ḍhæ̃ṛôs
olive জলপাই jɔlpai
onion পেঁয়াজ pẽŷaj, পিয়াজ, piŷaj

orange কমলা kɔmla
papaya পেঁপে pẽpe
pear নাসপাতি naspati
pea কলাই kɔlai, মটর mɔṭôr
pepper গোল মরিচ gol môric
pineapple আনারস anarɔs
pomegranate ডালিম ḍalim
pomelo জামবুরা jambura
potato আলু alu
pumpkin কুমড়া kumṛa
radish মূলা mūla (BD), মূলো mūlo (PB)
raisin কিশমিশ kiśmiś
seed বীচি bīci
sesame seed তিল til
snakebean পটোল pɔṭol
snakegourd চিচিঙ্গা ciciṅga

spice মসলা mɔsla; **mixed spices** গরম মসলা gɔrôm mɔsla
spinach পালং শাক palôṃ śa:k
sugar-cane আখ akh
sweet potato মিষ্টি আলু miṣṭi alu
tamarind তেঁতুল tẽtul
tomato টোমেটো ṭomeṭo
turmeric হলুদ hôlud
turnip শালগম shalgɔm
vegetable সবজি sôbji; **green vegetables** শাক সবজি śa:k sôbji
walnut কাঠবাদাম kaṭhbadam
watermelon তরমুজ tôrmuj
wood-apple বেল bel

Exercises: Unit 10

A lot of new structures! To help you practice them, here is an overview before you get started on the exercises. The exercises are deliberately a bit repetitive to help you remember the structures.

impact	structure	example
ability	IP + পারা	তোমরা কি আসতে পারবে? *Will you be able to come?*
inception	IP + লাগা	আমরা কাজ করতে লাগলাম। *We started working.*
need	VN genitive + দরকার	তার আর আসার দরকার নেই। *He doesn't need to come anymore.*
need	gen. subject, 3rd ps of লাগা	আমার তিন কেজি লাগবে। *I need three kilos.*
ought to	VN + উচিত	এটা করা উচিত নয়। *One shouldn't do that.*
obligation	IP + 3rd ps of হওয়া	তোমাকে আর একটু থাকতে হবে। *You will have to stay a bit longer.*
passive	VN + 3rd ps of হওয়া	তার কথা বলা হবে। *He will be talked about.*
permission	IP + দেওয়া	আমি তাকে চলে যেতে দিয়েছি। *I have permitted him to leave.*
possibility	VN + 3rd ps of যাওয়া	এ ব্যাপারে কিছু করা যায় না। *There is nothing to be done in this matter.*
purpose	IP with যাওয়া, আসা etc	আমরা তো এখানে খেতে আসিনি। *But we didn't come here to eat.*
simultaneous event	doubled IP	সে কাঁদতে কাঁদতে এই কথা বলল। *She was in tears as she said this.*
wish	IP + চাওয়া	আমি তোমার সঙ্গে দেখা করতে চাই। *I want to see you / meet with you.*

Exercise 10:1

The following sentences are similar to the ones given in the chart above, so you should have no problems tackling them. Translate the following sentences:

(i)   *Will he be able to go?*

(ii)   *Everybody is starting to laugh.* (হাসা = *laugh* / use present continuous)

(iii)   *Do you need to see the papers?* (use দরকার)

(iv)   *They will have to show me the tickets.*

(v)   *We will not be given food.*

(vi)   *Father will not allow him to stay the night.*

(vii)   *It is not possible to leave before morning.*

(viii) *We are going there to learn dancing.*

(ix)   *He eats while driving the car.* (গাড়ি চালানো = *drive a car*)

(x)   *They wanted to talk with you.* (use present perfect)

Exercise 10:2

Insert the correct verb form (VN, VN genitive, or IP) into the sentences below and translate:

(i)   এই রাস্তা দিয়ে _____ যায় না। (যাওয়া)

(ii)   কাজটা আজকে শেষ _____ হবে না। (করা)

(iii) আমাদের _____ সময় হয়ে গেছে। (যাওয়া)

(iv)   সে আমার সঙ্গে _____ চায় না। (কথা বলা)

(v)   এগুলো তাড়াতাড়ি _____ দরকার। (পাঠানো)

(vi)   আমাকে এখানে _____ দেবেন? (বসা)

(vii)   বাজারে আজকে কলা _____ যায় না। (পাওয়া)

(viii) তুমি কি গাজরের রস _____ পার না? (বানানো)

(ix)   তোমার এত সময় _____ উচিত নয়। (নষ্ট করা = *waste*)

(x)   আজকে _____ হবে না। (ছবি তোলা = *take pictures*)

Exercise 10:3

Complete the sentences, using the structures above, and translate:

(i)   তুমি কি কিছু করতে _____ ?

(ii)   আমার দুই কেজি গাজর _____ ।

(iii)   আমাকে তাড়াতাড়ি যেতে_____ ।

(iv)   আর একটু দুধ দেওয়া _____ ?

(v)   তুমি কি কিছু বলতে _____ ?

(vi)   আমি তাদের সিগারেট খেতে _____ না।

(vii)   সে তোমার সঙ্গে কথা বলতে _____ ।

(viii) তার আমাকে ভাল _____ ।

(ix)   আর কিছু বলার_____ নেই।

(x)   এই রাস্তাটায় এখন গাড়ি চালানো _____ না।

Exercise 10:4

Verbal noun or IP: To complete each sentence insert one of the two verb forms given in parentheses:

(i) তোমার সঙ্গে আবার _____ হবে।   (দেখা / দেখতে)

(ii) তাকে সাহায্য _____ আমার ইচ্ছা নেই।   (করার / করতে)

(iii) কাজটা আজকে শেষ _____ হবে না।   (করা / করতে)

(iv) এই রাস্তা দিয়ে _____ যায় না।   (যাওয়া / যেতে)

(v) বিকালে আবার বৃষ্টি _____ লাগল।   (পড়া / পড়তে)

(vi) সকাল পাঁচটায় ঘুম থেকে _____ হয়েছে।   (ওঠা / উঠতে)

(vii) ছেলেটির দুধ _____ ভালো লাগে না।   (খাওয়া / খেতে)

(viii) তারা কালকে মাছ _____ যাবে।   (ধরা / ধরতে)

(ix) আমি নিজে তাকে এই কথা _____ শুনেছি।   (বলা / বলতে)

(x) আমি চিঠিটা আজ _____ পারিনি।   (পাঠানো / পাঠাতে)

Exercise 10:5

Translate the following sentences:

(Note: Verbal noun with দরকার *need*, কথা *supposed to*, উচিত *should, ought to*: উচিত and কথা negate with নয়, দরকার negates with নেই. উচিত takes the nominative verbal noun, কথা take the genitive verbal noun. দরকার takes the genitive verbal noun in negative and past tense sentences and the nominative verbal noun in affirmative present tense sentences. Some additional vocabulary is given.)

(i)   I ought to have talked to you first.

(ii)   You don't need to explain all this to me.

(iii)   You are supposed to go today.

(iv)   You don't need to do this.

(v)   We should not have taken their food.

(vi)   You are not supposed to go out alone.

(vii)   We ought to believe him. (বিশ্বাস করা *believe*)

(viii) This matter should not be discussed with anyone else. (আলোচনা করা *discuss*)

(ix)   You shouldn't have complained. (অভিযোগ করা *complain*)

(x)   We needed to search the whole area. (খোঁজ করা *search*, পুরো এলাকা *whole area*)

(xi)   You didn't need to come.

(xii)   You weren't supposed to pay. (টাকা দেওয়া *pay*)

(xiii) You should have remembered what he said. (মনে রাখা *remember*)

(xiv)   I shouldn't have spent so much time with him. (সময় কাটানো *spend time*)

(xv)   What else will you need?

(xvi)   I won't need to write anything more today.

(xvii) Mother did not need to be told the whole story. (গল্প *story*)

(xviii) Why do you need to ask so many questions? (প্রশ্ন করা *ask questions*)

(xix)   Weren't you supposed to bring the umbrellas back?

(xx)   You should always follow your own heart. (lit: *move according to* (মত) *your own mind*)

Exercise 10: 6 Conjunct verbs

Now that you have learned about non-finite verb form in Bangla, you should be able to do this conjunct verb exercise. Conjunct verbs consist of noun-verb or adjective-verb combinations, e.g., *to work* in Bangla is কাজ করা *do work,* প্রশ্ন করা *ask* (noun-verb). *To clean* is পরিষ্কার করা *make clean* (adjective-verb). The vocabulary for this exercise (in Bangla alphabetical order) is given below – a more comprehensive list of conjunct verbs is given in Appendix 6 (page 338).

অপেক্ষা করা *wait*
আরম্ভ করা *start, begin*
আলোচনা করা *discuss*
আশা করা *expect, hope*
ক্ষতি করা *harm*
ক্ষমা করা *forgive*
খরচ করা *spend (money)*
গায়ে দেওয়া *put on, wear*
চেষ্টা করা *try*
টের পাওয়া *feel, be aware of, notice*

পরীক্ষা করা *examine*
বিয়ে করা *marry*
ভুল করা *make a mistake*
মন দেওয়া *concentrate*
রক্ষা করা *protect*
লক্ষ্য করা *notice*
সন্দেহ করা *doubt*
সহ্য করা *endure, tolerate, bear*
সাঁতার কাটা *swim*
সাহায্য করা *help*

Translate the following sentences:

(i)   She wants to protect her child.

(ii)   I have been waiting for you.

(iii)   I will wear the new sari today.

(iv)   I never make mistakes.

(v)   We did not expect this.

(vi)   Can't you forgive them?

(vii)   He doesn't spend a lot of money.

(viii) We need to discuss this.

(ix)   I can't bear the heat.

(x)   Will you promise me to come tomorrow?

(xi)   I can't help you any more.

(xii)   Have you started your new job?

(xiii) He has never got married.

(xiv)   She is trying to find a new house.

(xv)   *He doesn't concentrate on his studies.*

(xvi)   *The little boy hasn't learn to swim.*

(xvii) *I don't doubt that he is a very good person.*
        (sentence structure in Bangla: *He is a very good person. I don't doubt it.*)

(xviii) *Nobody wants to harm the children.*

(xix)   *Did you notice something when you arrived?*
        (Bangla: *at the time of your arriving*)

(xx)   *His statement* (তার কথা) *will have to be examined.*

UNIT 11

Dialogue

হোটেলে

নিনা: আপনাকে সাহায্য করতে পারি, স্যার?

রহমান সাহেব: হ্যাঁ, আমাদের একটা ডবল রুম দরকার, দুই রাতের জন্যে। হবে তো?

নিনা: আজকে জায়গা কম, স্যার। তবে আমাদের একতলাতে ছয় নম্বর খুব সুন্দর একটা রুম খালি আছে। এটাতে কিন্তু আপনাদের সুবিধা হবে কিনা আমি ঠিক বলতে পারছি না।

রহমান সাহেব: কেন? অসুবিধাটা কি?

নিনা: অসুবিধাটা আপনাদের পাশের ঘরের অতিথি, মিস্টার সেন। উনি আমাদের খুব পুরোনো অতিথি। অনেক বছর ধরে আসেন। এখন ভদ্রলোকের বয়স হয়ে গেছে আর উনি একটু অদ্ভুত হয়ে গেছেন। আপনাদের অসুবিধা হতে পারে।

রহমান সাহেব: কি রকম? আমাকে স্পষ্ট করে বলেন তো ভদ্রলোক কি করেন। ঘুমের মধ্যে খুব নাক ডাকেন নাকি?

নিনা: না না, এইরকম কিছু নয়, স্যার। কিন্তু ঘুমানোর আগে অন্তত আধা ঘণ্টা উনি গান করেন। বেশি জোরে নয় কিন্তু তাঁর গানের গলা নেই। শুনতে একটু খারাপ লাগবে।

রহমান সাহেব: কোন সময় ঘুমান?

নিনা: সাড়ে নয়টার পরে কোনও দিন আর গান করেন না।

রহমান সাহেব: আচ্ছা, তাহলে মনে হয় আমাদের কোনও অসুবিধা হবে না। আমার স্ত্রী এই ছুটিতে রোজ নানান রেস্তোরাঁতে খেতে চায়। এটা তার একটা শখ। মানে আমরা রাত দশটার আগে হোটেলে ফিরব না।

নিনা: সে তো খুব ভাল। তাহলে ছয় নম্বর রুমটা আপনাদের জন্যে নির্দিষ্ট করে দিচ্ছি। অবশ্য আপনাদের রুম ভাড়াটা একটু কমিয়ে দিচ্ছি। বুঝতে পারেন তো, স্যার, এমন মাননীয় পুরোনো অতিথিকে কিছু বলা যায় না।

রহমান সাহেব: না, তা তো অবশ্যই।

নিনা: আপনার মালপত্র এখানে রেখে যেতে পারেন। আমরা এগুলো রুমে দিয়ে আসব।

রহমান সাহেব: আচ্ছা। ধন্যবাদ। বিকালে আমরা কাপড় বদলাতে আসব।

নিনা: ধন্যবাদ। দেখা হবে।

রহমান সাহেব: দেখা হবে।

At a hotel

Nina: *Can I help you, Sir?*

Mr. Rahman: *We need a double room for two nights. Is that possible?*

Nina: *We don't have many rooms left. We have room 6, a very beautiful room on the ground floor. But I am not sure whether it will be suitable for you.*

Mr. Rahman: *Why? What's the problem with it?*

Nina: *There may be a problem with the gentleman in the room next to you, Mr. Sen. He is a regular guest and has been coming to us for many years. Now he is quite elderly and has become a little bit peculiar. That could be inconvenient for you.*

Mr. Rahman: *In what way? Just tell me straight what the gentleman does. Does he snore a lot?*

Nina: *No, no, it's nothing like that. But before he goes to sleep at night he sings for at least half an hour. Not very loudly, but his voice is not very good. Listening to it is not pleasant.*

Mr. Rahman: *What time does he go to sleep?*

Nina: *He never sings after half past nine.*

Mr Rahman: *Right, in that case I don't think we will have a problem at all. My wife wants to go out every night to try different restaurants during this holiday. It's a bit of a fancy with her. So we are unlikely to return to the hotel before 10 pm.*

Nina: *Oh, that's very good. In that case I will reserve room 6 for you. I will of course give it to you at a reduced price. I'm sure you understand that with an old honored guest like Mr. Sen it is impossible to say anything.*

Mr. Rahman: *Of course, of course, I quite understand.*

Nina: *You can leave your luggage here now if you like and we will take it to the room.*

Mr. Rahman: *Yes, that suits us fine. We'll be back this afternoon to get changed for the evening.*

Nina: *Yes, thank you. Goodbye for now.*

Mr. Rahman: *Bye, see you later.*

Vocabulary: Dialogue

হোটেল hoṭel *n.* hotel

স্যার syar *n.* sir

ডবল রুম ḍɔbôl rum *adj.* double room

একতলা æktɔla *n.* ground floor

খালি khali *adj.* empty

সুবিধা subidha *n.* convenience

অসুবিধা ɔsubidha *n.* inconvenience

অতিথি ôtithi *n.* guest

পুরানো purano *adj.* old

অদ্ভুত ɔdbhut *adj.* strange, peculiar

রকম rɔkôm *n.* kind, type

স্পষ্ট spɔṣṭô *adj.* clear

স্পষ্টভাবে spɔṣṭôbhabe *adv.* clearly, frankly

আধা adha *num.* half

নাক nak *n.* nose

ডাকা ḍaka *vb.* call

নাক ডাকা nak ḍaka *vb.* snore

ঘুমানো ghumano *vb.* sleep

আধা adha *num.* half

গান gan *n.* song

গান করা gan kɔra *vb.* sing

জোরে jore *adv.* loud, loudly, forcefully

গলা gɔla *n.* throat, voice

সাড়ে saṛe *num.* half past

রোজ roj *adv.* daily

নানান nanan *adj.* various

রেস্তোরাঁ resṭorã *n.* restaurant

শখ śɔkh *n.* interest, fancy, obsession

ফেরা phera *vb.* return, come back

নির্দিষ্ট nirdiṣṭô *adj.* fixed, determined

নির্দিষ্ট করা nirdiṣṭô kɔra *vb.* fix, determine, appoint

কমানো kɔmano *vb.* reduce

মালপত্র malpɔtrô *n.* luggage

কাপড় kapôṛ *n.* clothes

বদলানো bɔdlano *vb.* change

Grammar 25: Conditional participles (CP)

(Note: The formation of the conditional participle is given in Unit 6.)

The conditional participle can be used for expressing temporal *when* as well as for conditional *if* events:

তুমি বাজারে গেলে আমিও তোমার সঙ্গে যাব।
When (or if) you go to the market, I will go with you.

We had two examples of conditional participles in Unit 5 in the zoo story:

আগে জানালে আমিও তোমার সঙ্গে যেতাম।
If you had told me before, I would have come with you.

তাহলে তোমাকে নিয়ে গেলে তুমি আমাদের আইসক্রিম খাওয়াবে?
So then if we take you, will you give us ice cream to eat?

তা হলে is itself a conditional participle meaning *if this is so*. You will notice that in these two examples the conditional phrases আগে জানালে and তোমাকে নিয়ে গেলে do not actually have any expressed subjects. This shows the economy and adaptability of the conditional participle. The subject and the time frame for it are given in the rest of the sentence:

তুমি কলকাতায় গেলে এই হোটেলে থাকতে পারবে।
If you go to Kolkata, you can stay in this hotel.

or, when the main verb is in the past habitual:

তুমি কলকাতায় গেলে এই হোটেলে থাকতে পারতে।
If you had gone to Kolkata, you could have stayed in this hotel.

(Note: There will be more on the uses of the past habitual tense in Unit 12.)

When ও (see Unit 7) follows a conditional participle it adds a concessive *even if / even though* element:

কলকাতা গেলেও তুমি তার সঙ্গে দেখা করতে পারবে না।
Even if you go to Kolkata you won't be able to meet with him.

The conditional participle of the zero verb is হলে from হওয়া *be, become*:

আজ রবিবার হলেও কাজটা করতে হবে।
Even though it is Sunday today, the work has to be done.

The conditional participle of আছ- *be present, exist* is থাকলে from থাকা *stay:*

তোমার সময় থাকলে আমাদের বাড়িতে আসবে?
If you have time, will you come to our house?

When the conditional participle is negated, the negator না precedes it:

তোমার আজ সময় না থাকলে আমরা কালকে দেখা করতে পারব।
If you don't have time today, we can meet tomorrow.

The English translations in the following four examples show the versatility of the conditional participle. All these sentences start with the same conditional clause:

তুমি চলে গেলে কিছু হবে না।
It doesn't matter if you leave.

তুমি চলে গেলে ওরা সঙ্গে সঙ্গে ঝগড়া করতে লাগবে।
They will start arguing as soon as you leave.

তুমি চলে গেলে আমিও আর থাকতাম না।
If you left I wouldn't stay either.

তুমি চলে গেলে বাবা খুব রাগ করতেন।
If you had left, father would have been very angry.

Narrative

অসময়ের শাসন

একটি ছেলে একদিন স্কুল থেকে একা বাড়ি ফিরছিল। পথের পাশে একটা বড় পুকুর। তাতে অনেক পদ্ম ফুল ফুটেছে। তা দেখে ছেলেটির পদ্মফুল নেওয়ার ইচ্ছা হল। সে ভেবেছিল – হাঁটু-জলে নেমে হাত বাড়িয়ে দু-একটা ফুল তুলে নেবে। কিন্তু তা করতে গিয়ে সে গলা-জলে পড়ে গেল। পুকুরের কাদা-মাটিতে তার পা বসে যাচ্ছিল; তা ছাড়া সাঁতারও জানত না। তাই সে জল থেকে উঠে আসতে পারছিল না। তখন ভয় পেয়ে সে 'বাঁচাও, বাঁচাও!' বলে চিৎকার করতে লাগল।

এমন সময় একজন বয়স্ক লোক সেই পথ দিয়ে যাচ্ছিলেন। চিৎকার শুনে তিনি এসে পুকুরের পাড়ে দাঁড়িয়ে ছেলেটিকে বকাবকি করতে লাগলেন, 'সাঁতার জান না তো পুকুরে নামতে গেলে কেন? ভয়ডর নেই? এতটুকু ছেলে, ভাদ্রমাসের ভরা পুকুরে একা নামে? বলি, স্নান করার শখ, না পদ্ম তোলার শখ? এখন শখ মিটেছে? বাড়ি গিয়ে তোমার বাবাকে বলছি – এমন ছেলেকে শাসন করেন না কেন?'

ভদ্রলোক এক নিঃশ্বাসে এতগুলো কথা বললেন। ছেলেটি মিনতি করে বলল, 'আগে আমাকে জল থেকে ওঠান। আমি বেঁচে থাকলে শাসন করার অনেক সময় পাবেন।'

Untimely punishment

One day a boy was on his way back home from school. At the side of the path there was a big lake in which many water-lilies were floating in full bloom. When he saw them, the boy wanted to take some. He thought, "I will wade in up to my knees, stretch out my hand and grab a couple of flowers." But when he did so, he sank into the water up to his throat. His feet got stuck in the mud at the bottom of the lake and he didn't know how to swim. So he was unable to pull himself up out of the lake. He got frightened and started shouting "Help, help!"

At that time, an elderly gentleman was walking along the path. When he heard the shouting, he stood by the side of the lake and started telling the boy off. "If you can't swim why did you go into the lake? Aren't you afraid? Such a small boy, going on his own into a lake in full spate in the month of Bhadro! Did you want to have a bath or was it for picking some flowers? Have you had your fill now? I will go to your house and tell your father that a boy like you should be punished."

The gentleman said all of this without a break. The boy said humbly, "Please get me out of the water first. If I make it out alive, there will be plenty of time to punish me."

Vocabulary: Narrative

অসময় ɔsômôŷ *n.* inconvenient time

শাসন śasôn *n.* punishment

ফেরা phera *vb.* return

পদ্ম ফুল pɔdmô phul *n.* water-lily

ভাবা bhaba *vb.* think

হাঁটু hãṭu *n.* knee

জল jɔl *n.* water

নামা nama *vb.* get down, descend

হাত বাড়ানো hat baṛano *vb.* stretch out one's arm

তোলা tola *vb.* lift, pluck

গলা-জলে gɔla-jɔle *adv.* water up to one's neck

কাদা kada *n.* mud

পা pa *n.* foot, leg

বসা bɔsa *vb.* sit, sink down, settle, get stuck

তা ছাড়া ta chaṛa *conj.* besides, in addition

বাঁচানো bãcano *vb.* rescue, save

চিৎকার করা ciṭkar kɔra *vb.* shout

বয়স্ক bɔŷôskô *adj.* elderly

বকাবকি bɔkabôki *n.* reprimanding, telling off

বকাবকি করা bɔkabôki kɔra *vb.* reprimand, tell off

ভয়ডর bhɔŷḍɔr *n.* fear

এতটুকু ætôṭuku *adj.* so small

ভাদ্রমাস bhadrômas *n.* Bhadro (*month / August-September, the end of the rainy season*)

ভরা bhɔra *adj.* full

স্নান snan *n.* bath

মিটানো miṭano *vb.* fulfill, accomplish, satisfy

নিঃশ্বাস niḥśvas *n.* breath

এতগুলো ætôgulo *adj.* so many

কড়া kɔra *adj.* harsh, severe

মিনতি minôti *n.* humble request

ওঠানো oṭhano *vb.* lift up, pull out

বেঁচে থাকা bæ̃ce thaka *vb.* stay alive, survive

Grammar 26: Conditional sentences with যদি *if*

Conditional যদি structures are our first look at complex sentences. Complex sentences consist of a main clause and a subordinate clause. For conditional structures, the subordinate clause with যদি usually comes first. The main clause usually starts with তাহলে *if this is so* or *then*. There are some alternative conjunctions such as তবে *but*.

We have already seen the use of the conditional participle above (Grammar 25):

কেউ ইংল্যান্ডে গেলে আচারটা নিয়ে যেতে পারবে।
If someone goes to England, he/she can take the chutney.

Alternatively we can use a structure with যদি *if*. Here is how the sentence reads with যদি:

কেউ যদি ইংল্যান্ডে যায়, তাহলে আচারটা নিয়ে যেতে পারবে।

The sentence pattern for conditional *if* sentences is set out below. Unlike most other structures in Bangla, conditional sentences have a fixed time sequence, depending on the type of conditional we are using.

1. simple conditional

subordinate (conditional) clause	main clause
subj + যদি + না + vb (present simple)	তাহলে + subj + vb (pr s or future tense)
সে যদি আসে	তাহলে আমি খুশি হব।
If he comes	*I will be happy.*
সে যদি না আসে	তাহলে আমি আরও খুশি হব।
If he doesn't come	*I will be even happier.*

2. hypothetical conditional

subordinate (conditional) clause	main clause
subj + যদি + না + vb (past habitual)	তাহলে + subj + vb (past habitual)
সে যদি এখানে থাকত	তাহলে সে আমাকে সাহায্য করত।
If he had been here,	*he would have helped me.*
সে যদি এখানে না থাকত	তাহলে কেউ আমাকে সাহায্য করত না।
If he had not been here,	*nobody would have helped me.*

This means that only the present simple (for simple conditionals) or the past habitual (for hypothetical conditionals) are used in যদি clauses. Substitutions are the same as for the conditional participle: থাকা for আছ- and হওয়া for the zero verb. না precedes the verb in the conditional clause:

তোমার টাকা যদি না থাকে... *if you do not have any money...*
ধান যদি ভাল না হয়... *if the rice does not grow well...*

In hypothetical আছ- and হওয়া contexts, the past habitual form of থাকা in the main clause is often replaced by a past simple ছিল-. This applies to conditional participles as well as to যদি sentences.

তুমি না থাকলে এসব সম্ভব ছিল না।
If you hadn't been there, all this would not have been possible.

Do you notice how neat and compact the Bangla sentence is compared to the English one?

Here are ten more conditional examples with either the conditional participle or যদি structures, just for you to see how the structures work. The English translations do not always contain a conditional.

বেশি আম খেলে তোমার অসুখ হবে।
If you eat too many mangoes, you will get sick. = Eating too many mangoes will make you sick.

আমি যদি সাহায্য করি তাহলে তুমি কাজটা করতে পারবে।
You will be able to do the work if I help you. = You will be able to do the work with my help.

আমার যদি অনেক টাকা থাকত তাহলে তোমাদের সবাইকে ছুটিতে নিয়ে যেতাম।
If I had a lot of money, I would take you all on holiday.

আমি বেঁচে থাকলে শাসন করার অনেক সময় পাবেন।
If I survive, you will have plenty of time for punishment.

তুমি যদি এইভাবে ব্যবহার কর তাহলে কেউ তোমার সঙ্গে কথা বলবে না। (ব্যবহার = *behavior*)
If you behave like this, no one will talk to you.

তোমার টাকা যদি থাকে তাহলে আমাকে কিছু দাও।
If you have money, give me some.

ছেলেটি যদি পরীক্ষায় পাশ করে তাহলে বাবা তাকে ইটালিতে নিয়ে যাবেন।
If the boy passes his exams, the father will take him to Italy.

তুমি যদি আমাকে না বল তাহলে আমি কি করে বুঝব?
If you don't tell me, how can I understand?

তার শরীর খারাপ হলে তাকে ওষুধ খাওয়াতে হবে।
If he is ill, he will have to be given medicine.

তুমি মন দিয়ে কাজ করলে কাজটা তাড়াতাড়ি শেষ করতে পারবে।
You will be able to finish the work quickly if you concentrate. (মন দেওয়া = *concentrate*)

Additional Vocabulary: Common adjectives

We have seen quite a few adjectives throughout the previous units. Here we have assembled them all together, in English alphabetical order, to help you with your vocabulary learning.

bad খারাপ kharap

beautiful সুন্দর sundôr

big বড় bɔrô

bitter তিতা tita (BD), তিতো tito (PB)

black কালো kalo

blind অন্ধ ɔndhô

blue নীল nīl

bright উজ্জ্বল ujjvɔl

brown বাদামি badami

calm শান্ত śantô

clean পরিষ্কার pôriṣkar

clear স্পষ্ট spɔṣṭô

clever চালাক calak

cold ঠাণ্ডা ṭhaṇḍa, শীত śī:t

correct ঠিক ṭhi:k

dark অন্ধকার ɔndhôkar

deaf কালা kala

different ভিন্ন bhinnô

difficult কঠিন kôṭhin

dirty ময়লা mɔyla

dry শুকনা śukna (BD), শুকনো śukno (PB)

easy সহজ sɔhôj

empty খালি khali

excellent চমৎকার cɔmôtkar

expensive দামি dami

fair(-skinned) ফরসা phɔrsa

fast জোরে jore

fat মোটা moṭa

frightening ভয়ঙ্কর bhɔŷôṅkôr

full ভরা bhɔra

gentle কোমল komôl, ভদ্র bhɔdrô

golden সোনার sonar

good ভাল bhalô, ভালো bhalo

green সবুজ sôbuj

happy খুশি khuśi

hard শক্ত śɔktô

heavy ভারী bharī

hot গরম gɔrôm

impossible অসম্ভব ɔsɔmbhôb

last গত gɔtô

left বাঁ bã, বাম bam

light হালকা halka

long লম্বা lɔmba

loud জোরে jore

new নতুন nôtun

next আগামী agamī

normal সাধারণ sadharô

old পুরানো purano, বুড়া buṛa (BD), বুড়ো buṛo (PB)

peaceful শান্ত śantô

pink গোলাপি golapi

poor গরীব gôrīb

possible সম্ভব sɔmbhôb

raw কাঁচা kãca

red লাল la:l

rich ধনী dhônī

right *(correct)* ঠিক ṭhi:k; *(not left)* ডান ḍan

ripe পাকা paka

rotten পচা pɔca

round গোল gol

sad দুঃখিত duḥkhitô

same একই eki

separate আলাদা alada

short খাটো khaṭo

simple সহজ sɔhôj

slow ধীরে dhīre

small ছোট choṭô

soft নরম nɔrôm

sour টক ṭɔk

strange অদ্ভুত ɔdhbhut

strong শক্ত śɔktô

stupid বোকা boka

sweet মিষ্টি miṣṭi

thin পাতলা patla, রোগা roga

tired ক্লান্ত klantô

ugly বিশ্রী biśrī, নোংরা nɔṃra (nongra)

unbearable অসহ্য ɔsɔhyô (ɔshɔjjho)
unripe কাঁচা kãca
unusual অসাধারণ ɔsadharôṇ
usual সাধারণ sadharôṇ
violent উদ্দাম uddam
weak দুর্বল durbɔl

wet ভিজা bhija
white সাদা sada
wild উদ্দাম uddam
yellow হলুদ hôlud, হলদে hɔlde
young তরুণ tôruṇ

Some adjectives form their opposite by prefixing অ- (before consonants) or অন- (before vowels). In our list we have সম্ভব *possible* and অসম্ভব *impossible* as well as সাধারণ *normal, usual* and অসাধারণ *unusual*. The word for *many* in Bangla is অনেক = অন-এক = *not one*.

Exercises: Unit 11

Exercise 11:1
Write ten conditional যদি – তাহলে *sentences of your own.*

The যদি structure in the past habitual lends itself to *what if* musings of the type *If I could see into the future, if I could go back ten years,* etc. For your first exercise write ten complete sentences of this type. You have the structure: both verbs, in the subordinate clause and in the main clause need to be in the past habitual. And you have now reached the stage where you should be able to create your own sentences.

Exercise 11:2
Change the following conditional participles into যদি *structures and translate the sentences. The first four sentences are from our dialogues. Remember that you will need a personal verb ending and you will need to take your clue from the main clause to decide on the tense in the* যদি *clause.*

Example: তোমাকে নিয়ে গেলে …   → আমরা যদি তোমাকে নিয়ে যাই … *if we take you with us*

(i)   ভাল লোক পেলে একটু বলবেন।

(ii)   খাবারগুলো রেখে গেলে সব নষ্ট হয়ে যাবে।

(iii)   চিড়িয়াখানায় গেলে হাতি দেখতে পারব।

(iv)   গাজর থাকলে আমি ছয় কেজি নেব।

(v)   কিছু না করলে অবস্থাটা আরও খারাপ হয়ে যাবে।   (অবস্থা = *situation*)

(vi)   বাংলাদেশে থাকলে এত কষ্ট করে বাংলা শিখতে হত না।
        (Note: there is an obligation structure here!)

(vii) দরজাটার চাবি না থাকলে ভিতরে যেতে পারব না।

(viii) বৃষ্টি হলে আমরা নৌকায় যাব না।

(ix)   সে মাংস না খেলে তার জন্যে আলাদা রান্না করতে হবে।

(x)   বাংলা কথা বলতে না পারলে, কারও সঙ্গে গল্প করতে পারতে না।

Exercise 11:3
Translate the following sentences – you can use either conditional participles or যদি
*structures. Translating these sentences is a good challenge for you. Take your time and
follow the steps set out in Unit 6 (Grammar 10: Making Sentences), one by one: first
assembling your vocabulary, then ordering your components and fitting them into the
conditional sentence patterns given above. Some sentences contain impersonal structures
(Unit 10) and, of course, non-finite verb forms (Unit 9 and 10). Good luck!*

Example: *If we go to the zoo, we will have some ice cream.*
চিড়িয়াখানায় গেলে আমরা আইসক্রিম খাব।

(i)   *If you come tomorrow, I will take you to the market.*

(ii)   *If they don't have any potatoes, we will eat rice.*

(iii)   *If you are feeling cold, I will close the window.*

(iv)   *If they live in Dhanmondi (*ধানমণ্ডি*), they will know the road.*

(v)   *If it doesn't rain today, we will go out on a boat.*

(vi)   *If the shirt is too big, you can give it to your brother.*

(vii)   *If you need more money, you should look for a job. (*খোঁজা *= look for, search)*

(viii) *If you don't eat, you will get ill.*

(ix)   *If you live in a hot country, you have to drink plenty of water.*

(x)   *If you want, we can go out today. (*বেড়ানো *= go out, visit)*

(xi)   *If I lived in Bangladesh, I would be very happy.*

(xii)   *If you don't like the red one, you can take the green one.*

(xiii) *If he is late, we will not wait for him.*

(xiv)   *If they don't use the new words, they will not be able to learn the language.*

(xv)   *If you don't concentrate, you will not be able to finish the job.*

(xvi)   *Even if we told them the truth, they wouldn't believe us.*

(xvii)   *Even if you don't come with us, we will go to the cinema.*

(xviii) *If you want to live in Bangladesh, you will need to speak Bangla.*

(xix)   *If you don't ask, you won't learn.*

(xx)   *If we get there too late, they won't give us a room.*

UNIT 12

Dialogue

মাথা ব্যথা

ডাক্তার: সালাম ওয়ালিকুম। কেমন আছেন?

রোগী:   ওয়ালিকুম সালাম। আমার অবস্থা বেশি ভাল নয়।

ডাক্তার: কেন? কি হয়েছে?

রোগী:   আমার প্রায়ই খুব মাথা ব্যথা হয়।

ডাক্তার: মাথা ব্যথাটা কবে থেকে?

রোগী:   প্রায় দুই সপ্তাহ ধরে প্রতিদিন সকালে ঘুম থেকে ওঠার পর এই ব্যথা হয়। তারপরে, দিন যেতে যেতে আস্তে আস্তে কমে যায়।

ডাক্তার: আগের তুলনায় আপনার প্রতিদিনের নিয়মে কোনও পরিবর্তন হয়েছে?

রোগী:   পরিবর্তন হয়েছে অবশ্যই! আমি বিয়ে করেছি।

ডাক্তার: বিয়ে করেছেন? তা তো সুখের খবর। কিন্তু তার সঙ্গে মাথা ব্যথার সম্পর্ক স্পষ্ট দেখা যায় না। কথাটা আর একটু বুঝিয়ে বলতে পারেন?

রোগী:   আমি ঠিক জানি না। সে জন্যে তো আপনার কাছে এসেছি। তবে আমার বউয়ের পারফিউম নিয়ে আমার খুব কষ্ট হয়। আমি যেন নিঃশ্বাস নিতে পারি না। আমি তাকে অবশ্য কিছু বলিনি। নতুন বিয়ে তো। আপনি কি মনে করেন এটা থেকে আমার মাথা ব্যথা হতে পারে?

ডাক্তার: খুব সম্ভবত। পারফিউমের মধ্যে অনেক কিছু থাকে যার বিরুদ্ধে মানুষের অ্যালার্জি থাকতে পারে। আপনার বউকে এই কথা না বললে হবে না। ও তো নিজেও দেখে আপনার কষ্ট হচ্ছে। আর পারফিউম তেমন দরকারি জিনিসও নয়। স্বামীর শরীরের তুলনায় কিছু নয় আসলে। একটা কাজ করুন, আপনি নিজে কিছু বলতে না চাইলে, আপনার বউকে আগামী সপ্তাহে আমার কাছে নিয়ে আসুন। আমি তাকে সব বুঝিয়ে দেব। এতে রাজি আছেন তো?

রোগী:   খুব ভাল, ডাক্তার সাহেব। আমি তাই করব। আপনাকে অনেক ধন্যবাদ। আগামী সপ্তাহে তাহলে দেখা হবে।

ডাক্তার: আচ্ছা। দেখা হবে। খোদা হাফেজ।

রোগী:   খোদা হাফেজ।

Headache

Doctor: *Good afternoon. How are you?*

Patient: *Good afternoon. I am not all that well.*

Doctor: *Why? What is the matter?*

Patient: *I often have a very bad headache.*

Doctor: *How long have you had the headache?*

Patient: *For almost two weeks. Every day when I wake up in the morning I have this pain. Then in the course of the day it gradually eases off.*

Doctor: *Compared to before, has there been a change in your daily routine?*

Patient: *Yes, of course there has been a change. I've got married!*

Doctor: *You got married? Oh, well that's good news. But I can't quite see a link between that and your headache. Can you tell me a bit more?*

Patient: *I don't really know. That's why I've come to see you. But I have a big problem with my wife's perfume. It's as if I can't breathe and I get this headache. I haven't said anything to her, of course, we've only just got married! But do you think that could be the cause of my headache?*

Doctor: *Quite possibly. There are lots of ingredients in perfume which people can be allergic to. You will have to talk to your wife. Surely she realizes herself that you are suffering. And perfume is not so important – certainly not compared to her husband's health. Let's do it like this: If you don't want to tell your wife yourself, then bring her to see me next week and I will explain everything to her. Agreed?*

Patient: *Very good, doctor. That's what I will do. Thank you very much. I will see you next week then.*

Doctor: *Yes, see you. Goodbye.*

Patient: *Goodbye.*

Vocabulary: Dialogue

মাথা ব্যথা matha bytha (bætha) *n.* headache

প্রতিদিন prôtidin *adv.* every day

দিন যেতে যেতে din yete yete *phr.* as the day goes on

কমে যাওয়া kôme yaoŷa *cvb.* get less, reduce

তুলনা tulôna *n.* comparison

নিয়ম niŷôm *n.* routine, system

পরিবর্তন pôribɔrtôn *n.* change

বিয়ে biŷe *n.* marriage

বিয়ে করা biŷe kɔra *vb.* get married

সুখ sukh *n.* happiness

সম্পর্ক sɔmpɔrkô *n.* relationship

বাড়ানো baɽano *vb.* extend, increase

কথা বাড়ানো kɔtha baɽano *vb.* elaborate

পারফিউম parphium *n.* perfume

যেন yænô *conj.* as if, like, so that

সম্ভবত sɔmbhôbɔtô *adv.* possibly

বিরুদ্ধে biruddhe *pp.* against

অ্যালার্জি aylarji (ælarji) *n.* allergy

দরকারি dɔrkari *adj.* necessary, important

শরীর śôrīr *n.* health, body

আগামী agamī *adj.* next

বুঝিয়ে দেওয়া bujhiŷe deoŷa *cvb.* explain

আলাদা alada *adj.* separate

খোদা হাফেজ khoda haphej *phr.* good-bye (*lit:* God be with you)

Additional Vocabulary: Body and health

allergy আলার্জি alarji

arm বাহু bahu; হাত ha:t

back পিঠ pi:ṭh

blood রক্ত rɔktô

body গা ga:; শরীর śôrīr, দেহ dehô

breast বুক bu:k

breath নিঃশ্বাস niḥśvas (nisshash)

chest বুক bu:k

cold সর্দি sordi (shordi)

cough কাশি kaśi

diarrhea আমাশা amaśa

doctor ডাক্তার ḍaktar

dysentry আমাশা amaśa

ear কান ka:n

examine পরীক্ষা করা pôrīkṣa kɔra

eye চোখ co:kh

face মুখ mu:kh

fever জ্বর jɔr

finger আঙুল aṅul

flu সর্দি sordi (shordi)

foot পা pa:

hair চুল cu:l

hand হাত ha:t

head মাথা matha

health স্বাস্থ্য svasthyô; শরীর śôrīr

heart হৃদয় hṙidɔŷ (ridɔŷ)

hip পাছা pacha

ill অসুস্থ ɔsustho

illness অসুখ ɔsukh

infection সংক্রমণ sɔṃkrômôn

leg পা pa

lungs ফুসফুস phusphus

medicine ওষুধ oṣudh

midriff কোমর komôr

mouth মুখ mu:kh

neck ঘাড় ghaṛ

nose নাক nak

nurse সেবিকা sebika

pain ব্যথা bytha (bætha)

patient রোগী rogi

pregnant গর্ভবতী gɔrbhôbôtī

shoulder কাঁধ kãdh

skin চামড়া camṛa

spine মেরুদণ্ড merudɔnḍô

stomach পেট peṭ

throat গলা gɔla

toe পায়ের আঙুল paŷer aṅul

tongue জিভ jibh

tooth দাঁত dãt

treatment চিকিৎসা cikiṭsa

vaccination টিকা ṭika

waist কোমর komôr

Grammar 27: Bangla tense use

As in most languages, tense is built into the Bangla verbal system. Every finite verb form contains a tense element. Unlike English, Bangla does not have a sequence of tense except in a very limited range of structures such as conditional sentences. Bangla tenses can freely interact with one another.

Here is a sentence with a past perfective and a future tense verb. In the English translation the future tense has to be rendered with a *would* structure.

সে কথা দিয়েছিল যে সে তাদের আইসক্রিম খাওয়াবে। (কথা দেওয়া = *promise*)
He promised that he would feed them ice cream.

Bangla tense use is largely guided by actual time rather than by correlation between the tenses. There are three important considerations about the Bangla tense system as a whole:

Tenseless elements
Bangla has some common structures that are, to all intents and purposes, tenseless. The two negative verbs নেই *is absent* and ন– *is not* as well as zero verb equational structures and the existential verb আছ– are essential and tenseless features of the language that regularly occur in past tense contexts.

Compare: আমরা সবাই সেখানে ছিলাম কিন্তু তুমি নেই।
with: আমরা সবাই ছিলাম সেখানে কিন্তু তুমি ছিলে না।
            We were all there but you were absent.

The sentence with নেই has considerably more impact, immediacy, and expressiveness than the past tense version.

Non-finite verb forms
One of the main tasks of non-finite verb forms is to provide time relationships within sentences. The perfective participle takes care of preceding events, the imperfective participle can cover simultaneous events as well as future intentions. A genitive verbal noun followed by সময় sômôŷ *time* (রওনা দেওয়ার সময়ে *at the time of departure*) specifies points in time. The conditional participle can provide a time frame for whichever tense the finite verb occurs in. These readily available devices not only reduce the need for conjunctions in Bangla but also make a significant contribution to the flexibility of the Bangla tense system.

Principles of well-soundedness (phonaesthetics)
Due to the regularity of Bangla verb tense endings (গেল, দিল, হল, বলল), a string of verbs all in the same tense can sound quite monotonous. Flexible word order as well as frequent tense changes liven up narrative texts and provide pleasing variety to the ear.

Each tense in Bangla has particular designated tasks.

Present Simple: করি, যাও, দেয়, আসেন

The present simple is used for:

General, timeless statements:

> সূর্য পূর্বে ওঠে। *The sun rises in the East.*
> শীতকালের পরে বসন্ত আসে। *Spring comes after winter.*

Regularly occurring events:

> সে অনেক বই পড়ে। *She reads a lot of books.*
> সে সোমবারে বাজারে যায়। *He goes to the market on Monday.*

Ongoing states, feelings or experiences:

> আমি তাকে চিনি না। *I don't know him.*
> সে তার বাচ্চাকে নিয়ে চিন্তা করে। *He worries about his child.*

Ongoing states with explicit starting points in the past:

> আমি তিন বছর আগে থেকে এখানে আছি। *I have been here for three years.*

Present activities (English uses the present continuous here.):

> তারা ভাত খায়। *They are having dinner.*

Dates of births, deaths, or other events:

> রংপুর জেলায় আঠার-শ-আশি সালে বেগুম রোকেয়ার জন্ম হয়।
> *Begum Rokeya was born in the district of Rongpur in 1880.*
>
> আমি প্রথম বাংলা শিখতে শুরু করি ১৯৯১ সালে।
> *I first started learning Bangla in 1991.*

Past tense narratives invariably jump to the present simple for sentences of this kind. The year gives us what we need to know so the tense of the sentence becomes unimportant.

The present simple is used in modal clauses with যদি *if,* যেন *so that,* যাতে *so that,* পাছে *lest, so that not.*

. . . .

Present Continuous: করছি, যাচ্ছ, দিচ্ছে, আসছেন

The present continuous is the tense for present ongoing actions and events as well as for regularly intermittent events in the present. Note that Bangla uses the present continuous with verbs like পারা *be able to,* বোঝা *understand,* চাওয়া *want,* ভাবা *think,* হওয়া *be, become,* লাগা *feel* where English would often use the present simple.

For present ongoing events:

> বৃষ্টি হচ্ছে। *It is raining.*
> আমি নিঃশ্বাস নিতে পারছি না। *I can't breathe.*

For imminent future events:

> বাবা আজ আসছেন। *Father is coming today.*
> ওরা বাসা বদল করছে। *They are moving.* (বদল করা = *change*)

For events and states that started in the past:

> কতদিন ধরে চলছে এসব? *How long has all this been going on?*

Like the present simple, the present continuous can turn up in past tense contexts to provide liveliness.

• •

Present Perfect: করেছি, গিয়েছ, দিয়েছে, এসেছেন

The present perfect is one of the past tenses in Bangla. It combines the ability to relate past events that happened fairly recently and past events whose effects are still felt in the present. In negation the present perfect verb forms change to present simple verb forms followed by নি.

> affirmative: আমি কাপড় ধুয়েছি। *I have washed the clothes.*
> negative: আমি কাপড় ধুই নি। *I have not washed the clothes.*

recent past events: তার গতকাল একসিডেন্ট হয়েছে। *She had an accident yesterday.*

past events with effects on the present:

> রাস্তায় অনেক পানি জমেছে। (জমা = *gather, collect*)
> *A lot of water has accumulated in the road.* = *The road is flooded.*

> আপনি বদলে গিয়েছেন। *You have changed.*

The present perfect is used in some contexts to describe an event where English is more likely to give the after-state in the present simple, particularly with things coming to an end or to fruition:

> দোকানটা বন্ধ হয়েছে। *The shop has closed down.*
> সন্ধ্যা হয়ে গেছে। *It is evening.*
> তার অসুখ হয়েছে। *She is ill.*

• •

Future Tense: করব, যাবে, দেবে, অসবেন

The future tense covers everything that comes later, whether we start in the present or in the distant past. This is one of the reasons why Bangla tense use seems capricious at times, when it is, in fact, remarkably consistent. The future tense has an in-built modal potential in the sense that everything we say about the future is, in effect, a prediction, an intention, a promise or some such.

Future actions, events and states:

আমি পুরা দুই মাস থাকব। *I will stay a full two months.*
আবার নতুন ফুল ফুটবে। *New flowers will bloom again.*

Predictions, assumptions, intentions, requests, and probabilities (Many of these uses are modal.):

সে এরইমধ্যে বাসায় গিয়ে থাকবে। *She will have reached home by now.*

তাদের মনে হল মেয়েটির বয়স বছর বারো হবে।
They thought that the girl must be about twelve.

Intentions, requests, wishes, expressions of politeness, etc.:

কি বলব? *What can I say?* or *What should I say?*
পানি খাব। *I would like some water.*
আর কি লাগবে? *What else do you need?*
আসতে পারব? *Can I come in?*

. . . .

Past Simple: করলাম, গেলে, দিল, আসলেন

The past simple is the usual tense in narrative contexts. Of the five past tenses (present perfect, past simple, past continuous, past perfect, and past habitual), the past simple is the least marked. It can be used for events and actions in the distant or the recent past and it can be accompanied by a time adverbial specifying the time of the event.

Past actions, events, and states:

সে বিয়ে টিকল না। *That marriage didn't last.*
সব মিলিয়ে গেল আস্তে আস্তে। *Gradually everything fell into place.*

Immediate past or immediate future events:
(Note: This is an idiomatic use of the past simple which is common in spoken language and is always restricted to informal, simple, single remarks. Essentially the tense context is removed in these uses.)

আমি চললাম। *I'm off.*
খুশি হলাম। *I'm delighted.*
কিছু না খেয়ে গেলেন? *Are you leaving without eating anything?*

ছিল– *was* is the past tense of আছ ach– and also of the zero verb:

আমার কিন্তু ভয় ছিল না। *But I wasn't afraid.*
কথাটা তার মনে ছিল। *He remembered that.*
যখন ছোট ছিলাম ... *When I was little ...*

. . . .

Past Continuous: করছিলাম, যাচ্ছিলে, দিচ্ছিল, আসছিলেন

The past continuous either accompanies another past tense, or a perfective participle, to describe events that were occurring simultaneously, or it can describe ongoing processes or events in the past. The past continuous is also used to make requests or demands more polite:

With another past tense:

সে যখন এল তখন আমরা ছবি দেখছিলাম।
We were watching a film when he arrived.

Past processes (This is a very common use with verbs describing mental activity, ability and such like. They are often equivalent to the simple past in English.):

ভাবছিল কিভাবে সে বইটা হাতে পাবে।
She was wondering how to get hold of the book.

মেয়েটিকে তিনি একেবারে ভুলতে পারছিলেন না।
He was quite unable to forget the girl.

Politeness (This use is equivalent to the English shift from simple present *I want* to the more polite *I would like.* It is restricted to first person and is very common with caoŷa *want.*):

আমি তার সঙ্গে একটু কথা বলতে চাইছিলাম।
I would like to speak to him for a bit.

• •

Past Perfect: করেছিলাম, গিয়েছিলে, দিয়েছিল, এসেছিলেন

The past perfect is used for completed events or actions in the past which no longer have a direct bearing on the present:

Events described in the past perfect do not have to be in the distant past:

ও সকালে এসেছিল। *He came this morning.*

and they do not need to be linked to subsequent events:

আমি সে দিন ভুল করেছিলাম। *I made a mistake that day.*

What distinguishes the past perfect from both the past simple and the present perfect is the completedness of the related event.

For the sentence *He came this morning,* Bangla has the following options:

present perfect: সে সকালে এসেছে। (implies that he is still here)
past simple: সে সকালে এল। (relates the event without any inferences)
past perfect: সে সকালে এসেছিল। (implies that he came and left again)

The past perfect implies that the event is over:

কলকাতায় তিন বছরের মধ্যে সে পাঁচবার বাসা বদলিয়েছিল।
Within three years in Kolkata he moved (houses) five times.

The past perfect shares its negation with the present perfect:

তিনি কিছু একটা বলতে চেয়েছিলেন কিন্তু সুযোগ পাননি। (সুযোগ = *chance, opportunity*)
He wanted to say something but he didn't get a chance.

. . . .

Past Habitual: করতাম, যেতে, দিত, অসতেন

The past habitual has two distinct uses:

Habitual actions or events in the past, equivalent to the English *use to*. This use of the past habitual often includes a fairly precise time frame.

> ছোটবেলায় সবাই তাকে সাহায্য করত।
> *Everyone used to help him in his childhood.*

> সে দিনগুলোতে আমার এমন রাগ হত না।
> *I didn't use to get so angry in those days.*

> স্বামীকে তিনি চিরদিন দারুণ ভয় করতেন।
> *She was always extremely scared of her husband.*

The past habitual is rarely the main tense in narrative contexts but it mixes easily with ছিল and its variants:

> উনি যখন ইংল্যান্ডে ছিলেন তখন গান লিখতেন।
> *He used to write songs while he lived in England.*

The past habitual is used for hypothetical (modal) language use:

এই কথা সে কখনও বলত না।   *He would never say that.*
কেউ ওখানে রাত্রে থাকত না।   *No one would spend the night there.*

The past habitual is used with jana *know* to convey a past simple meaning:

আমি তা জানতাম না।   *I didn't know that.*

The past habitual is used in conditional sentences:

> তুমি যদি রাত্রে আসতে তাহলে নিজের চোখে দেখতে পারতে।
> *If you had come last night, you would have seen it with your own eyes.*

Here is a comparison of a perfective participle in a simple past sentence, on the one hand, and a past conditional structure with a conditional participle on the other.

past simple:	তুমি মনে কষ্ট পাবে জেনে এই কথা বললাম না।
	I didn't tell you because I knew that it would upset you.
past habitual:	তুমি মনে কষ্ট পাবে জানলে এই কথা বলতাম না।
	I wouldn't have said this if I had known that it would upset you.

Narrative

Note: This little anecdote is told about the famous Hindu monk and teacher Svami Vivekananda স্বামী বিবেকানন্দ, who even in his childhood as simply Noren Datta (Dotto) showed
remarkable fearlessness. The name Vivekananda consists of the noun বিবেক bibek *knowledge, awareness* and the noun আনন্দ anôndô *joy*, and means *joy of awareness*.(The passage
shows very clearly how flexible tense use is in Bangla. We go seamlessly from past simple
to present continuous, from past simple to present perfect and from past simple to present
simple. Once you have read and understood the passage, read it again carefully, paying
particular attention to the verb tenses.)

ভয় নেই

রামরতনবাবুর বাড়ির সামনে বিশেষ একটা গাছ ছিল। গাছের একটা ডাল এমন নিচে, মাটির কাছে যে তার
উপরে বসে দোল খাওয়া খুব সুবিধার। নরেন নামে একজন দুষ্টু ছেলে তার বন্ধুদের সঙ্গে রোজ সন্ধ্যাবেলায়
সেখানে বসে গল্প করে খেলত।

রামরতনবাবু এতে একটুও খুশি নন। তিনি ভয় দেখিয়ে ছেলেদের তাড়ানোর জন্যে একটা ভূতের গল্প
বললেন। তিনি বললেন : ভূত একদিন তাঁর সামনে উপস্থিত হয়ে বলল: 'আমি এই গাছের মালিক আছুন্ন
আর এখানে কারও বসা নিষেধ। আর কখনও কোনও দিন আসবে না। নাহলে আমি তোমাকে খেয়ে ফেলব।'

রামরতনবাবু বললেন, 'আমি আর কখনও এই ডালের উপরে বসিনি। তোমাদেরও খুব বিপদ।'

ছেলেরা ছটফট করে উঠে যে যার বাড়িতে চলে গেল। রামরতনবাবুকে আর জ্বালায়নি।

এক মাস পরে সন্ধ্যাবেলায় রামরতনবাবু বাড়ি ফিরতে ফিরতে নরেনকে দেখলেন। ছেলেটি ঠিক সেই গাছের
ডালের উপরে বসে আস্তে আস্তে গান গেয়ে দোল খাচ্ছে। 'কি রে? কি করছিস? আছুন্ন যদি আসে?'

নরেন বলল, 'আসলে আছুন্ন গত রাত্রে আমার কাছে এসেছিল। বলল, 'আমি এই গাছের মালিক আছুন্ন।
ভয় নেই। কিছু হবে না। অনেক বছর আগে এক রাত্রে আমার মেজাজ খুব খারাপ ছিল বলে একজন ছোট
ছেলেকে আমি খুব ভয় দেখালাম। বেচারা এত ভয় পেয়ে গেছে যে সে একবারও আর এই জায়গায় ফিরে
আসেনি। আজকালের ছেলেরা যে এত সহজে ভয় করে না তা দেখে আমি খুব খুশি।'

রামরতনবাবু তার কোনও উত্তর খুঁজে পাননি। সেদিন থেকে তিনি সন্ধ্যাবেলায় প্রায়ই ছেলেদের সঙ্গে বসে
ভূতের গল্প বলতেন।

Fearless

*There was a special tree in front of Ramroton Babu's house. One of its branches was so
low and close to the ground that it was very handy for sitting on and for swinging on it.*

*A naughty boy named Noren and his friends used to come in the evenings to sit there and
chat and play. Ramroton Babu was not at all happy about this. In order to chase the boys
away he frightened them by telling them a ghost story. A ghost appeared before him one
day and said, "I am Achunno, the master of this tree. No one is allowed to sit on it. Don't
ever come back or else I will swallow you up."*

*Ramroton Babu said, "I have never sat on that tree branch again and all of you are also
in great danger!"*

The boys went away, each to their own home. They didn't bother Ramroton Babu again.

A month later, one evening when Ramroton Babu was on his way home, he suddenly saw Noren sitting on that exact branch. The boy was swinging and singing quietly to himself. "What the ...! What are you doing? What if Achunno comes back?"

Noren said, "Actually, Achunno appeared to me here last night. He said, 'I am Achunno, the master of this tree. Don't be scared. Nothing will happen. One day, a long time ago, I was in a particularly foul mood and threatened a little boy. The poor thing was so frightened that he never came back to this place. I am very pleased to see that boys nowadays are not so easily scared off.'"

Ramroton Babu had no reply to this. From that day on he often sat down with the boys in the evening and told them ghost stories.

Vocabulary: Narrative

ভয় নেই bhɔŷ nei *phr.* have no fear, don't worry

রামরতন ramrɔtôn *name* Ramroton

বাবু babu *n.* Mister (Mr.)

ছিল chilô *vb.* was

ডাল ḍal *n.* branch

নিচে nice *adv.* low

দোল খাওয়া dol khaoŷa *vb.* swing

নরেন nɔren *name* Noren

ভয় দেখানো bhɔŷ dækhano *vb.* frighten, scare

তাড়ানো taṛano *vb.* chase away

ভূত bhūt *n.* ghost

উপস্থিত upôsthit *adj.* present

উপস্থিত হওয়া upôsthit hɔoŷa *vb.* appear

মালিক malik *n.* owner, landlord

আছুন্ন achunnô *name* Achunno

খেয়ে ফেলা kheŷe phæla *cvb.* eat up, gobble up

বিপদ bipɔd *n.* danger

জ্বালানো jvalano *vb.* annoy, irritate

গান গাওয়া gan gaoŷa *vb.* sing a song

কি রে? ki re? *expr.* What on earth?

যদি yôdi *conj.* if

কিছু হবে না। kichu hɔbe na *phr.* Nothing will happen = Everything is fine

বলে bôle *conj.* because

ভয় পাওয়া bhɔŷ paoŷa *vb.* get scared

বেচারা becara *n.* poor boy

ফিরে আসা phire asa *cvb.* return, come back

আজকাল ajkal *adv.* nowadays

ভয় করা bhɔŷ kɔra *vb.* be afraid

ভয় পাওয়া bhɔŷ paoŷa *vb.* be afraid

উত্তর uttôr *n.* reply, answer

খোঁজা khõja *vb.* search

খুঁজে পাওয়া khũje paoŷa *cvb.* find (after searching)

ভূতের গল্প bhūter gɔlpô *n.* ghost stories

Exercises: Unit 12

Exercise 12:1
*Note: This is just a practice exercise to build up your competence and confidence.
Remember (or check!) the past and future tense of* আছ- *and the zero verb (Unit 8,
Grammar 17) and the formation of the present perfect negative (Unit 7, Grammar 12).*

Change these present simple sentences to the tenses indicated in parentheses:

(i)   সে রাজশাহীতে আছে। (future)

(ii)   আমি বাজারে যাই। (past perfect)

(iii)   সে আমার সঙ্গে থাকে। (past continuous)

(iv)   ছোট বোনের কথা মনে পড়ে। (present perfect)

(v)   সাঈদার সঙ্গে একটু কথা বলি। (future)

(vi)   তার ঢাকায় ভাল লাগে না। (present perfect!)

(vii)   ওরা সাপ দেখে ভয় করে। (past perfect)

(viii) ব্যাপারটা জরুরি। (past simple)

(ix)   সেটা আমার মনে নেই। (past simple)

(x)   চিঠিটা পাঠাও। (future)

(xi)   মা রুটি বানায়। (present perfect)

(xii)   মেয়েটি কথা বলতে পারে না। (present continuous)

(xiii) তুমি কেমন আছ? (past simple)

(xiv)   আমরা ছুটিতে আছি। (past simple)

(xv)   তারা পুকুরে সাঁতার কাটে। (present perfect)

(xvi)   আমি কোনও খারাপ খাবার খাই না। (present perfect)

(xvii) গাজর খুব তাড়তাড়ি শেষ হয়ে যায়। (future)

(xviii) সে সকাল ৫টায় ওঠে। (past habitual)

(xix)   এক তলাতে একটা ঘর খালি আছে। (past simple)

(xx)   সে একটা রেস্তোরাঁতে খেতে চায়। (past perfect)

Exercise 12:2
Translate the sentences, paying particular attention to the verb tenses. Remember that the past simple is mainly used in narrative contexts. For isolated sentences like the ones below, use the past perfect (e.g., sentence xiii):

(i)   *We eat rice every day.*

(ii)   *He didn't understand me.*

(iii)   *At that time I was listening to the song.*

(iv)   *He ate up all the mangoes.*

(v)   *We have to finish the work by the end of this week.*

(vi)   *The cat is sleeping underneath the table.*

(vii)   *There is no hospital in this street.*

(viii) *I have been here all my life.*

(ix)   *He went to the market this morning.*

(x)   *I would have gone with you.*

(xi)   *We didn't see any tigers.*

(xii)   *He sat by the river all day long.*

(xiii)   *She wanted to stay here.*

(xiv)   *You didn't need to wait for me.*

(xv)   *I have thrown the rotten vegetables away.*

(xvi)   *I went to Italy five years ago.*

(xvii)   *He would never say such a thing.*

(xviii) *Did you know about this?*

(xix)   *I was in a bad mood.*

(xx)   *What did you ask him.*

UNIT 13

Dialogue: কোন দিকে *Which way?*
Vocabulary: Dialogue
Grammar 28: Compound and complex sentences and conjunctions
Narrative: ঋতু *Seasons*
Vocabulary: Narrative
Additional Vocabulary: Nature words
Grammar 29: Correlative structures
Exercises

Dialogue

কোন দিকে?

দুজন ভদ্রলোক রাস্তায় কথা বলছেন:

ক: মাফ করুন। এখানে কাছাকাছি ওষুধের দোকান কোথাও আছে বলতে পারেন?

খ: ওষুধের দোকান? খুব কাছে পাবেন না। তবে বাজারের পাশাপাশি দুটো ওষুধের দোকান আছে।

ক: বাজার কত দূর?

খ: এই তো, সামনের মোড়টা পার হয়ে একটু এগিয়ে গেলে একটা স্কুল পড়বে। তার পাশ দিয়ে বাঁদিকে যে রাস্তাটা চলে গেছে সেটা ধরে একটু এগোলে বাজার। হেঁটে গেলে মিনিট পাঁচেক লাগবে।

ক: হেঁটে যেতে হবে?

খ: না, আপনি রিকশায় যেতে পারেন। রিকশা আবার সদর রাস্তা দিয়ে যায় না। গলিঘুঁজি দিয়ে নিয়ে যাবে।

ক: তার চেয়ে হেঁটে যাওয়াই ভাল। আচ্ছা, বাজার যখন, তখন তো মুদির দোকানও থাকবে, তাই না?

খ: হ্যাঁ, তা তো আছে। একটা-আধটা নয়, দশ-বারো। শুধু মুদির দোকান কেন, কাঁচা সবজি, মাছ, মাংস, ফুল, ফলের দোকান তো পাবেন। তাছাড়াও পাবেন কাপড়, বাসন, বিছানা, জুতো, দরজি, বই-খাতা ও গয়নার দোকান।

ক: আসলে আমার জুতোর ফিতে গেছে ছিঁড়ে।

খ: ও, আচ্ছা। আপনি ঢোকার মুখেই দেখতে পাবেন একটা লোক জুতো সারাচ্ছে। ও জুতো রংও করে দেয়।

ক: বাঃ। আপনার সঙ্গে দেখা হওয়ায় আমার খুব উপকার হল।

খ: না, না, ও কথা বলছেন কেন? এ কাজ তো যে কোনও লোকেরই করা উচিত। আপনি কি এখানে নতুন এসেছেন?

ক: হ্যাঁ।

খ: কলকাতা কেমন লাগে?

ক: এমনিতে তো ভালই। খেলাধুলো, নাচ-গান, থিয়েটার, সিনেমা নিয়ে সারা শহরটা মেতে আছে। তবে এখানে রাস্তা কম, তার চেয়েও কম ফাঁকা জায়গা। আর সবচেয়ে কম গাছপালা।

Which way?

Two gentlemen talk in the street:

A: *Excuse me. Do you know if there is a pharmacy nearby?*

B: *A pharmacy? You won't find one very close to here. But there are two pharmacies right next to the market.*

A: *How far away is the market?*

B: *Well, if you cross the next junction and carry on for a bit there is a school. The road that turns left from the school will take you to the market. It's a five minute walk.*

A: *Do I have to walk?*

B: *No, you can take a rickshaw. But rickshaws don't go along the main roads. They will take you round the backroads.*

A: *In that case I may as well walk. OK, where there is a market, there will be a grocery shop, right?*

B: *Yes, certainly. Not just one or two but ten shops or more. And not just a grocery shop, but you can get fresh vegetables, fish, meat, flowers, fruit. There are also clothes, dishes, bedding, shoes, tailors, book and stationery shops, jewelers.*

A: *Actually, my shoelace is torn.*

B: *Ah well, right at the entrance to the market there is a man who repairs shoes. He also dyes shoes.*

A: *Wow! How lucky I am to have met you. That's been very useful.*

B: *No, no, don't talk like that. Anybody ought to do the same. Have you only just arrived here?*

A: *Yes.*

B: *How do you like Kolkata?*

A: *On the whole I like it very much. All over the town there is great enthusiasm for sports, dance and music, theater and cinema. But there is a lack of roads. Even worse, there are no open spaces. And worst of all is the lack of trees and plants.*

Vocabulary: Dialogue

কাছাকাছি kachakachi *adv.* close by
ওষুধ oṣudh *n.* medicine
পাশাপাশি paśapaśi *adv.* side by side
মোড় moṛ *n.* crossing, junction
পার হওয়া par hɔoŷa *vb.* cross, go past
এগনো egôno* *vb.* go forward, advance
হেঁটে যাওয়া hẽṭe yaoŷa *cvb.* walk
পাঁচেক pãcek *num.* about five
সদর রাস্তা sɔdôr rasta *n.* main road
গলিঘুঁজি gôlighũji *n.* lanes and by-lanes
যখন – তখন yɔkhôn – tɔkhôn *conj.* when
  – then
মুদির দোকান mudir dokan *n.* grocery shop
একটা-আধটা ӕkṭa-adhṭa *num.* one or two
খান দশ-বারো khan dɔś-baro *num.* almost
  a dozen
কাঁচা kãca *adj.* raw, fresh
সবজি sôbji *n.* vegetables
বাসন basôn *n.* dishes
বিছানা bichana *n.* bed
জুতো juto *n.* shoe, জুতা juta *n.* shoes
দরজি dôrji *n.* tailor

বই-খাতা bôi–khata *n.* books and notebooks
গয়না gɔŷna *n.* jewelry
ফিতে phite *n.* string
জুতোর ফিতে jutor phite *n.* shoelace
ছেঁড়া chẽṛa *vb.* tear
ছিঁড়ে যাওয়া chĩṛe yaoŷa *cvb.* get torn, get
  ripped
ঢোকা ḍhoka *vb.* enter
মুখ mukh *n.* face, mouth, opening
ঢোকার মুখে ḍhokar mukhe *adv.* right by the
  entrance
সারানো saranô *vb.* mend, repair
রং করে দেওয়া rɔṁ kôre deoŷa *vb.* dye,
  color
উপকার upôkar *n.* favor, benefit
এমনি emni *adv.* overall, just like that
খেলাধুলা khӕladhula *n.* sport
থিয়েটার thiŷeṭar *n.* theater
সিনেমা sinema *n.* cinema
মেতে → মাতা mata *vb.* be excited, go mad
ফাঁকা phãka *adj.* open, empty
গাছ-পালা gach-pala *n.* trees and plants

---

* এগনো is a slightly unusual verb in its conjugation. It has the inherent vowel in the second syllable where other verbs have আ a. The imperfective participle is এগুতে egute, the conditional participle এগুলে egule. This conjugation is more common in Paschim Banga than in Bangladesh and can be used for other extended verbs like ঘুমনো ghumôno instead of ঘুমানো ghumano for *sleep*, বেড়নো beṛano *go out, visit*, ফুরনো phurôno *run out, finish*.

Grammar 28: Compound and complex sentences and conjunctions

We have already seen a number of conjunctions throughout the previous units. Here we take a closer look at them. Conjunctions are joining words that link together sentences or parts of sentences. Bangla distinguishes coordinating conjunctions from subordinating conjunctions. The preferred way for Bangla to form its complex sentences is with relative–correlative structures. (These will be dealt with in Grammar 29, page 237.)

Coordinating conjunctions (linking two equal elements)

When coordinating conjunctions link two sentences we get two main clauses – this sentence structure is called compound.

ও *and, also*	তার বউ ও দুটি ছেলেমেয়ে *his wife and two children* আমরা বাংলায়ও টেবিল বলি। *We also say tebil in Bangla.*
আর *and*	ইনি আমার বাবা আর উনি আমার মা। *This is my father and that is my mother.*
আবার *and, again*	কালকে সকালে আবার পাওয়া যাবে। *(They) will be available again tomorrow morning.*
বা *or*	উনি আজকে বা কালকে আসবেন। *He will come today or tomorrow.*
না *or*	সে যাবে না থাকবে এখনও বলেনি। *He hasn't said yet whether he will go or stay.*
কিনা *whether ... or not*	আমি ওখানে আছি কিনা ... *whether I am there or not ...*
নাকি *or*	সে হেঁটে যাবে নাকি রিকশায় উঠবে ঠিক নেই। *It is not yet decided whether he will walk or go on a rickshaw.*
কিন্তু *but*	বাংলাদেশ মুসলমানের দেশ কিন্তু আমরা খ্রিস্টান। *Bangladesh is a Muslim country but we are Christians.*
তবে *but*	তবে আমাদের একতলাতে ছয় নম্বর খুব সুন্দর একটা রুম খালি আছে। *But on the ground floor we have a very beautiful room free, number six.*
কারণ *because*	আমরা বাংলায়ও টেবিল বলি কারণ এটা বিদেশি জিনিস। *We also say tebil in Bangla because it is a foreign thing.* (কারণ is a noun meaning *reason*.)

তাহলে *then, in that case* (lit: *if this is so*)

> তুমি যাবে না? তাহলে আমি একা যাব।
> *Are you not going? Then I will go by myself.*

না হলে *otherwise*

> তাড়াতাড়ি তৈরি হও। নাহলে আমি তোমাকে রেখে যাব।
> *Get ready quickly. Otherwise I will go without you.*

তাই *so, therefore*

> তার অসতে দেরি হয়েছে। তাই খারাপ লাগছে।
> *She was late arriving. Therefore she felt bad.*

তারপর *then, afterwards*

> প্রতিদিন সকালে এই ব্যথা হয়। তারপরে, দিন যেতে যেতে কমে যায়।
> *Every morning I have this headache. Then in the course of the day it subsides.*

Single subordinating conjunctions
(introducing subordinate clauses)

There are only a few single subordinating conjunctions in Bangla. The much more common way of linking subordinate clauses to main clauses is with a two-part correlative structure (see Grammar 29, page 237).

যে ye is a relative pronoun *(he, who)*, an intensifier for indefinites (Unit 7, Grammar 13), as well as a conjunction meaning *that*. The subordinate clause containing যে usually precedes the main clause. In the dialogue in Unit 8 we had the sentence:

> লোকটা যে এত কথা বলতে পারে কে জানত।
> the.man that so.much word say.IP he.can who would.know
> *Who would have thought that the man could talk so much?*

Occasionally the main clause comes first as in the narrative in Unit 10:

> মা বলেছে যে আমাদের বাড়ির কাছের নদীর ধারে
> mother she.has said that our home.GEN near.GEN river.GEN side.LOC
>
> সূর্যোদয় খুব সুন্দর দেখা যায়।
> sunrise very beautiful see.VN it.goes
> *Mother said that you could see the sunshine beautifully from the riverbank close to our house.*

(For correlative uses of যে see Grammar 29, page 237.)

. . . .

বলে *that, because*

বলে is actually the perfective participle of the verb বলা *speak, say* and, unlike other conjunctions, it comes **after** the finite verb. It can imply either *that* or *because*. Due to its position after the main verb, বলে as a conjunction makes for unobtrusive and elegant sentence structuring.

আমার মেজাজ খুব খারাপ ছিল বলে একজন ছোট ছেলেকে আমি ভয় দেখালাম।
Because I was in such a foul mood, I scared a little boy.
Lit.: *My mood was bad having said a little boy I scared.*

তুমি আসবে বলে কথা দিয়েছ।
you   will come having said you have given word
You promised that you would come.

আজকে ছুটি বলে আমরা কোথাও যাব না।
today   holiday having said we   somewhere will go not
We won't be going anywhere today because it is a holiday.

• • • • • • • • • • • • • • • • • • •

যেন *as if, so that*

আমি যেন নিঃশ্বাস নিতে পারি না।
It's as if I couldn't breathe.

বর্ষা পুরো দেশকে যেন নতুন জলে স্নান করায়।
It's as if the monsoon bathes the whole country in fresh water.

Narrative

Note: This type of story about the seasons in Bengal is typically found in school books. In this narrative the word "Bangladesh" is used in a geographical, not in a political, sense and refers to the whole of Bengal, i.e., Bangladesh and Paschim Banga (West Bengal).

ঋতু

আমাদের বাংলাদেশে ঋতুর সংখ্যা ছয়টা। প্রত্যেকটি ঋতু তার নিজের রং টং দিয়ে আমাদের মনে দাগ কাটে। ঋতুর এমন চমৎকার বৈচিত্র্য পৃথিবীতে কম দেখা যায়।

গ্রীষ্ম

প্রচণ্ড উত্তাপ এবং ঘূর্ণিঝড় গ্রীষ্মকালের ঋতু আরম্ভ হয়। সুফলা মাটি রোদে শুকিয়ে যায়। এ সময় নদী ও পুকুরে পানি এত কমে যায় যে গ্রামে দেখা দেয় খাবার পানির অভাব। তবে গ্রীষ্ম যে শুধু দুঃখ বয়ে আনে তা নয়। গ্রীষ্মকাল আমাদের জন্যে আনে নানা সুমিষ্ট ফল যেমন আম, কাঁঠাল, লিচু, কলা, জাম।

বর্ষা

এরপর বর্ষা। আকাশ তখন ঘন ঘন কালো মেঘে আচ্ছন্ন হয়ে পড়ে, ঝড়ো বাতাসও হয়। বর্ষা তার অবিরাম বৃষ্টি নিয়ে পুরো দেশকে যেন নতুন জলে স্নান করায়। বর্ষার আগমনে বাংলাদেশ আবার ফিরে পায় তার জীবন। গাছ–পালা আবার সবুজ হয়ে ওঠে, নদ–নদী, খাল–বিল ভরে যায় পানিতে। বর্ষা বাংলাদেশের জন্যে অনেক সময় দুঃখও বয়ে নিয়ে আসে। অতিরিক্ত বৃষ্টির ফলে বন্যা হয় প্রায় প্রতি বছর। তখন গ্রামের বাড়ি, শহরের বস্তি, রাস্তা, ফসল, এমনকি মানুষের আশা সব নষ্ট হয়ে উঠতে পারে।

শরৎ

বর্ষার পরে আসে শরৎ। শরতের নীল আকাশে তুলার মত ভেসে বেড়ায় মেঘ। বিচিত্র দেশী ফুল তাদের সুগন্ধ নিয়ে ফুটে ওঠে। সমস্ত প্রকৃতিতে নেমে আসে একটি নির্মল প্রশান্ত রূপ।

হেমন্ত

হেমন্ত সোনালি সম্ভাবনার ঋতু। হেমন্ত ফসল তোলার ঋতু। বাংলার কৃষকের মুখে এ সময় ফুটে ওঠে হাসি – ধান কাটা শুরু হবে এই আশায়। এই সময় পাকা ধানে ভরে ওঠে কৃষকের উঠান। হেমন্ত ঋতু প্রকৃতির পরিপূর্ণতার রূপে সুন্দর।

শীত

হেমন্তের পর আসে শীত। শীতকালে উত্তরের হিমেল হাওয়ায় অনেক গাছের পাতা ঝরে যায়। তাপমাত্রা কমে যায়। সকালে কুয়াশা পড়ে। নানা শাক–সবজি, মজাদার পিঠা ও পায়েস তৈরির উৎসবে মেতে ওঠে সবাই। এই ঋতুতে গ্রামে গ্রামে মেলা হয়, বিয়ে হয় আর হয় নানা আনন্দের অনুষ্ঠান।

বসন্ত

বাংলার শেষ ঋতু হল বসন্ত। তখন প্রকৃতি সব মলিন, সব পচা জিনিস ফেলে নতুন হয়ে ওঠে। বসন্তকালে সুন্দর সুন্দর ফুল দেখে আমরা আনন্দিত হয়ে যাই। পলাশ শিমূল ফুলে প্রকৃতি সাজে। কোকিল ডাকে। কবির ভাষায় বসন্তকাল তাই 'ঋতুরাজ'।

Seasons

Our Bengal has six seasons. Each season makes an impression on our minds with its own colors and characteristics. Such a fantastic variety of seasons is rare to be seen in the world.

Summer
Summer starts with great heat and cyclones. The fertile ground dries out in the sun of Boisakh. At this time the water in rivers and lakes decreases so much that villages have a shortage of drinking water. But summertime does not only bring sorrow. It brings us all kinds of sweet fruits such as mangoes, jackfruit, lychees, bananas and plums.

Monsoon
Then comes the monsoon. The sky is filled with dense black clouds and there are stormy winds. The monsoon with its incessant rains seems to bathe the whole country in fresh water. At the arrival of the rains, Bengal is once again filled with new life. Plants and trees are turning green again, rivers and streams, canals and lakes are filling up with water. But the rainy season often also brings sorrow. As a result of too much rain there are floods almost every year. Then village houses, slums in the city, roads, harvests and even human hopes can be destroyed.

Early autumn
After the rainy season comes early autumn. Clouds float through the blue early autumn skies like cotton wool. Various indigenous flowers with their own sweet fragrance start blossoming. The whole of nature takes on an appearance of immaculate tranquility.

Late autumn
Late autumn is the season of golden opportunities. It is the harvest season. At this time smiles appear on the faces of the farmers in the expectation of the coming rice harvest. The farmers' courtyards are filled up with the ripened paddy. In late autumn nature is revealed in all its full beauty.

Winter
Late autumn is followed by winter. In the cold North winds many trees shed their leaves. The temperature falls and there is fog in the mornings. Various green vegetables, cakes and rice puddings are prepared for celebrations and feasts and everyone is in high spirits. In this season, there are fairs in the villages, weddings and various other joyful celebrations.

Spring
The last season in Bengal is spring. Nature throws out all dirty and rotten things and renews itself. We are glad to see the beautiful flowers. Nature is adorned by Palash and Shimul trees. The cuckoo calls. In the language of the poet spring is therefore the king of seasons.

Vocabulary: Narrative

ঋতু r̩tu (ritu) *n.* season

সংখ্যা sɔṁkhya *n.* number

রং rɔṁ *n.* color

দাগ dag *n.* mark, spot

দাগ কাটা dag kaṭa *vb.* make an impression

চমৎকার cɔmôṭkar *adj.* excellent, fantastic

বৈচিত্র্য boicitryô *n.* variety

পৃথিবী pr̩thibī *n.* world, earth

গ্রীষ্মকাল grīṣmôkal *n.* summer

প্রচণ্ড prôcɔṇḍô *adj.* fierce, severe

উত্তাপ uttap *n.* heat

ঘূর্ণিঝড় ghūrṇijhɔr̩ *n.* cyclone, tornado

আরম্ভ arɔmbhô *n.* beginning

সুফলা suphɔla *adj.* fertile

মাটি maṭi *n.* earth, soil

বৈশাখ boiśakh *n.* Baishakh *(month)*

রোদ rod *n.* sunlight, sunshine

শুকানো śukano *vb.* dry, dry out

কমা kɔma *vb.* reduce, decrease

অভাব ɔbhab *n.* lack, shortage

দুঃখ duḥkhô *n.* sorrow, misery, sadness

বয়ে আনা bôŷe ana *cvb.* bring, bring along

সুমিষ্ট sumiṣṭô *adj.* delicious and sweet

আম am *n.* mango

কাঁঠাল kãṭhal *n.* jackfruit

লিচু licu *n.* lychee

কলা kɔla *n.* banana

জাম jam *n.* berry

বর্ষা bɔrṣa *n.* monsoon

ঘন ghɔnô *adj.* dense

কালো kalo *adj.* black

মেঘ megh *n.* cloud

আচ্ছন্ন achɔnnô *adj.* overcast

হয়ে পড়া hôŷe pɔra *vb.* become

ঝড়ো jhɔr̩o *adj.* stormy

বাতাস batas *n.* wind

অবিরাম ɔbiram *adj.* incessant

বৃষ্টি br̩ṣṭi *n.* rain

পুরো puro *adj.* whole

যেন yænô *conj.* as if

জল jɔl *n.* water

স্নান snan *n.* bath

করানো kɔrano *vb.* cause to do

আগমন agômôn *n.* arrival

জীবন jībôn *n.* life

গাছ-পালা gach-pala *n.* trees and plants

সবুজ sôbuj *adj.* green

হয়ে ওঠা hôŷe oṭha *vb.* become

নদী nôdī *n.* river

নদ-নদী nɔd-nôdī *n.* rivers and streams

খাল khal *n.* canal

বিল bi:l *n.* lake, floodplain

ভরা bhɔra *vb.* fill, fill up

ভরে যাওয়া bhôre yaoŷa *vb.* get filled up

নিয়ে আসা niŷe asa *vb.* bring

অতিরিক্ত ôtiriktô *adj.* excessive

ফল phɔl *n.* result

বন্যা bɔnya *n.* flood

শহর śɔhôr *n.* town

বস্তি bôsti *n.* slum

ফসল phɔsôl *n.* harvest

আশা aśa *n.* hope

নষ্ট nɔṣṭô *adj.* spoiled, destroyed

শরৎ śɔrôṭ *n.* early autumn

নীল nīl *adj.* blue

আকাশ akaś *n.* sky

তুলা tula *n.* cotton-wool

বেড়ানো berano *vb.* move around

ভাসা bhasa *vb.* float

বিচিত্র bicitrô *adj.* various

দেশী deśī *adj.* indigenous

গন্ধ gɔndhô *n.* smell, fragrance

সুগন্ধ sugɔndhô *n.* nice smell, sweet fragrance

ফোটা phoṭa *vb.* blossom, bloom

ফুটে ওঠা phuṭe oṭha *cvb.* blossom, bloom

সমস্ত sɔmôstô *adj.* whole, entire

প্রকৃতি prôkr̊ti (prokriti) *n.* nature

নামা nama *vb.* get down, descend

নির্মল nirmɔl *adj.* pure, immaculate

প্রশান্ত prôśantô *adj.* peaceful

রূপ rūp *n.* appearance, shape

হেমন্ত hemôntô *n.* late autumn

সোনালি sonali *adj.* golden

সম্ভবনা sɔmbhɔbôna *n.* possibility

তোলা tola *vb.* lift, pick

কৃষক kr̊ṣôk (krishok) *n.* farmer

হাসি hasi *n.* smile, laugh

ধান dha:n *n.* paddy, rice in the field

কাটা kaṭa *vb.* cut

শুরু śuru *n.* beginning

পাকা paka *adj.* ripe, mature

উঠান uṭhan *n.* courtyard

পরিপূর্ণতা pôripūrṇota *n.* fullness, richness

শীত śī:t *adj.* cold

শীতকাল śī:tkal *n.* winter

উত্তর uttôr *n.* north

হিমেল himel *adj.* icy, cold

হাওয়া haoŷa *n.* wind, air, weather

পাতা pata *n.* leaf

ঝরা jhɔra *vb.* shed, fall

তাপমাত্রা tapmatra *n.* temperature

কুয়াশা kuŷaśa *n.* fog

পড়া pɔṛa *n.* fall

শাক-সবজি śak-sôbji *n.* leafy greens, spinach

মজাদার mɔjadar *adj.* delicious

পিঠা piṭha *n.* cake

পায়েস paŷes *n.* rice pudding

তৈরি toiri *n.* preparation

উৎসব utsɔb *n.* occasion, function

মেতে ওঠা mete oṭha *cvb.* be delighted

সবাই sɔbai *n.* everybody

মেলা mæla *n.* fair

বিয়ে biŷe *n.* wedding

আনন্দ anôndô *n.* joy, pleasure

অনুষ্ঠান ônuṣṭhan *n.* celebration

শেষ śeṣ *n.* end

বসন্ত bɔsôntô *n.* spring

মলিন môlin *adj.* dirty, unclean

পচা pɔca *adj.* rotten, spoiled

ফেলা phæla *vb.* throw, throw away

আনন্দিত anônditô *adj.* pleased, glad

পলাশ pɔlaś *n.* palas *(flower)*

শিমূল śimūl *n.* silk-cotton

সাজা saja *vb.* dress, decorate

কোকিল kokil *n.* cuckoo

ডাকা ḍaka *vb.* call

কবি kôbi *n.* poet

ভাষা bhaṣa *n.* language

তাই tai *conj.* so, therefore

ঋতুরাজ r̊turaj (rituraj) *n.* king of seasons

Additional Vocabulary: Nature words

air হাওয়া haoŷa, বাতাস batas
bay উপসাগর upôsagôr
Bay of Bengal বঙ্গোপসাগর bɔṅgôpsagôr
cloud মেঘ megh
comet ধূমকেতু dhūmketu
cold শীত śīt (shi:t)
cyclone ঘূর্ণিঝড় ghurṇijhɔṛ
darkness অন্ধকার ɔndhôkar
death মৃত্যু mṛtu (mritu)
desert মরুভূমি morubhūmi
drought অনাবৃষ্টি ɔnabṛṣṭi (ɔnabrishṭi)
dust ধুলা dhula
earth *(dirt/soil)* মাটি maṭi
fire আগুন agun
flood বন্যা bɔnya (bɔnna)
fog কুয়াশা kuŷaśa (kuwasha)
forest বন bon
full moon পূর্ণিমা purṇima
grass ঘাস ghas
heat গরম gɔrôm
Himalayas হিমালয় himalɔŷ
hurricane ঘূর্ণিঝড় ghurṇijhɔṛ
ice বরফ bɔrôph
iron লোহা loha
jungle জঙ্গল jɔṅgôl
land জমি jômi
light আলো alo
lightning বিজলি bijoli
life জীবন jībon
metal লোহা loha
monsoon বর্ষা bɔrṣa (bɔrsha)
moon চাঁদ cãd

mountain পাহাড় pahaṛ
nature প্রকৃতি prôkṛti (prokriti)
ocean সাগর sagôr, সমুদ্র sômudrô
plant চারা cara
rain বৃষ্টি bṛṣṭi (brishṭi)
river নদী nôdī (nodi)
riverbank পাড় paṛ
rock পাথর pathôr
sand বালু balu
sea সাগর sagôr, সমুদ্র sômudrô
season কাল kal, ঋতু ṛtu (ritu)
shade ছায়া chaŷa
sky আকাশ akaś
snow বরফ bɔrôph
soil মাটি maṭi
stars তারা tara
stone পাথর pathôr
storm ঝড় jhɔṛ
sun সূর্য shurjô
sunrise সূর্যোদয় shuryodɔŷ
sunset সূর্যাস্ত shuryastô
sunshine রোদ rod
thunder মেঘের ডাক megher ḍak
tornado ঘূর্ণিঝড় ghurṇijhɔṛ
tree গাছ ga:ch
universe বিশ্ব biśvô (bissho)
water জল jɔl (PB), পানি pani (BD)
wave ঢেউ ḍheu
weather আবহাওয়া abhaoŷa (abhaowa)
wind হাওয়া haoŷa, বাতাস batas
world পৃথিবী pṛthibī (prithibi), দুনিয়া duniŷa

Grammar 29: Correlative structures

The most common way to make complex sentences in Bangla is with correlative structures. The যদি – তাহলে structure (*Grammar 26, page 201*) is one type of correlative structure. Complex sentences consist of a main clause and a subordinate clause. In Bangla these sentences usually have two corresponding conjunctions, one in the subordinate clause that tends to precede the main clause, and one in the main clause. The relative conjunction in the subordinate clause always begins with য. The English sentence *I will be here when you come* would in Bangla literally be: *When you come, then I will be here*:

> তুমি যখন আসবে   তখন আমি এখানে থাকব।
> you when will come then I here will be
> *I will be here when you come.*

In our dialogues and narratives we have had the following examples of correlative structures:

Unit 7 (Narrative): যেমন – তেমন *as – as, such*

> আমার আপনাদের বাড়িতে যেমন ভাল ঘুম হয়েছে
> my   your   at home as   good sleep has happened
> তেমন জীবনে অন্য কোথাও হয়নি।
> so   in life other somewhere has not happened
> *In my whole life I have slept nowhere as well as I have in your home.*

Unit 10 (Dialogue): যা – তা *what – that*

> আমি যা বুঝি না,   তা আমার কাছে জাদু।
> I   what I understand not that my near magic
> *What I don't understand is magic to me.*

You will see that in this sentence the correlative elements are actually pronouns. There is a full set of relative pronouns that is equivalent to the 3rd person pronouns we saw in Unit 3. English question pronouns also function as relative pronouns whereas Bangla has a separate set of forms for relative uses. This has the advantage that these relative pronouns can stand alone without an accompanying noun. In English we have to say *the person who* or, less commonly, *he who* whereas all we need in Bangla is যে and its variants. Since English distinguishes neither ordinary from honorific nor singular from plural in its question pronouns, there is only one English equivalent for four forms in Bangla.

Animate relative pronouns:

	nominative *who*	genitive *whose*	objective *to whom*
sg. ord.	যে	যার	যাকে
sg. hon.	যিনি	যাঁর	যাঁকে
pl. ord.	যারা	যাদের	যাদের
pl. hon.	যাঁরা	যাঁদের	যাঁদের

Inanimate relative pronouns have only singular forms:

nom./obj.	*which*	genitive	*of which*	locative	*in which*
যা		যার		যাতে	

Below are the main correlatives in Bangla, starting with the pronouns. Although each relative pronoun has a designated partner, there are also plenty of examples with non-matching pairs. Correlatives include pronouns (যে – সে *he who*, যা – তা *that which*) and adverbs of time, place, and manner (যেখানে – সেখানে *where, there*, যখন – তখন *when, then*, যেমন – তেমন *in such a way*). The English translations for Bangla correlatives do not always contain relative structures.

যে – সে *he/she – who*

যে তোমাকে এই কথা বলেছে সে কি অন্য কিছু বলেনি?
Didn't the person who told you this say anything else?

যারা আমাকে সাহায্য করেছে তাদেরকে ধন্যবাদ।
Thank you to those who have helped me.

সে plus noun; or সেটা or তা *that – which*

তার মা যেদিন চলে গেছে সেদিন তার অসুখ হয়েছে।
She became ill on the day her mother left.

তুমি সকালে যে কথা বলেছিলে তা আর কখনও বলবে না।
Don't ever say again what you said this morning.

যেখানে – সেখানে *where*

মানুষ যেখানে খুব যত্ন করে মন দেয় সেখানে তার কাজ সফল হয়।
Human beings are successful in the areas where they give great care and attention. (যত্ন = *care*, সফল = *successful*)

আমি যেখানে যেতে চেয়েছিলাম সেখানে এখন আর কেউ নেই।
There is no one left at the place where I wanted to go.

যেদিন – সেদিন *that day*

মেয়েটি যেদিন আসবে সেদিন তাদের বিয়ে হবে।
They will get married on the day the girl arrives.

যেভাবে – সেভাবে *in that way*

বাপ-ঠাকুরদারা যেভাবে জীবন কাটিয়েছেন, আমিও সেভাবে কাটাই।
I spend my life the same way my father and grandfathers spent theirs.

যা – তা *what*

আজকালের ছেলেরা যে   এত সহজে ভয় করে না তা দেখে   আমি খুব খুশি।
today's   boys   what so easily fear do not that having seen I   very happy
I am very happy to see that the boys of today don't get scared so easily.

তুমি যা   বলেছ   আমি তাই   করেছি।
you what have said I   that.emp have done
I did just what you said.

যা হয়ে গেছে তা নিয়ে আর ভেবে লাভ নেই।   (লাভ = *profit, gain*)
There is no point in worrying about what has happened.

যখন – তখন *when*

বাজার যখন, তখন তো মুদির   দোকানও থাকবে, তাই   না?
market when then emp grocer's shop.also will.be that.emp not
There will also be a grocer's shop in the market, won't there?

বৃষ্টি যখন নামতে লাগল তখন তুমি কি রাস্তায় ছিলে?
Were you on the road when it started raining?

যত – তত *as much as*

যতটা খারাপ হবে সে ভেবেছিল, ততটা নয়।
It was not as bad as he had thought.

যতদিন – ততদিন *as long as, while*

আমি যতদিন   সেখানে ছিলাম ততদিন এত বেশি গরম ছিল   না।
I   as.long.as there   I.was so.long so much hot it.was. not
It wasn't so very hot while I was there.

যতদূর – ততদূর *as far as*

যতদূর যেতে হবে ততদূর আমরা যেতে রাজি আছি।
We are willing to go as far as we have to.

যদিও – তবুও *although, even though* (This pair is similar to **যদি – তাহলে** *if, then* but it does not have the same tense restrictions.)

আমি যদিও তোমার মা নই, তবুও তোমার জন্যে মায়ের মত চিন্তা করি।
Even though I am not your mother, I worry about you like a mother would.

যেমন – তেমন *such, as – as*

অফিসে সব কাজ যেমন চলা উচিত তেমনই চলছে।
In the office the work is going exactly as it is supposed to.

In short sentences and when the context is clear, the correlative is sometimes dropped:

যেদিকে   চাও   খালি লাল আর হলুদ।
Whichever.direction you look, just red   and yellow.
There is just red and yellow all around.

আমি চেষ্টা   করি   যেখানে   যাই হেঁটেই   যেতে।
I   attempt I.do wherever I.go walk.PP.emp go
Wherever I go I try to walk as much as possible.

Exercises: Unit 13

There is quite a lot of new information in this unit to get your head around and become used to, so the first exercise is to read through the correlative example sentences (and their translations) again very carefully and then progress in two stages in this exercise. First translate the very simple English sentence given for each correlative pair; then make up a sentence yourself modeled on the examples for each correlative pair. Don't be too ambitious with your sentences but keep it simple and make sure that all the elements in the sentence are correct.

For translating the English sentences, it may be helpful to separate the two component sentences, e.g.: *I don't know the person you were talking about.* This sentence has two components:

(a) *you were talking about him*: this is the subordinate clause and comes first in the Bangla sentence: তুমি তার কথা বলেছিলে

(b) I don't know him: আমি তাকে চিনি না।

In order to connect the sentences, the তার in (a) changes to যার and there we have it:

> তুমি যার কথা বলেছিলে তাকে আমি চিনি না।
> *The one you were talking about, I don't know him.*

You will notice that in the completed sentence, the object তাকে comes before the subject আমি. This is quite common in correlative structures – the connecting element between the two component sentences is often placed at the beginning of the main clause. (We will have a closer look at word order in Bangla in Unit 14.)

Exercise 13:1

Below are the correlatives pairs in the order they were introduced with a sentence to be translated. (Once you have done this then make up your own simple sentence using that correlative):

(i)   যে – সে *he/she who*

> *The man who came yesterday will come again tomorrow.*

(ii) সে plus noun or সেটা or তা *that – which*

> *I don't like the book I am reading.* (use যে বই – তা)

(iii) যেখানে – সেখানে *where – there*

> *There are a lot of snakes in the place where he is going.*

(iv) যেদিন – সেদিন *that day*

> *I will explain everything to her on the day you bring her here.*

(v) যেভাবে – সেভাবে *in that way*

   He talks the same way as his father does.

(vi) যা – তা *that which, what*

   I will give you what you want.

(vii) যখন – তখন *when – then*

   He will be here when you come.

(viii) যত – তত *as much as*

   You can eat as much as you like.

(ix) যতদিন – ততদিন *for as long as*   (look up the দরকার structure in Unit 10, Grammar 24)

   I will stay with you as long as you need me.

(x) যতদূর – ততদূর *as far as*

   We will help as far as possible. (সম্ভব = *possible*)

(xi) যদিও – তবুও *even though, although*

   Even though he left a long time ago, we still remember him. (মনে পড়া = *remember*)

(xii) যেমন – তেমন *such, as – as*

   He cannot work as well as you do.

Exercise 13:2

Write a short passage (of about 150 words) about yourself, a funny incident, or something interesting that happened to you. Try to incorporate the new structures you have learned, but stay within your comfort zone. There are no answer keys to this exercise but there is a short passage from my own experience with translation in the answer keys section.

UNIT 14

Dialogue: মজার ব্যাপার *That's funny!*
Vocabulary: Dialogue
Grammar 30: Word order
Narrative: পদ্মা *The Padma*
Vocabulary: Narrative
Additional Vocabulary: Abstract nouns
Exercises

Dialogue

মজার ব্যাপার

ক: মাফ করুন। আমাকে একটু সাহায্য করতে পারেন?

খ: হ্যাঁ, চেষ্টা করব। কি ব্যাপার?

ক: আমি একটা বাড়ি খুঁজছি। এই রাস্তার চৌদ্দ নম্বর বাসা কোথায় আপনি কি জানেন?

খ: চৌদ্দ নম্বর বাসায় যাচ্ছেন?

ক: হ্যাঁ, কিন্তু বাসাটা খুঁজে পাচ্ছি না। এইদিকে তের নম্বর আর ওইদিকে পনের নম্বর,
কিন্তু চৌদ্দ নম্বর নেই।

খ: তাই তো। এরই মধ্যে একটা মজার ব্যাপার আছে। শুনবেন?

ক: বলুন।

খ: গত বছর আমি ইংল্যান্ডে একটা শহরে ছিলাম যেখানে অনেক রাস্তায় তের নম্বর বাসা
নেই। কেননা তের নম্বরে অদ্ভুত একরকম কুসংস্কার থাকে। সে জন্যে রাস্তার মধ্যে
তের নম্বর বাদ দেওয়া হয়। কি আশ্চর্য, চিন্তা করুন। কেউ তের নম্বর বাসায় যেতে
চাইলে সেটা পাওয়া যাবে না।

ক: আসলে, ভাই, তের নম্বর বাসা না থাকলে তো খুঁজবে কে? কারও ঠিকানা হতে পারে
না তো। আমি কিন্তু চৌদ্দ নম্বর বাসাটা খুঁজছি। আপনি ... ?

খ: হা, হা, হা, ঠিক বলেছেন! মজার ব্যাপার তো। বাসাটা যদি না থাকে তাহলে মানুষও সে
বাসায় থাকবে না। আর যে না থাকে, তাকে অন্য মানুষ সে ঠিকানটাতে খুঁজবেও না।
ঠিকই। কি চালাকি! খুব ভাল লেগেছে আপনার সঙ্গে কথা বলতে। আসি এইবার?

ক: চৌদ্দ নম্বর বাসাটা চেনেন না তাহলে?

খ: চিনি না? চিনি না? কি বলছেন? চৌদ্দ নম্বর বাসায় তো আমিই থাকি। দুতলার
ফ্ল্যাট্টাতে। চলুন, রাস্তার ওপারে চলে যাই। এই যে চৌদ্দ নম্বর। আমাদের ওখানে
যাচ্ছেন, তা তো মজার ব্যাপার। শুরু থেকে বলেননি কেন?

ক: আমি তো জানতাম না এটাই আপনার বাসা। আমার ভাইয়ের কাছে যাচ্ছি। আপনি
নাকি তার প্রতিবেশী? আপনার কথা আমার ভাইয়ের কাছ থেকে অনেক শুনেছি।

খ: তাই নাকি? তা তো মজার ব্যাপার। হা, হা, হা ...

That's funny!

A: *Excuse me, could you help me, please?*

B: *Yes, sure, I'll try. What's the matter?*

A: *I'm looking for a house. Can you tell me where number fourteen is on this street?*

B: *You are going to number fourteen?*

A: *Yes, but I can't find the house. This way is number thirteen and that way is number fifteen. But there is no number fourteen.*

B: *You are right. There is a funny story about that kind of thing. Do you want to hear it?*

A: *Go on, tell me.*

B: *Last year I was in a town in England where they had no number thirteen in many streets. The reason is that there is some superstition about the number thirteen. So they left out the number thirteen in numbering the houses. It's amazing, don't you think? If someone wants to go to number thirteen, they won't find it.*

A: *Yes, but if there is no number thirteen, who would go looking for it? It wouldn't be anyone's address. But I am actually looking for number fourteen. Do you ...?*

B: *Ha, ha, ha, you are right. That's funny. If there is no house, then no one can live in that house either. And if there is no person, then no one will come looking for him at that address. Exactly! How clever! I have really enjoyed talking to you. Now I must go.*

A: *So you don't know where number fourteen is?*

B: *Do I not know? Me not know? I live at number fourteen myself! In the apartment on the second floor. Come on, it's on the other side of the road, right here. You are going to our house? That's funny! Why didn't you say so from the start?*

A: *I didn't know that you lived there, did I? I am going to see my brother. You must be his neighbor. I have heard a lot about you from my brother.*

B: *Really? That's funny! Ha, ha, ha ...*

Vocabulary: Dialogue

মজা mɔja *n.* fun, enjoyment

ব্যাপার byapar (bæpar) *n.* matter, business

মাফ maph *n.* pardon, forgiveness

মাফ করা maph kɔra *vb.* pardon, forgive

চেষ্টা ceṣṭa *n.* attempt

চেষ্টা করা ceṣṭa kɔra *vb.* try

চৌদ্দো couddo *num.* fourteen

বাসা basa *n.* house

তেরো tero *num.* thirteen

পনেরো pɔnero *num.* fifteen

কেননা kænôna *conj.* because

একরকম ækrɔkôm *adv.* a kind of

কুসংস্কার kusɔṁskar *n.* superstition

বাদ দেওয়া bad deoŷa *vb.* omit, leave out

আশ্চর্য aścɔryô *adj.* amazing, surprising

ঠিকানা ṭhikana *n.* address

চালাকি calaki *n.* cleverness

আসা asa *vb.* come, leave

এইবার eibar *adv.* this time

তলা tɔla *n.* floor, story

ফ্ল্যাট phlyaṭ (phlæṭ) *n.* apartment, flat

শুরু śuru *n.* beginning, start

Grammar 30: Word order

In English the standard order of sentence parts is S (subject) – V (verb) – O (object), whereas in Bangla the verb comes at the end and the object precedes it (S–O–V).

The English:	subject	verb	object
	I	*love*	*him.*

is in Bangla	subject	object	verb
	আমি	তাকে	ভালবাসি।
	I	*him*	*love*

	আমি	চিঠি	লিখি।		
	I	*letter*	*write*	=	*I write letters.*

This has various consequences for the way Bangla sentences are organized. In essence, sentences work backwards from the verb. The object belongs to the verb and comes immediately before it, so any additional items like time and place adverbs, question words, postpositional phrases, or conjunctions would naturally come between the subject and the object:

subject	time adverb	object	verb (plus negation)		
আমি	আজকে	কাজ	করব না।		
I	*today*	*work*	*will not do*	=	*I will not work today.*

subject	place adverb	object	verb		
আমি	এখানে	–	বসব।		
I	*here*		*will sit*	=	*I will sit here.*

subject	question word	object	verb		
তুমি	কোথায়	কাজ	কর?		
you	*where*	*work*	*do*	=	*Where do you work?*
সে	কেন		আসেনি?		
he	*why*		*did not come?*	=	*Why didn't he come?*

subject	postposition	object	verb		
সে	তোমার জন্যে	আম	নিয়ে এসেছে।		
she	*for you*	*mango*	*brought*	=	*She has brought mangoes for you.*

subject	conjunction	object	verb		
তুমি	যদি	সাহায্য	কর		
you	*if*	*help*	*do*	=	*if you help ...*
লোকটা	যে	এত কথা	বলতে পারে		
the man	*that*	*so many words*	*can say*	=	*that the man can talk so much ...*

This is the default way sentence parts are ordered in Bangla sentences. There is, however, another factor. Bangla nouns have case markings and Bangla verbs are fully conjugated so actual word order in sentences can be a lot freer than in a language like English that does without these features. Emphasized parts of the sentence can be shifted to the beginning of the sentence.

object first: তাকে আমি অনেক আগে থেকে চিনি।
                  I have known him for a long time.

                  খবরের কাগজ তারা আর পড়ে না।
                  They don't read newspapers any more.

When a subject is already known from the context it is often added after the verb at the end of the sentence:

subject at the end: কিছু বুঝিনি তো আমি।
                        But I didn't understand anything.

                        কি বলছ তুমি?
                        What are you saying.

Narrative

The Padma (pronounced pɔdda in Bangla) is one of the main rivers in Bangladesh. This passage indicates the immense importance of rivers in the region.

পদ্মা

আমি পদ্মা। আমার জন্মকথা নিয়ে লোকমুখে অনেক গল্প ছড়িয়ে আছে। কেউ বলে, আমি নাকি দেবতা শিবের কন্যা। গঙ্গা আমার মা। মায়ের জন্ম হিমালয়ে। আমাকে জন্ম দিয়ে মা গঙ্গা ঢুকে পড়ে পশ্চিম বাংলায়। আর আমি হয়তো বা পথ ভুল করে এসে পড়ি এই বাংলাদেশে। সে যাই হোক, জন্মের পর থেকে শুরু হয় আমার পথচলা।

এই চলার পথে অনেক নদীর সঙ্গে আমার মিতালি হয়েছে। ফরিদপুরের কাছে এসে আমি মিলেছি যমুনার সাথে। দুষ্টজনে যেতে যেতে এসে পড়ি চাঁদপুরে। সেখানে আমাদের দেখা হয় মেঘনার সাথে। তারপর তিনজনে গলাগলি করে ঝাঁপিয়ে পড়ি বঙ্গোপসাগরের বুকে। অসীম সাগরের বুকে মিশে যাওয়াতে নদীর আনন্দ।

লোকে বলে, নদী নাকি বাংলাদেশের প্রাণ। পৃথিবীর আর কোথাও এত নদী নেই। নদী বাঁচিয়ে রেখেছে বাংলাদেশকে, সৃষ্টি করেছে দেশের সৌন্দর্য। পৃথিবীর তিন ভাগ জল, এক ভাগ স্থল। একসময় নদী ছিল মানুষের চলাচলের একমাত্র পথ। তখন মোটরগাড়ি, রেলগাড়ি, উড়োজাহাজ কিছুই ছিল না। মানুষ নদীপথে ঘুরে বেড়াত দেশ থেকে দেশান্তরে। মানুষের একমাত্র ভরসা ছিল নদী। সারা দেশে যে এতসব নদনদী, এসব নদীর তীরে গড়ে উঠেছিল বাংলার প্রাচীন রাজধানি, শহর, নগর ও বন্দর। সেসব ইতিহাস লেখা আছে আমার বুকে।

কত রাজা এখানে রাজত্ব করে গেছে। আমি তো পথ দেখিয়ে এনেছি তাদের। এক রাজা যায়, এক রাজা আসে। বদলায় দেশের মানচিত্র। বাংলাদেশের মানচিত্রে আমার একটা বিশেষ স্থান আছে। এক ডাকে সবাই আমাকে চেনে।

শীতে আমি শান্ত, ঘুমিয়ে-থাকা মেয়ের মত। ঢেউ জাগে না তখন। উপরে নীল আকাশ। আমার বুকের আয়নাতে সে তার মুখ দেখে। মাঠ ভরা ধান। সোনার মত ধান চাষীর চোখে স্বপ্ন জাগায়। গর্বে ভরে ওঠে বুক।

কিন্তু সে সুখ বেশি দিন থাকে না। কারণ ধীরে ধীরে আমার রূপ বদলাতে থাকে। বৈশাখে আমি অস্থির হয়ে, বর্ষাকালে জেগে উঠি ভয়ংকরী রূপে। তখন আমি আর শান্ত থাকতে পারি না। আমার জোয়ার দুষ্পাশের সব কিছু ভাসিয়ে নিয়ে যায়। ভেঙে যায় সাজানো সংসার, ঘরবাড়ি আর জীবনের ব্যবস্থাগুলো। রাশি রাশি জল ডুবিয়ে দেয় ফসলের ক্ষেত। একদিন যা ছিল আমার গৌরব, তা আবার নষ্ট হয়ে যায় আমার শক্তিতে। এভাবে আমি জন্ম দিয়েছি কত নগর, আবার ধ্বংসও করেছি বহু জায়গা।
এ কেমন কপাল আমার !

Source: শাহীদা আখতার in: ধানশালিকের দেশ, p. 141 (extract)

The Padma

I am the Padma. There are lot of stories about my origins spread around. Some people say that I am the daughter of Lord Shiva. The Ganges is my mother. Mother was born in the Himalayas. After giving birth to me she enters West Bengal. And I, perhaps by mistake, finish up in Bangladesh. In any case, my journey begins from birth.

On the way I make friends with many rivers. Near Faridpur I merge with the Jamuna. Together we travel on to Chandpur. There we meet the Meghna. Then the three of us carry on closely entwined until we jump into the Bay of Bengal. To flow into the endless sea is a river's happiness.

People say that rivers are the life-force of Bangladesh. There is nowhere else in the world where there are so many rivers. Rivers have kept Bangladesh alive and given the country its beauty. The earth is three parts water and one part land. At one time rivers were the only way for people to get around. At that time there were no cars, trains or planes. People used the waterways to travel from one country to another. People were entirely dependent on rivers. With so many rivers in the country, the old capitals, towns and harbors were all built on the banks of the rivers. All this history is written on my body.

In the winter I am peaceful – like a sleeping girl. Waves don't rise at that time. The blue sky is above. Its face is mirrored on my body. The fields are full of paddy. From the golden rice-fields the farmers' eyes fill with dreams. I am filled with pride.

But this happiness does not last long, as my nature is gradually transformed. In Baisakh I become restless. In the rainy season I take on frightening features. I can't stay calm anymore then. My tide sweeps everything away on both sides. Tidy social structures, houses and life's arrangement are all destroyed. Wave after wave of water submerges the fields and harvests. What was once my glory is now devastated by my strength. Just as I have given birth to a great number of cities, so I have destroyed many places. What kind of a fate is that!

———————————

The passage about the Padma River is our first proper narrative text and takes us a little bit further than the dialogues so far. You should go through it carefully, paying attention to the way the sentence parts are arranged. At the end we have two sentences with interesting ordering. In sentence (1) the verb comes at the beginning and the multi-part subject follows it; in sentence (2) the object follows the verb:

(1) ভেঙে যায় সাজানো সংসার, ঘরবাড়ি আর জীবনের ব্যবস্থাগুলো।
Tidy social structures, houses and life's arrangement are all destroyed.

(2) রাশি রাশি জল ডুবিয়ে দেয় ফসলের ক্ষেত।
Wave after wave of water submerges the fields and harvests.

Vocabulary: Narrative

Note: There are a lot of new words here but you should now be able to make a sensible decision on which words you want to learn straightaway and which you can save for later.

পদ্মা pɔdma (pɔdda) *name* Padma (Podda) *(river)*

ছড়ানো chɔṛano *vb.* spread

দেবতা debôta *n.* god

শিব śib *name* Shiva *(god)*

কন্যা kɔnya (kɔnna) *n.* daughter

গঙ্গা gɔṅga *name* Ganges *(river)*

হিমালয় himalɔy *name* Himalayas *(mountain range)*

পশ্চিম বাংলা pôścim baṃla *name* Paschim Banga (West Bengal)

ভুল bhu:l *n.* mistake

ভুল করা bhu:l kɔra *vb.* make a mistake

ভুল করে bhu:l kôre *adv.* accidentally

যাই হোক yai hok *expr.* in any case

পথচলা pɔthcɔla *n.* journey

মিতালি mitali *n.* alliance

ফরিদপুর phôridpur *name* Faridpur *(town)*

যমুনা yômuna *name* Jamuna *(river)*

সাথে sathe *pp.* with

চাঁদপুর cãdpur *name* Chandpur *(town)*

মেঘনা meghna *name* Meghna *(river)*

গলাগলি করে gɔlagôli kôre *adv.* intertwined

বঙ্গোপসাগর bɔṅgôpsagôr *name* Bay of Bengal

বুক buk *n.* breast, chest

অসীম ɔsīm *adj.* endless

সাগর sagôr *n.* sea, ocean

মিশে যাওয়া miśe yaoẏa *cvb.* mingle, flow into

আনন্দ anôndô *n.* joy, pleasure

প্রাণ praṇ *n.* life

বাঁচানো bācano *vb.* save, rescue

বাঁচিয়ে রাখা bāciẏe rakha *cvb.* keep alive

সৃষ্টি sṛṣṭi (srishṭi) *n.* creation

সৃষ্টি করা sṛṣṭi (srishṭi) kɔra *vb.* create

সৌন্দর্য soundôryô *n.* beauty

ভাগ bhag *n.* part

স্থল sthɔl *n.* land, dry land

একমাত্র æ̃kmatro *adj.* only

চলাচল cɔlacɔl *n.* coming and going

মোটরগাড়ি moṭôrgaṛi *n.* motorcar

রেলগাড়ি relgaṛi *n.* train, railway

উড়োজাহাজ uṛojahaj *n.* airplane

দেশান্তর deśantôr *n.* another country

ভরসা bhɔrsa *n.* support, refuge, prop

নদনদী nôdnôdī *n.* waterways

তীর tīr *n.* bank (of a river)

গড়া gɔṛa *vb.* build, form

গড়ে ওঠা gôṛe oṭha *cvb.* be established, be built

প্রাচীন pracīn *adj.* old, ancient

রাজধানী rajdhanī *n.* capital

নগর nɔgôr *n.* town

ইতিহাস itihas *n.* history

রাজা raja *n.* king

রাজত্ব rajôtvô *n.* kingdom

বদলানো bɔdlano *vb.* change

মানচিত্র mancitrô *n.* map

স্থান sthan *n.* place

ডাক ḍak *n.* call

শান্ত śantô *adj.* peaceful

ঘুমিয়ে-থাকা ghumiẏe-thaka *adj.* sleeping

ঢেউ ḍheu *n.* wave

জাগা jaga *vb.* wake up, awake

নীল nīl *adj.* blue

আয়না aẏna *n.* mirror

ধান dhan *n.* paddy, rice

সোনা sona *n./adj.* gold

চাষী caṣī *n.* farmer

স্বপ্ন svɔpnô *n.* dream

জাগানো jagano *vb.* cause to wake, awaken

গর্ব gɔrbô *n.* pride

ধীরে dhīre *adv.* slowly, gradually

রূপ rūp *n.* shape, form

বৈশাখ boiśakh *n.* Baishakh *(first month of the Bengali year)*

অস্থির ɔsthir *adj.* restless

বর্ষাকাল bɔrṣakal *n.* rainy season, monsoon

জেগে ওঠা jege oṭha *cvb.* wake up

ভয়ংকর bhɔŷômkɔr *adj.* frightening

জোয়ার joŷar *n.* flow, tide

ভাসানো bhasano *vb.* cause to float

সাজানো sajano *vb.* equip, fit out

সংসার sɔṁsar *n.* world; family

ঘরবাড়ি ghɔrbaṛi *n.* houses, buildings

ব্যবস্থা bybôstha (bæbôstha) *n.* arrangement

রাশি raśi *n.* heap

ডুবিয়ে দেওয়া ḍubiŷe deoŷa *cvb.* cause to drown, wash away

ফসল phɔsôl *n.* harvest

ক্ষেত kṣet (khet) *n.* field

গৌরব gourob *n.* glory, pride

নষ্ট হওয়া nɔṣṭô hɔoŷa *vb.* get destroyed, get spoiled

ধ্বংস dhvɔṁsô *n.* destruction

বহু bôhu *adj.* many

কপাল kɔpal *n.* forehead; luck

Additional Vocabulary: Abstract nouns

If you have been learning your new words conscientiously as they appeared from unit to unit, you will notice that quite a few of these nouns are already familiar to you and also that there are plenty of other abstract nouns in the rest of the book. You are now moving from basic to intermediate vocabulary.

anger রাগ rag

beauty সৌন্দর্য soundôryô

beginning আরম্ভ arɔmbhô

belief বিশ্বাস biśvas (bisshash)

comfort আরাম aram

consideration বিবেচনা bibecôna

courage সাহস sahôs

culture সংস্কৃতি sɔṁskr̥ti (shongskriti)

death মৃত্যু mr̥tyu (mritu)

defeat পরাজয় pɔrajɔŷ

democracy গণতন্ত্র gɔṇôtɔntrô

destruction ধ্বংস dhvɔṁsô (dhɔngshô)

disappointment হতাশা hɔtaśa

doubt সন্দেহ sɔndehô

dream স্বপ্ন svɔpnô

end ইতি iti, শেষ śeṣ

future ভবিষ্যৎ bhôbiṣyɔṯ

gain লাভ labh

geography ভূগোল bhūgol

government সরকার sɔrkar

heaven স্বর্গ svɔrgô

hell নরক nɔrôk

history ইতিহাস itihas

hope আশা aśa

illusion মায়া maŷa

imagination কল্পনা kɔlpôna

independence স্বাধীনতা svadhīnôta

injustice অন্যায় ɔnyaŷ (onnay)

joy আনন্দ anôndô

justice ন্যায় nyaŷ (nay)

knowledge জ্ঞান jñan (gæn)

lie *(untruth)* মিথ্যা mithya (mittha)

life জীবন jībôn

loss লোকসান loksan

luck ভাগ্য bhagyô

memory স্মৃতি smr̥ti (sriti)

nature প্রকৃতি prôkr̥ti (prokriti)

neglect অবহেলা ɔbôhela

opinion মত mɔ:t

oppression অত্যাচার ɔtyacar

past অতীত ɔtīt

peace শান্তি śanti

reality বাস্তবতা bastôbôta

sadness দুঃখ duḥkhô

suffering কষ্ট kɔṣṭô

tradition ঐতিহ্য oitihyô (oitijjho)

trust আস্থা astha

truth সত্যি sôtyi

turmoil ঝামেলা jhamela

untruth মিথ্যা mithya (mittha)

victory জয় jɔŷ

wisdom বুদ্ধি buddhi

Exercises: Unit 14

Exercise 14:1
Answer the following questions in Bangla about the Narrative (পদ্মা):

(i)   গল্পটা বলেছে কে?

(ii)   পদ্মার মা-বাবার কথা কি বলা হয়েছে?

(iii) পদ্মা ফরিদপুর এসে আরও বড় হয়ে যায় কি করে?

(iv)   চাঁদপুরে কি হয়েছে?

(v)   বঙ্গোপসাগর কি?

(vi)   নদীকে বাংলাদেশের প্রাণ বলা হয় কেন?

(vii) শহর কেন নদীর তীরে গড়ে উঠল?

(viii) শীতকালে নদী শান্ত থাকে কি কারণে?

(ix)   বৈশাখ মাস কোন ঋতুতে হয়?

(x)   নদী গ্রীষ্মকালে বিপজ্জনক হয়ে যায় কেমন করে?

Exercise 14:2
Find a synonym (a word that means the same) for the following words:

(i)   কন্যা _____   (vi)   প্রাচীন _____

(ii)   মিতালি _____   (vii) স্থান _____

(iii) প্রাণ _____   (viii) বদলানো _____

(iv)   স্থল _____   (ix)   ক্ষেত _____

(v)   দেশান্তর _____   (x)   কপাল _____

Exercise 14:3
Opposites – give the Bangla equivalents of the English noun pairs:

(i)   life   death   _____   _____

(ii)   dream   reality   _____   _____

(iii)   beginning   end   _____   _____

(iv)   future   past   _____   _____

(v)   nature   culture   _____   _____

(vi)   gain   loss   _____   _____

(vii)   victory   defeat   _____   _____

(viii)   independence   oppression   _____   _____

(ix)   truth   lie   _____   _____

(x)   heaven   hell   _____   _____

(xi)   joy   sadness   _____   _____

(xii)   peace   turmoil   _____   _____

(xiii)   justice   injustice   _____   _____

(xiv)   belief   doubt   _____   _____

(xv)   comfort   suffering   _____   _____

BANGLA GRAMMAR OVERVIEW

This sections gives a brief overview of the main components of Bangla grammar and where in the book these components are featured.

Word Order
(Unit 14: Grammar 30)

Basic word order in Bangla is S (Subject) – O (Object) – V (Verb):

আমি কাজ করি।
ami   kaj   kôri
I   work do   = *I work.*

সে রিনাকে   ভালবাসে।
se rinake   bhalôbase
He Rina + obj. loves   =   *He loves Rina.*

Due to case endings and verb conjugation, word order in Bengali is relatively flexible.

Sentence Types
(Unit 2: Grammar 1; Unit 10: Grammar 24)

* Dynamic sentences have an active subject and a *doing* verb (with or without an object) whose ending agrees with the subject.

* Equational sentences such as *He is my friend* or *Today is Wednesday* have a zero verb in Bangla:

তুমি আমার বন্ধু।
tumi amar bôndhu
you   my   friend   =   *You are my friend.*

আজ বুধবার।
aj   budhbar
today Wednesday   =   *Today is Wednesday.*

* Existential/locative (*There are problems / We are here*) and possessive (*I have a bicycle*) structures are formed with the incomplete verb আছ ach– *be, exist*:

সমস্যা   আছে।
sɔmsya ache
problems exist   =   *There are problems.*

আমরা এখানে আছি।
amra ekhane achi
We   here   are   = *We are here.*

আমার সাইকেল আছে।
amar saikel ache
Of me bicycle exists = *I have a bicycle.*

- Impersonal structures are used particularly for expressing feelings and sensations. Impersonal structures do not have agreement between a nominative subject and the verb. The subject in these sentences is often in the genitive.

তার খারাপ লাগছে।
tar   kharap   lagche
of him bad   is attaching = *He is feeling ill.*

তোমার কি শীত করছে?
tomar ki śīt kôrche
of you what cold is making = *Are you feeling cold?*

তার ভয় করছে।
tar   bhɔŷ   kôrche
of him fear   is doing = *He is scared.*

Word Classes

Nouns
(Unit 4: Grammar 5; Unit 5: Grammar 6)

- Nouns have four cases: nominative, genitive, objective, locative. Inanimate nouns (things) do not usually take the object case ending. Animate nouns (people) do not usually take the locative.

nominative: sg.: no ending
             pl.: –রা –ra, –গুলো –gulo
                  বইগুলো bôigulo *books*, মেয়েরা meŷera *girls*

genitive: sg.: র –r, এর –er
                  বাবার babar *father's*, বাড়ির baṛir *of the home*, বোনের boner *sister's*
             pl.: –দের der, –গুলোর gulor
                  লোকদের lokder *of the people*, গানগুলোর gangulor *of the songs*

objective: sg.: –কে –ke
                  মানুষকে manuṣke *to the person*
             pl.: –দের –der, –দেরকে –derke, –গুলো / গুলিকে –gulo/ gulike
                  বাচ্চাদের baccader *to the children*,
                  ছেলেদেরকে chelederke *to the boys*,
                  গরুগুলিকে gôrugulike *to the cows*

locative: sg.: –এ e, –তে –te –য় –ŷ

গ্রামে grame *in the village,* নদীতে nodīte *on the river,*
থানায় thanaŷ *at the police-station*

pl.: –গুলো /গুলিতে –gulo/gulite
থালাগুলিতে thalagulite *on the plates*

- Classifiers –টা –ṭa, –টি –ṭi, –জন –jɔn, –খানা –khana, –গুলো –gulo, –গুলি –guli are attached to nouns to form definite and indefinite noun phrases and to distinguish singular and plural. They can, unlike articles in English, occur with possessive adjectives and demonstratives.

আমার এই কলমটা
amar ei kɔlômṭa
my   this pen + cl. = *this pen of mine*

When a quantifier *(much, many, some, a little)* or a numeral precedes the noun, the classifier is added to them, not to the noun:

অনেকটা ফল   ছয়জন সাংবাদিক
ɔnekṭa phɔl   chɔŷjɔn saṃbadik
much + Cl fruit = *a lot of fruit*   six + Cl journalist = six journalists

- Indefinite noun phrases are formed by adding the singular classifier to the word এক æk *(one)*, e.g.:

definite   indefinite

মানুষটি manuṣṭi *the person*   একটি মানুষ ekṭi manuṣ *a person*
কলমটা kɔlômṭa *the pen*   একটা কলম æktạ kɔlôm *a pen*
বইখানা bôikhana *the book*   একখানা বই ækkhana bôi *a book*

for plural indefinites no classifier is used, e.g.:

definite   indefinite

মানুষগুলো manuṣgulo *the people*   মানুষ manuṣ *people*
কলমগুলি kɔlômguli *the pens*   কলম kɔlôm *pens*

Pronouns
(Unit 3: Grammar 3; Unit 7: Grammar 13; Unit 13: Grammar 29)

Bangla has the following types of pronouns: personal, inanimate, interrogative (question) pronouns are introduced in Unit 3, Grammar 3 (page 56), indefinite pronouns in Unit 7, Grammar 13 (page 123), and relative pronouns in Unit 13, Grammar 29 (page 237).

Bangla pronouns do not distinguish male and female. সে se: (ordinary) and তিনি tini (honorific) can mean both *he* and *she.* Both second and third person pronouns distinguish between ordinary/familiar (তুমি tumi *you* and সে se *he, she*) and honorific/polite address (আপনি apni *you* and তিনি tini *he, she*). Third person forms additionally distinguish proximity: এ e *this one here,* ও o *that one there,* সে se: *he, she, it* (neutral). Pronoun charts are given in Unit 3.

In addition to the forms given in this book there is an intimate 2nd person তুই tui (sg.) and তোরা tora (pl.), that is used between school friends and siblings. Foreigners are unlikely to need these forms but it is good to be aware of them.

Verbs
(Unit 6: Grammar 9)

Unit 6 deals extensively with all aspects of verbs. Verb charts are given in Appendix 3. Bangla verb conjugation is very regular. Verbs are conjugated according to person and tense. There is no difference between singular and plural verb endings and no gender distinction either in pronouns or in verb forms. Second person polite and third person honorific conjugate the same.

There is a regular vowel shift from high to low stem in present simple verb forms:

আমি লিখি ami likhi *I write*   তুমি লেখ tumi lekho *you write*
আমি দেখি ami dekhi *I see*   তুমি দেখ tumi dækho *you see*
আমি বুঝি ami bujhi *I understand*   তুমি বোঝ tumi bojho *you understand*
আমি বলি ami boli *I say*   তুমি বল tumi bɔlo *you say*

Bengali has eight tenses: present simple, present continuous, present perfect, future tense, past simple, past continuous, past perfect, past habitual.

For specific verb forms the endings for tense and person are added to the stem of the verb.

Non-finite verb forms
Every Bengali verb has four non-finite verb forms: verbal noun (VN / Unit 10: Grammar 22, page 180), imperfective participle (IP / Unit 10: Grammar 23, page 181), perfective participle (PP / Unit 9: Grammar 19, page 155), and conditional participle (CP / Unit 11: Grammar 25, page 197). They have a variety of uses and occur in connection with finite (conjugated) verb forms. Non-finite verb forms play an important part in Bengali sentence dynamics.

Adjectives
(Unit 8: Grammar 15 and 16)

Adjectives can be used attributively before nouns:

একটা সুন্দর বাগান ækṭa sundôr bagan *a beautiful garden*
এই মিষ্টি আম ei miṣṭi a:m *this sweet mango*
আমার লাল শাড়ি amar la:l śaṛi *my red saree*

or predicatively in equational structures:

তাদের বাড়ি খুব ছোট। tader baṛi khub choṭô. *Their house is very small.*
আমার সাইকেল ভাঙা। amar saikel bhaṅa. *My bicycle is broken.*

Comparisons are formed with simple adjective forms:

তুমি আমার চেয়ে চালাক।
tumi amar ceye calak
you   than   me   clever = *You are cleverer than me.*

No comparative or superlative adjective forms need to be learned. Comparatives are formed with আরও aro *more* and চেয়ে ceye *more than*, superlatives with সবচেয়ে shɔbceye *than all*:

ভাল bhalô	আরও ভাল aro bhalô	সবচেয়ে ভাল sɔbceŷe bhalô
good	*better*	*best*

সে তোমার চেয়ে লম্বা। se tomar ceŷe lɔmba.
He is taller than you.

Equal comparisons are formed with the postposition মত mɔto *like*:

আকাশের মত বড় akaśer mɔto bɔrô *as big as the sky*
তোমার মত সুন্দর tomar mɔto sundôr *as beautiful as you*

Adverbs

• Adverbs can be formed from adjectives by adding করে kore *having done* or ভাবে bhabe *in the way*:

নরম nɔrôm *soft*	নরমভাবে nɔrômbhabe *softly*
ভাল bhalo *good*	ভাল করে bhalo kore *well*

• Adding এ *e* to some nouns and adjectives produces adverbs:

সহজ shɔhôj *easy*	সহজে shɔhôje *easily*
আসল asôl *actual*	আসলে asôle *actually*
গোপন gopon *hidden*	গোপনে gopone *secretly*

• Some adverbs are formed from nouns and adjectives by adding -ɔto:

বিশেষত biśeṣɔtô *especially*	সাধারণত sadharônɔtô *usually*
প্রধানত prôdhanɔtô *mainly*	সম্ভবত sɔmbhôbɔtô *possibly*

• But there are also a great number of underived adverbs, such as:

দারুণ darun *very*	আস্তে aste *slowly*	ধীরে dhīre *slowly*
খুব khub *very*	তাড়াতাড়ি taṛataṛi *quickly*	হঠাৎ hɔṭhat *suddenly*
বেশ beś *quite*	ভীষণ bhīṣôn *extremely*	প্রায় pray *almost*
শুধু śudhu *only*	মাত্র matrô *only*	কেবল kebôl *only*

Interrogatives
(Unit 4: Grammar 4)

Interrogatives do not make up a word class of their own. They are pronouns, adjectives, and adverbs. The main Bangla question words are:

কে ke: *who*   কি ki: *what*   কেন kæno *why*   কোন kon *which*
কোথায় kothay *where*   কবে kɔbe *when*   কখন kɔkhon *when*
কেমন kæmon *how*   কত kɔto *how much*   কয়টা kɔyṭa *how many*

Postpositions
(Unit 5: Grammar 7)

Postpositions are equivalent to prepositions *(in, on, with, over, for,* etc.) and appear after the noun they position. Most Bengali spatial postpositions are locative noun forms and require a preceding genitive:

টেবিলের   উপরে
ṭebiler   upore
of the table   on top   =   *on the table*

• Some postpositions are derived from verbs — the preceding noun is in the nominative:

ছুরি   দিয়ে
churi diye
knife   having given = with   =   *with a knife*

রান্না-ঘর   থেকে
ranna-ghɔr theke
kitchen   having stayed = from   =   *from the kitchen*

• There are also some non-derived postpositions whose case uses need to be learned:

মত mɔto *as, like* (with preceding genitive):
বিজলির মত bijolir mɔto *like lightning*

পর্যন্ত porjonto *until* (with preceding nominative):
সোমবার পর্যন্ত shombar porjonto *until Monday*

জন্য jɔnno, জন্যে jɔnne *for* (with preceding genitive):
তোমার জন্যে tomar jɔnne *for you*

Conjunctions (joining words)
(Unit 13: Grammar 28)

Bengali has three ways of joining sentences:

• with coordinating conjunctions to connect two main clauses, e.g.:

আর ar *and,* এবং ebɔng *and,* কিন্তু kintu *but,* বা ba *or,* কারণ karon *because,*
সুতরাং sutôrang *hence, therefore,* কাজেই kajei *so, therefore,*
তাই tai *so, therefore,* তবে tɔbe *but,* তারপর tarpɔr *then, afterwards*

- with single subordinating conjunctions (there are very few of those) to join a subordinate clause to a main clause:

  যে je *that*, যেন jæno *so that*, যাতে jate *so that*, পাছে pache *so that not*, বলে bole *that*

- with correlative conjunctions or pronouns

  Correlative structures usually have a preceding subordinate clause, with a relative conjunction/pronoun, followed by the correlative pronoun/conjunction introducing the main clause. Correlatives are explained in Unit 13: Grammar 29 (page 237). Here are the main correlative pairs:

যখন	তখন	*when*
যত	তত	*as much as*
যদি	তাহলে / তবে	*if – then* (conditional)
যদিও	তবুও	*although*
যা	তা	*what*
যে	সে	*who*
যে	তা	*what – that*
যেমন	তেমন	*such, as – as*
যেখানে	সেখানে	*where*
যেদিন	সেদিন	*that day*
যেভাবে	সেভাবে	*in that way*

Particles

Particles are words that are not syntactically necessary but have a decisive influence on the perspective or attitude of a sentence or statement. They are not usually translatable as individual words but gain their meaning in context. Common particles are:

তো to	তোমাকেই তো সবই বলি।	tomake to sɔbi boli	*But I tell you everything.*
ই i	আমি কিছুই করিনি।	ami kichui korini	*I didn't do anything at all.*
ও o	তিনি তাও জানতেন না।	tini tao janten na	*He didn't even know that.*
তা ta	তা কি বলছ?	ta ki bolcho	*What exactly are you saying?*
বা ba	তুমিই বা যাবে কেন?	tumii ba jabe kæno	*Why on earth would you go?*
যে je	তার সঙ্গে আজ দেখা হয়নি যে।	tar shɔngge a:j dækha hɔyni je	*I didn't see him today — that's why ...*

Onomatopoeia

One characteristic feature of Bengali is its rich stock of onomatopoeia, words that represent sounds, emotions, and visual and other sensory impressions. These words are often doubled to make one word. Onomatopoeia add color and spice to the language and are an essential ingredient of Bengali literature. Onomatopoeia are not dealt with in this book as they belong to a more advanced stage of learning. Here are some examples:

আমি থরো থরো কম্পমান।   ami thɔro thɔro kɔmpôman
I was shivering violently.

ফিসফিস করে বলল।   phishphish kore bollo.
He spoke in a whisper.

বাচ্চাটি ভয়ে হাউমাউ করে কেঁদে উঠল।   baccaṭi bhɔŷe haumau kôre kẽde uṭhlô.
The child was so scared that he started wailing.

সব ব্যাপারে এত খুঁতখুঁত হলে চলে না।   sɔb byapare etô khũtkhũt hôle cɔle na.
It won't do to be so petty about everything.

পুকুরের জল টলমল।   pukurer jɔl ṭɔlmɔl.
The water of the lake was churning.

সারা শহর থমথম হয়ে আছে।   sara śɔhor thɔmthɔm hôŷe ache.
The whole town was eerily silent.

Syntactic economy

Bangla sentences and phrases apply a NEED-TO-KNOW principle, which means that necessary information is given only once. This principle applies throughout the language. In the English sentence *I have three books* there are two indicators for the plural: the number three and the plural s-ending on books. In Bangla we follow the NEED-TO-KNOW principle and say *I have three book.* In order to avoid doubling of information, sentences containing specific dates or years usually keep their verbs in the present simple tense, so in Bangla we say *I am born in 1976.* Bangla employs classifiers rather than articles to distinguish singular vs. plural and definite vs. indefinite. Classifiers work together with numbers, quantifiers, and case endings to make noun phrases. Again this system is designed according to the NEED-TO-KNOW principle, whereas in English every noun has to be marked as either definite or indefinite.

ANSWER KEY TO EXERCISES

Unit 1

Exercise 1:1a

মা ma, পা pa:, গা ga:, মামা mama, মাল mal, মালা mala, লাল lal, কাল kal, গাল gal, চাল cal, দল dɔl, কল kɔl, ফল phɔl, চলা cɔla, কলা kɔla, গলা gɔla, তলা tɔla, বলা bɔla, মশা mɔśa, শসা śɔsa, কষা kɔṣa, দশা dɔśa, রাত rat, ভাত bhat, সাত sat, হাত hat, কাথা katha, কান kan, টান ṭan, গান gan, ধান dhan, থানা thana, দাম dam, নাম nam, আম am, খাম kham, তামা tama, থামা thama, নামা nama, আর ar, কার kar, তার tar, বার bar, তারা tara, মারা mara, কারা kara, সারা sara, হারা hara, চিনি cini, কিনি kini, তিনি tini, তিমি timi, চিঠি ciṭhi, দুপুর dupur, নুপুর nupur, পুকুর pukur, কুকুর kukur, সকাল sɔkal, বিকাল bikal

Exercise 1:1b *(each row across are answers to a column in the exercise)*

গান, বাগান, মা, মাল, লাল, আম, আমি, আমার, আমরা, রাত, দিন
মালি, লিপি, নাক, কান, চাঁদ, কাটা, হাঁটা, আসা, মিনিট, বিকাল, মাস

কলা, গলা, গরম, খবর, সকল, নরম
কলম, শহর, বছর, অনেক, অলস

কুকুর, পুকুর, দুপুর, খুব, উকিল
আগুন, গুলি, মুখ, চুল

ছেলে, এলোমেলো, মেলা, মেঝে
বেলা, থেকে, গেলে

Exercise 1:2a

(i) দেরি   (ii) গলি   (iii) চুমু   (iv) মেঝে   (v) চাবি   (vi) পারি   (vii) বালু   (viii) ভাল   (ix) চাকা   (x) শুনি   (xi) ছেলে   (xii) খারাপ   (xiii) চামচ   (xiv) কাগজ   (xv) নতুন   (xvi) গোলাপী   (xvii) কমলা   (xviii) বিমান   (xix) মানুষ   (xx) পুরুষ

Exercise 1:3a

(i) কেউ   (ii) দুই   (iii) খাই   (iv) দই   (v) বিয়ে   (vi) মেয়ে   (vii) পাওয়া   (viii) ধোয়া   (ix) দেওয়াল   (x) শিয়াল

Exercise 1:3b

(i) maŷer (ii) dui (iii) paoŷa (iv) kheŷal (v) jɔŷ (vi) reoŷaj (vii) niu (viii) khai (ix) kauke (x) hôŷe (xi) rehai (xii) iurop

Exercise 1:3c

(i) শোয়া (ii) উপায় (iii) দায়ী (iv) ক্রিয়া (v) রুই (vi) দেওয়াল (vii) মেয়াদ (viii) হওয়া (ix) রায় (x) শয়তান

Exercise 1:3d

(i) উনুন (ii) ইনি (iii) এলেবেলে (iv) ওরা (v) ইতিহাস (vi) আমার (vii) অমর (viii) তৈরি (ix) নৌকা (x) উপকার

Exercise 1:4a

(i) ছাত্র (ii) শক্তি (iii) সঙ্গে (iv) গ্রাম (v) বিশ্বাস (vi) শান্তি (vii) শুক্রবার (viii) আন্দাজ (ix) মিষ্টি (x) আস্তে

Exercise 1:4b

(i) ন্ন (উন্নতি)   (ii) স্ত (রাস্তা)   (iii) ন (অন্তর)   (iv) গ (সঙ্গে)   (v) ত (উত্তর)   (vi) ন্দ (সুন্দর)
(vii) ষ (অক্ষর)   (viii) জ (বিজ্ঞান)   (ix) দ্ধ (বুদ্ধি)   (x) ম্প (কম্প)

Exercise 1:5

(i) প্র (প্রতি)   (ii) গ (গৃ/hm)   (iii) র্ম (ধর্ম)   (iv) ত (মাত্রা)   (v) র (তর্ক)   (vi) র্শ (আদর্শ)
(vii) ব্র (ব্রিজ)   (viii) য (পর্যন্ত)   (ix) ত (মুহূর্ত)   (x) ভ্র (ভ্রমণ)

Unit 2

Exercise 2:1: Grammar practice

(i) c   (ii) a   (iii) c   (iv) b   (v) a

Exercise 2:2: Script practice

(i) কয়েকটা   (ii) এগুলো   (iii) তোমাকে   (iv) এতে   (v) জিনিস   (vi) বাংলায়
(vii) অনেক   (viii) কলম   (ix) ছবি   (x) কমপিউটার

Unit 3

Exercise 3:1

(i) আমার *my*   (ii) কারা *who (pl.)*   (iii) ওরা *they*   (iv) তোমার *your*   (v) উনি *he (hon.)*
(vi) তুমি *you*   (vii) তোমাকে *you (obj.)*   (viii) আমরা *we*   (ix) কে *who*   (x) তাদের *their, them*

Exercise 3:2

(i)   এটা কি তোমার কলম? *Is this your pen?*
(ii)   তোমার বাবা কি সাংবাদিক? *Is your father a journalist?*
(iii)   তোমার কি তিনটি ছোট বোন আছে? *Do you have three little sisters?*
(iv)   মহিষ কি খুব বড়? *Are water buffaloes very big?*
(v)   তোমার কি কয়েকটা ছবি আছে? *Do you have a few pictures?*
(vi)   এগুলো কি তোমার পড়ার টেবিলের জিনিস? *Are these the things on your desk?*
(vii)   উনার নাম কি সিলভিয়া? *Is her name Sylvia?*
(viii)   এটা কি একটা গ্রামের ছবি? *Is this a picture of a village.*
(ix)   তাদের কি অনেক শক্তি আছে? *Are they very strong?*
(x)   এইবার কি আমার পালা? *Is it my turn now?*

Exercise 3:3

গা	লি	তো	কু	পি	উ
এক	আ	মার	অন	ভা	নি
কো	থাক	হে	তা	দের	সা
আ	শো	টি	যে	ঠো	উন
মা	মূ	তু	মি	সু	ই
দের	নীল	বন	থে	ও	রা
যা	কা	রা	আম	ভুল	প্র
ছি	হয়	ত	রা	আ	মি

Exercise 3:4

(i) *This is very big.*

(ii) *Is this your picture?*

(iii) *I don't know.*

(iv) *She is my sister.*

(v) *What is his name?*

(vi) *I don't have a brother.*

(vii) *Your sister is young.*

(viii) *His father's name is Luis.*

(ix) *My mother works in an office.*

(x) *He is their only son.*

Exercise 3:5

(i) আমার তিনটি বোন খুব ছোট।

(ii) সে আমার ভাই।

(iii) এটা একটা নদী।

(iv) আমার কয়েকটা জিনিস আছে।

(v) এখানে অনেক কলম আছে।

(vi) আমরা এটা ইংরেজিতে বলি।

(vii) আমার বোন নেই।

(viii) এখানে একটা পুকুর আছে।

(ix) তারা কারা?

(x) তোমার নাম কি?

Unit 4

Exercise 4:1

(i)   What is Bimol's daughter's name?

(ii)   How far is Chapra from Kolkata?

(iii)   Where is Bimol's house?

(iv)   At what time do they phone?

(v)   At whose house is Saida?

(vi)   What is Saida's mother's name?

(vii)   Who is Rohim?

(viii) What are the mangoes in Bimol's garden like?

(ix)   How many papaya trees are there in the garden?

(x)   At what time will Rohim come to their house?

Exercise 4:2

(i)   বিমলের বাগানে একটা আম গাছ আছে।

(ii)   বিমলের ছেলের নাম ফটিক।

(iii)   শালিনির বয়স দেড় বছর।

(iv)   ঘরের সামনে বারান্দা।

(v)   বিমলের গ্রামের নাম ছাপড়া।

(vi)   পেঁপে গাছের ফল পেঁপে।

(vii)   না, বিমলেরর আম গাছটার আমগুলো বেশি মিষ্টি নয়।

(viii) বিমলের বাড়িতে তার বউ আর দুটি ছেলেমেয়ে আছে।

(ix)   বাড়ির মাঝখানে উঠান।

(x)   রান্নাঘর বারান্দর ডান দিকে।

Exercise 4:3

(i)   মায়ের বাগান *mother's garden*

(ii)   বিমলের বাড়ি *Bimol's homestead*

(iii)   ঘরের দেওয়াল *the walls of the building*

(iv)   উঠানের পাশে *to the side of the courtyard*

(v)   মেয়ের নাম *the girl's name*

(vi)   বাগানের গাছ *trees in the garden*

(vii)   গাছের ফল *fruits on the trees*

(viii) গ্রামের দক্ষিণে *to the south of the village*

(ix)   ছেলের বয়স *the boy's age*

(x)   চাচার বাড়িতে *the uncle's house*

Exercise 4:4

গাছ *tree*   কলম *pen*   গ্রাম *village*   আম *mango*   বাগান *garden*   বাড়ি *house*
ছবি *picture*   নদী *river*   ফল *fruit*   পুকুর *lake*   রাত *night*   রাস্তা *road*   দিন *day*
বারান্দা *verandah*   উঠান *courtyard*

Unit 5

Exercise 5:1

(i)   *my pens*
(ii)   *the girl*
(iii)   *his wife's name*
(iv)   *a small garden*
(v)   *many banana plants*

(vi)   *my younger sister*
(vii)   *two rickshaws*
(viii)   *this big road*
(ix)   *dogs*
(x)   *the books*

(xi)   অনেক মেয়ে or অনেকগুলো মেয়ে
(xii)   এক বছর
(xiii)   তার বাগানে
(xiv)   তার মায়ের বাগানে
(xv)   সাপগুলো

(xvi)   কয়টি বোন
(xvii)   একজন সাংবাদিক
(xviii)   তোমার ভাইয়েরা
(xix)   তিন দিন
(xx)   এই গ্রামটা

Exercise 5:2

See translations in the dialogues and narratives.

Exercise 5:3

(i)   *for you*
(ii)   *in front of the house*
(iii)   *like my pen*
(iv)   *to the right of the verandah*
(v)   *with his younger sisters*
(vi)   *from Kolkata*
(vii)   *among the fruit trees*
(viii)   *in the middle of the day*
(ix)   *from (a person)*
(x)   *within the town*
(xi)   *three years ago*
(xii)   *from next month*
(xiii)   *until night*
(xiv)   *outside the courtyard*
(xv)   *northwards*

(xvi)   বাড়ির কাছে
(xvii)   টেবিলের নিচে
(xviii)   ট্রেনের ভিতরে
(xix)   গতকাল পর্যন্ত
(xx)   তখন থেকে
(xxi)   গ্রামের পিছনে
(xxii)   তোমার বাবার সঙ্গে
(xxiii)   আমার বড় ভাইয়ের মত
(xxiv)   রাতের আগে
(xxv)   শহরের দিকে
(xxvi)   পশ্চিমে
(xxvii)   সোমবারের পরে
(xxviii)   শনিবার পর্যন্ত
(xxix)   সকাল থেকে রাত পর্যন্ত
(xxx)   পূর্বে or পূর্বের দিকে

Unit 6

Exercise 6:1

(i) তোলে   (ii) থেমেছি   (iii) শোনে   (iv) পেরেছি   (v) জানি
(vi) ঢুকি   (vii) পড়ে   (viii) এনেছি   (ix) ঘুরি   (x) কেটেছি

Exercise 6:2

(i) চেনা   (ii) শোনা   (iii) দেখা   (iv) আসা   (v) লেখা
(vi) পড়া   (vii) বোঝা   (viii) আনা   (ix) বসা   (x) ফেরা

Exercise 6:3

(i) এসেছি   (ii) থেকেছি   (iii) শুনেছি   (iv) দেখেছি   (v) করেছি
(vi) রেখেছি   (vii) জেনেছি   (viii) পড়েছি   (ix) ধরেছি   (x) কিনেছি

Exercise 6:4

(i)   আমি একটা কলম কিনেছি।
(ii)   আমি ছবিটা দেখেছি।
(iii)   ওরা ছবিটা দেখবে।
(iv)   আমরা এই কলমগুলি কিনব না।
(v)   ও আসবে না। or উনি আসবে না।
(vi)   তুমি কি আসবে? or আপনি কি আসবেন?
(vii)   উনি সকালে অফিসে যাবেন।
(viii) আমি তোমাকে তাদের নাম বলব।
(ix)   তারা ছবিগুলো দেখছে।
(x)   আমরা অফিসে যাব না।
(xi)   সে সকালে এসেছে।
(xii)   সে তোমাকে তার নাম বলবে।
(xiii) এই কলমটা তোমার কি ভাল লাগে?
(xiv)   সে আইসক্রিম কিনবে।
(xv)   আমি ছেলেটিকে দেখেছি।
(xvi)   আমরা মেয়েটিকে দেখেছি / দেখলাম।
(xvii) ছেলেটি সকালে আসবে।
(xviii) ও আইসক্রিম খাচ্ছে।
(xix)   আইসক্রিমটা তাদের ভাল লেগেছে।
(xx)   আপনারা অফিসে আসবেন।

Exercise 6:5

(i)   আমি / আমরা   *I am / we are going to Bonpara.*
(ii)   আপনি / আপনারা   *Have you eaten?*
(iii)   তুমি   *You will write the letter.*
(iv)   সে   *She is not here.*
(v)   তুমি   *Can you give me ten taka?*
(vi)   তুমি   *Will you come tomorrow afternoon?*
(vii)   সে   *Where does she work?*
(viii) আমি   *I went to the market with my father.*
(ix)   আমি   *I don't know your brother.*
(x)   আমার   *I don't have a car.*
(xi)   উনি   *He lives in Kolkata.*
(xii)   তুমি   *Will you not go to the office?*
(xiii) আমি   *I will phone you.*
(xiv)   আমিনা বেগুম   *Amina Begum has told Rohim about Saida.*
(xv)   তার   *She has two children.*
(xvi)   তুমি   *What did you tell her?*
(xvii) তিনি   *He gets up very early.*
(xviii) আমরা   *We don't eat meat.*
(xix)   তাদের   *They like buffalos very much.*
(xx)   তারা   *They are my friends.*

Unit 7

Exercise 7:1

(i)   তার আমাকে ভাল লাগে।

(ii) আমাদের আরও সময় লাগবে।

(iii) তার হাতে লেগেছে।

(iv) গ্রামটা তার কেমন লাগে?

(v)   খাবার তোমার কেমন লেগেছে?

(vi) তাদের আরও জায়গা লাগবে।

(vii) তোমার কি আরাম লাগছে?

(viii) তার প্রতিবেশীকে তার ভাল লাগে না।

(ix) তার বাগানটা খুব সুন্দর লাগছে।

(x)   এই কাজটা তার খারাপ লাগে।

Exercise 7:2

(i)   আমরা টেবিল বলি না।

(ii)   আমার ভাই নেই।

(iii) এটা বিদেশি জিনিস নয়।

(iv)   তার নাম লুইস নয়।

(v)   আমি একমাত্র ছেলে নই।

(vi)   সাঈদা চলে যায়নি।

(vii) ছোট বোনের কথা মনে পড়ে না।

(viii) আমগাছটার আম মিষ্টি নয়।

(ix)   সে তার চাচার বাড়িতে থাকে না।

(x)   আমার এখানে ভাল লাগেনি।

(xi)   সে রাজশাহীতে যায়নি।

(xii) উনি একটা অফিসে চাকরি করেন না।

(xiii) তারা ছোট নয়।

(xiv) উনি তোমার বাবা নন।

(xv)   আমরা তাই আশা করিনি।

Exercise 7:3

(i)   তুমি আমার ভাই নও।

(ii)   আমার গাড়ি নেই।

(iii) আমার ক্লান্ত লাগছে না।

(iv)   আমরা আমেরিকান নই।

(v)   তার ব্যান্ডেজ লাগবে না।

(vi)   গাড়িটা বাইরে নেই।

(vii) আমার হাতে ব্যথা লাগে না। (ব্যথা = *pain*)

(viii) তার আমাকে ভাল লাগে না।

(ix)   তার আর কিছু লাগবে না।

(x)   তারা বাড়িতে নেই।

Exercise 7:4

(i)   He didn't tell me anything.

(ii)   Do you have any money?

(iii) I am not going anywhere.

(iv)   There aren't any banana trees in Bimol's garden.

(v)   I have never seen the lake.

(vi)   I put the flowers somewhere. *(use present perfect)*

(vii) Nothing can be done.

(viii) He couldn't find anyone at their house. (find = পাওয়া)

(ix)   Did you want to tell me something?

(x)   Has anyone seen my sister today?

(xi)   সে কারও সঙ্গে থাকে না।

(xii) আর কখনও এই কথা বলবে না। *(neg. imperative)*

(xiii) তার কোনও ভাইবোন নেই।

(xiv) সাঈদা কোথাও গিয়েছে নাকি?

(xv)   কেউ এখানে নেই।

(xvi) আমি কিছু শুনিনি।

(xvii) আমরা কোনও গরুর মাংস খাই নি।

(xviii) তুমি কখনও ভারতে গিয়েছ? (ভারত = India)

(xix) তাদের কোনও সবজি ভাল লাগে না।

(xx)   এখানে কোথাও একটা দোকান আছে?

Exercise 7:5

(i) বিকালে

(ii) শুক্রবারে

(iii) দুপুরে

(iv) সকালে

(v) সোমবারে

(vi) বাগানে / বাগানের ভিতরে

(vii) শহরের বাইরে

(viii) রাস্তায়

(ix) রাতে / রাত্রে

(x) এই মাসে

Unit 8

Exercise 8:1

(i) তারা বেশি মাংস খায় না।

(ii) উনি অনেক বাগানের কাজ করেন।

(iii) সার্টটা বেশি বড়।

(iv) গতকাল অনেক লোক এখানে ছিল।

(v) সে আর চা খাবে না।

(vi) আমার আরও থালা দরকার।

(vii) খাবারটা বেশি ভাল ছিল না।

(viii) আমার পরিবারে বেশি মানুষ নেই।

(ix) তারা আরও মাছ ধরেনি।

(x) আমাকে আরও আম দিতে পারেন?

Exercise 8:2

(i) সবচেয়ে   *I had the best sleep here.*

(ii) মত   *Cows are not as strong as buffalos.*

(iii) চেয়ে   *In Bimol's garden there are more banana plants than papaya trees.*

(iv) সবচেয়ে   *I like your garden the best.*

(v) চেয়ে   *A new Buick costs a lot more than ten taka.*

(vi) চেয়ে   *Biplob talks more than Prodip.*

(vii) সবচেয়ে   *They liked the elephants best.*

(viii) আরও   *My master is more stupid.*

(ix) মত   *There is no one like us.*

(x) চেয়ে   *Mr. Khan is a lot younger than Mr. Choudhuri.*

Exercise 8:3

(i) আরও কিছু প্রশ্ন

(ii) বেশি খাবার

(iii) আর একটা চাবি

(iv) আরও দুইটা দেশ

(v) একটু সাহায্য

(vi) *a long way away*

(vii) *a few hours*

(viii) *later*

(ix) *nothing*

(x) *who else?*

Exercise 8:4

(i) সে তার ভাইয়ের মত নয়।

(ii) দিল্লি এখান থেকে আরও অনেক দূরে।

(iii) তোমার কি আরও টাকা আছে?

(iv) সে সবার চেয়ে বেশি খায়।

(v) আমি তোমার চেয়ে কম পড়ি।

(vi) আমগাছটা বাগানের মধ্যে সবচেয়ে বড় গাছ।

(vii) রাজনা তার মায়ের চেয়ে সুন্দর।

(viii) তার লেখা সবচেয়ে ভাল।

(ix) আমরা তাদের চেয়ে অনেক ফল খাই।

(x) আপনি আরও সবজি নেবেন?

(xi) *She got the best sleep here.*

(xii) *My mother's cooking is better.*

(xiii) *She can't speak Bangla as well as you.*
(xiv)   *In this place the trees are smaller.*
(xv)   *He has many more brothers and sisters than me.*
(xvi)   *I can't talk like him.*
(xvii) *You have to work more.*
(xviii) *a lot more beautiful than our village*
(xix)   *Nothing is bigger than an elephant.*
(xx)   *Who are the most stupid people?*

Exercise 8:5

(i)   সওয়া একটা
(ii)   আড়াইটা
(iii) এগারোটায়
(iv)   তিনটা দশ

(v)   চার ঘণ্টা
(vi)   দেড় ঘণ্টা
(vii) পৌনে পাঁচটা

(viii) পৌনে বারোটায়
(ix)   আটটা বিশ
(x)   দেড়টায়

Unit 9

Exercise 9:1

(i)   উনি রিকশায় উঠে পড়ে গিয়েছিলেন।
       He fell off as he was getting on the rickshaw.
(ii)   আমরা চিড়িয়াখানায় গিয়ে অনেক পশু দেখেছি।
       We went to the zoo and saw many animals.
(iii) সে তার সাইকেল নিয়ে অফিসে যাবে।
       He will go to the office on his bike.
(iv)   আমরা নাস্তা খেয়ে বাইরে যাব।
       We will go out after we have eaten breakfast.
(v)   উনি কুষ্টিয়ায় গিয়ে নতুন গাছ কিনেছেন।
       He went to Kustia to buy a new tree.
(vi)   তুমি চিঠিটা লিখে আমার কাছে পাঠাবে।
       You will send me the letter when you have written it.
(vii) ওরা সাপটা দেখে ভয় পেয়ে গেছে।
       They were afraid when they saw the snake.
(viii) আমি ঢাকায় গিয়ে লেখাপড়া করব।
       I will go to Dhaka to study.
(ix)   মেয়েটি কাছে এসে তাঁর হাত ধরে তাঁকে টান দিয়েছে।
       The girl came close, took his hand and pulled him.
(x)   বাবা দেরি করে সন্ধ্যাবেলায় বাসায় ফিরে এসেছেন।
       Father was late coming home in the evening.

Exercise 9:2

(i)   আমার ঘুম ভেঙে গেছে। *My sleep was broken. = I woke up.*
(ii)   উনি আমাকে পাঠিয়ে দেবেন। *He will send me.*
(iii) আমি তোমাকে নিয়ে যাব না। *I won't take you with me.*
(iv)   আমরা মোটা হয়ে যাচ্ছি। *We are getting fat.*
(v)   সে রিকশা থেকে পড়ে গেছিল। *He fell off the rickshaw.*
(vi)   একটা গোলাপ ফুল ফুটে উঠেছে । *A rose has blossomed.*
(vii) দিনটা আস্তে আস্তে আরও খারাপ হয়ে যাচ্ছে । *The day is gradually getting worse.*

(viii) সে চা খাওয়া ছেড়ে দিয়েছে। *She has given up drinking tea.*

(ix) গতকালের ভাত ফেলে দাও। *Throw the rice from yesterday away.*

(x) আমাকে এখানে নামিয়ে দেবেন? *Will you drop me off here?*

(xi) সে তার মনের কথা লুকিয়ে রাখে। *He keeps his feelings hidden.*

(xii) আমরা আমগুলো খেয়ে ফেলেছি। *We have eaten up the mangoes.*

(xiii) সে আবার ভাল হয়ে উঠেছে। *He has recovered again.*

(xiv) তুমি সকালে কোন সময় জেগে ওঠ? *What time do you get up in the morning?*

(xv) বাচ্চাটি ঘুমিয়ে পড়েছে। *The baby has fallen asleep.*

Exercise 9:3

(i) আমি তোমাকে জানাবো।

(ii) এই চিঠিটা আজকে পাঠাতে হবে।

(iii) আমি সেটা তোমাকে বুঝিয়ে দিতে পারি না।

(iv) ডাক্তারকে দেখিয়েছ?

(v) সে আমাদের আইসক্রিম খাওয়াবে।

(vi) সে তার নিজের রুটি বানায়।

(vii) উনি আমার হাতে মলম লাগিয়েছেন।

(viii) আমি সারাদিন ঘুমিয়েছিলাম।

(ix) সে গাড়ি চালাতে পারে না।

(x) ওরা সকালে এসে গেছে।

(xi) *They didn't bother me.*

(xii) *He has reduced the price of potatoes.*

(xiii) *He teaches me Bangla.*

(xiv) *She loses a lot of things.*

(xv) *They don't save their money.*

(xvi) *He showed us the road.*

(xvii) *How are you* (or: *is he/she) going to escape from here?*

(xviii) *He will read the letter to us.*

(xix) *I am making arrangements to wake him up.*

(xx) *They plant trees in their own garden.*

Review Exercises

Review Exercise 1. Script

(i) স্ত = ন + ত + উ   কিন্তু

(ii) ত্র = ত + র   মাত্র

(iii) ম্ভ = ম + ভ   সম্ভব

(iv) ক্ষ = ক + ষ   ক্ষতি

(v) স্ত = স + ত   আস্তে

(vi) জ্ঞ = জ + ঞ   বিজ্ঞান

(vii) ণ্ড = ণ + ড   ঠাণ্ডা

(viii) ষ্ট = ষ + ট   কষ্ট

(ix) স্ত = স + স + উ   প্রস্তুত

(x) র্থ = র + থ   অর্থ

Review Exercise 2: Vocabulary

স্বাদ *taste*, কেন *why*, কিছু *some, something*, লোক *person*, গল্প *story*, মাথা *head*, একসঙ্গে *together*, মাছ *fish*, জানালা *window*, কাউকে *to someone*, প্রায় *almost*, বুধবার *Wednesday*, পুকুর *pond, lake*, দূর *distance*, তাড়াতাড়ি *quickly*

much অনেক, *seven* সাত, *day* দিন, *play* খেলা, *meat* মাংস, *garden* বাগান, *town* শহর, *time* সময়, *only* শুধু, *until* পর্যন্ত, *beautiful* সুন্দর, *bad* খারাপ, *usually* সাধারণত, *help* সাহায্য, *green* সবুজ

animal	people	colors	nature words
ঘোড়া	আপা	কালো	আকাশ
পাখি	দাদা	সবুজ	ঘাস
বাঘ	পিসি	সাদা	জমি
হাঁস	মামা	হলুদ	বৃষ্টি
verbs	adjectives	postpositions	pronouns
আসা	ক্লান্ত	পর্যন্ত	আমাদের
চালানো	খুশি	পিছনে	এরা
পাওয়া	গরম	থেকে	কারা
বসা	চমৎকার	সামনে	তা
things	abstract nouns	food	parts of the body
কলম	অসুবিধা	ডাল	গলা
ঘড়ি	কথা	ডিম	চামড়া
চাবি	খবর	দুধ	চোখ
চামচ	ঘটনা	নুন	পা

Review Exercise 3: Mixed grammar

Postpositions:

(i)   ছয়টার পরে

(ii) গ্রামের মাঝখানে

(iii) রবিবারের আগে

(iv) সকাল পর্যন্ত

(v)   শহরের বাইরে

(vi) *inside the mind/heart*

(vii) *without you*

(viii) *for them*

(ix) *from 5 o'clock*

(x)   *westwards*

Pronouns:

(i)   সে / তারা রাজশাহীতে গিয়েছে।

(ii) আমরা রোজ টেলিফোন করি।

(iii) আপনি / উনি চা খাবেন?

(iv) তুমি / তোমরা ভাত খেয়েছ?

(v)   সে / তারা ছবি দেখছে।

(vi) সে / তারা গ্রামে থাকে।

(vii) আমি / আমরা বাইরে যাইনি।

(viii) আপনি / তিনি চিন্তা করেন না।

(ix) আপনি / আপনারা জমিতে কাজ করেন।

(x)   আমরা ছুটিতে যাচ্ছি।

Classifiers:

(i)   তিনটা রাস্তা

(ii) পাঁচ মিনিট

(iii) লাল কলমটা

(iv) একটা ছোট বাচ্চা

(v)   কিছুটা বৃষ্টি

(vi) সবগুলো বই

(vii) কয়েকটা মেয়ে

(viii) দশ মাইল

(ix) এই দুইটা নদী

(x)   একটু সময়

Imperfective participles:

(i)   আমি কাজ করতে পারি।   *I can work*

(ii) আমি সেটা বুঝতে পারি না।   *I can't understand this.*

(iii) আমি কি আসতে পারি?   *May I come in?*

(iv) আমি চার দিন থাকতে পারি।   *I can stay for four days.*

(v)   আমি টাকা দিতে পারি না।   *I can't pay.*

Perfective participles:

(i)   সে কাজ শেষ করে চলে গেছে। *He left when he had finished the work.*

(ii) তুমি জিনিসটা না বুঝে ভুল করেছ। *You made a mistake because you misunderstood.*

(iii) তোমরা এসে সব নিজের চোখে দেখবে। *When you come you will see it all for yourselves.*

(iv) আমি কলকাতায় থেকে অনেক কিছু শিখেছি। *I learned a lot while I was in Kolkata.*

(v)   আমি টাকা দিয়ে তাদের সাহায্য করেছি। *I helped them by paying.*

Unit 10

Exercise 10:1

(i)   সে কি যেতে পারবে?

(ii) সবাই হাসতে লাগছে।

(iii) কাগজগুলো তোমার কি দেখা দরকার?

(iv) তাদের টিকিটগুলো আমাকে দেখাতে হবে।

(v)   আমাদের খাবার দেওয়া হবে না।

(vi) বাবা তাকে রাতে থাকতে দেবেন না।

(vii) সকালের আগে চলে যাওয়া যাবে না।

(viii) আমরা ওখানে নাচ শিখতে যাচ্ছি।

(ix) সে খেতে খেতে গাড়ি চালায়।

(x)   ওরা আপনার সঙ্গে কথা বলতে চেয়েছে।

Exercise 10:2

(i)   যাওয়া   *It is not possible to go this way.*

(ii)   করতে   *The work doesn't have to be finished today.*

(iii) যাওয়ার   *It is time for us to leave.*

(iv)   কথা বলতে   *He doesn't want to talk to me.*

(v)   পাঠানো   *These need to be sent quickly.*

(vi)   বসতে   *Will you allow me to sit here.*

(vii) পাওয়া   *There are no bananas in the market today.*

(viii) বানাতে   *Don't you know how to prepare carrot juice?*

(ix)   নষ্ট করা   *You shouldn't waste so much time.*

(x)   ছবি তুলতে   *No pictures need to be taken today.*

Exercise 10:3

(i)   তুমি কি কিছু করতে পার না?   *Can't you do something?*

(ii)   আমার দুই কেজি গাজর দরকার।   *I need two kilos of carrots.*

(iii) আমাকে তাড়াতাড়ি যেতে হবে।   *I need to go quickly.*

(iv)   আর একটু দুধ দেওয়া যাবে?   *Can I have some more milk?*

(v)   তুমি কি কিছু বলতে চাও?   *Do you want to say something?*

(vi)   আমি তাদের সিগারেট খেতে দেই না।   *I don't allow them to smoke.*

(vii) সে তোমার সঙ্গে কথা বলতে চায়।   *He wants to talk to you.*

(viii) তার আমাকে ভাল লাগে না।   *She doesn't like me.*

(ix)   আর কিছু বলার দরকার নেই।   *Nothing more needs to be said.*

(x)   এই রাস্তাটায় এখন গাড়ি চালানো যাবে না।   *It is not possible to drive down this road now.*

Exercise 10:4

(i)   তোমার সঙ্গে আবার দেখা হবে।

(ii)   তাকে সাহায্য করার আমার ইচ্ছা নেই।

(iii) কাজটা আজকে শেষ করতে হবে না।

(iv)   এই রাস্তা দিয়ে যাওয়া যায় না।

(v)   বিকালে আবার বৃষ্টি পড়তে লাগল।

(vi)   সকাল পাঁচটায় ঘুম থেকে উঠতে হয়েছে।

(vii) ছেলেটির দুধ খেতে ভালো লাগে না।

(viii) তারা কালকে মাছ ধরতে যাবে।

(ix)   আমি নিজে তাকে এই কথা বলতে শুনেছি।

(x)   আমি চিঠিটা আজ পাঠাতে পারিনি।

Exercise 10:5

(i)   প্রথমে তোমার সঙ্গে কথা বলা উচিত ছিল।

(ii)   তোমার এসব আমাকে বুঝিয়ে দেওয়ার দরকার নেই।

(iii)   তোমার আজ যাওয়ার কথা।

(iv)   সেটা তোমার করার দরকার নেই।

(v)   তাদের খাবার আমাদের নেওয়া উচিত ছিল না।

(vi)   তোমার একা বাইরে যাওয়ার কথা নয়।

(vii)   তাকে আমাদের বিশ্বাস করা উচিত।

(viii)   ব্যাপারটা অন্য কারও সঙ্গে আলোচনা করা উচিত নয়।

(ix)   তোমার অভিযোগ করা উচিত ছিল না।

(x)   পুরো এলাকাটা খোঁজ করতে হবে।

(xi)   তোমার আসার দরকার ছিল না।

(xii)   তোমার টাকা দেওয়ার কথা ছিল না।

(xiii)   তার কথা তোমার মনে রাখা উচিত ছিল।

(xiv)   আমার তার সঙ্গে এত সময় কাটানো উচিত ছিল না।

(xv)   তোমার আর কি দরকার হবে?

(xvi)   আমার আজ আর কিছু লেখার দরকার নেই।

(xvii)   মাকে পুরা গল্পটা বলার দরকার ছিল না।

(xviii) তোমার এত প্রশ্ন করার দরকার কি?

(xix)   তোমার কি ছাতিগুলো ফিরিয়ে নিয়ে আসার কথা ছিল না?

(xx)   তোমার সব সময় নিজের মনের মত চলা উচিত।

Exercise 10:6

(i)   সে তার বাচ্চাকে রক্ষা করতে চায়।

(ii)   আমি তোমার জন্যে অপেক্ষা করেছি।

(iii)   নতুন শাড়িটা আমি আজকে গায়ে দেব।

(iv)   আমি কখনও ভুল করি না।

(v)   আমরা সেটা আশা করিনি।

(vi)   তুমি কি তাদের ক্ষমা করতে পার না?

(vii)   সে বেশি টাকা খরচ করে না।

(viii)   সেটা আমাদের আলোচনা করতে হবে।

(ix)   গরম আমি সহ্য করতে পারি না।

(x)   তুমি যে কালকে আসবে, কথা দিচ্ছ?

(xi)   আমি তোমাকে আর সাহায্য করতে পারি না।

(xii)   তুমি কি তোমার নতুন চাকরি আরম্ভ করেছ?

(xiii)   সে কখনও বিয়ে করেনি।

(xiv)   সে একটা নতুন বাড়ি খুঁজতে চেষ্টা করছে।

(xv)   সে তার পড়ার দিকে মন দেয় না।

(xvi)   ছোট ছেলেটি সাঁতার কাটতে শেখেনি।

(xvii)   উনি যে খুব ভাল একজন মানুষ, আমি তা সন্দেহ করি না।

(xviii) কেউ বাচ্চাদের ক্ষতি করতে চায় না।

(xix)   তোমার আসার সময়ে কিছু লক্ষ্য করেছ?

(xx)   তার কথা পরীক্ষা করতে হবে।

Unit 11

Exercise 11:1
(**Note:** the possibilities are endless; these are just some examples.)

(i) আমি পাখি হলে উড়ে যেতাম।
If I was a bird I would fly.

(ii) তুমি অনেক ধনী হলে কি করতে?
What would you do if you were very rich?

(iii) আমি যদি দশ বছর পিছনে যেতে পারতাম, তাহলে অনেক কিছু বদলাতাম।
If I could go back ten years, I would change a lot of things.

(iv) লোকে যদি একজন অন্যজনকে আরও ভাল বুঝত, এত ঝগড়া করত না।
If people understood one another better, they wouldn't quarrel so much.

(v) আমরা মাংস আরও কম খেলে আমাদের স্বাস্থ্য আরও ভাল থাকত।
If we ate less meat, we would be healthier.

(vi) চিড়িয়াখানায় যদি হাতি থাকত তাহলে আমরা খুব খুশি হতাম।
We would have been very happy if there had been elephants at the zoo.

(vii) সে তার পরীক্ষায় পাস করলে বিশ্ববিদালয়ে যেতে পারত।
If he had passed his exams, he could have gone to university.

(viii) এত সময় নষ্ট না করলে আমি আরও অনেক কিছু করতে পারতাম।
I could do a lot more if I didn't waste so much time.

(ix) আমরা গাড়ি চালানো ছেড়ে দিলে পৃথিবীর জন্য আর অনেক উপকার হত।
It would be much more beneficial for the earth if we stopped driving cars.

(x) খাবারটা ভাল না লাগলে আমি সেটা খেতাম না।
I wouldn't eat the food if I didn't like it.

Exercise 11:2
(i) আপনি যদি একজন ভাল লোক পান, তাহলে একটু বলবেন।

(ii) আমরা যদি খাবারগুলো রেখে যাই, তাহলে সব নষ্ট হয়ে যাবে।

(iii) আমরা যদি চিড়িয়াখানায় যাই, তাহলে হাতি দেখতে পারব।

(iv) গাজর যদি থাকে, তাহলে ছয় কেজি নেব।

(v) আমরা যদি কিছু না করি, তাহলে অবস্থাটা আরও খারাপ হয়ে যাবে।

(vi) আমি যদি বাংলাদেশে থাকতাম, তাহলে এত কষ্ট করে বাংলা শিখতে হত না।

(vii) দরজারটার চাবি যদি না থাকে, তাহলে ভিতরে যেতে পারব না।

(viii) বৃষ্টি যদি হয়, তাহলে আমরা নৌকায় যাব না।

(ix) সে যদি মাংস না খায়, তাহলে তার জন্য আলাদা রান্না করতে হবে।

(x) তুমি যদি বাংলা কথা বলতে না পারতে, তাহলে কারও সঙ্গে গল্প করতে পারতে না।

Exercise 11:3
(i) কালকে আসলে আমি তোমাকে বাজারে নিয়ে যাবে।

(ii) তাদের আলু যদি না থাকে, তাহলে আমরা ভাত খাব।

(iii) তোমার শীত লাগলে, আমি জানালাটা বন্ধ করব।

(iv) তারা ধানমণ্ডিতে থাকলে রাস্তাটা চিনবে।

(v) বৃষ্টি যদি আজ না হয়, তাহলে আমরা নৌকায় যাব।

(vi) সার্টটা বেশি বড় হলে তোমার ভাইকে দিতে পারবে।

(vii) আরও টাকা যদি দরকার হয়, তাহলে তোমার একটা চাকরি খোঁজা উচিত।

(viii) না খেলে অসুখ হবে।

(ix) গরম দেশে থাকলে অনেক পানি খেতে হয়।

(x)   তুমি যদি চাও তাহলে আমরা বেড়াতে যেতে পারব।
(xi)   বাংলাদেশে যদি থাকতাম তাহলে আমি খুব খুশি হতাম।
(xii)   লালটা তোমার ভাল না লাগলে, সবুজটা নিতে পারবে।
(xiii)   তার যদি দেরি হয়, তাহলে আমরা তার জন্যে অপেক্ষা করব না।
(xiv)   নতুন শব্দগুলো যদি ব্যবহার না কর, তাহলে ভাষাটা শিখতে পারবে না।
(xv)   মন না দিলে কাজটা শেষ করতে পারবে না।
(xvi)   তাদের সত্যি বললেও তারা আমাদের বিশ্বাস করত না।
(xvii)   তুমি আমাদের সঙ্গে না গেলেও আমরা সিনেমা দেখতে যাব।
(xviii)   বাংলাদেশে থাকতে চাইলে, বাংলা কথা বলা দরকার।
(xix)   প্রশ্ন না করলে শিখবে না।
(xx)   ওখানে দেরিতে পৌঁছিয়ে গেলে ওরা আমাদের জায়গা (or একটা ঘর) দেবে না।

Unit 12

Exercise 12:1

(i)   সে রাজশাহীতে থাকবে।
(ii)   আমি বাজারে গিয়েছিলাম।
(iii)   সে আমার সঙ্গে থাকছিল।
(iv)   ছোট বোনের কথা মনে পড়েছে।
(v)   সাঈদার সঙ্গে একটু কথা বলব।
(vi)   তার ঢাকায় ভাল লাগেনি।
(vii)   ওরা সাপ দেখে ভয় করেছিল।
(viii)   ব্যাপারটা জরুরি ছিল।
(ix)   সেটা আমার মনে ছিল না।
(x)   চিঠিটা পাঠাবে।

(xi)   মা রুটি বানিয়েছে।
(xii)   মেয়েটি কথা বলতে পারছে না।
(xiii)   তুমি কেমন ছিলে?
(xiv)   আমরা ছুটিতে ছিলাম।
(xv)   তারা পুকুরে সাঁতার কেটেছে।
(xvi)   আমি কোনও খারাপ খাবার খাই নি।
(xvii)   গাজর খুব তাড়তাড়ি শেষ হয়ে যাবে।
(xviii)   সে সকাল ৫টায় উঠত।
(xix)   এক তলাতে একটা ঘর খালি ছিল।
(xx)   সে একটা রেস্টোরাঁতে খেতে চেয়েছিল।

Exercise 12:2

(i)   আমরা প্রতিদিন ভাত খাই।
(ii)   সে আমাকে বোঝেনি।
(iii)   সে সময়ে আমি গানটা শুনছিলাম।
(iv)   সে সবগুলো আম খেয়ে ফেলেছে।
(v)   কাজটা আমাদেরব এই সপ্তাহের মধ্যে শেষ করতে হবে।
(vi)   বিড়ালটা টেবিলের নিচে ঘুমাচ্ছে।
(vii)   এই রাস্তায় কোনও হাসপাতাল নেই।
(viii)   আমি এখানে সারা জীবন আছি।
(ix)   সে সকালে বাজারে গিয়েছিল।
(x)   আমি তোমার সঙ্গে যেতাম।
(xi)   আমরা কোনও বাঘ দেখিনি।
(xii)   সে সারাদিন নদীর কাছে (ধারে) বসেছিল।
(xiii)   সে এখানে থাকতে চেয়েছিল।
(xiv)   তোমার আমার জন্যে অপেক্ষা করার দরকার ছিল না।
(xv)   আমি পচা সবজিগুলো ফেলে দিয়েছি।
(xvi)   আমি পাঁচ বছর আগে ইটালিতে গিয়েছিলাম।
(xvii)   সে এই কথা কখনও বলত না।
(xviii)   তুমি কি সেটা জানতে?
(xix)   আমার মেজাজ খারাপ ছিল।
(xx)   তুমি তাকে কি প্রশ্ন করেছিলে?

Unit 13

Exercise 13:1

(i)   যে গতকাল এসেছিল, সে কালকে আবার আসবে।

(ii)   আমি যে বইটা পড়ছি তা আমার ভাল লাগে না।

(iii)   সে যেখানে যাচ্ছে সেখানে অনেক সাপ আছে।

(iv)   আপনি যেদিন তাকে এখানে নিয়ে আসবেন, সেদিন আমি তাকে সব বুঝিয়ে দেব।

(v)   তার বাবা যেভাবে কথা বলেন সেও ঠিক সেভাবে কথা বলে।

(vi)   তুমি যা চাও তা আমি তোমাকে দেব।

(vii)   তুমি যখন আসবে তখন সে এখানে থাকবে।

(viii) তুমি যত খেতে চাও তত খেতে পার।

(ix)   তোমার যতদিন আমাকে দরকার হবে, ততদিন আমি থাকব।

(x)   যতদূর সম্ভব, ততদূর আমরা সাহায্য করব।

(xi)   সে যদিও অনেক আগে চলে গেছে, তার কথা তবুও এখনও মনে পড়ে।

(xii)   তুমি যেমন কাজ কর, তেমন সে কাজ করতে পারে না।

Exercise 13:2

Sample paragraph with translation

বাংলা কথা বলা

তুমি বাংলাদেশে গেলে মানুষ আশা করবে না যে তুমি বাংলা কথা বলতে পারবে। শহরে অনেকে ইংরেজি কথা বলতে পারে। ইংরেজি বা অল্প বাংলা পারলে সামলানো যায় – অনেকে তোমার সঙ্গে তাদের ইংরেজির কথা বলা চর্চা করতে চাইবে। কিন্তু বড় শহরের বাইরে গেলে বাংলার দরকার পড়বে। তাও মানুষের বিশ্বাস হয় না যে তুমি বাংলা পার, নিজের কানে শুনলেও।

এক দিন আমি বাস স্ট্যান্ডে দাঁড়িয়ে ছিলাম। একজন লোক আমার কাছে এসে স্বাভাবিক প্রশ্নগুলো জিজ্ঞেস করতে লাগল। 'আপনি কোন দেশের? কত দিন বাংলাদেশে আছেন? এখানে কি করেন? বিয়ে হয়েছে? কষজন বাচ্চা? বাংলাদেশ কেমন লাগে?'

আমি কিছুক্ষণ ধরে তার সঙ্গে আলাপ করে তার সব প্রশ্ন উত্তর দিলাম। আরও অনেক লোক এসে আমাদের কথা শুনল। হঠাৎ, শেষে, লোকটি আমাকে জিজ্ঞেস করল 'আপনি কি বাংলা বলতে পারেন?' পুরা আলাপ তো বাংলায় ছিল – আমার কি বলার কথা ছিল? আমি বললাম 'আপনি কি বাংলা বুঝতে পারেন?' তারপরে আমরা সবাই হেসে ফেললাম।

When you go to Bangladesh the people there will not expect you to know Bengali. In the towns many people speak English, so you can manage with English or just a little Bengali—many people will want to try their English with you. But outside the big towns you will need Bengali. Still people find it difficult to believe that you can speak it, even when they hear it themselves.

Once I was waiting at a bus stop. A man came up to me and started asking me the usual questions. "Where are you from? How long have you been in Bangladesh? What are you doing here? Are you married? How many children do you have? How do you like Bangladesh?" I talked to him for a few minutes, answering all his questions, and many more people came and stood listening to the conversation. Suddenly, at the end, he asked me: "Can you speak Bengali?" The whole conversation had been in Bengali—what was I supposed to say to this? I asked him back: "Can you understand Bengali?" Then we were all laughing.

Unit 14

Exercise 14:1
(i)   পদ্মা নদী গল্পটা বলেছে।

(ii)   বলা হয় যে পদ্মার মা গঙ্গা আর তার বাবা দেবতা শিব।

(iii)   পদ্মা ফরিদপুর এসে যমুনার সাথে মিলে যায়।

(iv)   চাঁদপুরে তিনটি নদীর মিল হয় : মেঘনা, পদ্মা আর যমুনা মিলে একটা বড় বড় নদী সৃষ্টি করে।

(v)   বাংলাদেশের দক্ষিণের যে সাগর থাকে তার নাম বঙ্গোপসাগর।

(vi)   নদীকে বাংলাদেশের প্রাণ বলা হয় কারণ নদী সারা দেশকে জীবন দেয়।

(vii)   শহর নদীর তীরে গড়ে উঠল কারণ মানুষ পানি ছাড়া বাঁচতে পারে না।

(viii)   শীতকালে বৃষ্টি হয় না বলে নদীর পানি খুব কম থাকে।

(ix)   বৈশাখ মাস বসন্ত কালে হয়, এপ্রিল মাসে।

(x)   গ্রীষ্মকালে হিমালয় থেকে অনেক পানি নেমে আসে, নদীর পানি অনেক। সে জন্যে বিপজ্জনক হয়ে যায়।

Exercise 14:2
(i)	কন্যা	মেয়ে	(vi)	প্রাচীন	পুরানো
(ii)	মিতালি	সম্পর্ক	(vii)	স্থান	জায়গা
(iii)	প্রাণ	জীবন	(viii)	বদলানো	পরিবর্তন
(iv)	স্থল	জমি	(ix)	ক্ষেত	মাঠ
(v)	দেশান্তর	অন্য দেশ	(x)	কপাল	ভাগ্য

Exercise 14:3
(i)	জীবন	মৃত্যু	(ix)	সত্যি	মিথ্যা
(ii)	স্বপ্ন	বাস্তবতা	(x)	স্বর্গ	নরক
(iii)	আরম্ভ	শেষ, ইতি	(xi)	আনন্দ	দুঃখ
(iv)	ভবিষ্যৎ	অতীত	(xii)	শান্তি	ঝামেলা
(v)	প্রকৃতি	সংস্কৃতি	(xiii)	ন্যায়	অন্যায়
(vi)	লাভ	লোকসান	(xiv)	বিশ্বাস	সন্দেহ
(vii)	জয়	পরাজয়	(xv)	আরাম	কষ্ট
(viii)	স্বাধীনতা	অত্যাচার			

DICTIONARIES

Using Bangla Dictionaries
Bangla–English Dictionary
English–Bangla Dictionary

USING BANGLA DICTIONARIES

Moving from a beginner to intermediate level, you will want to be able to use dictionaries in order to look up unfamiliar words. Here are some guidelines to help build up your confidence. In trying to look up a word that you have heard spoken, there are certain areas of possible confusion and it is good to be aware of them.

- some are related to inaccurate hearing:
  - hearing the difference between aspirated and non-aspirated sounds
  - hearing the difference between dental and palatal sounds
  - hearing the difference between র r and ড় ṛ
  - hearing the difference between long ও (o) or অ (ô) and short অ (ɔ)

- some are related to the order of letters in the dictionary:
  - words starting with nasalized (*chondrobindu*) consonants come **before** unnasalized words, e.g.:
    খসা . . . খাই . . . খাঁচা . . . খাঁটি . . . খাক
  - conjunct letters come **after** consonant-vowel combinations, e.g.:
    বসত . . . বসন্ত . . . বসা . . . বসু . . . বস্তি
    but watch out for alternative spellings:
    দরকার . . . দরখাস্ত . . . দরজা . . . দরিদ্র . . . দর্জি . . . দর্শন
  - ক্ষ consists of ক + ষ and comes in the dictionary between ক and খ.
  - জ্ঞ consists of জ + ঞ and comes after the জ + vowel combinations and before জ + bophola.
  - ণ comes after the palatal plosives (ট, ঠ, ড, ঢ); ন comes after the dental plosives (ত, থ, দ, ধ).
  - ৎ comes straight after the full vowels (সওয়াল, সংকট); ঙ, ঞ and ৯ come (in that order) between ঘ and চ.

  Note that the order of letters in dictionaries can vary a bit. In the new Adhikary dictionary, combinations of letters with bophola, e.g., ধ্বংস, come after ধ + ʃ and after ধ + র.

- most are related to unpredictable spellings:
  - short ই i and long ঈ ī, short উ u and long ঊ ū: sound and spelling don't match. Spellings have to be learned. Remember that both short u and short i are much more common than their long counterparts.
  - স, শ, ষ — this is a matter of memorizing (or a knowledge of Sanskrit!). ষ is rare at the beginning of words, except for numbers relating to six (ষোলো ṣolo *sixteen*, ষাট ṣaːṭ *sixty*)

- an æ sound can be written in three ways: এ (দেখ), ্য (ব্যস্ত), or ্যা (ব্যাকরণ)

- a ri sound can be written in three ways: ঋ (বৃষ্টি), রি (ত্রিশ), or রী (স্ত্রী)

- জ and য sound the same. All 'grammatical words' (relative pronouns, conjunctions, adverbs) are spelled with য (যা, যখন, যেমন, যদি) but also যাওয়া *go*.

- a jj sound can be spelled in three ways: জ্জ(লজ্জা) or য্য (সাহায্য) or হ্য (সহ্য)

- ন and ণ sound the same, but ণ does not occur at the beginning of words.

- ঙ, ৎ and ঙ sound the same. Spellings need to be learned. ৎ is never followed by a vowel.

- silent letters like bophola, mophola, jophola, particularly with the first letter of a word, can cause great problems if they slip your mind. Try to learn these spellings straightaway, e.g.: স্বপ্ন svɔpnô (shopno) *dream*, স্বর্গ svɔrgô (shɔrgo) *heaven*, স্বামী svamī (shami) *husband*, স্বাদ svad (sha:d) *taste*, স্বাভাবিক svabhabik (shabhabik) *normal*, স্বীকার svīkar (shikar) *admission*, স্মরণ smɔrôn (shɔrôn) *memory*, স্মৃতি smṙti (sriti) *memory*, záhlh jvala (jala) *bother*, ব্যথা bytha (bætha) *pain*, ব্যাপার byapar (bæpar) *matter*, ব্যক্তি bykti (bekti) *person*, etc.

Dictionary order of letters

Vowels

অ   আ   ই   ঈ   উ   ঊ
ঋ   এ   ঐ   ও   ঔ

Between vowels and consonants

ৎ   ঃ   ঁ

Consonants *(read across and then down)*

ক (ক্ষ)	খ	গ	ঘ	ঙ (ক্ক, ঙ্গ)
চ	ছ	জ (জ্ঞ)	ঝ	এঃ (ঞ্চ, ঞ্জ)
ট	ঠ	ড ড়	ঢ ঢ়	ণ
ত, ৎ	থ	দ	ধ	ন
প	ফ	ব	ভ	ম
য য়	র	ল		
শ	ষ	স	হ	

BANGLA – ENGLISH DICTIONARY

অ

অংশ ɔmśô *n.* part
অংশ নেওয়া ɔmśô neoŷa *vb.* take part
অক্ষর ôkṣôr *n.* letter, syllable
অঙ্ক ɔṅkô *n.* maths
অঞ্চল ɔñcɔl *n.* area
অজানা ɔjana *adj.* unknown
অতিথি ôtithi *n.* guest
অতিরিক্ত ôtiriktô *adj.* excessive
অতীত ôtīt *n.* past
অত্যাচার ɔtyacar *n.* oppression
অদ্ভুত ɔdbhut *adj.* strange, peculiar
অধিকার ôdhikar *n.* right, privilege
অনাবৃষ্টি ɔnabr̥ṣṭi *n.* drought
অনুষ্ঠান ônuṣṭhan *n.* celebration
অনেক ɔnek *adj.* much, many
অনেক দূরে ɔnek dūre *adv.*. very far
অন্তত ɔntôtô *adv.* at least
অন্ধ ɔndhô *adj.* blind
অন্ধকার ɔndhôkar *n.* darkness
অন্য ɔnyô *adj.* other
অন্যজন ɔnyôjɔn *n.* the other one/person
অন্যায় ɔnyaŷ (onnay) *n.* injustice, wrong
অপরাধ ɔpôradh *n.* crime, offense
অপেক্ষা করা ɔpekṣa kɔra *vb.* wait
অফিস ɔphis *n.* office
অবশেষে ɔbôśeṣe *adv.* finally
অবশ্য ɔbôśyô *adv.* of course
অবস্থা ɔbôstha *n.* situation
অবহেলা ɔbôhela *n.* neglect
অবিরাম ɔbiram *adj.* incessant
অভাব ɔbhab *n.* lack, shortage
অভিজ্ঞতা ôbhijñôta (obhiggota) *n.* experience
অভিযোগ ôbhiyog *n.* complaint
অমর ɔmɔr *adj.* immortal
অলস ɔlôs (ɔlôsh) *adj.* lazy
অল্প ɔlpô *adj.* a little bit
অশ্লীল ɔślīl *adj.* obscene
অসময় ɔsômôŷ *n.* inconvenient time

অসহ্য ɔsɔhyô (ɔshôjjhô) *adj.* unbearable
অসাধারণ ɔsadharôṇ *adj.* unusual
অসীম ɔsīm *adj.* endless
অসুখ ɔsukh *n.* illness
অসুবিধা ɔsubidha *n.* inconvenience
অসুস্থ ɔsusthô *adj.* ill
অস্থির ɔsthir *adj.* restless
অহঙ্কার ɔhɔṅkar *n.* pride

আ

আইসক্রিম aiskrim *n.* ice cream
আংটি amṭi (angṭi) *n.* ring
আকাশ akaś *n.* sky
আক্রমণ akrômôn *n.* attack
আখ akh *n.* sugar-cane
আগমন agômôn *n.* arrival
আগামী agamī *adj.* next
আগামীকাল agamīkal *adv.* tomorrow
আগুন agun *n.* fire
আগে age *adv./pp.* earlier, before
আঘাত aghat *n.* blow, shock
আঙুর aṅur (anggur) *n.* grape
আঙুল aṅul (anggul) *n.* finger
আচার acar *n.* chutney
আচ্ছন্ন acchɔnnô *adj.* overcast
আচ্ছা accha *excl.* OK
আছ- ach- *vb.* be present, exist
আজ a:j *adv.* today
আজকাল ajkal *adv.* nowadays
আজকে ajke *adv.* today
আট aṭ *num.* eight
আড্ডা aḍḍa *n.* social gathering
আড়াই aṛai *num.* two and a half
আতাফল ataphɔl *n.* custard apple
আদা ada *n.* ginger
আধ adh *num.* half
আধা adha *num.* half
আত্মা atma (atta) *n.* soul
আত্মীয় atmīŷô (attiyo) *n.* relative
আনন্দ anôndô *n.* joy, pleasure
আনন্দিত anônditô *adj.* pleased, delighted

আন্ডারগ্রাউন্ড anḍargraunḍ *n.* underground
আনা ana *vb.* bring
আনারস anarɔs *n.* pineapple
আপনারা apnara *pr. (pl., pol.)* you
আপনি apni *pr. (sg., pol.)* you
আপা apa *n.* elder sister *(M.)*
আপেল apel *n.* apple
আবার abar *adv.* again
আবহাওয়া abhaoẏa *n.* weather
আব্বা abba *n.* father
আম a:m *n.* mango
আমরা amra *pr.* we
আমাশা amaśa *n.* diarrhea, dysentry
আমি ami *pr.* I
আমেরিকান amerikan *adj.* American
আম্মা amma *n.* mother
আয়না aẏna *n.* mirror
আর ar *conj.* and, more
আরও aro *adv.* more
আরম্ভ arômbhô *n.* beginning, start
আরম্ভ করা arômbhô kɔra *vb.* begin, start
আরাম aram *n.* rest, relaxation
আরে are *excl. expr.* of exasperation
আরে না are na *excl.* not at all
আলনা alna *n.* rack
আলমারি almari *n.* cupboard
আলাদা alada *adj.* separate
আলাপ alap *n.* conversation, introduction
আলু alu *n.* potato
আলো alo *n.* light
আলোচনা alocôna *n.* discussion
আলোচনা করা alocôna kɔra *vb.* discuss
আশা aśa *n.* hope
আশা করা aśa kɔra *vb.* hope
আশ্চর্য aścɔryô *adj.* amazing, surprising
আষাঢ় aṣaṛh *n.* Asharh *(Bengali month)*
আসলে asôle *adv.* actually
আসা asa *vb.* come
আস্তে আস্তে aste aste *adv.* gradually, slowly
আস্থা astha *n.* trust
অ্যালার্জি aylarji (ælarji) *n.* allergy

ই

ই i *emp.* emphasizer
ইংরেজি imreji (ingreji) *n./adj.* English
ইংল্যান্ড imlyanḍ *name* England

ইঁদুর ĩdur *n.* mouse
ইঙ্গিত iṅgit *n.* sign, hint
ইচ্ছা iccha (BD), ইচ্ছে icche (PB) *n.* wish
ইঞ্জিন iñjin *n.* engine
ইট i:ṭ *n.* brick
ইটালি iṭali *name* Italy
ইতি iti *n.* end
ইতিহাস itihas *n.* history
ইত্যাদি ityadi (ittadi) *adv.* etcetera, and so on
ইনশা–আল্লাহ। inśa allah *expr.* God willing!

ঈগল īgôl *n.* eagle
ঈশ্বর īśvôr (isshor) *n.* God

উকিল ukil *n.* lawyer
উকুন ukun *n.* louse
উচিত ucit *adj.* fitting, proper
উজ্জ্বল ujjvôl (ujjol) *adj.* bright
উট u:ṭ *n.* camel
উঠান uṭhan *n.* courtyard
উঠে যাওয়া uṭhe yaoẏa *vb.* come off;
    disappear, vanish
উড়োজাহাজ uṛojahaj *n.* airplane
উৎসব utsɔb *n.* ceremony
উত্তর uttôr *n.* answer, reply
উত্তর দেওয়া uttôr deoẏa *vb.* reply, answer
উত্তর uttôr *n.* north
উত্তাপ uttap *n.* heat
উদ্দাম uddam *adj.* violent, wild
উদ্দেশ্য uddeśyô (uddesho) *n.* purpose, aim
উদ্বিগ্ন udbignô *adj.* worried
উনার unar *pr. (hon.)* his, her
উনি, ইনি uni, ini *pr. (hon.)* he, she
উনিশ uniś *num.* nineteen
উপকার upôkar *n.* favor, benefit
উপকারি upôkari *adj.* beneficial
উপর upôr *pp.* on, on top of
উপসাগর upôsagôr *n.* bay
উপস্থিত upôsthit *adj.* present
উপস্থিত হওয়া upôsthit hɔoẏa *vb.* appear
উপহার upôhar *n.* present, gift
উপায় upaẏ *n.* means, way
উভয় ubhɔẏ *n.* both (people)

ঋ

ঋতু ŕtu (ritu) *n.* season
ঋণ ŕṇ (rin) *n.* debt, loan

এ

এ, এই e, ei *adj.* this
এইবার eibar *adv.* this time
এই মাত্র ei matrô *adv.* just now
এই যে ei ye *phr.* here, look
এক æk *num.* one
একই eki *adj.* same
একজন ækjɔn *adj./n.* one (person)
একটা ækṭa *adj.* one, a
একটা-আধটা ækṭa-adhṭa *num.* one or two
একটু ekṭu *adj.* a little bit
একতলা æktɔla *n.* ground floor
একদম ækdɔm *adv.* altogether, completely
একবার ækbar *adv.* once, one time
একমাত্র ækmatro *adj.* only
একরকম ækrɔkôm *adv.* a kind of
এক শ æk śô *num.* one hundred
একসঙ্গে eksɔṅge *adv.* together
একসিডেন্ট eksideṇṭ *n.* accident
একা æka *adv.* alone
একেবারে ækebare *adv.* completely, totally
এখন ækhôn *adv.* now
এখনও ækhônô *adv.* yet, still
এখানে ekhane *adv.* here
এগোনো egôno *vb.* go forward, advance
এগারো egaro *num.* eleven
এগুলো egulo *n.* these (things)
এটা æṭa *pr.* this (thing)
এত ætô *adj./adv.* so much, so many
এতগুলো ætôgulo *adj.* so many
এতটুকু ætôṭuku *adj.* so small
এতে ete *pr.* in this
এমন æmôn *adv.* such, so
এমনি emni *adv.* overall, just like that
এয়ারমেল eŷarmel *n.* airmail
এরমধ্যে ermôdhye *adv.* in the meantime, by then
এরইমধ্যে erimôdhye *adv.* in the meantime, by then
এলাকা elaka *n.* area
এলাচ elac *n.* cardamom
এসব esɔb *n.* all this

ঐ

ঐতিহ্য oitihyô (oitijjho) *n.* tradition

ও

ও o *pr.* he, she; *conj.* also, even
ওইদিকে oidike *adv.* that way, over there
ওখানে okhane *adv.* there
ওজন ojôn *n.* weight
ওঠা oṭha *vb.* get up
ওঠানো oṭhano *vb.* cause to wake up, lift up, pull out
ওড়না orna *n.* scarf, headscarf
ওমা oma *excl.* My goodness!
ওয়ালিকুম সালাম oŷalikum salam *phr.* God be with you! *(Muslim greeting reply)*
ওরা ora *pr.* they
ওষুধ oṣudh *n.* medicine

ক (ক্ষ)

কখন kɔkhôn *qu.* when
কখনও kɔkhônô *adv.* ever
কখনও না kɔkhônô na *adv.* never
কচ্ছপ kɔcchop *n.* turtle
কঠিন kôṭhin *adj.* difficult
কড়াই kɔṛai *n.* frying pan
কত kɔtô *qu.* how much
কতদিন kɔtôdin *qu.* for how long
কথা kɔtha *n.* word, fact
কথা দেওয়া kɔtha deoŷa *vb.* promise
কথা বলা kɔtha bɔla *vb.* talk
কথা বাড়ানো kɔtha baṛano *vb.* elaborate
কথা রাখা kɔtha rakha *vb.* keep promise
কন্যা kɔnya (kɔnna) *n.* daughter
কপাল kɔpal *n.* forehead, luck
কফি kôphi *n.* coffee
কবি kôbi *n.* poet
কবে kɔbe *qu.* when
কম kɔm *adj./adv.* less
কমপিউটার kɔmpiuṭar *n.* computer
কমলা kɔmla *n./adj.* orange
কমা kɔma *vb.* reduce, decrease
কমানো kɔmano *vb.* reduce
কমে যাওয়া kôme yaoŷa *cvb.* get less, reduce
কম্প kɔmpô *n.* tremor
কম্বল kɔmbôl *n.* blanket

কয়জন kɔŷjɔn *qu.* how many (people)
কয়টা বাজে? kɔŷṭa baje *phr.* what time is it?
কয়েক kɔŷek *adj.* a few
করা kɔra *vb.* do
করানো kɔrano *vb.* cause to do
কর্মচারী kɔrmôcarī *n.* employee
কল kɔl *n.* machine, water pump
কলকাতা kôlkata *name* Kolkata
কলম kɔlôm *n.* pen
কলসি kôlsi *n.* water jug
কলা kɔla *n.* banana
কলেজ kɔlej *n.* college
কল্পনা kɔlpôna *n.* imagination
কল্পনা করা kɔlpôna kɔra *vb.* imagine
কষ্ট kɔṣṭô *n.* trouble, hardship, suffering
কষ্ট পাওয়া kɔṣṭô paoŷa *vb.* be upset, suffer
কাঁচা kāca *adj.* raw, unripe
কাঁচা মরিচ kāca môric *n.* green chili
কাঁঠাল kāṭhal *n.* jackfruit
কাঁদা kāda *vb.* cry, weep
কাঁধ kādh *n.* shoulder
কাকা kaka *n.* uncle *(father's younger brother) (H.)*
কাগজ kagôj *n.* paper
কাগজি বাদাম kagôji badam *n.* almond
কাচ kac *n.* glass
কাছ থেকে kach theke *pp.* from (a person)
কাছাকাছি kachakachi *adv.* close by
কাছে kache *pp.* near, to
কাজ kaj *n.* work
কাজ করা kaj kɔra *vb.* work
কাটা kaṭa *vb.* cut
কাটা চামচ kaṭa camôc *n.* fork
কাঠবাদাম kaṭhbadam *n.* walnut
কাদা kada *n.* mud
কান ka:n *n.* ear
কানের ফুল kaner phul *n.* earring
কাপড় kapôṛ *n.* clothes
কামড় kamôṛ *n.* bite
কারণ karôṇ *n.* reason
কারা kara *pr. (pl.)* who
কাল kal *n.* season
কালকে kalke *n.* tomorrow, yesterday
কালো kalo *adj.* black
কাশি kaśi *n.* cough
কি ki *qu.* what

কি করে ki kôre *qu.* how, by what transport
কি দিয়ে ki diŷe *qu.* with what
কি রে ki re *expr.* what on earth ...
কি হয়েছে? ki hôŷeche? *phr.* what has happened?
কিছু kichu *adj.* some; *n.* something
কিছু হবে না kichu hɔbe na *phr.* nothing will happen = everything is fine
কিন্তু kintu *conj.* but
কিমা kima *n.* minced meat
কিশমিশ kiśmiś *n.* raisin
কুকুর kukur *n.* dog
কুমড়া kumṛa *n.* pumpkin
কুমির kumir *n.* crocodile
কুঁড়ে ঘর kūṛe ghɔr *n.* thatched hut
কুয়াশা kuŷaśa (kuwasha) *n.* fog, mist
কুষ্টিয়া kuṣṭiŷa *name* Kustia *(town)*
কুসংস্কার kusɔṃskar *n.* superstition
কৃষক kr̥ṣôk (krishok) *n.* farmer
কৃষি kr̥ṣi (krishi) *n.* agriculture
কে ke *qu.* who
কেচি keci (BD) কাঁচি kāci (PB) *n.* scissors
কেজি keji *n.* kilogram
কেটলি keṭli *n.* kettle
কেন kænô *qu.* why
কেননা kænôna *conj.* because
কেনা kena *vb.* buy
কেনাকাটা kenakaṭa *n.* shopping
কেমন kæmôn *qu.* how
কোকিল kokil *n.* cuckoo
কোথাও kothao *adv.* somewhere, anywhere
কোথায় kothaŷ *qu.* where
কোন kon *qu.* which
কোনও kono *adj.* any
কোমর komôr *n.* waist, midriff
কোমল komôl *adj.* soft, gentle
ক্রিয়া kriŷa *n.* work
ক্লান্ত klantô *adj.* tired
ক্লাব klab *n.* club
ক্ষতি kṣôti (khoti) *n.* harm
ক্ষতিকর kṣôtikɔr *adj.* harmful
ক্ষতি করা kṣôti kɔra *vb.* do harm
ক্ষমা kṣôma (khoma) *n.* forgiveness
ক্ষমা করা kṣôma kɔra *vb.* forgive
ক্ষুর kṣur (khur) *n.* razor
ক্ষেত kṣet (khet) *n.* field

খ

খড় khɔṛ *n.* straw

খবর khɔbôr *n.* news

খবরের কাগজ khɔbôrer kagôj *n.* newspaper

খরগোশ khɔrgoś (khɔrgosh) *n.* rabbit

খরচ করা khɔrôc kɔra *vb.* spend (money)

খরিদ্দার khôriddar *n.* customer

খাওয়া khaoŷa *vb.* eat, drink, consume

খাওয়ানো khaoŷano *vb.* feed, give to eat

খাট kha:ṭ *n.* bed

খাটো khaṭo *adj.* short

খাতা khata *n.* notebook

খাপ্পা khappa *adj.* angry

খাবার khabar *n.* food

খাবার ঘর khabar ghɔr *n.* dining room

খারাপ kharap *adj.* bad

খাল kha:l *n.* canal

খালি khali *adj.* empty, free; *adv.* only

খাসির মাংস khasir maṃsô *n.* lamb

খিদে khide (PB), খিদা khida (BD) *n.* hunger

খুঁজে পাওয়া khũje paoŷa *cvb.* find (after searching)

খুব. khub *adv.* very

খুশি khuśi *adj.* happy

খেজুর khejur *n.* date

খেলা khæla *vb.* play

খেলা করা khæla kɔra *vb.* play

খেলাধুলা khæladhula *n.* sport

খেয়ে ফেলা kheŷe phæla *cvb.* eat up, gobble up

খোঁজ করা khõj kɔra *vb.* search

খোঁজা khõja *cvb.* search

খোদা হাফেজ khoda haphej *phr.* good-bye (*lit:* God be with you)

খ্রিস্টান khrisṭan *n., adj.* Christian

গ

গঙ্গা gɔṅga *name* Ganges (river)

গড়া gɔṛa *vb.* build, form

গড়ে ওঠা gôṛe oṭha *cvb.* be established, be built

গত gɔtô *adj.* last

গতকাল gɔtôkal *adv.* yesterday

গণতন্ত্র gɔṇôtɔntrô *n.* democracy

গন্ধ gɔndhô *n.* smell, scent, fragrance

গভীর gôbhīr *adj.* deep

গয়না gɔŷna *n.* jewelry

গরম gɔrôm *adj.* hot

গরম গেঞ্জি gɔrôm geñji *n.* pullover

গরম মসলা gɔrôm mɔsla *n.* hot spices

গরীব gôrīb *adj.* poor

গরু gôru *n.* cow, cattle

গরুর মাংস gorur maṃsô *n.* beef

গর্ত gɔrtô *n.* hole

গর্ব gɔrbô *n.* pride

গর্ভবতী gɔrbhôbôti *adj.* pregnant

গলা gɔla *n.* throat

গলাগলি করে gɔlagôli kôre *adv.* intertwined

গলা gɔla *n.* throat, voice

গলা-জলে gɔla-jɔle *adv.* water up to one's neck

গলিঘুঁজি gôlighũji *phr.* lanes and by-lanes

গল্প gɔlpô *n.* story

গল্প করা gɔlpô kɔra *vb.* chat

গাঁ gã *n.* village

গা ga *n.* body

গায়ে লাগা gaŷe laga *vb.* fit

গাছ gach *n.* tree

গাছ-পালা gach-pala *n.* trees and plants

গাজর gajôr *n.* carrot

গাড়ি gaṛi *n.* car, vehicle

গাড়ি চালানো gaṛi calano *vb.* drive (a car)

গাঢ় garhô *adj.* intense, thick

গাধা gadha *n.* donkey

গান gan *n.* song

গান করা gan kɔra *vb.* sing

গান গাওয়া gan gaoŷa *vb.* sing a song

গামছা gamcha *n.* towel

গালিচা galica *n.* carpet

গুছানো guchano *vb.* tidy up

গুজব gujôb *n.* gossip

গুড় guṛ *n.* molasses

গুরুত্ব gurutvô (gurutto) *n.* importance, weight

গুহা / গুহা guha *n.* cave

গেঞ্জি geñji *n.* vest

গেট geṭ *n.* gate

গেলাস gelas *n.* glass

গোঁফ gõph *n.* moustache

গোয়াল goŷal (gowal) *n.* cowshed

গোল gol *adj.* round

গোল মরিচ gol môric *n.* pepper

গোলাপ golap *n.* rose

গোলাপি golapi *adj.* pink
গৌরব gourob *n.* glory, pride
গ্রন্থ grônthô *n.* book
গ্রহণ করা grôhôṇ kɔra *vb.* accept
গ্রাম gram *n.* village
গ্রীষ্মকাল grīṣmôkal *n.* summer

ঘ

ঘটনা ghɔṭôna *n.* event
ঘড়ি ghôṛi *n.* clock, watch
ঘণ্টা ghɔṇṭa *n.* hour
ঘন ghɔnô *adj.* dense
ঘনিষ্ঠ ghôniṣṭô *adj.* close
ঘর ghɔr *n.* house, room
ঘরবাড়ি ghɔrbaṛi *n.* houses, buildings
ঘাড় gha:ṛ *n.* neck
ঘাস ghas (gha:sh) *n.* grass
ঘুঘু ghughu *n.* dove
ঘুম ghum *n.* sleep
ঘুমানো ghumano *vb.* sleep
ঘুমিয়ে-থাকা ghumiŷe-thaka *adj.* sleeping
ঘূর্ণিঝড় ghūrṇijhɔr *n.* cyclone, tornado
ঘোড়া ghoṛa *n.* horse
ঘোরা ghora *vb.* move, turn

চ

চটি côṭi *n.* sandals
চট্টগ্রাম cɔṭṭôgram *name* Chittagong
চড়া cɔṛa *vb.* ride
চমৎকার cɔmôṯkar *adj.* splendid, wonderful
চর্চা cɔrca *n.* practice
চলা cɔla *vb.* move, go
চলাচল cɔlacɔl *n.* coming and going
চলে যাওয়া côle yaoŷa *cvb.* go away
চশমা cɔśma *n.* glasses
চাওয়া caoŷa *vb.* want
চাঁদ cãd *n.* moon
চাঁদপুর cãdpur *name* Chandpur *(town)*
চাদর cadôr *n.* sheet
চাকর cakôr *n.* servant
চাকরি cakri *n.* job
চাকরি করা cakri kɔra *vb.* do a job, work
চাচা caca *n.* uncle *(father's younger brother)*
চাবি cabi *n.* key
চামচ camôc *n.* spoon
চামড়া camṛa *n.* skin

চারা cara *n.* plant, seed
চাল cal (chal) *n.* roof
চালাক calak *adj.* clever
চালাকি calaki *n.* cleverness
চাষী caṣī *n.* farmer
চিকিৎসা cikiṯsa *n.* treatment
চিচিঙ্গা ciciṅga *n.* snakegourd
চিঠি ciṭhi *n.* letter
চিড়িয়াখানা ciṛiŷakhana *n.* zoo
চিৎকার করা ciṯkar kɔra *vb.* shout
চিরদিন cirôdin *adv.* forever
চিরুনি ciruni *n.* comb
চিহ্ন cihnô (cinhô) *n.* sign
চুপ cup *adj.* quiet
চুমু cumu *n.* kiss
চুল cul *n.* hair
চুলা cula *n.* oven
চেনা cena *vb.* know, recognize
চেয়ার ceŷar *n.* chair
চেষ্টা ceṣṭa *n.* attempt
চেষ্টা করা ceṣṭa kɔra *vb.* try
চেহারা cehara *n.* appearance
চোখ cokh *n.* eye
চৌকি couki *n.* bedstead

ছ

ছড়ানো chɔṛano *vb.* spread
ছবি chôbi *n.* picture
ছবি তোলা chôbi tola *vb.* take pictures
ছাগল chagôl *n.* goat
ছাড়া chaṛa *pp.* except, without
ছাড়া chaṛa *vb.* leave, let go
ছাতি chati *n.* umbrella
ছাত্র chatrô *n.m.* student
ছাত্রী chatrī *n.f.* student
ছাদ cha:d *n.* roof
ছায়া chaŷa *n.* shade
ছিঁড়ে যাওয়া chĩṛe yaoŷa *cvb.* get torn, get
  ripped
ছুটি chuṭi *n.* holiday
ছুরি churi *n.* knife
ছেঁড়া chẽṛa *vb.* tear
ছেলে chele *n.* boy, son
ছেলেমেয়ে chelemeŷe *n.* children
ছোঁয়া chõŷa *vb.* touch
ছোট choṭô *adj.* small

জ (জ্ঞ)

জগ jɔg *n.* jug
জগৎ jɔgôt̪ *n.* world
জঙ্গল jɔṅgôl *n.* jungle
জন্ম jɔnmô *n.* birth
জন্য, জন্যে jônyô, jônye (jonne) *pp.* for
জমজ jɔmôj *n.* twins
জমা jɔma *vb.* collect, gather
জমি jômi *n.* land
জয় jɔŷ *n.* victory
জরুরি jôruri *adj.* urgent
জল (PB) jɔl *n.* water
জলপাই jɔlpai *n.* olive
জলসা jɔlsa *n.* concert
জাগা jaga *vb.* wake up, awake
জাগানো jagano *vb.* cause to wake, awaken
জাদু jadu *n.* magic
জানা jana *vb.* know, find out
জানানো janano *vb.* inform, let know
জানালা janala *n.* window
জাম jam *n.* berry
জামবুরা jambura *n.* pomelo
জামাকাপড় jamakapôṛ *n.* clothes
জায়গা jaŷga *n.* place, space
জায়ফল jaŷphɔl *n.* nutmeg
জাহাজ jahaj *n.* ship
জিজ্ঞাসা jijñasa (jiggasha) *n.* question
জিনিস jinis *n.* thing
জিভ ji:bh *n.* tongue
জিরা jira *n.* cumin
জীবজন্তু jībjôntu *n.* animal
জীবন jībôn *n.* life
জুঁই jūi *n.* jasmine
জুতা, জুতো juta, juto *n.* shoe, shoes
জেগে ওঠা jege oṭha *cvb.* wake up
জেলা jela *n.* district
জোনাকি jonaki *n.* firefly
জোয়ার joŷar *n.* flow, tide
জোরে jore *adv.* loud; fast; strong
জ্ঞান jñan (gæn) *n.* knowledge
জ্বর jvɔr (jɔr) *n.* fever
জ্বালানো jvalano *vb.* ignite, annoy, irritate

ঝ

ঝগড়া jhɔgṛa *n.* quarrel, argument
ঝড় jhɔr *n.* storm
ঝড়ো jhɔro *adj.* stormy
ঝরা jhɔra *vb.* shed, fall
ঝাঁপানো jhãpano *vb.* jump, burst
ঝাড়ু jharu *n.* broom
ঝামেলা jhamela *n.* hassle, upset
ঝিনুক jhinuk *n.* oyster
ঝুড়ি jhuri *n.* basket

ট

টক ṭɔk *adj.* sour
টয়লেট ṭɔŷleṭ *n.* toilet
টাকা ṭaka *n.* taka *(currency of Bangladesh)*
টাকা দেওয়া ṭaka deoŷa *vb.* pay
টাটকা ṭaṭka *adj.* fresh
টান ṭan *n.* pull, attraction
টান দেওয়া ṭan deoŷa *vb.* pull
টিকা ṭika *n.* vaccination
টিকিট ṭikiṭ *n.* ticket
টুপি ṭupi *n.* hat
টেকা ṭeka *vb.* last, continue
টেবিল ṭebil *n.* table
টের পাওয়া ṭer paoŷa *vb.* feel, notice
টেলিফোন ṭeliphon *n.* telephone
টোমেটো ṭomeṭo *n.* tomato
ট্রেন ṭren *n.* train

ঠ

ঠকা ṭhɔka *vb.* cheat
ঠাকুরমা ṭhakurma *n.* grandmother *(father's mother)* *(H.)*
ঠাট্টা ṭhaṭṭa *n.* joke, mockery
ঠাণ্ডা ṭhanḍa *adj.* cold
ঠিক ṭhik *adj.* correct, right, exactly
ঠিক আছে ṭhik ache *phr.* OK, alright
ঠিক করা ṭhik kɔra *vb.* put straight
ঠিকানা ṭhikana *n.* address
ঠেলাগাড়ি ṭhelagaṛi *n.* pushcart

ড

ডজন ḍɔjôn *n.* dozen

ডবল রুম ḍɔbôl rum *n.* double room

ডাক ḍak *n.* call

ডাক দেওয়া ḍak deoŷa *vb.* call

ডাকটিকিট ḍakṭikiṭ *n.* postage stamp

ডাকা ḍaka *vb.* call

ডাক্তার ḍaktar *n.* doctor

ডান ḍan *adj.* right *(not left)*

ডান দিকে ḍan dike *pp.* to the right

ডানা ḍana *n.* wing

ডাব ḍa:b *n.* green coconut

ডাল ḍal *n.* lentil

ডাল ḍal *n.* branch

ডালিম ḍalim *n.* pomegranate

ডিঙ্গি ḍiṅgi *n.* small boat, dinghy

ডিম ḍim *n.* egg

ডুবিয়ে দেওয়া ḍubiŷe deoŷa *cvb.* cause to drown, wash away

ডুমুর ḍumur *n.* fig

ডেকচি ḍekci *n.* pot (for cooking)

ঢ

ঢাকা ḍhaka *name* Dhaka *(cap. of Bangladesh)*

ঢেঁড়স ḍhẽros *n.* lady's fingers, okra

ঢেউ ḍheu *n.* wave

ঢোকা ḍhoka *vb.* enter

ঢোকার মুখে ḍhokar mukhe *adv.* by the entrance

ত

তখন tɔkhôn *adv.* then

তখনও tɔkhôno *adv.* still

তন্দ্রা tɔndra *n.* sleep

তবে tɔbe *conj.* but

তরমুজ tôrmuj *n.* watermelon

তরুণ tôrun *adj.* young

তলা tɔla *n.* floor, story

তা ta *pr.* it, that

তা ছাড়া ta chaṛa *conj.* besides, in addition

তাই tai *conj.* so, therefore

তাই না? tai na? *phr.* isn't that so?

তাই নাকি? tai naki? *phr.* is that so?

তাকানো takano *vb.* look at

তাড়াতাড়ি taṛataṛi *adv.* quickly

তাড়ানো taṛano *vb.* chase away

তাদের → তারা tader *pr.* their, them

তার → সে tar *pr.* his, her

তার ঠিক নেই tar ṭhik nei *phr.* it is uncertain

তারা tara *n.* star

তারিখ tarikh *n.* date

তালা tala *n.* lock

তালাক talak *n.* divorce

তাহলে tahôle *conj.* in that case, then

তিতা tita *adj.* bitter

তিমি timi *n.* whale

তিল til *n.* sesame

তীর tīr *n.* bank (of a river)

তুফান tuphan *n.* typhoon

তুলনা tulôna *n.* comparison

তুলা tula *n.* cotton-wool

তৃপ্ত tṛptô (tripto) *adj.* satisfied

তেঁতুল tẽtul *n.* tamarind

তেজপাতা tejpata *n.* bay leaf

তেমন tæmôn *adv.* so, so much

তেল tel *n.* oil

তৈরি toiri *adj.* prepared, built, made

তো to *emph* but

তোমাকে → তুমি tomake → tumi *pr. (sg, fam.)* you

তোমার → তুমি tomar → tumi *pr. (sg, fam.)* you

তোয়ালে toŷale *n.* towel

তোলা tola *vb.* lift, pluck

থ

থলি thôli *n.* bag

থাকা thaka *vb.* stay

থাক thak *vb.* stay; leave it!

থানা thana *n.* police station

থামা thama *vb.* stop

থালা thala *n.* plate

থিয়েটার thiŷeṭar *n.* theater

থেকে theke *pp.* from

দ

দক্ষিণ dôkṣiṇ (dokkhin) *n.* south

দড়ি dôri *n.* rope

দণ্ড dɔṇḍô *n.* staff, pole

দরকার dɔrkar *n.* need
দরকারি dɔrkari *adj.* necessary, important
দরজা dɔrja *n.* door
দরজি dôrji *n.* tailor
দশ dɔʃ (dɔsh) *num.* ten
দাঁড়ানো dãṛano *vb.* stand, wait
দাঁত dãt *n.* tooth
দাগ dag *n.* mark, stain
দাগ কাটা dag kaṭa *vb.* make an impression
দাদা dada *n.* older brother
দাম da:m *n.* price
দামি dami *adj.* expensive
দারচিনি darcini *n.* cinnamon
দারুণ daruṇ *adj.* excellent
দারোয়ান daroẏan *n.* porter, guard
দিক dik *n.* direction
দিকে dike *pp.* towards
দিগন্ত digôntô *n.* horizon
দিচ্ছি → দেওয়া dicchi → deoẏa *vb.* give
দিদি didi *n.* older sister *(H.)*
দিদিমা didima *n.* maternal grandmother
দিন di:n *n.* day
দিন যেতে যেতে di:n yete yete *phr.* in the
    course of the day *(lit.: day going going)*
দিয়ে diẏe *pp.* with *(instrumental)*
দীপ dīp *n.* lamp
দীর্ঘ dīrghô *adj.* long
দুঃখ duḥkhô *n.* sadness, sorrow
দুঃখ করা duḥkhô kɔra *vb.* regret
দুঃখিত duḥkhitô *adj.* sad
দুজন dujɔn *adj./n.* two (persons)
দুধ du:dh *n.* milk
দুনিয়া duniẏa *n.* world
দুপুর dupur *n.* midday
দুর্বল durbɔl *adj.* weak
দুষ্টু duṣṭu *adj.* naughty
দূর dūr *n.* distance
দূর dūr *excl.* no way!
দূরত্ব dūrôtvô (durotto) *n.* distance
দেওয়া deoẏa *vb.* give; allow
দেওয়াল deoẏal (deowal) *n.* wall
দেখা dækha *vb.* see, look at
দেখানো dækhano *vb.* show
দেখা পাওয়া dækha paoẏa *vb.* detect, spot,
    get to see
দেড় deṛ *num.* one and a half
দেবতা debôta *n.* god

দেরাজ deraj *n.* drawer
দেরি deri *n.* delay
দেরি করা deri kɔra *vb.* delay, be late
দেশ deʃ *n.* country
দেশলাই deʃôlai *n.* matches
দেশান্তর deʃantôr *n.* another country
দেশী deʃī *adj.* indigenous
দেহ dehô *n.* body
দৈনিক doinik *adj.* daily
দোকান dokan *n.* shop
দোকানদার dokandar *n.* shopkeeper
দোতালা dotala *n.* second floor
দোল খাওয়া dol khaoẏa *vb.* swing
দোষ doṣ *n.* fault
দ্বিতীয় dvitīẏô *num.* second

ধ

ধনিয়া dhôniẏa *n.* coriander
ধনী dhônī *adj.* rich
ধন্যবাদ dhɔnyôbad *expr.* thanks, thank you
ধরন dhɔrôn *n.* type, kind
ধরা dhɔra *vb.* hold, catch
ধরে dhôre *pp.* during, for *(time)*
ধর্ম dhɔrmô *n.* religion
ধাক্কা dhakka *n.* push
ধান dha:n *n.* paddy, rice
ধার dhar *n.* bank *(of a river)*, side
ধীরে dhīre *adv.* slowly, gradually
ধুতি dhuti *n.* dhoti
ধুলা dhula *n.* dust
ধোয়া dhoẏa *vb.* wash
ধ্বংস dhvɔṃsô *n.* destruction

ন

নগদ nɔgôd *n.* cash
নগর nɔgôr *n.* town
নড়াচড়া nɔṛacɔra *vb.* move, move around
নতুন nôtun *adj.* new
নদনদী nôdnôdī *n.* waterways
নদী nôdī *n.* river
নদ-নদী nɔd-nôdī *n.* rivers and streams
নরক nɔrôk *n.* hell
নরম nɔrôm *adj.* soft, gentle
নলকূপ nɔlkūp *n.* tubewell
নষ্ট nɔṣṭô *adj.* spoiled

নষ্ট করা nɔṣṭô kɔra *vb.* spoil, destroy

নষ্ট হওয়া nɔṣṭô hɔoŷa *vb.* get destroyed, get spoiled

না na *adv.* no, not

না হলে na hôle *conj.* otherwise

নাক nak *n.* nose

নাক ডাকা nak ḍaka *vb.* snore

নাচ nac *n./vb.* dance

নাটক naṭôk *n.* drama

নানা, নানান nana, nanan *adj.* various

নাম nam *n.* name

নামা nama *vb.* get down, descend

নারিকেল narikel *n.* coconut

নার্সিং narsiṃ (narsing) *n.* nursing

নাসপাতি naspati *n.* pear

নাস্তা nasta *n.* breakfast

নিঃশ্বাস niḥśvas (nisshash) *n.* breath

নিচে nice *adv.* low

নিজ nij *pr.* own, self

নিমন্ত্রণ nimôntroṇ *n.* invitation

নিয়ম niŷôm *n.* routine, system

নিয়ে niŷe *pp.* with, about

নিয়ে → নেওয়া neoŷa *vb.* take

নিয়ে আসা niŷe asa *vb.* bring

নিয়ে যাওয়া niŷe yaoŷa *cvb.* take along

নিদিষ্ট nirdiṣṭô *adj.* fixed, confirmed

নিদিষ্ট করা nirdiṣṭô kɔra *vb.* confirm, fix

নির্মল nirmɔl *adj.* pure, immaculate

নিশ্চয় niścɔŷ (nishcɔŷ) *adv.* of course

নিষেধ niṣedh *n.* prohibition

নীল nīl *adj.* blue

নুন nun *n.* salt

নূপুর nūpur *n.* ankle-bells

নেই nei *vb.* be absent, not exist

নেওয়া neoŷa *vb.* take

নোংরা noṃra *adj.* dirty, ugly

নৌকা nouka *n.* boat

ন্যায় nyaŷ (nay) *n.* justice

প

পকেট pɔkeṭ *n.* pocket

পচা pɔca *adj.* rotten, spoiled

পটোল pɔṭol *n.* snakebean

পড়া pɔṛa *vb.* read, study

পড়া pɔṛa *vb.* fall

পড়ে যাওয়া pôṛe yaoŷa *cvb.* fall off, fall down

পণ্ডিত pôṇḍit *n.* scholar

পথ pɔth *n.* way, road

পথচলা pɔthcɔla *n.* journey

পদ্ম ফুল pɔdmô phul *n.* lotus

পদ্মা pɔdma (pɔdda) *name* Padma (Podda) (river)

পরদা pɔrda *n.* curtain

পরা pɔra *vb.* wear

পরাজয় pɔrajɔŷ *n.* defeat

পরিপূর্ণতা pôripūrṇota *n.* fullness, richness

পরিবর্তন pôribɔrtôn *n.* change

পরিবার pôribar *n.* family

পরিশ্রম pôriśrôm *n.* hard work

পরিষ্কার pôriṣkar *adj.* clean

পরিষ্কার করা pôriṣkar kɔra *vb.* clean

পরীক্ষা করা pôrīkṣa kɔra *vb.* examine

পরে pɔre *pp.* after

পর্যন্ত pôryôntô (porjonto) *pp.* until

পরশু দিন pôrśudin *n.* day after tomorrow

পলাশ pɔlaś *n.* palas (flower)

পশু pôśu *n.* animal

পশ্চিম pôścim *n.* west

পশ্চিম বাংলা pôścim baṃla *name* West Bengal

পা pa *n.* foot, leg

পাউডার pauḍar *n.* powder

পাওয়া paoŷa *vb.* get, receive

পেলে → পাওয়া paoŷa *vb.* get, find

পাওয়া যায় paoŷa yaŷ *vb.* is available

পাঁচ pãc *num.* five

পাঁচেক pãcek *num.* about five

পাকা paka *adj.* ripe

পাখা pakha *n.* fan

পাখি pakhi *n.* bird

পাছা pacha *n.* hip

পাট pa:ṭ *n.* jute

পাঠানো paṭhano *vb.* send

পাঠিয়ে দেওয়া paṭhiŷe deoŷa *vb.* send

পাড় paṛ *n.* riverbank

পাতলা patla *adj.* thin (material)

পাতা pata *n.* leaf

পাথর pathôr *n.* stone

পানি (BD) pani *n.* water

পায়খানা paŷkhana *n.* feces

পায়জামা paŷjama *n.* pajamas

পায়েস paŷes *n.* rice pudding

পার হওয়া par hɔoŷa *vb.* cross, go past

পারফিউম parphium *n.* perfume

পারসেল parsel *n.* parcel

পারা para *vb.* be able to, can

পালং শাক palôm śa:k *n.* spinach

পালা pala *n.* turn

পালানো palano *vb.* flee, escape

পাশাপাশি paśapaśi *adv.* side by side

পাশে paśe *pp.* alongside, on the side

পাহাড় pahaṛ *n.* mountain

পিঁপড়া pīpṛa (BD), পিঁপড়ে pīpṛe (PB) *n.* ant

পিছনে, পেছনে pichône, pechône *pp.* behind

পিঠ pi:ṭh *n.* back

পিঠা piṭha *n.* cake

পিরিচ piric *n.* saucer

পিসি pisi *n.* aunt *(father's sister) (H.)*

পুকুর pukur *n.* pond, lake

পুদিনা pudina *n.* mint

পুরা pura (BD), পুরো puro (PB) *adj.* whole, complete

পুরানো purano *adj.* old *(for things)*

পুরুষ puruṣ *n.* man, male human being

পূর্ণিমা pūrṇima *n.* full moon

পূর্ব pūrbô *adj.* east

পৃথিবী pṛthibī (prithibi) *n.* world

পেঁপে pēpe *n.* papaya, pawpaw

পেঁয়াজ pēŷaj *n.* onion

পেট peṭ *n.* stomach

পেনসিল pensil *n.* pencil

পেয়ারা peŷara *n.* guava

পোকা poka *n.* insect

পোষাক poṣak *n.* dress *(attire)*

পৌঁছানো pōuchano *vb.* arrive

পৌনে poune *adj.* quarter to

প্যাক করা pyak kɔra *vb.* pack

প্যান্ট pyanṭ (pænṭ) *n.* trousers, pants

প্রকৃতি prôkṛti (prokriti) *n.* nature

প্রচণ্ড prôcɔṇḍô *adj.* fierce, severe

প্রজাপতি prôjapôti *n.* butterfly

প্রতি prôti *adj.* each, every

প্রতিদিন prôtidin *adv.* every day

প্রতিবেশী prôtibeśi *n.* neighbor

প্রথম prôthôm *adj.* first

প্রথমে prôthôme *adv.* at first

প্রমাণ prômaṇ *n.* proof, evidence

প্রশান্ত prôśantô *adj.* peaceful

প্রশ্ন prôśnô *n.* question

প্রশ্ন করা prôśnô kɔra *vb.* ask question

প্রসঙ্গত prôsɔŋgôtô *adv.* by the way

প্রস্তুত prôstut *adj.* ready, prepared

প্রাচীন pracīn *adj.* old, ancient

প্রাণ praṇ *n.* life

প্রায় praŷ *adv.* almost

প্রায়ই praŷi *adv.* often

প্রিয় priŷô *adj.* favorite, well-liked

প্লাবন plabôn *n.* flood

ফ

ফরসা phɔrsa *adj.* fair (skinned)

ফরিদপুর phôridpur *name* Faridpur *(town)*

ফল phɔl *n.* fruit, result

ফলগাছ phɔlgach *n.* fruit tree

ফসল phɔsôl *n.* harvest

ফাইল phail *n.* file

ফাঁকা phãka *adj.* open, empty

ফিতা, ফিতে phita, phite *n.* string, ribbon; lace

ফিরে আসা phire asa *cvb.* return, come back

ফুটবল phuṭbɔl *n.* football, soccer

ফুটি phuṭi *n.* melon

ফুটে ওঠা phuṭe oṭha *cvb.* blossom, bloom

ফুফু phuphu *n.* aunt *(father's sister) (M.)*

ফুর্তি phurti *n.* fun, enjoyment

ফুল phul *n.* flower

ফুলকপি phulkôpi *n.* cauliflower

ফুসফুস phusphus *n.* lungs

ফেরত দেওয়া pherôt deoŷa *vb.* return, give back

ফেরা phera *vb.* return

ফেরি pheri *n.* ferry

ফেলা phæla *vb.* throw, throw away

ফোটা phoṭa *vb.* blossom

ফ্রক phrɔk *n.* dress *(girl's)*

ফ্ল্যাট phlyaṭ (phlæṭ) *n.* flat

ব

বই bôi *n.* book

বই-খাতা bôi-khata *n.* books and notebooks

বউ, বৌ bou *n.* wife

বকাবকি bɔkabôki *n.* telling off, reprimand

বকাবকি করা bɔkabôki kɔra *vb.* tell off, reprimand

বঙ্গোপসাগর bɔŋgôpsagôr *name* Bay of Bengal

বছর bɔchôr *n.* year
বড় bɔṛô *adj.* big
বড় ভাই bɔṛô bhai *n.* older brother *(M.)*
বদল করা bɔdôl kɔra *vb.* change, exchange
বদলানো bɔdlano *vb.* change, transform
বন bôn *n.* forest
বন্ধ bɔndhô *adj.* closed
বন্ধ করা bɔndhô kɔra *vb.* close
বন্ধু bôndhu *n.* friend
বন্যা bônya *n.* flood
বয়স bɔŷôs (bɔyosh) *n.* age
বয়স্ক bɔŷôskô *adj.* elderly
বয়াম bɔŷam *n.* jar
বয়ে আনা bôŷe ana *cvb.* bring, bring along
বরই bɔroi *n.* jujube
বরফ bɔrôph *n.* ice, snow
বরবটি bɔrbôṭi *n.* green bean
বর্ষা bɔrṣa *n.* rainy season, monsoon
বলা bɔla *vb.* say, speak
বলে bôle *vb. part.* called
বলে bôle *conj.* because
বসন্ত bɔsôntô *n.* spring *(season)*
বসা bɔsa *vb.* sit, sink down, settle, get stuck
বস্তি bôsti *n.* slum
বহু bôhu *adj.* many
বা ba *conj.* or
বাইরে baire *pp.* outside
বাংলা bamla *adj./n.* Bangla
বাংলাদেশ bamladeś *name* Bangladesh
বাঃ bah *excl.* wow, oh, ah
বাঁ bã *n.* left *(not right)*
বাঁ দিকে bã dike *pp.* to the left
বাঁচা bãca *vb.* survive
বাঁচানো bãcano *vb.* rescue, save
বাঁচিয়ে রাখা bãciŷe rakha *cvb.* keep alive
বাঁধাকপি bãdhakôpi *n.* cabbage
বাঁশ bãś *n.* bamboo
বাকি baki *adj.* left-over
বাগান bagan *n.* garden
বাঘ bagh *n.* tiger
বাঙালি baṅali (banggali) *adj.* Bengali
বাচ্চা bacca *n.* child
বাজা baja *vb.* strike (of a clock)
বাজার bajar *n.* market
বাটি baṭi *n.* bowl
বাড়ানো baṛano *vb.* extend, increase
বাড়ি baṛi *n.* home, village home

বাতাস batas *n.* wind
বাতি bati *n.* lamp
বাদ দেওয়া bad deoŷa *vb.* omit, leave out
বাদাম badam *n.* peanut, groundnut
বাদামি badami *adj.* brown
বানর banôr *n.* monkey
বানানো banano *vb.* prepare, make
বান্ধবী bandhôbī *n.f.* friend
বাবা baba *n.* father
বাবু babu *n.* Mister
বারান্দা baranda *n.* verandah
বালতি balti *n.* bucket
বালিশ baliś *n.* pillow
বালু balu (BD), বালি bali (PB) *n.* sand
বাসন basôn *n.* dishes
বাসা basa *n.* house
বাস্তবতা bastôbôta *n.* reality
বাহু bahu *n.* arm
বিউইক biuik *n.* Buick
বিকাল bikal (BD), বিকেল bikel (PB) *n.*
  afternoon
বিঘা bigha *n.* bigha *(land measure)*
বিচার bicar *n.* judgement
বিচিত্র bicitrô *adj.* various
বিছানা bichana *n.* bed
বিজলি bijoli *n.* lightning
বিজ্ঞাপন bijñapɔn (biggapɔn) *n.*
  advertisement
বিড়াল biṛal *n.* cat
বিদায় bidaŷ *n.* farewell
বিদায় দেওয়া bidaŷ deoŷa *vb.* say farewell
বিদেশি bideśi *n.* foreigner; *adj.* foreign
বিদ্যা bidya (bidda) *n.* learning
বিদ্যুৎ bidyuṯ *n.* lightning, electricity
বিপদ bipɔd *n.* danger
বিবেচনা bibecôna *n.* consideration
বিমান biman *n.* airplane
বিয়ে biŷe *n.* marriage, wedding
বিয়ে করা biŷe kɔra *vb.* get married
বিরুদ্ধে biruddhe *pp.* against
বিল bi:l *n.* floodplane
বিশ biś *num.* twenty
বিশেষ biśeṣ *adj.* special
বিশ্ব biśvô *n.* universe
বিশ্বাস biśvas (bisshash) *n.* belief
বিশ্বাস করা biśvas kɔra *vb.* believe
বিশ্রাম biśram *n.* rest, pause

বিশ্রী biśrī *adj.* ugly

বিস্কুট biskuṭ *n.* biscuit

বিশ্রাম biśram *n.* rest, relaxation

বীচি bīci *n.* seed

বুক buk *n.* breast, chest

বুঝিয়ে দেওয়া bujhiẏe deoẏa *cvb.* explain

বুড়া bura (BD), বুড়ো buṛo (PB) *adj.* old (about people)

বুদ্ধি buddhi *n.* wisdom

বুধবার budhbar *n.* Wednesday

বৃষ্টি br̥ṣṭi (brishṭi) *n.* rain

বৃহস্পতিবার br̥hôspôtibar (brihôshpôtibar) *n.* Thursday

বেঁচে থাকা bēce thaka *vb.* stay alive, survive

বেগুন begun *n.* aubergine, eggplant

বেচা bæca *vb.* sell

বেচারা becara *n.* poor boy

বেড়ানো beṛano *vb.* visit, go out

বেড়াল beṛal *n.* cat

বেল bel *n.* wood-apple

বেশ beś *adv.* quite

বেশি beśi *adj.* much, too much

বেশি করে beśi kôre *adv.* much, a lot

বৈচিত্র্য boicitryô *n.* variety

বৈশাখ boiśakh *n.* Baishakh (*first month of the Bengali year*)

বোকা boka *adj.* stupid

বোঝা bojha *vb.* understand

বোঝানো bojhano *vb.* explain

বোতল botôl *n* bottle

বোতাম botam *n.* button

বোন bon *n.* sister

বউ, বৌ bôu, bou *n.* wife

ব্যক্তি bykti (bekti) *n.* person

ব্যথা bytha (bætha) *n.* pain

ব্যবস্থা bybôstha (bæbostha) *n.* arrangement

ব্যস্ত bystô (bæsto) *adj.* busy

ব্যবহার bybôhar (bæbohar) *n.* behavior

ব্যাং byaṃ (bæng) *n.* frog

ব্যাপার byapar (bæpar) *n.* matter

ব্রাহ্ম (brahmô) brammo *name* Brahman

ব্লাউজ blauj *n.* blouse

ভ

ভদ্রমহিলা bhɔdrômôhila *n.* lady

ভদ্রলোক bhɔdrôlok *n.* gentleman

ভবিষ্যৎ bhôbiṣyɔt *n.* future

ভয় bhɔẏ *n.* fear

ভয় করা bhɔẏ kɔra *vb.* be afraid

ভয় দেখানো bhɔẏ dækhano *vb.* frighten, scare

ভয় নেই bhɔẏ nei *phr.* have no fear, don't worry

ভয় পাওয়া bhɔẏ paoẏa (paowa) *vb.* be scared, be afraid

ভয়ংকর bhɔẏôṃkɔr *adj.* frightening

ভয়ডর bhɔẏḍɔr *n.* fear

ভরসা bhɔrsa *n.* support, refuge, prop

ভরা bhɔra *adj.* full, filled

ভরে যাওয়া bhôre yaoẏa *vb.* get filled up

ভাই bhai *n.* brother

ভাইবোন bhaibon *n.* brothers and sisters

ভাগ bhag *n.* part

ভাগ্য bhagyô *n.* luck, fate

ভাঙা bhaṅa (bhangga) *vb.* break, destroy

ভাড়া bhaṛa *n.* rent, hire

ভাড়া দেওয়া bhaṛa deoẏa *vb.* rent out

ভাত bhat *n.* (cooked) rice

ভদ্রমাস bhadrômas *n.* Bhadro (*month / August-September, the end of the rainy season*)

ভাবা bhaba *vb.* think

ভারী bharī *adj.* heavy

ভাল bhalô *adj.* good, nice

ভালবাসা bhalôbasa, ভালোবাসা bhalobasa *vb.* love

ভালভাবে bhalôbhabe *adv.* well, thoroughly

ভাল লাগা bhalô laga *vb.* like

ভাষা bhaṣa *n.* language

ভাসানো bhasano *vb.* cause to float

ভিজা, ভিজে bhija, bhije *adj.* wet

ভিতরে bhitôre *pp.* inside

ভিন্ন bhinnô *adj.* different

ভীতি bhīti *n.* fear

ভীষণ bhīṣôṇ *adv.* extremely

ভুট্টা bhuṭṭa *n.* corn, maize

ভুল bhul *n.* mistake

ভুল করা bhul kɔra *vb.* make a mistake

ভুল করে bhul kôre *adv.* accidentally

ভুলে যাওয়া bhule yaoẏa *cvb.* forget
ভূগোল bhūgol *n.* geography
ভূত bhūt *n.* ghost
ভূতের গল্প bhūter gɔlpô *n.* ghost stories
ভূমি bhūmi *n.* earth, land
ভেঙে যাওয়া bheṅge yaoẏa *cvb.* get broken, be destroyed
ভেঙে পড়া bheṅe pɔṛa *cvb.* get broken
ভেড়া bhæṛa *n.* sheep
ভোর bhor *n.* dawn
ভোলা bhola *vb.* forget

ম

মই môi *n.* ladder
মক্কা mɔkka *n.* maize
মঙ্গল mɔṅgôl (mɔnggol) *n.* benefit
মঙ্গলবার mɔṅgôlbar *n.* Saturday
মঞ্চ mɔñcô *n.* stage
মজা mɔja *n.* fun
মজাদার mɔjadar *adj.* delicious
মটর mɔṭôr *n.* pea
মত mɔtô *pp.* like, about
মত mɔ:t *n.* opinion
মদ mɔd *n.* alcohol
মধু môdhu *n.* honey
মধ্যে môdhye *pp.* within, among
মন môn *n.* mind, heart
মন দেওয়া môn deoẏa *vb.* concentrate
মনে আছে mône ache *vb.* remember, be aware of
মনে করা mône kɔra *vb.* think
মনে নেই mône nei *vb.* not remember, be unaware of
মনে পড়া mône pɔṛa *vb.* miss (someone)
মনে রাখা mône rakha *vb.* remember
মনে হয় mône hɔẏ *phr.* it is in the mind = I think
মন্ত্রী môntri *n.* minister
মন্দ mɔndô *adj.* bad, evil
ময়লা mɔẏla *adj.* dirty
মরা mɔra *vb.* die
মরিচ môric (BD) *n.* chili
মরুভূমি môrubhūmi *n.* desert
মর্যাদা mɔryada (mɔrjada) *n.* dignity
মলম mɔlôm *n.* paste, ointment
মলিন môlin *adj.* dirty, unclean

মশা mɔśa *n.* mosquito
মসজিদ môsjid *n.* mosque
মসলা mɔsla *n.* spice
মহিলা môhila *n.* woman
মহিষ môhiṣ (mohish) *n.* water buffalo
মা ma *n.* mother
মাংস maṃsô (mangsho) *n.* meat
মাকড়সা makôrsa *n.* spider
মাখন makhôn *n.* butter
মাছ mach *n.* fish
মাছি machi *n.* fly
মাঝ majh *n.* middle
মাঝখানে majhkhane *pp.* in the middle of
মাঝে মাঝে majhe majhe *adv.* sometimes
মাটি maṭi *n.* earth, soil
মাঠ maṭh *n.* field
মাত্র matrô *adv.* only
মাথা matha *n.* head
মাথা খারাপ matha kharap *phr.* are you crazy?
মাথা ব্যথা matha bytha (bætha) *n.* headache
মানচিত্র mancitro *n.* map
মাননীয় manônīẏô *adj.* respectable, honorable
মানিব্যাগ manibyag *n.* purse
মানুষ manuṣ *n.* person, human being
মানে mane *n.* meaning
মাফ maph *n.* pardon, forgiveness
মাফ করা maph kɔra *vb.* pardon, forgive
মাফলার maphlar *n.* scarf
মা–বাবা ma–baba *n.* parents
মামা mama *n.* uncle *(maternal)*
মায়া maẏa *n.* illusion
মারা mara *vb.* hit, strike
মারা যাওয়া mara yaoẏa *vb.* die
মালপত্র malpɔtrô *n.* luggage
মালা mala *n.* necklace
মালি mali *n.* gardener
মালিক malik *n.* owner, landlord
মাস ma:s *n.* month
মিটানো miṭano *vb.* fulfill, satisfy, accomplish
মিতালি mitali *n.* alliance
মিথ্যা mithya (mittha) *n.* lie, untruth
মিনতি minôti *n.* humble request
মিনিট miniṭ *n.* minute
মিলানো milano *vb.* balance, correspond
মিশে যাওয়া miśe yaoẏa *cvb.* mingle, flow into

মিষ্টি miṣṭi (mishti) *adj.* sweet; *n.* sweets
মিষ্টি আলু miṣṭi alu *n.* sweet potato
মুক্তি mukti *n.* freedom
মুখ mukh *n.* face, mouth, opening
মুগ্ধ mugdhô *adj.* fascinated, enchanted
মুদির দোকান mudir dokan *n.* grocery store
মুরগি murgi *n.* chicken
মুর্গির মাংস murgir maṃsô *n.* chicken
মুশকিল muśkil *n.* problem, difficulty
মুসলমান musôlman *n./adj.* Muslim
মুহূর্ত muhūrtô *n.* moment
মূলা mūla *n.* radish
মূল্য mūlyô *n.* value
মৃত্যু mṛtyu (mrittu) *n.* death
মেঘ megh *n.* cloud
মেঘনা meghna *name* Meghna *(river)*
মেঘের ডাক megher ḍak *n.* thunder
মেজাজ mejaj *n.* mood, temper
মেঝে mejhe *n.* floor
মেতে ওঠা mete oṭha *cvb.* be delighted
মেতে → মাতা mete → mata *vb.* be excited, go mad
মেয়ে meẏe *n.* girl, daughter
মেরুদণ্ড merudɔṇḍô *n.* spine
মেলা mæla *n.* fair, exhibition
মোজা moja *n.* socks
মোট moṭ *adv.* in total
মোটরগাড়ি moṭôrgaṛi *n.* motorcar, car, automobile
মোটা moṭa *adj.* overweight, fat
মোড় moṛ *n.* crossing, junction
মোড়া moṛa *n.* cane chair
মোমবাতি mombati *n.* candle
মৌমাছি moumachi *n.* bee
ম্যাডাম myaḍam *n.* madam

য

যখন – তখন yɔkhôn – tɔkhôn *conj.* when – then
যত্ন yɔtnô *n.* care
যদি yôdi *conj.* if
যমুনা yômuna *name* Jamuna *(river)*
যা ya *pr.* what
যাই হোক yai hok *expr.* in any case
যাওয়া yaoẏa *vb.* go
যাত্রা yatra (jatra) *n.* journey

যুক্তি yukti *n.* reason
যে ye *conj.* that
যেতে → যাওয়া yete → yaoẏa *vb.* go
যেন yænô *conj.* as if, like, so that
যেমন yæmôn *conj.* as
যেমন – তেমন yæmôn – tæmôn *conj.* as – as

র

রং rɔṃ *n.* color
রংপুর rɔṃpur *name* Rangpur
রকম rɔkôm *n.* kind, type
রক্ষা করা rôkṣa kɔra *vb.* protect
রবিবার rôbibar *n.* Sunday
রং rɔṃv (rɔng) *n.* color
রং করে দেওয়া rɔṃ kôre deoẏa *vb.* dye, color
রকম rɔkôm *n.* kind, type
রক্ত rɔktô *n.* blood
রবিবার rôbibar *n.* Sunday
রস rɔs *n.* juice
রসুন rôsun *n.* garlic
রাখা rakha *vb.* keep, put, put away
রাগ rag *n.* anger
রাজত্ব rajôtvô *n.* kingdom
রাজধানী rajdhanī *n.* capital
রাজশাহী rajshahī *n.* Rajshahi *(town)*
রাজা raja *n.* king
রাজি raji *adj.* agreed, willing
রাত rat *n.* night
রাত্রে ratre *adv.* at night
রান্না ranna *n.* cooking
রান্না করা ranna kɔra *vb.* cook
রান্না ঘর ranna ghɔr *n.* kitchen
রাশি raśi *n.* heap, mass
রাস্তা rasta *n.* road
রিকশা rikśa *n.* rickshaw
রুটি ruṭi *n.* bread
রূপ rūp *n.* shape, form, appearance
রেখে আসা rekhe asa *cvb.* leave, leave behind
রেখে যাওয়া rekhe yaoẏa *cvb.* leave behind
রেস্তোরাঁ restorā *n.* restaurant
রেলগাড়ি relgaṛi *n.* train, railway
রোগ rog *n.* illness, disease
রোগা roga *adj.* thin, emaciated
রোগী rogī *n.* patient

রোজ roj *adv.* daily
রোদ rod *n.* sunlight, sunshine

ল

লংকা lɔṃka (lɔnka) (PB) *n.* chili
লক্ষ করা lôkṣô kɔra *vb.* notice, observe
লজ্জা lɔjja *n.* embarrassment
লবঙ্গ lɔbôṅgô *n.* clove
লবণ lɔbôṇ *n.* salt
লম্বা lɔmba *adj.* long
লাউ lau *n.* gourd
লাগা laga *vb.* be attached; start
লাগানো lagano *vb.* plant; employ
লাঠি laṭhi *n.* stick
লাফ laph *n.* jump
লাভ labh *n.* profit
লাল la:l *adj.* red
লিচু licu *n.* lychee
লুব্ধ lubdho *adj.* enticing
লেখা lekha *vb.* write
লেখাপড়া lekhapɔra *n.* studying, education
লেবু lebu *n.* lemon
লোক lok *n.* person, man
লোকসান loksan *n.* loss
লোভ lobh *n.* greed
লোহা loha *n.* iron

শ

শক্ত śɔktô *adj.* hard, strong
শক্তি śôkti *n.* strength
শখ śɔkh *n.* hobby
শত্রু śôtru *n.* enemy
শনিবার śônibar *n.* Saturday
শব্দ śɔbdô *n.* sound, word
শরৎ śɔrôṯ *n.* early autumn
শরীর śôrīr *n.* health; body
শসা śɔsa *n.* cucumber
শহর śɔhôr *n.* town
শাক সবজি śa:k sôbji *n.* green vegetables
শাড়ি, শাড়ী śaṛi, śaṛī *n.* saree
শান্ত śantô *adj.* calm, peaceful
শান্তি śanti *n.* peace
শালগম shalgɔm *n.* turnip
শাসন śasôn *n.* punishment, discipline
শাস্তি দেওয়া śasti deoẏa *vb.* punish

শিব śib *name* Shiva (god)
শিমূল śimūl *n.* silk-cotton
শিয়াল śiẏal *n.* fox, jackal
শিল śil *n.* grinding stone
শিশি śiśi *n.* small glass bottle
শিশু śiśu *n.* baby, infant
শীত śī:t *adj.* cold; *n.* winter
শীতকাল śī:tkal *n.* winter
শুকনা śukna *adj.* dry
শুকানো śukano *vb.* dry, dry out
শুক্রবার śukrôbar *n.* Friday
শুধু śudhu (shudhu) *adv.* only
শুনতে → শোনা śunte → śona *vb.* hear, listen
শুরু śuru *n.* beginning, start
শুরু করা śuru kɔra *vb.* begin, start
শুরুতে śurute *adv.* at first
শূকর śūkôr (shukor) *n.* pig
শূকরের মাংস śūkôrer maṃsô *n.* pork
শূন্য śūnyô (shunno) *num.* zero
শেখা śekha *vb.* learn
শেষ śeṣ (shesh) *n.* end
শেষ করা śeṣ kɔra *vb.* finish
শেষে śeṣe *n.* finally
শেষ হয়ে যাওয়া śeṣ hôẏe yaoẏa *vb.* run out, come to an end, be finished
শোধ śodh *n.* repayment
শোনা śona *vb.* hear, listen
শোবার ঘর śobar ghɔr *n.* bedroom
শোয়া śoẏa *vb.* lie down
শ্রেষ্ঠ śreṣṭhô (sreshto) *adj.* best
শ্লিষ্ট śliṣṭô (slishto) *adj.* joined

ষ

ষাঁড় ṣāṛ *n.* ox
ষাট ṣaṭ *num.* sixty
ষোলো ṣolo *num.* sixteen

স

সওয়া sɔoẏa *n.* plus one quarter
সংক্রমণ sɔṃkrômôn *n.* infection
সংখ্যা sɔṃkhya *n.* number
সংসার sɔṃsar *n.* world; family
সংস্কৃতি sɔṃskr̥ti (shongskriti) *n.* culture
সকাল sɔkal *n.* morning

সকাল সকাল sɔkal sɔkal *adv.* early

সঙ্গে sɔŋge (shɔngge) *pp.* with

সঙ্গে সঙ্গে sɔŋge sɔŋge *adv.* immediately

সত্যি sôtyi *n.* truth

সত্ত্বেও sɔttveo (shɔtteo) *pp.* in spite of

সদর রাস্তা sɔdôr rasta *n.* main road

সন্দেহ sɔndehô (shɔndeho) *n.* doubt

সন্দেহ করা sɔndehô kɔra *vb.* doubt, be suspicious

সন্ধ্যা sɔndhya (shɔndha) *n.* evening

সন্ধ্যাবেলা sɔndhyabæla *n.* evening time

সপ্তাহ sɔptahô *n.* week

সফল sɔphɔl *adj.* effective, successful

সব sɔb *adj.* all

সবচেয়ে sɔbceẏe *pp.* than all

সব জায়গায় sɔb jaẏga *adv.* everywhere

সব মিলে sɔb mile *adv.* all together

সব সময় sɔb sômôẏ *n.* always

সবজি sôbji *n.* vegetables

সবাই sɔbai *n.* everybody

সবুজ sôbuj *adj.* green

সময় sɔmɔẏ *n.* time

সময় কাটানো sɔmɔẏ kaṭano *vb.* spend time

সমস্ত sɔmôstô *adj.* whole, entire

সমস্যা sɔmôsya *n.* problem

সমুদ্র sɔmudrô *n.* sea, ocean

সম্পর্ক sɔmpɔrkô *n.* relationship

সম্প্রতি sɔmprôti *adv.* recently

সম্ভব sɔmbhôb *adv.* possible

সম্ভবত sɔmbhôbɔtô *adv.* possibly

সম্ভাবনা sɔmbhabôna *n.* possibility

সম্মান sɔmman *n.* respect

সরকার sɔrkar *n.* government

সরিষা sôriṣa (shorisha) *n.* mustard

সর্দি sôrdi (shordi) *n.* cold, flu

সহজ sɔhôj *adj.* easy, simple

সহজে sɔhôje *adv.* easily

সহ্য sɔhyô (shɔjjhô) *n.* endurance

সহ্য করা sɔhyô kɔra *vb.* bear, tolerate, endure

সাইকেল saikel *n.* bicycle

সাইজ saij *n.* size

সাংবাদিক saṃbadik *n.* journalist

সাঁতার কাটা sãtar kaṭa *vb.* swim

সাজা saja *vb.* dress, decorate

সাগর sagôr *n.* sea, ocean

সাজানো sajano *vb.* equip, fit out

সাড়ে saṛe *num.* plus one half, half past

সাড়ে নয়টা saṛe nɔẏṭa *num.* half past nine

সাথে sathe *pp.* with

সাদা sada *adj.* white

সাধারণ sadharôṇ *adj.* normal

সাধারণত sadharôṇôtô *adv.* usually

সাপ sap *n.* snake

সাবান saban *n.* soap

সামনে samne (shamne) *pp.* in front of

সামনে samne (shamne) *adj.* next

সামনে মাস samne mas *phr.* next month

সারা sara *adj.* whole

সারাদিন saradin *adv.* all day

সারানো sarano *vb.* mend, repair

সার্ট sarṭ (sharṭ) *n.* shirt

সালাম ওয়ালিকুম salam oẏalikum *phr.* God be with you! *(Muslim greeting)*

সাহস sahôs *n.* courage

সাহায্য sahayyô *n.* help

সাহায্য করা sahayyô kɔra *vb.* help, assist

সিংহ simhô (shingho) *n.* lion

সিঁড়ি sĩṛi *n.* stairs

সিনেমা sinema *n.* cinema

সীম sīm *n.* broad bean

সীমা sīma (shima) *n.* limit, border

সুখ sukh *n.* happiness

সুগন্ধ sugɔndhô *n.* nice smell, sweet fragrance

সুন্দর sundôr (shundor) *adj.* beautiful

সুফলা suphɔla *adj.* fertile

সুবিধা subidha *n.* convenience

সুমিষ্টি sumiṣṭi *adj.* delicious and sweet

সুযোগ suyog *n.* chance, opportunity

সূচি sūci *n.* needle

সূর্য sūryô *n.* sun

সূর্যাস্ত sūryastô *n.* sunset

সূর্যোদয় sūryodɔẏ *n.* sunrise

সৃষ্টি sṛṣṭi (srishṭi) *n.* creation

সৃষ্টি করা sṛṣṭi (srishṭi) kɔra *vb.* create

সে se *pr.* he, she, it

সে জন্য / জন্যে se jônyô, jônye *conj.* therefore, that's why, for that reason

সেতু setu (shetu) *n.* bridge

সেবিকা sebika *n.* nurse

সৈনিক soinik *n.* soldier

সোজা soja *adv.* straight

সোনা sona *n.* gold

সোনার sonar *adj.* golden
সোমবার sombar *n.* Monday
সৌন্দর্য soundôryô *n.* beauty
স্কুল skul, ইস্কুল iskul *n.* school
স্ত্রী strī *n.* wife
স্থল sthɔl *n.* land, dry land
স্থান sthan *n.* place
স্নান snan *n.* bath
স্পষ্ট spɔṣṭô *adj.* clear
স্পষ্টভাবে spɔṣṭôbhabe *adv.* clearly, frankly
স্বপ্ন svɔpnô *n.* dream
স্বর্গ svɔrgô *n.* heaven
স্বাদ svad (sha:d) *n.* taste
স্বাধীনতা svadhīnôta *n.* independence
স্বাভাবিক svabhabik *adj.* usual, normal
স্বামী svamī (shami) *n.* husband
স্বাস্থ্য svasthyô (shastho) *n.* health
স্মরণ smɔrôṇ (shɔrôn) *n.* memory
স্মৃতি smṛti (sriti) *n.* memory
স্যার syar *n.* sir

হ

হওয়া hɔôŷa (hɔowa) *vb.* be, become, happen, occur
হঠাৎ hɔṭhaṯ *adv.* suddenly
হতাশ hɔtaś (hɔtash) *adj.* disappointed, dejected
হতাশা hɔtaśa *n.* disappointment
হতে পারে hôte pare *phr.* perhaps, maybe
হয়তো hɔŷto *adv.* perhaps
হয়ে hôŷe *pp.* in place of
হয়ে ওঠা hôŷe oṭha *vb.* become
হয়ে পড়া hôŷe pɔṛa *vb.* become
হয়ে যাওয়া hôŷe yaôŷa *cvb.* occur, happen, come to pass
হরিণ hôriṇ *n.* deer

হলদে hɔlde *adj.* yellow (PB)
হলুদ hôlud *adj.* yellow (B)
হাওয়া haoŷa *n.* air, wind
হাঁড়ি hāṛi *n.* pan
হাঁটা hāṭa *vb.* walk
হাঁটু hāṭu *n.* knee
হাঁস hās *n.* duck
হাত hat *n.* hand
হাত বাড়ানো hat baṛano *vb.* stretch out one's arm
হাতে লাগা hate laga *vb.* hurt one's hand
হাতা hata *n.* ladle
হাতি hati *n.* elephant
হাতুড়ি haturi *n.* hammer
হায় হায় haŷ haŷ *phr.* oh dear! *(expression of dismay)*
হার har *n.* necklace, chain
হারা hara *vb.* be lost
হারানো harano *vb.* lose
হারিকেন hariken *n.* lantern
হালকা halka *adj.* light (in weight)
হালি (BD) hali *num.* group of four
হাসপাতাল haspatal *n.* hospital
হাসা hasa *vb.* laugh, smile
হাসি hasi *n.* smile, laugh
হাসিমুখে hasimukhe *adv.* smiling, happily
হিমালয় himalɔŷ *name* Himalayas *(mountain range)*
হিমেল himel *adj.* icy, cold
হকুম / হুকুম hukum *n.* order, command
হৃদয় ṛdɔŷ (ridɔŷ) *n.* heart
হেঁটে যাওয়া hēṭe yaôŷa *cvb.* walk
হেমন্ত hemôntô *n.* late autumn
হৈচৈ hoicoi *n.* fuss, uproar
হোটেল hoṭel *n.* hotel
হাঁ hyæ̃ (hæ̃) *adv.* yes

ENGLISH – BANGLA DICTIONARY

Note: There is not always a one-to-one correspondence between English and Bangla words. What English expresses with an adjective will in Bangla often require a verbal structure, e.g., "He is afraid" is in Bangla তার ভয় করছে tar bhɔŷ kôrche (*lit:* of him fear is making). It is therefore important to be flexible in using this dictionary. Once you have found the Bangla equivalent of an English entry, always make sure to look up the Bangla entry to check you have the right word and the appropriate word class.

A

a *adj.* একটা ækṭa

a lot *adv.* বেশি করে beśi kôre

able to: be able to *vb.* পারা para

about *pp.* মত mɔtô, নিয়ে niŷe

absent: be absent *vb.* নেই nei

accept *vb.* গ্রহণ করা grôhôṇ kɔra

accident *n.* একসিডেন্ট eksiḍenṭ

accidentally *adv.* ভুল করে bhul kôre

accomplish *vb.* মিটানো miṭano

actually *adv.* আসলে asôle

addition: in addition *conj.* তা ছাড়া ta chaṛa

address *n.* ঠিকানা ṭhikana

advance *vb.* এগনো egôno

advertisement *n.* বিজ্ঞাপন bijñapɔn (biggapɔn)

aeroplane *n.* উড়োজাহাজ uṛojahaj, বিমান biman

afraid: be afraid *vb.* ভয় করা bhɔŷ kɔra

after *pp.* পরে pɔre

afternoon *n.* বিকাল bikal

again *adv.* আবার abar

against *pp.* বিরুদ্ধে biruddhe

age *n.* বয়স bɔŷôs (bɔyosh)

agreed *adj.* রাজি raji

agriculture *n.* কৃষি kṛṣi (krishi)

ah *excl.* বাঃ baḥ

aim *n.* উদ্দেশ্য uddeśyô (uddesho)

air *n.* হাওয়া haoŷa

airmail *n.* এয়ারমেল eŷarmeil

airplane *n.* উড়োজাহাজ uṛojahaj, বিমান biman

alcohol *n.* মদ mɔd

all *adj.* সব sɔb

all day *adv.* সারাদিন saradin

all this *n.* এসব esɔb

all together *adv.* সব মিলে sɔb mile

allergy *n.* অ্যালার্জি aylarji (ælarji)

alliance *n.* মিতালি mitali

allow *vb.* দেওয়া deoŷa

almond *n.* কাগজি বাদাম kagôji badam

almost *adv.* প্রায় praŷ

alone *adv.* একা æka

alongside *pp.* পাশে paśe

also *conj.* ও o

altogether *adv.* একদম ækdɔm

always *n.* সব সময় sɔb sômôŷ

amazing *adj.* আশ্চর্য aścɔryô

American *adj.* আমেরিকান amerikan

among *pp.* মধ্যে môdhye

ancient *adj.* প্রাচীন pracīn

and *conj.* আর ar

anger *n.* রাগ rag

angry *adj.* খাপ্পা khappa

animal *n.* জীবজন্তু jībjôntu, পশু pôśu

ankle-bells *n.* নূপুর nūpur

annoy *vb.* জ্বালানো jvalano

answer *n.* উত্তর uttôr; *vb.* উত্তর দেওয়া uttôr deoŷa

ant *n.* পিঁপড়া pīpṛa

any *adj.* কোনও kono

anywhere *adv.* কোথাও kothao

appear *vb.* উপস্থিত হওয়া upôsthit hɔoŷa

appearance *n.* চেহারা cehara, রূপ rūp

apple *n.* আপেল apel

area *n.* অঞ্চল ɔñcɔl, এলাকা elaka

argument *n.* ঝগড়া jhɔgṛa

arm *n.* বাহু bahu

arrangement *n.* ব্যবস্থা bybôstha (bæbostha)

arrival *n.* আগমন agômôn

arrive *vb.* পৌছানো pôuchano

as *conj.* যেমন yæmôn

as – as *conj.* যেমন – তেমন yæmôn – tæmôn

as if *conj.* যেন yænô

Asharh *(Bengali month)* *n.* আষাঢ় aṣaṛh

ask question *vb.* প্রশ্ন করা prôśnô kɔra

assist *vb.* সাহায্য করা sahayyô kɔra

at first *adv.* প্রথমে prôthôme, শুরুতে śurute

at least *adv.* অন্তত ɔntôtô

attached: be attached *vb.* লাগা laga

attack *n.* আক্রমণ akrômôn

attempt *n.* চেষ্টা ceṣṭa

attraction *n.* টান ṭan

aubergine (eggplant) *n.* বেগুন begun

aunt *n.* See Appendix 7, kinship terms

autumn *n.* **early autumn** শরৎ śɔrôṯ, **late autumn** হেমন্ত hemôntô

available: is available *vb.* পাওয়া যায় paoẏa yaẏ

awake *vb.* জাগা jaga

awaken *vb.* জাগানো jagano

aware: be aware of *vb.* মনে আছে mône ache

B

baby *n.* শিশু śiśu

back *n.* পিঠ pi:ṭh

bad *adj.* খারাপ kharap; *(evil)* মন্দ mɔndô

bag *n.* থলি thôli

Baishakh *(first month of the Bengali year)* *n.* বৈশাখ boiśakh

balance *vb.* মিলানো milano

bamboo *n.* বাঁশ bãś

banana *n.* কলা kɔla

Bangla *adj./n.* বাংলা bamla

Bangladesh *name* বাংলাদেশ bamladeś

bank (of a river) *n.* তীর tīr, ধার dhar

basket *n.* ঝুড়ি jhuri

bath *n.* স্নান snan

bay *n.* উপসাগর upôsagôr

bay leaf *n.* তেজপাতা tejpata

Bay of Bengal *name* বঙ্গোপসাগর bɔṅgôpsagôr

be *vb.* হওয়া hɔoẏa (hɔowa)

  be able to *vb.* পারা para

be absent *vb.* নেই nei

be afraid *vb.* ভয় করা bhɔẏ kɔra, ভয় পাওয়া bhɔẏ paoẏa (paowa)

be attached *vb.* লাগা laga

be delighted *cvb.* মেতে ওঠা mete oṭha

be excited, go mad *vb.* মেতে → মাতা mete → mata

be lost *vb.* হারা hara

be present, exist *vb.* আছ- ach-

be scared *vb.* ভয় পাওয়া bhɔẏ paoẏa (paowa), ভয় করা bhɔẏ kɔra

be upset *vb.* কষ্ট পাওয়া kɔṣṭô paoẏa

bean *n.* *(broad bean)* সীম sīm; *(green bean)* বরবটি bɔrbôṭi

bear *vb.* সহ্য করা sɔhyô kɔra

beautiful *adj.* সুন্দর sundôr (shundor)

beauty *n.* সৌন্দর্য soundôryô

because *conj.* কেননা kænôna, বলে bôle

become *vb.* হয়ে ওঠা hôẏe oṭha, হয়ে পড়া hôẏe pɔra, হওয়া hɔoẏa (hɔowa)

bed *n.* খাট kha:ṭ, বিছানা bichana

bedroom *n.* শোবার ঘর śobar ghɔr

bedstead *n.* চৌকি couki

bee *n.* মৌমাছি moumachi

beef *n.* গরুর মাংস gorur maṃsô

before *pp.* আগে age

begin *vb.* আরম্ভ করা arômbhô kɔra, শুরু করা śuru kɔra

beginning *n.* আরম্ভ arômbhô, শুরু śuru

behavior *n.* ব্যবহার bybôhar (bæbohar)

behind *pp.* পিছনে pichône, পেছনে pechône

belief *n.* বিশ্বাস biśvas (bisshash)

believe *vb.* বিশ্বাস করা biśvas kɔra

beneficial *adj.* উপকারি upôkari

benefit *n.* মঙ্গল mɔṅgôl (mɔnggol), উপকার upôkar

Bengali *adj.* বাঙালি baṅali (banggali)

berry *n.* জাম jam

besides *conj.* তা ছাড়া ta chara

best *adj.* শ্রেষ্ঠ śreṣṭhô (sreshto)

Bhadro *(month / August-September, the end of the rainy season)* *n.* ভদ্রমাস bhadrômas

bicycle *n.* সাইকেল saikel

big *adj.* বড় bɔrô

bigha *(land measure)* *n.* বিঘা bigha

bird *n.* পাখি pakhi

birth *n.* জন্ম jɔnmô

biscuit *n.* বিস্কুট biskuṭ

bite *n.* কামড় kamôṛ

bitter *adj.* তিতা tita

black *adj.* কালো kalo

blanket *n.* kôbl kɔmbôl

blind *adj.* aí ɔndhô

blood *n.* রক্ত rɔktô

bloom *cvb.* ফুটে ওঠা phuṭe oṭha

blossom *vb.* ফোটা phoṭa; *cvb.* ফুটে ওঠা phuṭe oṭha

blouse *n.* ব্লাউজ blauj

blow *n.* আঘাত aghat

blue *adj.* নীল nīl

boat *n.* নৌকা nouka / **small boat** *n.* দিঘি dighi

body *n.* গা ga, দেহ dehô, শরীর śôrīr

book *n.* গ্রন্থ grônthô, বই bôi

books and notebooks *n.* বই-খাতা bôi-khata

border *n.* সীমা sīma (shima)

both (people) *n.* উভয় ubhôy

bottle *n.* বোতল botôl / **small glass bottle** *n.* শিশি śiśi

bowl *n.* বাটি baṭi

boy *n.* ছেলে chele / **poor boy** *n.* বেচারা becara

Brahman *name* ব্রাহ্ম (brahmô) brammo

branch *n.* ডাল ḍal

bread *n.* রুটি ruṭi

break *vb.* ভাঙা bhaṅa (bhangga)

breakfast *n.* নাস্তা nasta

breast *n.* বুক buk

breath *n.* নিঃশ্বাস niḥśvas (nisshash)

brick *n.* ইট i:ṭ

bridge *n.* সেতু setu (shetu)

bright *adj.* উজ্জ্বল ujjvôl (ujjol)

bring *vb.* আনা ana, নিয়ে আসা niẏe asa / **bring along** *cvb.* বয়ে আনা bôẏe ana

broom *n.* ঝাড়ু jhaṛu

brother *n.* ভাই bhai; *(older brother)* দাদা dada, *(M.)* বড় ভাই bɔṛô bhai

brothers and sisters *n.* ভাইবোন bhaibon

brown *adj.* বাদামি badami

bucket *n.* বালতি balti

Buick *n.* বিউইক biuik

build *vb.* গড়া gɔṛa

buildings *n.* ঘরবাড়ি ghɔrbaṛi

built *adj.* তৈরি toiri / **be built** *cvb.* গড়ে ওঠা gôre oṭha

burst *vb.* ঝাঁপানো jhãpano

busy *adj.* ব্যস্ত bystô (bæsto)

but *conj.* কিন্তু kintu, তবে tɔbe; *emph.* তো to

butter *n.* মাখন makhôn

butterfly *n.* প্রজাপতি prôjapôti

button *n.* বোতাম botam

buy *vb.* কেনা kena

by the way *adv.* প্রসঙ্গত prôsɔṅgôtô

by then *adv.* এরমধ্যে ermôdhye, এরইমধ্যে erimôdhye

C

cabbage *n.* বাঁধাকপি bãdhakôpi

cake *n.* পিঠা piṭha

call *n.* ডাক ḍak; *vb.* ডাক দেওয়া ḍak deoẏa, ডাকা ḍaka

called *vb. part* বলে bôle

calm *adj.* শান্ত śantô

camel *n.* উট u:ṭ

can *vb.* পারা para

canal *n.* খাল kha:l

candle *n.* মোমবাতি mombati

cane chair *n.* মোড়া moṛa

capital *n.* রাজধানী rajdhanī

car *n.* গাড়ি gaṛi

cardamom *n.* এলাচ elac

care *n.* যত্ন yɔtnô

carpet *n.* গালিচা galica

carrot *n.* গাজর gajôr

cash *n.* নগদ nɔgôd

cat *n.* বিড়াল biṛal, beṛal

catch *vb.* ধরা dhɔra

cattle *n.* গরু gôru

cauliflower *n.* ফুলকপি phulkôpi

cause to do *vb.* করানো kɔrano

    cause to drown *cvb.* ডুবিয়ে দেওয়া ḍubiẏe deoẏa

    cause to float *vb.* ভাসানো bhasano

    cause to wake up *vb.* ওঠানো oṭhano

    cause to wake *vb.* জাগানো jagano

cave *n.* গুহা / গুহা guha

celebration *n.* অনুষ্ঠান ônuṣṭhan

ceremony *n.* উৎসব uṯsɔb

chain (*necklace*) *n.* হার har

chair *n.* চেয়ার ceŷar

chance *n.* সুযোগ suyog

Chandpur (*town*) *name* চাঁদপুর cãdpur

change *n.* পরিবর্তন pôribɔrtôn; *vb.*
(*exchange*) বদল করা bɔdôl kɔra;
(*transform*) বদলানো bɔdlano

chase away *vb.* তাড়ানো taɽano

chat *vb.* গল্প করা gɔlpô kɔra

cheat *vb.* ঠকা ṭhɔka

chest (*anat.*) *n.* বুক buk

chicken *n.* মুরগি murgi, মুর্গির মাংস murgir
maṃsô

child *n.* বাচ্চা bacca

children *n.* ছেলেমেয়ে chelemeŷe

chili *n.* মরিচ môric / **green chili** *n.* কাঁচা
মরিচ kãca môric

Chittagong *name* চট্টগ্রাম cɔṭṭôgram

Christian *n./adj.* খ্রিস্টিয়ান khrisṭiŷan

chutney *n.* চাটনি caṭni

cinema *n.* সিনেমা sinema

cinnamon *n.* দারচিনি darcini

clean *adj.* পরিষ্কার pôriṣkar; *vb.* পরিষ্কার
করা pôriṣkar kɔra

clear *adj.* স্পষ্ট spɔṣṭô

clearly *adv.* স্পষ্টভাবে spɔṣṭôbhabe

clever *adj.* চালাক calak

cleverness *n.* চালাকি calaki

clock *n.* ঘড়ি ghôɽi

close *adj.* ঘনিষ্ঠ ghônisṭô; *vb.* বন্ধ করা
bɔndhô kɔra

close by *adv.* কাছাকাছি kachakachi

closed *adj.* বন্ধ bɔndhô

clothes *n.* কাপড় kapôɽ, জামাকাপড়
jamakapôɽ

cloud *n.* মেঘ megh

clove *n.* লবঙ্গ lɔbôṅgô

club *n.* ক্লাব klab

coconut *n.* নারিকেল narikel / **green coconut**
n. ডাব ḍa:b

coffee *n.* কফি kôphi

cold *adj.* ঠাণ্ডা ṭhaṇḍa. শীত śī:t; *n.* (*illness*)
সর্দি sôrdi (shordi); (*icy temperature*) শীত
śī:t, হিমেল himel

collect *vb.* জমা jɔma

college *n.* কলেজ kɔlej

color *n.* রং rɔṃv (rɔng), রং rɔṃ; *vb.* রং করা
rɔṃ kɔra

comb *n.* চিরুনি ciruni

come *vb.* আসা asa

come back *cvb.* ফিরে আসা phire asa

come off *vb.* উঠে যাওয়া uṭhe yaoŷa

come to pass *cvb.* হয়ে যাওয়া hôŷe yaoŷa;
vb. হওয়া hɔowa (hɔowa)

come to an end *vb.* শেষ হয়ে যাওয়া śeṣ
hôŷe yaoŷa

coming and going *n.* চলাচল cɔlacɔl

command *n.* হুকুম / হুকুম hukum

comparison *n.* তুলনা tulôna

complaint *n.* অভিযোগ ôbhiyog

complete *adj.* পুরা pura (BD), পুরো puro
(PB)

completely *adv.* একেবারে æekebare, একদম
æekdɔm

computer *n.* কমপিউটার kɔmpiuṭar

concentrate *vb.* মন দেওয়া môn deoŷa

concert *n.* জলসা jɔlsa

confirm *vb.* নির্দিষ্ট করা nirdisṭô kɔra

confirmed *adj.* নির্দিষ্ট nirdisṭô

consideration *n.* বিবেচনা bibecôna

consume *vb.* খাওয়া khaoŷa

continue *vb.* টেকা ṭeka

convenience *n.* সুবিধা subidha

conversation *n.* আলাপ alap

cook *vb.* রান্না করা ranna kɔra

cooking *n.* রান্না ranna

coriander *n.* ধনিয়া dhôniŷa (BD), ধনে
dhône (PB)

corn *n.* ভুট্টা bhuṭṭa

correct *adj.* ঠিক ṭhik

correspond (*balance with*) *vb.* মিলানো
milano

cotton-wool *n.* তুলা tula

cough *n.* কাশি kaśi

country *n.* দেশ deś / **another country** *n.*
দেশান্তর deśantôr

courage *n.* সাহস sahôs

courtyard *n.* উঠান uṭhan

cow *n.* গরু gôru

cowshed *n.* গোয়াল goŷal (gowal)

crazy: are you crazy? মাথা খারাপ? matha
kharap

create *vb.* সৃষ্টি করা sṛṣṭi (srishṭi) kɔra

creation *n.* সৃষ্টি sṛṣṭi (srishṭi)

crime *n.* অপরাধ ɔpôradh

crocodile *n.* কুমির kumir
cross *vb.* পার হওয়া par hɔoŷa
crossing *n.* মোড় moṛ
cry *vb.* কাঁদা kãda
cuckoo *n.* কোকিল kokil
cucumber *n.* শসা ŝɔsa
culture *n.* সংস্কৃতি sɔmskṙti (shongskriti)
cumin *n.* জিরা jira
cupboard *n.* আলমারি almari
curtain *n.* পরদা pɔrda
custard apple *n.* আতাফল ataphɔl
customer *n.* খরিদ্দার khôriddar
cut *vb.* কাটা kaṭa
cyclone *n.* ঘূর্ণিঝড় ghūrṇijhɔṛ

D

daily *adj.* দৈনিক doinik
daily *adv.* রোজ roj
dance *n., vb.* নাচ nac
danger *n.* বিপদ bipɔd
darkness *n.* অন্ধকার ɔndhôkar
date *n.* খেজুর khejur
date *n.* তারিখ tarikh
daughter *n.* কন্যা kɔnya (kɔnna), মেয়ে meŷe
dawn *n.* ভোর bhor
day *n.* দিন di:n
day after tomorrow *n.* পরশু দিন pôrśudin
death *n.* মৃত্যু mṙtyu (mrittu)
debt *n.* ঋণ ṙṇ (rin)
decorate *vb.* সাজা saja
decrease *vb.* কমা kɔma
deep *adj.* গভীর gôbhīr
deer *n.* হরিণ hôriṇ
defeat *n.* পরাজয় pɔrajɔŷ
dejected *adj.* হতাশ hɔtaś (hɔtash)
delay *n.* দেরি deri; *vb.* দেরি করা deri kɔra
delicious *adj.* মজাদার mɔjadar
delicious and sweet *adj.* সুমিষ্ট sumiṣṭô
delighted *adj.* আনন্দিত anônditô / be
   delighted *cvb.* মেতে ওঠা mete oṭha
democracy *n.* গণতন্ত্র gɔṇôtɔntrô
dense *adj.* ঘন ghɔnô
descend *vb.* নামা nama
desert *n.* মরুভূমি môrubhūmi
destroy *vb.* ভাঙা bhaṅa (bhangga), নষ্ট করা nɔṣṭô kɔra

destruction *n.* ধ্বংস dhvɔṃsô
detect *vb.* দেখা পাওয়া dækha paoŷa
Dhaka *(capital of Bangladesh) name* ঢাকা ḍhaka
dhoti *n.* ধুতি dhuti
diarrhea *n.* আমাশা amaśa
die *vb.* মরা mɔra, মারা যাওয়া mara yaoŷa
different *adj.* ভিন্ন bhinnô
difficult *adj.* কঠিন kôṭhin
difficulty *n.* মুশকিল muśkil
dignity *n.* মর্যাদা mɔryada (mɔrjada)
dinghy *n.* দিঘি dighi
dining room *n.* খাবার ঘর khabar ghɔr
direction *n.* দিক dik
dirty *adj.* ময়লা mɔŷla, নোংরা noṃra, মলিন môlin
disappear *vb.* উঠে যাওয়া uṭhe yaoŷa
disappointed *adj.* হতাশ hɔtaś (hɔtash)
disappointment *n.* হতাশা hɔtaśa
discipline *n.* শাসন ŝasôn
discuss *vb.* আলোচনা করা alocôna kɔra
discussion *n.* আলোচনা alocôna
disease *n.* রোগ rog
dishes *n.* বাসন basôn
distance *n.* দূর dūr, দূরত্ব dūrôtvô
district *n.* জেলা jela
divorce *n.* তালাক talak
do *vb.* করা kɔra
do a job *vb.* চাকরি করা cakri kɔra
do harm *vb.* ক্ষতি করা kṣôti kɔra
doctor *n.* ডাক্তার ḍaktar
dog *n.* কুকুর kukur
donkey *n.* গাধা gadha
door *n.* দরজা dɔrja
double room *n.* ডবল রুম ḍɔbôl rum
doubt *n.* সন্দেহ sɔndehô (shɔndeho); *vb.* সন্দেহ করা sɔndehô kɔra
dove *n.* ঘুঘু ghughu
dozen *n.* ডজন ḍɔjôn
drama *n.* নাটক naṭôk
drawer *n.* দেরাজ deraj
dream *n.* স্বপ্ন svɔpnô
dress *n.* *(attire)* পোষাক poṣak; *(girl's)* ফ্রক phrɔk; *vb.* সাজা saja
drink *vb.* খাওয়া khaoŷa
drive (a car) *vb.* গাড়ি চালানো gaṛi calano
drought *n.* অনাবৃষ্টি ɔnabṙṣṭi

drown *vb.* ডুবে যাওয়া ḍube yaoŷa / **cause to drown** *cvb.* ডুবিয়ে দেওয়া ḍubiŷe deoŷa

dry *adj.* শুকনা śukna*vb.* শুকানো śukano

duck *n.* হাঁস hãs

during *pp.* ধরে dhôre

dust *n.* ধুলা dhula

dye *vb.* রং করা rɔm kɔra

dysentry *n.* আমাশা amaśa

E

each *adj.* প্রতি prôti

eagle *n.* ঈগল īgôl

ear *n.* কান ka:n

earlier *adv.* আগে age

early *adv.* সকাল সকাল sɔkal sɔkal

earring *n.* কানের ফুল kaner phul

earth *n.* ভূমি bhūmi; *(soil)* মাটি maṭi / **what on earth ...** *expr.* কি রে ki re

easily *adv.* সহজে sɔhôje

east *adj.* পূর্ব pūrbô

easy *adj.* সহজ sɔhôj

eat *vb.* খাওয়া khaoŷa

eat up *cvb.* খেয়ে ফেলা kheŷe phæla

education *n.* লেখাপড়া lekhapɔra

effective *adj.* সফল sɔphɔl

egg *n.* ডিম ḍim

eggplant *n.* বেগুন begun

eight *num.* আট aṭ

elaborate *vb.* কথা বাড়ানো kɔtha baṛano

elderly *adj.* বয়স্ক bɔŷôskô

electricity *n.* বিদ্যুৎ bidyuṯ

elephant *n.* হাতি hati

eleven *num.* এগারো egaro

emaciated *adj.* রোগা roga

embarrassment *n.* লজ্জা lɔjja

employ *vb.* লাগানো lagano

employee *n.* কর্মচারী kɔrmôcarī

empty *adj.* খালি khali, ফাঁকা phãka

enchanted *adj.* মুগ্ধ mugdhô

end *n.* ইতি iti, শেষ śeṣ (shesh) / **come to an end** *vb.* শেষ হয়ে যাওয়া śeṣ hôŷe yaoŷa

endless *adj.* অসীম ɔsīm

endurance *n.* সহ্য sɔhyô (shɔjjhô)

endure *vb.* সহ্য করা sɔhyô kɔra

enemy *n.* শত্রু śôtru

engine *n.* ইঞ্জিন iñjin

England *name* ইংল্যান্ড iṃlyanḍ

English *adj.* ইংরেজি iṃreji (ingreji)

enjoyment *n.* ফুর্তি phurti

enter *vb.* ঢোকা ḍhoka

enticing *adj.* লুব্ধ lubdho

entire *adj.* সমস্ত sɔmôstô

entrance *n.* প্রবেশ prôbeś / **by the entrance** *adv.* ঢোকার মুখে ḍhokar mukhe

equip *vb.* সাজানো sajano

escape *vb.* পালানো palano

establish *vb.* গড়া gɔra / **be established** *cvb.* গড়ে ওঠা gôre oṭha

etcetera (etc.) *adv.* ইত্যাদি ityadi (ittadi)

even *conj.* ও o

evening *n.* সন্ধ্যা sɔndhya (shɔndha)

evening time *n.* সন্ধ্যাবেলা sɔndhyabæla

event *n.* ঘটনা ghɔṭôna

ever *adv.* কখনও kɔkhôno

every *adj.* প্রতি prôti

every day *adv.* প্রতিদিন prôtidin

everybody *n.* সবাই sɔbai

everywhere *adv.* সব জায়গায় sɔb jaŷga

evidence *n.* প্রমাণ prôman

evil *adj.* মন্দ mɔndô

exactly *adj.* ঠিক ṭhik

examine *vb.* পরীক্ষা করা pôrīkṣa kɔra

excellent *adj.* দারুণ darun

except *pp.* ছাড়া chaṛa

excessive *adj.* অতিরিক্ত ôtiriktô

exchange *vb.* বদল করা bɔdôl kɔra

excited *adj.* মেতে / **be excited** *vb.* মাতা mata

exhibition *n.* মেলা mæla

exist *vb.* আছ- ach- / **not exist** *vb.* নেই nei

expensive *adj.* দামি dami

experience *n.* অভিজ্ঞতা ôbhijñôta (obhiggota)

explain *cvb.* বুঝিয়ে দেওয়া bujhiŷe deoŷa

explain *vb.* বোঝানো bojhano

extend *vb.* বাড়ানো baṛano

extremely *adv.* ভীষণ bhīṣôn

eye *n.* চোখ cokh

F

face *n.* মুখ mukh

fact *n.* কথা kɔtha

fair (-skinned) *adj.* ফরসা phɔrsa; *n.* মেলা mæla

fall *vb.* পড়া pɔṛa; *(shed)* ঝরা jhɔra

fall down *cvb.* পড়ে যাওয়া pôṛe yaoŷa

fall off *cvb.* পড়ে যাওয়া pôṛe yaoŷa

family *n.* পরিবার pôribar, সংসার sɔṃsar

fan *n.* পাখা pakha

far *adj.* দূরে dūre

farewell *n.* বিদায় bidaŷ / **say farewell** *vb.* বিদায় দেওয়া bidaŷ deoŷa

Faridpur *(town) name* ফরিদপুর phôridpur

farmer *n.* কৃষক kr̥ṣôk (krishok), চাষী caṣī

fascinated *adj.* মুগ্ধ mugdhô

fast *adj.* জোরে jore

fat *adj.* মোটা moṭa

fate *n.* ভাগ্য bhagyô

father *n.* আব্বা abba, বাবা baba

fault *n.* দোষ doṣ

favor *n.* উপকার upôkar

favorite *adj.* প্রিয় priŷô

fear *n.* ভয় bhɔŷ, ভয়ডর bhɔŷḍɔr, ভীতি bhīti / **have no fear** *phr.* ভয় নেই bhɔŷ nei

feces *n.* পায়খানা paŷkhana

feed *vb.* খাওয়ানো khaoŷano

feel *vb.* টের পাওয়া ṭer paoŷa

ferry *n.* ফেরি pheri

fertile *adj.* সুফলা suphɔla

fever *n.* জ্বর jvɔr (jɔr)

few (a few) *adj.* কয়েক kɔŷek

field *n.* ক্ষেত kṣet (khet), মাঠ maṭh

fierce *adj.* প্রচণ্ড prôcɔṇḍô

fig *n.* ডুমুর ḍumur

file *n.* ফাইল phail

filled *adj.* ভরা bhɔra

finally *adv.* অবশেষে ɔbôṣeṣe; শেষে śeṣe

find *vb.* পাওয়া paoŷa; *(after searching)* *cvb.* খুঁজে পাওয়া khũje paoŷa / **find out** *vb.* জানা jana

finger *n.* আঙুল aṅul (anggul)

finish *vb.* শেষ করা śeṣ kɔra / **be finished** *vb.* শেষ হয়ে যাওয়া śeṣ hôŷe yaoŷa

fire *n.* আগুন agun

firefly *n.* জোনাকি jonaki

first *adj.* প্রথম prôthôm / **at first** *adv.* প্রথমে prôthôme, শুরুতে śurute

fish *n.* মাছ mach

fit *vb.* গায়ে লাগা gaŷe laga

fit out *vb.* সাজানো sajano

fitting *adj.* উচিত ucit

five *num.* পাঁচ pãc / **about five** *num.* পাঁচেক pãcek

fix *(confirm)* *vb.* নির্দিষ্ট করা nirdiṣṭô kɔra

fixed *(confirmed)* *adj.* নির্দিষ্ট nirdiṣṭô

flat *n.* ফ্ল্যাট phlyaṭ (phlæṭ)

flee *vb.* পালানো palano

float *vb.* ভাসা bhasa / **cause to float** *vb.* ভাসানো bhasano

flood *n.* প্লাবন plabôn, বন্যা bônya

floodplane *n.* বিল bi:l

floor *n.* মেঝে mejhe; *(level of a building)* তলা tɔla

flow *n.* জোয়ার joŷar / **flow into** *cvb.* মিশে যাওয়া miśe yaoŷa

flower *n.* ফুল phul

fly *n.* মাছি machi

fog *n.* কুয়াশা kuŷaśa (kuwasha)

food *n.* খাবার khabar

foot *n.* পা pa

football (soccer) *n.* ফুটবল phuṭbɔl

for *pp.* জন্য, জন্যে jônyô, jônye (jonne), ধরে dhôre

for how long *qu.* কতদিন kɔtôdin

forehead *n.* কপাল kɔpal

foreign *adj.* বিদেশি bideśi

foreigner *n.* বিদেশি bideśi

forest *n.* বন bôn

forever *adv.* চিরদিন cirôdin

forget *cvb.* ভুলে যাওয়া bhule yaoŷa; *vb.* ভোলা bhola

forgive *vb.* ক্ষমা করা kṣôma kɔra, মাফ করা maph kɔra

forgiveness *n.* ক্ষমা kṣôma (khoma), মাফ maph

fork *n.* কাঁটা চামচ kãṭa

form *vb.* গড়া gɔṛa; *n.* রূপ rūp

four *num.* চার car / **group of four** *num.* হালি hali

fox *n.* শিয়াল śiŷal

fragrance *n.* গন্ধ gɔndhô / **sweet fragrance** *n.* সুগন্ধ sugɔndhô

frankly *adv.* স্পষ্টভাবে spɔṣṭôbhabe

free *adj.* খালি khali

freedom *n.* মুক্তি mukti

fresh *adj.* টাটকা ṭaṭka

Friday *n.* শুক্রবার śukrôbar

friend *n.* বন্ধু bôndhu, *n.f.* বান্ধবি bandhôbi

frighten *vb.* ভয় দেখানো bhôẏ dækhano

frightening *adj.* ভয়ংকর bhôẏôṁkɔr

frog *n.* ব্যাং byaṁ (bæng)

from *pp.* থেকে theke; **from (a person)** কাছ থেকে kach theke

fruit *n.* ফল phɔl

fruit tree *n.* ফলগাছ phɔlgach

frying pan *n.* কড়াই kɔṛai

fulfill *vb.* মিটানো miṭano

full *adj.* ভরা bhɔra

full moon *n.* পূর্ণিমা pūrṇima

fullness *n.* পরিপূর্ণতা pôripūrṇôta

fun *n.* মজা mɔja, ফুর্তি phurti

fuss *n.* হৈচৈ hoicoi

future *n.* ভবিষ্যৎ bhôbiṣyɔṯ

G

Ganges *(river) name* গঙ্গা gɔṅga

garden *n.* বাগান bagan

gardener *n.* মালি mali

garlic *n.* রসুন rôsun

gate *n.* গেট geṭ

gather *vb.* জমা jɔma

gentle *adj.* নরম nɔrôm, কোমল komôl

gentleman *n.* ভদ্রলোক bhɔdrôlok

geography *n.* ভূগোল bhūgol

get *vb. (receive)* পাওয়া paoẏa, *(find)* পেলে → পাওয়া paoẏa

  get broken *cvb.* ভেঙে পড়া bheṅe pɔṛa, ভেঙে যাওয়া bheṅge yaoẏa

  get destroyed *vb.* নষ্ট হওয়া nɔṣṭô hɔoẏa

  get down *vb.* নামা nama

  get filled up *vb.* ভরে যাওয়া bhôre yaoẏa

  get less *cvb.* কমে যাওয়া kôme yaoẏa

  get married *vb.* বিয়ে করা biẏe kɔra

  get spoiled *vb.* নষ্ট হওয়া nɔṣṭô hɔoẏa

  get torn *cvb.* ছিঁড়ে যাওয়া chĩṛe yaoẏa

  get up *vb.* ওঠা oṭha

ghost *n.* ভূত bhūt

ghost stories *n.* ভূতের গল্প bhūter gɔlpô

gift *n.* উপহার upôhar

ginger *n.* আদা ada

girl *n.* মেয়ে meẏe

give *vb.* দিচ্ছি → দেওয়া dicchi → deoẏa

give back *vb.* ফেরত দেওয়া pherôt deoẏa

glass *n.* কাচ kac, গেলাস gelas

glasses *n.* চশমা cɔśma

glory *n.* গৌরব gourob

go *vb.* যাওয়া yaoẏa, চলা cɔla

  go away *cvb.* চলে যাওয়া côle yaoẏa

  go forward *vb.* এগনো egôno

  go past *vb.* পার হওয়া par hɔoẏa

  go out *vb.* বেড়ানো beṛano

goat *n.* ছাগল chagôl

gobble up *cvb.* খেয়ে ফেলা kheẏe phæla

God *n.* ঈশ্বর īśvôr (isshor) / *(Muslim greeting)* **God be with you!** *phr.* সালাম ওয়ালিকুম salam oẏalikum / *(Muslim greeting reply)* **God be with you!** *phr.* ওয়ালিকুম সালাম oẏalikum salam / **God willing!** *expr.* ইনশা-আল্লাহ inśa–allah

god *n.* দেবতা debôta

gold *n.* সোনা sona

golden *adj.* সোনার sonar

good *adj.* ভাল bhalô

goodbye *(lit: God be with you)* *phr.* খোদা হাফেজ khoda haphej

gossip *n.* গুজব gujôb

gourd *n.* লাউ lau

government *n.* সরকার sɔrkar

gradually *adv.* আস্তে আস্তে aste aste, ধীরে dhīre

grandmother *(paternal)* *(H.)* *n.* ঠাকুরমা ṭhakurma; *(maternal)* দিদিমা didima

grape *n.* আঙুর aṅur (anggur)

grass *n.* ঘাস ghas (gha:sh)

greed *n.* লোভ lobh

green *adj.* সবুজ sôbuj

green chili *n.* কাঁচা মরিচ kãca môric

green coconut *n.* ডাব ḍa:b

green vegetables *n.* শাক সবজি śa:k sôbji

grinding stone *n.* শিল śil

grocery store *n.* মুদির দোকান mudir dokan

ground floor *n.* একতলা æktɔla

guard *n.* দারোয়ান daroẏan

guava *n.* পেয়ারা peẏara

guest *n.* অতিথি ôtithi

H

hair *n.* চুল cul

half *num.* আধ adh, আধা adha / **half past** সাড়ে saṛe / **half past nine** সাড়ে নয়টা saṛe nɔŷta / **plus one half** সাড়ে saṛe

hammer *n.* হাতুড়ি hatuṛi

hand *n.* হাত hat

happen *vb.* হওয়া hɔoŷa (hɔowa); *cvb.* হয়ে যাওয়া hôŷe yaoŷa

happily *adv.* হাসিমুখে hasimukhe

happiness *n.* সুখ sukh

happy *adj.* খুশি khuśi

hard *adj.* শক্ত śɔkto

hard work *n.* পরিশ্রম pôriśrôm

hardship *n.* কষ্ট kɔṣṭô

harm *n.* ক্ষতি kṣôti (khoti)

harmful *adj.* ক্ষতিকর kṣôtikɔr

harvest *n.* ফসল phɔsôl

hassle *n.* ঝামেলা jhamela

hat *n.* টুপি ṭupi

he *(hon.) pr.* উনি uni, ইনি ini; সে se, ও o

head *n.* মাথা matha

headache *n.* মাথা ব্যথা matha bytha (bætha)

headscarf *n.* ওড়না oṛna

health *n.* স্বাস্থ্য svasthyô (shastho), শরীর śôrīr

heap *n.* রাশি raśi

hear *vb.* শোনা śona

heart *n.* হৃদয় ṛdɔŷ (ridɔŷ), মন môn

heat *n.* উত্তাপ uttap, গরম gɔrôm

heaven *n.* স্বর্গ svɔrgô

heavy *adj.* ভারী bharī

hell *n.* নরক nɔrôk

help *n.* সাহায্য sahayyô; *vb.* সাহায্য করা sahayyô kɔra

her *pr.* তার → সে tar; *(hon.)* উনার unar

here *adv.* এখানে ekhane / **here, look** *phr.* এই যে ei ye

Himalayas *(mountain range) name* হিমালয় himalɔŷ

hint *n.* ইঙ্গিত iṅgit

hip *n.* পাছা pacha

hire *n.* ভাড়া bhaṛa

his *pr.* তার → সে tar; *(hon.)* উনার unar

history *n.* ইতিহাস itihas

hit *vb.* মারা mara

hobby *n.* শখ śɔkh

hold *vb.* ধরা dhɔra

hole *n.* গর্ত gɔrtô

holiday *n.* ছুটি chuṭi

home *n.* বাড়ি baṛi

honey *n.* মধু môdhu

honorable *adj.* মাননীয় manônīŷô

hope *n.* আশা aśa; *vb.* আশা করা aśa kɔra

horizon *n.* দিগন্ত digôntô

horse *n.* ঘোড়া ghoṛa

hospital *n.* হাসপাতাল haspatal

hot *adj.* গরম gɔrôm

hot spices *n.* গরম মসলা gɔrôm mɔsla

hotel *n.* হোটেল hoṭel

hour *n.* ঘণ্টা ghɔnṭa

house *n.* বাসা basa

house *n.* ঘর ghɔr

houses *n.* ঘরবাড়ি ghɔrbaṛi

how *qu.* কেমন kæmôn; *(by what transport)* কি করে ki kôre

how many (people) *qu.* কয়জন kɔŷjɔn

how much *qu.* কত kɔtô

human being *n.* মানুষ manuṣ

humble request *n.* মিনতি minôti

hunger *n.* খিদে, খিদা khide, khida

husband *n.* স্বামী svamī (shami)

I

I *pr.* আমি ami

ice *n.* বরফ bɔrôph

ice cream *n.* আইসক্রিম aiskrim

icy *adj.* হিমেল himel

if *conj.* যদি yôdi

ignite *vb.* জ্বালানো jvalano

ill *adj.* অসুস্থ ɔsusthô

illness *n.* অসুখ ɔsukh

illness *n.* রোগ rog

illusion *n.* মায়া maŷa

imagination *n.* কল্পনা kɔlpôna

imagine *vb.* কল্পনা করা kɔlpôna kɔra

immaculate *adj.* নির্মল nirmɔl

immediately *adv.* সঙ্গে সঙ্গে sɔṅge sɔṅge

immortal *adj.* অমর ɔmɔr

importance *n.* গুরুত্ব gurutvô (gurutto)

important *adj.* দরকারি dɔrkari

impression: make an impression *vb.* দাগ কাটা dag kaṭa

in *pp. Note: There is no word for 'in' in Bangla. English prepositions, such as* *in, at, on, are done with locative endings on nouns, e.g.,* ḅalu *sand,* ḅalute *in the sand.*

in any case *expr.* যাই হোক yai hok
in front of *pp.* সামনে samne (shamne)
in place of *pp.* হয়ে hôŷe
in spite of *pp.* সত্ত্বেও sɔttveo (shɔtteo)
in that case *conj.* তাহলে tahôle
in the course of the day (*lit.:* day going going) *phr.* দিন যেতে যেতে di:n yete yete
in the meantime *adv.* এরমধ্যে ermôdhye, এরইমধ্যে erimôdhye
in the middle of *pp.* মাঝখানে majhkhane
in this *pr.* এতে ete
in total *adv.* মোট moṭ
incessant *adj.* অবিরাম ɔbiram
inconvenience *n.* অসুবিধা ɔsubidha
inconvenient time *n.* অসময় ɔsômôŷ
increase *vb.* বাড়ানো baṛano
independence *n.* স্বাধীনতা svadhīnôta
indigenous *adj.* দেশী deśī
infant *n.* শিশু śiśu
infection *n.* সংক্রমণ sɔṃkrômôn
inform *vb.* জানানো janano
injustice *n.* অন্যায় ɔnyaŷ (onnay)
insect *n.* পোকা poka
inside *pp.* ভিতরে bhitôre
intense *adj.* গাঢ় gaṛhô
intertwined *adv.* গলাগলি করে gɔlagôli kôre
introduction *n.* আলাপ alap
invitation *n.* নিমন্ত্রণ nimôntron
iron *n.* লোহা loha
irritate *vb.* জ্বালানো jvalano
is that so? *phr.* তাই নাকি tai naki / **isn't that so?** *phr.* তাই না? tai na?
it *pr.* সে se, তা ta
Italy *name* ইটালি iṭali

J

jackal *n.* শিয়াল śiŷal
jackfruit *n.* কাঁঠাল kāṭhal
Jamuna (*river*) *name* যমুনা yômuna
jar *n.* বয়াম bɔŷam
jasmine *n.* জুঁই jūi
jewelry *n.* গয়না gɔŷna
job *n.* চাকরি cakri

joined *adj.* শ্লিষ্ট śliṣṭô (slishṭo)
joke *n.* ঠাট্টা ṭhaṭṭa
journalist *n.* সাংবাদিক saṃbadik
journey *n.* পথচলা pɔthcɔla, যাত্রা yatra (jatra)
joy *n.* আনন্দ anôndô
judgement *n.* বিচার bicar
jug *n.* জগ jɔg
juice *n.* রস rɔs
jujube *n.* বরই bɔroi
jump *n.* লাফ laph; *vb.* ঝাঁপানো jhāpano
junction *n.* মোড় mor
jungle *n.* জঙ্গল jɔṅgôl
just like that *adv.* এমনি emni
just now *adv.* এই মাত্র ei matrô
justice *n.* ন্যায় nyaŷ (nay)
jute *n.* পাট pa:ṭ

K

keep *vb.* রাখা rakha
   keep alive *cvb.* বাঁচিয়ে রাখা bāciŷe rakha
   keep promise *vb.* কথা রাখা kɔtha rakha
kettle *n.* কেটলি keṭli
key *n.* চাবি cabi
kilogram *n.* কেজি keji
kind *n.* (*type*) রকম rɔkôm, ধরন dhɔrôn / **kind of** *adv.* একরকম ækrɔkôm
king *n.* রাজা raja
king of seasons *n.* ঋতুরাজ ṛturaj (rituraj)
kingdom *n.* রাজত্ব rajôtvô
kiss *n.* চুমু cumu
kitchen *n.* রান্না ঘর ranna ghɔr
knee *n.* হাঁটু hāṭu
knife *n.* ছুরি churi
know *vb.* জানা jana, চেনা cena / **let know** *vb.* জানানো janano
knowledge *n.* জ্ঞান jñan (gæn)
Kolkata *name* কলকাতা kôlkata
Kustia (*town*) *name* কুষ্টিয়া kuṣṭiŷa

L

lack *n.* অভাব ɔbhab
ladder *n.* মই môi
ladle *n.* হাতা hata
lady *n.* ভদ্রমহিলা bhɔdrômôhila

lady's fingers (okra) *n.* ঢেঁড়স ḍhẽṛos

lake *n.* পুকুর pukur

lamb *n.* খাসির মাংস khasir maṃsô

lamp *n.* দীপ dīp, বাতি bati

land *n.* জমি jômi, স্থল sthɔl, ভূমি bhūmi

landlord *n.* মালিক malik

lanes and by-lanes *phr.* গলিঘুঁজি gôlighūji

language *n.* ভাষা bhasa

lantern *n.* হারিকেন hariken

last *adj.* গত gɔtô; *vb.* টেকা ṭeka

late: be late *vb.* দেরি করা deri kɔra

late autumn *n.* হেমন্ত hemôntô

laugh *vb.* হাসা hasa, লহাসি hasi

lawyer *n.* উকিল ukil

lazy *adj.* অলস ɔlôs (ɔlôsh)

leaf *n.* পাতা pata

learn *vb.* শেখা śekha

learning *n.* বিদ্যা bidya (bidda)

least: at least *adv.* অন্তত ɔntôtô

leave *cvb.* রেখে আসা rekhe asa; *vb.* ছাড়া chaṛa

    leave behind *cvb.* রেখে যাওয়া rekhe yaoŷa, রেখে আসা rekhe asa

    leave it *vb.* থাক thak

    leave out *vb.* বাদ দেওয়া bad deoŷa

left *(opp. of right)* *n./adj.* বাঁ bā / **to the left** *pp.* বা দিকে bā dike

left-over *adj.* বাকি baki

leg *n.* পা pa

lemon *n.* লেবু lebu

lentil *n.* ডাল ḍal

less *adj./adv.* কম kɔm

let go *vb.* ছাড়া chaṛa

letter *n.* চিঠি ciṭhi; *(of alphabet)* অক্ষর ôkṣôr (ôkkhôr)

lie *(untruth)* *n.* মিথ্যা mithya (mittha)

lie down *vb.* শোয়া śoŷa

life *n.* জীবন jībôn, প্রাণ praṇ

lift *vb.* তোলা tola

lift up *vb.* ওঠানো oṭhano

light *n.* আলো alo; *adj. (in weight)* হালকা halka

lightning *n.* বিজলি bijoli, বিদ্যুৎ bidyut

like *vb.* ভাল লাগা bhalô laga; *pp.* মত mɔtô; *conj.* যেন yænô

limit *n.* সীমা sīma (shima)

lion *n.* সিংহ simhô (shingho)

listen *vb.* শোনা śona

little bit *adj.* অল্প ɔlpô, একটু ekṭu

loan *n.* ঋণ r̥ṇ (rin)

lock *n.* তালা tala

long *adj.* দীর্ঘ dīrghô, লম্বা lɔmba

look at *vb.* তাকানো takano, দেখা dækha

lose *vb.* হারানো harano

loss *n.* লোকসান loksan

lost *adj.* হারানো harano / **be lost** *vb.* হারা hara

lotus *n.* পদ্ম ফাল pɔdmô phul (pɔddô)

loud *adj.* জোরে jore

louse *n.* উকুন ukun

love *vb.* ভালবাসা bhalôbasa, ভালোবাসা bhalobasa

low *adv.* নিচে nice

luck *n.* ভাগ্য bhagyô, কপাল kɔpal

luggage *n.* মালপত্র malpɔtrô

lungs *n.* ফুসফুস phusphus

lychee *n.* লিচু licu

M

machine *n.* কল kɔl

mad *adj.* পাগল pagôl / **go mad** *vb.* মেতে → মাতা mete → mata

madam *n.* ম্যাডাম myaḍam

made *adj.* তৈরি toiri

magic *n.* জাদু jadu

maize *n.* মক্কা mɔkka

make *vb.* বানানো banano

man *(male human being)* *n.* পুরুষ puruṣ, *(person)* লোক lok

mango *n.* আম a:m

many *adj.* বহু bôhu, অনেক ɔnek

map *n.* মানচিত্র mancitro

mark *n.* দাগ dag

market *n.* বাজার bajar

marriage *n.* বিয়ে biŷe / **get married** *vb.* বিয়ে করা biŷe kɔra

mass *(heap)* *n.* রাশি raśi

matches *n.* দেশলাই deśôlai

math *n.* অঙ্ক ɔṅkô

matter *n.* ব্যাপার byapar (bæpar)

maybe *phr.* হতে পারে hôte pare

meaning *n.* মানে mane

means *n.* উপায় upaŷ

meat *n.* মাংস mamsô (mangsho)

medicine *n.* ওষুধ osudh

Meghna *(river) name* মেঘনা meghna

melon *n.* ফুটি phuṭi

memory *n.* স্মরণ smɔrôṇ (shɔrôn), স্মৃতি smŕti (sriti)

mend *vb.* সারানো saranô

midday *n.* দুপুর dupur

middle *n.* মাঝ majh / **in the middle of** *pp.* মাঝখানে majhkhane

midriff *n.* কোমর komôr

milk *n.* দুধ du:dh

minced meat *n.* কিমা kima

mind *n.* মন môn / **it is in the mind = I think** *phr.* মনে হয় mône hɔŷ

mingle *cvb.* মিশে যাওয়া miśe yaoŷa

minister *n.* মন্ত্রী môntri

mint *n.* পুদিনা pudina

minute *n.* মিনিট miniṭ

mirror *n.* আয়না aŷna

miss (someone) *vb.* মনে পড়া mône pɔṛa

mist *n.* কুয়াশা kuŷaśa (kuwasha)

mistake *n.* ভুল bhul / **make a mistake** *vb.* ভুল করা bhul kɔra

Mister (Mr.) *n.* বাবু babu

mockery *n.* ঠাট্টা ṭhaṭṭa

molasses *n.* গুড় guṛ

moment *n.* মুহূর্ত muhūrtô

Monday *n.* সোমবার sombar

monkey *n.* বানর banôr

monsoon *n.* বর্ষা bɔrṣa

month *n.* মাস ma:s / **next month** *phr.* সামনের মাস samne mas

mood *n.* মেজাজ mejaj

moon *n.* চাঁদ cãd / **full moon** *n.* পূর্ণিমা pūrṇima

more *adv.* আরও aro, আর ar

morning *n.* সকাল sɔkal

mosque *n.* মসজিদ môsjid

mosquito *n.* মশা mɔśa

mother *n.* আম্মা amma, মা ma

motorcar *n.* মোটরগাড়ি moṭôrgaṛi

mountain *n.* পাহাড় pahaṛ

mouse *n.* ইঁদুর ĩdur

moustache *n.* গোঁফ gõph

mouth *n.* মুখ mukh

move *vb. (go)* চলা cɔla; *(turn)* ঘোরা ghora

/ **move around** *vb.* নড়াচড়া করা nɔṛacɔṛa kɔra

much *adv.* বেশি করে beśi kôre; *adj.* অনেক ɔnek, বেশি beśi / **too much** *adj.* বেশি beśi

mud *n.* কাদা kada

Muslim *n./adj.* মুসলমান musôlman

mustard *n.* সরিষা sôriṣa (shorisha)

my goodness! *excl.* ওমা oma

N

name *n.* নাম nam

nature *n.* প্রকৃতি prôkŕti (prokriti)

naughty *adj.* দুষ্টু duṣṭu

near *pp.* কাছে kache

necessary *adj.* দরকারি dɔrkari

neck *n.* ঘাড় gha:r

necklace *n.* মালা mala

necklace *n.* হার har

need *n.* দরকার dɔrkar

needle *n.* সূচি sūci

neglect *n.* অবহেলা ɔbôhela

neighbor *n.* প্রতিবেশী prôtibeśi

never *adv.* কখনও না kɔkhôno na

new *adj.* নতুন nôtun

news *n.* খবর khɔbôr

newspaper *n.* খবরের কাগজ khɔbôrer kagôj

next *adj.* আগামী agamī, সামনে samne (shamne) / **next month** *phr.* সামনের মাস samner mas

nice *adj.* ভাল bhalô / **nice smell** *n.* সুগন্ধ sugɔndhô

night *n.* রাত rat / **at night** *adv.* রাত্রে ratre

nineteen *num.* উনিশ uniś

no, not *adv.* না na / **no way!** *excl.* দূর dūr

normal *adj.* সাধারণ sadharôṇ

north *n.* উত্তর uttôr

nose *n.* নাক nak

not *adv.* না na / **not at all** *excl.* আরে না are na / **not remember** *vb.* মনে নেই mône nei

notebook *n.* খাতা khata

nothing *n.* কিছু না kichu na

notice *vb.* লক্ষ করা lôkṣô kɔra, টের পাওয়া ṭer paoŷa

now *adv.* এখন æxkhôn / **just now** *adv.* এই মাত্র ei matrô

nowadays *adv.* আজকাল ajkal
number *n.* সংখ্যা sɔṃkhya
nurse *n.* সেবিকা sebika
nursing *n.* নার্সিং narsiṃ (narsing), সেবা seba
nutmeg *n.* জায়ফল jaŷphɔl

O

obscene *adj.* অশ্লীল ɔślīl
observe *vb.* লক্ষ করা lôkṣô kɔra
occur *cvb.* হয়ে যাওয়া hôŷe yaoŷa; *vb.* হওয়া hɔoŷa (hɔowa)
ocean *n.* সমুদ্র sɔmudrô, সাগর sagôr
of course *adv.* অবশ্য ɔbôśyô, নিশ্চয় niścɔŷ (nishcɔŷ)
offense *(crime)* *n.* অপরাধ ɔpôradh
office *n.* অফিস ɔphis
often *adv.* প্রায়ই praŷi
oh! *excl.* বাঃ baḥ
oh dear! *(expression of dismay)* *phr.* হায় হায় haŷ haŷ
oil *n.* তেল tel
ointment *n.* মলম mɔlôm
OK / okay *excl./phr.* আচ্ছা accha, ঠিক আছে ṭhik ache
okra *n.* ঢেঁড়স ḍhē̃ros
old *adj.* *(of people)* বুড়া buṛa (BD), বুড়ো buṛo (PB); *(of things)* পুরানো purano; *(ancient)* প্রাচীন pracīn *(H)*, আপা apa *(M)*
olive *n.* জলপাই jɔlpai
omit *vb.* বাদ দেওয়া bad deoŷa
on: on top of *pp.* উপর upôr
once *adv.* একবার ækbar
one *num.* এক æk; **one (person)** *adj./n.* একজন ækjɔn; *adj.* একটা ækṭa / **one or two** *num.* একটা-আধটা ækṭa-adhṭa
one and a half *num.* দেড় deṛ
one hundred *num.* এক শ æk śô
onion *n.* পেঁয়াজ pẽŷaj
only *adj.* একমাত্র ækmatro; *adv.* খালি khali, মাত্র matrô, শুধু śudhu (shudhu)
open *adj.* ফাঁকা phã̄ka
opening *n.* মুখ mukh
opinion *n.* মত mɔːt
opportunity *n.* সুযোগ suyog
oppression *n.* অত্যাচার ɔtyacar

or *conj.* বা ba
orange *n., adj.* কমলা kɔmla
order *(command)* *n.* হুকুম / হুকুম hukum
other *adj.* অন্য ɔnyô / **the other one/person** *n.* অন্যজন ɔnyôjɔn
otherwise *conj.* না হলে na hôle
out: go out *vb.* বেড়ানো beṛano
outside *pp.* বাইরে baire
oven *n.* চুলা cula, উনুন unun
over there *adv.* ওইদিকে oidike
overall *adv.* এমনি emni
overcast *adj.* আচ্ছন্ন acchɔnnô
overweight *adj.* মোটা moṭa
own *pr.* নিজ nij
owner *n.* মালিক malik
ox *n.* ষাঁড় ṣãṛ
oyster *n.* ঝিনুক jhinuk

P

pack *vb.* প্যাক করা pyak kɔra
paddy (rice paddy) *n.* ধান dha:n
Padma (Podda) *(river) name* পদ্মা pɔdma (pɔdda)
pain *n.* ব্যথা bytha (bæthа)
pajamas *n.* পায়জামা paŷjama
palas *(flower)* *n.* পলাশ pɔlaś
pan *n.* হাঁড়ি hã̄ri
pants *n.* প্যান্ট pyanṭ (pænṭ)
papaya *n.* পেঁপে pẽpe
paper *n.* কাগজ kagôj
parcel *n.* পারসেল parsel
pardon *vb.* মাফ করা maph kɔra; *n.* মাফ maph
parents *n.* মা-বাবা ma-baba
part *n.* ভাগ bhag
past *n.* অতীত ɔtīt
paste *n.* মলম mɔlôm
patient *n.* রোগী rogī
pause *n.* বিশ্রাম biśram
pawpaw *n.* পেঁপে pẽpe
pay *vb.* টাকা দেওয়া ṭaka deoŷa
pea *n.* মটর mɔṭôr
peace *n.* শান্তি śanti
peaceful *adj.* প্রশান্ত prôśantô, শান্ত śantô
peanut *n.* বাদাম badam
pear *n.* নাসপাতি naspati

peculiar *adj.* অদ্ভুত ɔdbhut

pen *n.* কলম kɔlôm

pencil *n.* পেনসিল pensil

pepper *n.* গোল মরিচ gol môric

perfume *n.* পারফিউম parphium

perhaps *adv.* হয়তো hɔŷto; *phr.* হতে পারে hôte pare

person *n.* ব্যক্তি bykti (bekti); *(human being)* মানুষ manuṣ; *(man)* লোক lok

pickle *n.* আচার acar

picture *n.* ছবি chôbi

pig *n.* শূকর śūkôr (shukor)

pillow *n.* বালিশ baliś

pineapple *n.* আনারস anarɔs

pink *adj.* গোলাপি golapi

place *n.* স্থান sthan, জায়গা jaŷga / **in place of** *pp.* হয়ে hôŷe

plant *vb.* লাগানো lagano; *n.* চারা cara

plate *n.* থালা thala

play *vb.* খেলা khæla, খেলা করা khæla kɔra

pleased *adj.* আনন্দিত anônditô

pleasure *n.* আনন্দ anôndô

pluck *vb.* তোলা tola

plus one half *n.* সাড়ে saṛe

plus one quarter *n.* সওয়া sɔŷa

pocket *n.* পকেট pɔkeṭ

poet *n.* কবি kôbi

pole *n.* দণ্ড dɔṇḍô

police station *n.* থানা thana

pomegranate *n.* ডালিম ḍalim

pomelo *n.* জাম্বুরা jambura

pond *n.* পুকুর pukur

poor *adj.* গরীব gôrīb / **poor boy** *n.* বেচারা becara

pork *n.* শূকরের মাংস śūkôrer maṃsô

porter *n.* দারোয়ান daroŷan

possibility *n.* সম্ভাবনা sɔmbhabôna

possible *adv.* সম্ভব sɔmbhôb

possibly *adv.* সম্ভবত sɔmbhôbɔtô

postage stamp *n.* ডাকটিকিট ḍakṭikiṭ

pot *(cooking) n.* ডেকচি ḍekci

potato *n.* আলু alu

powder *n.* পাউডার pauḍar

practice *n.* চর্চা cɔrca

pregnant *adj.* গর্ভবতী gɔrbhôbôti

prepare *vb.* বানানো banano

prepared *adj.* তৈরি toiri, প্রস্তুত prôstut

present *adj.* উপস্থিত upôsthit / **be present** *vb.* আছ- ach-; *n. (gift)* উপহার upôhar

price *n.* দাম da:m

pride *n.* অহঙ্কার ɔhɔŋkar, গৌরব gourob, গর্ব gɔrbô

privilege *n.* অধিকার ôdhikar

problem *n.* সমস্যা sɔmôsya, মুশকিল muśkil

profit *n.* লাভ labh

prohibition *n.* নিষেধ niṣedh

promise *vb.* কথা দেওয়া kɔtha deoŷa / **keep promise** *vb.* কথা রাখা kɔtha rakha

proof *n.* প্রমাণ prômaṇ

prop *n.* ভরসা bhɔrsa

proper *adj.* উচিত ucit

protect *vb.* রক্ষা করা rôkṣa kɔra

pull *vb.* টান দেওয়া ṭan deoŷa; *n.* টান ṭan

pull out *vb.* ওঠানো oṭhano

pullover *n.* গরম গেঞ্জি gɔrôm geñji

pumpkin *n.* কুমড়া kumṛa

punish *vb.* শাস্তি দেওয়া śasti deoŷa

punishment *n.* শাসন śasôn

pure *adj.* নির্মল nirmɔl

purpose *n.* উদ্দেশ্য uddeśyô (uddesho)

purse *n.* মানিব্যাগ manibyag

push *n.* ধাক্কা dhakka

pushcart *n.* ঠেলাগাড়ি ṭhelagaṛi

put; put away *vb.* রাখা rakha

put straight *vb.* ঠিক করা ṭhik kɔra

Q

quarrel *n.* ঝগড়া jhɔgṛa

quarter: plus one quarter *n.* সওয়া sɔŷa

quarter to *adj.* পৌনে poune

question *n.* জিজ্ঞাসা jijñasa (jiggasha), প্রশ্ন prôśnô

quickly *adv.* তাড়াতাড়ি taṛataṛi

quiet *adj.* চুপ cup

quite *adv.* বেশ beś

R

rabbit *n.* খরগোশ khɔrgôś (khɔrgosh)

rack *n.* আলনা alna

radish *n.* মূলা mūla

railway *n.* রেলগাড়ি relgaṛi

rain *n.* বৃষ্টি bṛṣṭi (brishti)

rainy season *n.* বর্ষা bɔrṣa

raisin *n.* কিশমিশ kiśmiś

Rajshahi *(town) name* রাজশাহী rajshahī

Rangpur *name* রংপুর rɔmpur

raw *adj.* কাঁচা kãca

razor *n.* ক্ষুর kṣur (khur)

read *vb.* পড়া pɔṛa

ready *adj.* প্রস্তুত prôstut

reality *n.* বাস্তবতা bastôbôta

reason *n.* কারণ karôṇ, যুক্তি yukti / **for that reason** *conj.* সে জন্য se jônyô, জন্যে jônye

receive *vb.* পাওয়া paoŷa

recently *adv.* সম্প্রতি sɔmprôti

red *adj.* লাল la:l

reduce *vb.* কমানো kɔmano, কমা kɔma; *cvb.* কমে যাওয়া kôme yaoŷa

refuge *n.* ভরসা bhɔrsa

regret *vb.* দুঃখ করা duḥkhô kɔra

relationship *n.* সম্পর্ক sɔmpɔrkô

relative *n.* আত্মীয় atmīŷô (attiyo)

relaxation *n.* আরাম aram, বিশ্রাম biśram

religion *n.* ধর্ম dhɔrmô

remember *vb.* মনে রাখা mône rakha, মনে আছে mône ache / **not remember** *vb.* মনে নেই mône nei

rent *n.* ভাড়া bhaṛa / **rent out** *vb.* ভাড়া দেওয়া bhaṛa deoŷa

repair *vb.* সারানো saranô

repayment *n.* শোধ śodh

reply *vb.* উত্তর দেওয়া uttôr deoŷa; *n.* উত্তর uttôr

reprimand *vb.* বকাবকি করা bɔkabôki kɔra; *n.* বকাবকি bɔkabôki

request: humble request *n.* মিনতি minôti

rescue *vb.* বাঁচানো bãcano

respect *n.* সম্মান sɔmman

respectable *adj.* মাননীয় manônīŷô

rest *n.* বিশ্রাম biśram

rest *n.* আরাম aram, বিশ্রাম biśram

restaurant *n.* রেস্টোরাঁ restôrã

restless *adj.* অস্থির ɔsthir

result *n.* ফল phɔl

return *vb.* ফেরা phera; *(give back)* ফেরত দেওয়া pherôt deoŷa; *cvb. (come back)* ফিরে আসা phire asa

ribbon *n.* ফিতা phita, ফিতে phite

rice *n.* ধান dha:n / **cooked rice** *n.* ভাত bhat

rice pudding *n.* পায়েস paŷes

rich *adj.* ধনী dhônī

richness *n.* পরিপূর্ণতা pôripūrṇota

rickshaw *n.* রিকশা rikśa

ride *vb.* চড়া cɔṛa

right *adj. (correct)* ঠিক ṭhik; *(opp. of left)* ডান ḍan / **to the right** *pp.* ডান দিকে ḍan dike; *n.* অধিকার ôdhikar

ring *n.* আংটি aṃṭi (angṭi)

ripe *adj.* পাকা paka

river *n.* নদী nôdī

riverbank *n.* পাড় paṛ

rivers and streams *n.* নদ-নদী nɔd-nôdī

road *n.* রাস্তা rasta, পথ pɔth / **main road** *n.* সদর রাস্তা sɔdôr rasta

roof *n.* চাল cal (chal), ছাদ cha:d

room *n.* ঘর ghɔr

rope *n.* দড়ি dôṛi

rose *n.* গোলাপ golap

rotten *adj.* পচা pɔca

round *adj.* গোল gol

routine *n.* নিয়ম niŷôm

run out *vb.* শেষ হয়ে যাওয়া śeṣ hôŷe yaoŷa

S

sad *adj.* দুঃখিত duḥkhitô

sadness *n.* দুঃখ duḥkhô

salt *n.* নুন nun, লবণ lɔbôṇ

same *adj.* একই eki

sand *n.* বালু balu

sandals *n.* চটি côṭi

saree *n.* শাড়ি śari, শাড়ী śarī

satisfied *adj.* তৃপ্ত tṛptô (tripto)

satisfy *vb.* মিটানো miṭano

Saturday *n.* মঙ্গলবার mɔṅgôlbar, শনিবার śônibar

saucer *n.* পিরিচ piric

save *vb. (rescue)* বাঁচানো bãcano

say *vb.* বলা bɔla / **say farewell** *vb.* বিদায় দেওয়া bidaŷ deoŷa

scare *vb.* ভয় দেখানো bhɔŷ dækhano

scared: be scared *vb.* ভয় পাওয়া bhɔŷ paoŷa (paowa), ভয় করা bhɔŷ kɔra

scarf *n.* মাফলার maphlar, ওড়না orna

scholar *n.* পণ্ডিত pônḍit

school *n.* স্কুল skul, ইস্কুল iskul

scissors *n.* কেঁচি keci (BD), কাঁচি kāci (PB)

sea *n.* সমুদ্র sɔmudrô, সাগর sagôr

search *vb.* খোঁজা khõja, খোঁজ করা khõj kɔra

season *n.* কাল kal, ঋতু r̥tu (ritu)

second *num.* দ্বিতীয় dvitīŷô / **second floor** *n.* দোতালা dotala

see *vb.* দেখা dækha

seed *n.* বীচি bīci, চারা cara

self *pr.* নিজ nij

sell *vb.* বেচা bæca

send *vb.* পাঠানো pathano, পাঠিয়ে দেওয়া pathiŷe deoŷa

separate *adj.* আলাদা alada

servant *n.* চাকর cakôr

sesame *n.* তিল til

settle *vb.* বসা bɔsa

severe *adj.* প্রচণ্ড prôcɔɳɖô

shade *n.* ছায়া chaŷa

shape *n.* রূপ rūp

she *pr. (hon.)* উনি uni, ইনি ini; সে se, ও o

shed *vb.* ঝরা jhɔra

sheep *n.* ভেড়া bhæra

sheet *n.* চাদর cadôr

ship *n.* জাহাজ jahaj

shirt *n.* সার্ট sart (shart)

Shiva *(god) name* শিব śib

shock *n.* আঘাত aghat

shoe(s) *n.* জুতা juta (BD), জুতো juto (PB)

shop *n.* দোকান dokan

shopkeeper *n.* দোকানদার dokandar

shopping *n.* কেনাকাটা kenakata

short *adj.* খাটো khato

shortage *n.* অভাব ɔbhab

shoulder *n.* কাঁধ kādh

shout *vb.* চিৎকার করা citkar kɔra

show *vb.* দেখানো dækhano

side *n.* ধার dhar / **side by side** *adv.* পাশাপাশি paśapaśi / **on the side** *pp.* পাশে paśe

sign *n.* চিহ্ন cihnô (cinhô); *(hint)* ইঙ্গিত iṅgit

silk-cotton *n.* শিমুল śimūl

simple *adj.* সহজ sɔhôj

sing *vb.* গান করা gan kɔra / **sing a song** *vb.* গান গাওয়া gan gaoŷa

sink down *vb.* বসা bɔsa

sir *n.* স্যার syar

sister *n.* বোন bon / **older sister** *(M.)* আপা apa, *(H.)* দিদি didi

sit *vb.* বসা bɔsa

situation *n.* অবস্থা ɔbôstha

sixteen *num.* ষোলো solo

sixty *num.* ষাট sat

size *n.* সাইজ saij

skin *n.* চামড়া camra

sky *n.* আকাশ akaś

sleep *n.* ঘুম ghum, তন্দ্রা tɔndra; *vb.* ঘুমানো ghumano

sleeping *adj.* ঘুমিয়ে-থাকা ghumiŷe-thaka

slowly *adv.* ধীরে dhīre, আস্তে আস্তে aste aste

slum *n.* বস্তি bôsti

small *adj.* ছোট chɔtô

smell *n.* গন্ধ gɔndhô / **nice smell** *n.* সুগন্ধ sugɔndhô

smile *n.* হাসি hasi, হাসা hasa

smiling *adv.* হাসিমুখে hasimukhe

snake *n.* সাপ sap

snakebean *n.* পটোল pɔtol

snakegourd *n.* চিচিঙ্গা ciciṅga

snore *vb.* নাক ডাকা nak ɖaka

snow *n.* বরফ bɔrôph

so *conj.* তাই tai; *adv.* তেমন tæmôn, এমন æmôn / **is that so?** *phr.* তাই নাকি tai naki / **isn't that so?** *phr.* তাই না? tai na?

so many *adj./adv.* এতগুলো ætôgulo, এত ætô

so much *adj./adv.* এত ætô, তেমন tæmôn

so small *adj.* এতটুকু ætôtuku

so that *conj.* যেন yænô

soap *n.* সাবান saban

soccer *n.* ফুটবল phutbɔl

social gathering *n.* আড্ডা aɖɖa

socks *n.* মোজা moja

soft *adj.* নরম nɔrôm, কোমল komôl

soil *n.* মাটি mati

soldier *n.* সৈনিক soinik

some *adj.* কিছু kichu

something *n.* কিছু kichu

sometimes *adv.* মাঝে মাঝে majhe majhe

somewhere *adv.* কোথাও kothao

son *n.* ছেলে chele

song *n.* গান gan

sorrow *n.* দুঃখ duḥkhô

soul *n.* আত্মা atma (atta)

sound *n.* শব্দ śɔbdô

sour *adj.* টক ṭɔk

south *n.* দক্ষিণ dôksin (dokkhin)

space *n. (place)* জায়গা jaŷga

speak *vb.* বলা bɔla

special *adj.* বিশেষ biśeṣ

spend (money) *vb.* খরচ করা khɔrôc kɔra

spend time *vb.* সময় কাটানো sɔmɔŷ kaṭano

spice *n.* মসলা mɔsla / **hot spices** *n.* গরম মসলা gɔrôm mɔsla

spider *n.* মাকড়সা makôrsa

spinach *n.* পালং শাক palôm śa:k

spine *n.* মেরুদণ্ড merudɔṇḍô

splendid *adj.* চমৎকার cɔmôṭkar

spoil *vb.* নষ্ট করা nɔṣṭô kɔra

spoiled *adj.* নষ্ট nɔṣṭô, পচা pɔca

spoon *n.* চামচ camôc

sport *n.* খেলাধুলা khæladhula

spread *vb.* ছড়ানো chɔrano

spring *(season) n.* বসন্ত bɔsôntô

staff *n.* দণ্ড dɔṇḍô

stage *n.* মঞ্চ mɔñcô

stain *n.* দাগ dag

stairs *n.* সিঁড়ি sĩṛi

stamp (postage stamp) *n.* ডাকটিকিট ḍakṭikiṭ

stand *vb.* দাঁড়ানো dãṛano

star *n.* তারা tara

start *vb.* লাগা laga, আরম্ভ করা arômbhô kɔra, শুরু করা śuru kɔra; *n.* আরম্ভ arômbhô, শুরু śuru

stay *vb.* থাকা thaka, থাক thak

stay alive *vb.* বেঁচে থাকা bẽce thaka

stick *n.* লাঠি laṭhi

still *adv.* তখনও tɔkhôno, এখনও ækhônô

stomach *n.* পেট peṭ

stone *n.* পাথর pathôr

stop *vb.* থামা thama

storm *n.* ঝড় jhɔr

stormy *adj.* ঝড়ো jhɔṛo

story *n.* গল্প gɔlpô

straight *adv.* সোজা soja

strange *adj.* অদ্ভুত ɔdbhut

straw *n.* খড় khɔr

strength *n.* শক্তি śôkti

stretch out one's arm *vb.* হাত বাড়ানো hat baṛano

strike *vb. (of a clock)* বাজা baja; *(hit)* মারা mara

string *n.* ফিতা phita, ফিতে phite

strong *adj.* শক্ত śɔktô, জোরে jore

stuck: get stuck *vb.* বসা bɔsa

student *n. (f.)* ছাত্রী chatrī, *(m.)* ছাত্র chatrô

study *vb.* পড়া pɔra

studying *n.* লেখাপড়া lekhapɔra

stupid *adj.* বোকা boka

successful *adj.* সফল sɔphɔl

such *adv.* এমন æmôn

suddenly *adv.* হঠাৎ hɔṭhaṭ

suffer *vb.* কষ্ট পাওয়া kɔṣṭô paoŷa

suffering *n.* কষ্ট kɔṣṭô

sugar-cane *n.* আখ akh

summer *n.* গ্রীষ্মকাল grīṣmôkal

sun *n.* সূর্য sūryô

Sunday *n.* রবিবার rôbibar

sunlight *n.* রোদ rod

sunrise *n.* সূর্যোদয় sūryodɔ̂ŷ

sunset *n.* সূর্যাস্ত sūryastô

sunshine *n.* রোদ rod

superstition *n.* কুসংস্কার kusɔṃskar

support *n.* ভরসা bhɔrsa

surprising *adj.* আশ্চর্য aścɔryô

survive *vb.* বাঁচা bãca, বেঁচে থাকা bẽce thaka

suspicious *adj.* সন্দেহজনক sɔndehôjɔnôk / **be suspicious** *vb.* সন্দেহ করা sɔndehô kɔra

sweet potato *n.* মিষ্টি আলু miṣṭi alu

sweet(s) *adj./n.* মিষ্টি miṣṭi (mishṭi)

swim *vb.* সাঁতার কাটা sãtar kaṭa

swing *vb.* দোল খাওয়া dol khaoŷa

syllable *n.* অক্ষর ôkṣôr

system *n.* নিয়ম niŷôm

T

table *n.* টেবিল ṭebil

tailor *n.* দরজি dôrji

taka *(currency of Bangladesh) n.* টাকা ṭaka

take *vb.* নিয়ে → নেওয়া neoŷa

take along *cvb.* নিয়ে যাওয়া niŷe yaoŷa

take part *vb.* অংশ নেওয়া ɔmśô neoŷa

take pictures *vb.* ছবি তোলা chôbi tola

talk *vb.* কথা বলা kɔtha bɔla

tamarind *n.* তেঁতুল tẽtul

taste *n.* স্বাদ svad (sha:d)

tear *vb.* ছেঁড়া chẽra

tear *n* চোখের জল cokher jɔl

telephone *n.* টেলিফোন ṭeliphon

tell off *vb.* বকাবকি করা bɔkabôki kɔra

telling off *n.* বকাবকি bɔkabôki

temper *n.* মেজাজ mejaj

ten *num.* দশ dɔś (dɔsh)

than all *pp.* সবচেয়ে sɔbceŷe

thank you *expr.* ধন্যবাদ dhɔnyôbad

thanks *expr.* ধন্যবাদ dhɔnyôbad

that *conj.* যে ye; *pr.* তা ta / **so that** *conj.* যেন yænô / **that's why** *conj.* সে জন্য se jônyô, জন্যে jônye / **that way** *adv.* ওইদিকে oidike

thatched hut *n.* কুঁড়ে ঘর kũre ghɔr

theater *n.* থিয়েটার thiŷeṭar

their *pr.* তাদের → তারা tader

them *pr.* তাদের → তারা tader

then *adv.* তখন tɔkhôn; *conj.* তাহলে tahôle / **by then** *adv.* এরমধ্যে ermôdhye, এরইমধ্যে erimôdhye / **when – then** *conj.* যখন – তখন yɔkhôn – tɔkhôn

there *adv.* ওখানে okhane / **over there** *adv.* ওইদিকে oidike

therefore *conj.* সে জন্য se jônyô, জন্যে jônye, তাই tai

these (things) *n.* এগুলো egulo

they *pr.* ওরা ora

thick *adj.* গাঢ় gaṛhô

thin *adj.* (*material*) পাতলা patla; (*emaciated*) রোগা roga

thing *n.* জিনিস jinis

think *vb.* ভাবা bhaba, মনে করা mône kɔra / **it is in the mind = I think** *phr.* মনে হয় mône hɔŷ

this *adj.* এ, এই e, ei / **in this** *pr.* এতে ete / **this (thing)** *pr.* এটা æṭa / **this time** *adv.* এইবার eibar

thoroughly *adv.* ভালভাবে bhalôbhabe

throat *n.* গলা gɔla

throw *vb.* ফেলা phæla / **throw away** *vb.* ফেলা phæla

thunder *n.* মেঘের ডাক megher ḍak

Thursday *n.* বৃহস্পতিবার br̊hôspôtibar (brihôshpôtibar)

ticket *n.* টিকিট ṭikiṭ

tide *n.* জোয়ার joŷar

tidy up *vb.* গুছানো guchano

tiger *n.* বাঘ bagh

time *n.* সময় sɔmɔŷ / **what time is it?** *phr.* কয়টা বাজে? kɔŷṭa baje

tired *adj.* ক্লান্ত klantô

to *pp.* কাছে kache

today *adv.* আজ a:j, আজকে ajke

together *adv.* একসঙ্গে eksɔṅge

toilet *n.* টয়লেট ṭɔŷleṭ

tolerate *vb.* সহ্য করা sɔhyô kɔra

tomato *n.* টোমেটো ṭomeṭo

tomorrow *adv.* আগামীকাল agamīkal; কালকে kalke (*Note: this also means yesterday*)

tongue *n.* জিভ ji:bh

tooth *n.* দাঁত dãt

top: on top of *pp.* উপর upôr

tornado *n.* ঘূর্ণিঝড় ghūrṇijhɔr

total *n.* মোট moṭ

totally *adv.* একেবারে ækebare

touch *vb.* ছোঁয়া chõŷa

towards *pp.* দিকে dike

towel *n.* গামছা gamcha, তোয়ালে toŷale

town *n.* নগর nɔgôr, শহর śɔhôr

tradition *n.* ঐতিহ্য oitihyô (oitijjho)

train *n.* ট্রেন ṭren, রেলগাড়ি relgari

transform *vb.* বদলানো bɔdlano

treatment *n.* চিকিৎসা cikiṯsa

tree *n.* গাছ gach

trees and plants *n.* গাছ-পালা gach-pala

tremor *n.* কম্প kɔmpô

trouble *n.* কষ্ট kɔṣṭô

trousers *n.* প্যান্ট pyanṭ (pænṭ)

trust *n.* আস্থা astha

truth *n.* সত্যি sôtyi

try *vb.* চেষ্টা করা ceṣṭa kɔra

tubewell *n.* নলকূপ nɔlkūp

turn *n.* পালা pala; *vb.* ঘোরা ghora

turnip *n.* শালগম shalgɔm

turtle *n.* কচ্ছপ kɔcchop

twenty *num.* বিশ biś (BD), কুড়ি kuri (PB)

twins *n.* জমজ jɔmôj

two (persons) *adj., n.* দুজন dujɔn

two and a half *n.* আড়াই aṛai

type *n.* ধরন dhɔrôn, রকম rɔkôm

typhoon *n.* তুফান tuphan

U

ugly *adj.* বিশ্রী biśrī, নোংরা nomra

umbrella *n.* ছাতি chati, ছাতা chata

unaware (of): be unaware of *vb.* মনে নেই mône nei

unbearable *adj.* অসহ্য ɔsɔhyô (ɔshôjjhô)

uncertain *adj* অনিশ্চিত ɔniścitô / **it is uncertain** *phr.* তার ঠিক নেই tar ṭhik nei

uncle *n. See Appendix 7, kinship terms*

unclean *adj.* মলিন môlin

underground *n.* আন্ডারগ্রাউন্ড anḍargraunḍ

understand *vb.* বোঝা bojha

universe *n.* বিশ্ব biśvô

unknown *adj.* অজানা ɔjana

unripe *adj.* কাঁচা kāca

until *pp.* পর্যন্ত pôryôntô (porjonto)

unusual *adj.* অসাধারণ ɔsadharôṇ

uproar *n.* হৈচৈ hoicoi

upset *n.* ঝামেলা jhamela / **be upset** *vb.* কষ্ট পাওয়া kɔṣṭô paoŷa

urgent *adj.* জরুরি jôruri

usual *adj.* স্বাভাবিক svabhabik

usually *adv.* সাধারণত sadharôṇôtô

V

vaccination *n.* টিকা ṭika

value *n.* মূল্য mūlyô

vanish *vb.* উঠে যাওয়া uṭhe yaoŷa

variety *n.* বৈচিত্র্য boicitryô

various *adj.* নানা nana, নানান nanan

various *adj.* বিচিত্র bicitrô

vegetables *n.* সবজি sôbji

vehicle *n.* গাড়ি gari

verandah *n.* বারান্দা baranda

very *adv.* খুব. khub

very far *adv.* অনেক দূরে ɔnek dūre

vest *n.* গেঞ্জি geñji

victory *n.* জয় jɔŷ

village *n.* গাঁ gā, গ্রাম gram

violent *adj.* দ্দাম uddam

visit *vb.* বেড়ানো beṛano

voice *n.* গলা gɔla

W

waist *n.* কোমর komôr

wait *vb.* অপেক্ষা করা ɔpekṣa kɔra, দাঁড়ানো dāṛano

wake up *vb.* জাগা jaga; *cvb.* জেগে ওঠা jege oṭha / **cause to wake up** *vb.* ওঠানো oṭhano, জাগানো jagano

walk *vb.* হাঁটা hāṭa; *cvb.* হেঁটে যাওয়া hēṭe yaoŷa

wall *n.* দেওয়াল deoŷal (deowal)

walnut *n.* কাঠবাদাম kaṭhbadam

want *vb.* চাওয়া caoŷa

wash *vb.* ধোয়া dhoŷa / **wash away** *cvb.* ডুবিয়ে দেওয়া ḍubiŷe deoŷa

watch *(timepiece) n.* ঘড়ি ghôri

water *n.* জল jɔl, পানি pani / **water up to one's neck** *phr.* গলা-জলে gɔla-jɔle

water buffalo *n.* মহিষ môhiṣ (mohish)

water jug *n.* কলসি kôlsi

water pump *n.* কল kɔl

watermelon *n.* তরমুজ tôrmuj

waterways *n.* নদনদী nôdnôdī

wave *n.* ঢেউ ḍheu

way *n. (path, road)* পথ pɔth; *(means)* উপায় upaŷ / **no way!** *excl.* দূর dūr

we *pr.* আমরা amra

weak *adj.* দুর্বল durbɔl

wear *vb.* পরা pɔra

weather *n.* আবহাওয়া abhaoŷa

wedding *n.* বিয়ে biŷe

Wednesday *n.* বুধবার budhbar

week *n.* সপ্তাহ sɔptahô

weep *vb.* কাঁদা kāda

weight *n.* ওজন ojôn; *(importance)* গুরুত্ব gurutvô (gurutto)

well *adv.* ভালভাবে bhalôbhabe

well-liked *adj.* প্রিয় priŷô

west *n.* পশ্চিম pôścim

West Bengal *name* পশ্চিম বাংলা pôścim bamla

wet *adj.* ভিজা bhija, ভিজে bhije

whale *n.* তিমি timi

what *qu.* কি ki; *rel. pr.* যা ya / **what has happened?** *phr.* কি হয়েছে? ki hôŷeche? / **what on earth ...** *expr.* কি রে ki re / **what time is it?** *phr.* কয়টা বাজে? kɔŷṭa baje /

with what *qu.* কি দিয়ে ki diẏe

when *qu.* কখন kɔkhôn, কবে kɔbe / **when – then** *conj.* যখন– তখন yɔkhôn – tɔkhôn

where *qu.* কোথায় kothaẏ

which *qu.* কোন kon

white *adj.* সাদা sada

who *qu.* কে ke; *(pl.) pr.* কারা kara

whole *adj.* পুরা pura (BD), পুরো puro (PB), সারা sara, সমস্ত sɔmôstô

why *qu.* কেন kænô / **that's why** *conj.* সে জন্য se jônyô, জন্যে jônye

wife *n.* বউ, বৌ bou, স্ত্রী strī

wild *adj.* উদ্দাম uddam

willing *adj.* রাজি raji

wind *n.* বাতাস batas, হাওয়া haoẏa

window *n.* জানালা janala

wing *n.* ডানা ḍana

winter *n.* শীতকাল śī:tkal; *adj./ n.* শীত śī:t

wisdom *n.* বুদ্ধি buddhi

wish *n.* ইচ্ছা iccha

with *pp.* সঙ্গে sɔṅge (shɔngge), সাথে sathe; *(instrumental)* দিয়ে diẏe; নিয়ে niẏe / **with what** *qu.* কি দিয়ে ki diẏe

within *pp.* মধ্যে môdhye

without *pp.* ছাড়া chaṛa

woman *n.* মহিলা môhila

wonderful *adj.* চমৎকার cɔmôtkar

wood-apple *n.* বেল bel

word *n.* কথা kɔtha, শব্দ śɔbdô

work *n.* কাজ kaj, ক্রিয়া kriẏa; *vb.* কাজ করা kaj kɔra, চাকরি করা cakri kɔra

world *n.* জগৎ jɔgôt, দুনিয়া duniẏa, পৃথিবী pr̥thibī (prithibi); সংসার sɔṃsar

worried *adj.* উদ্বিগ্ন udbignô

worry *vb.* চিন্তা করা cinta kɔra / **don't worry** *phr.* ভয় নেই bhɔẏ nei

wow! *excl.* বাঃ baḥ

write *vb.* লেখা lekha

wrong *n.* অন্যায় ɔnyaẏ (onnay)

Y

year *n.* বছর bɔchôr

yellow *adj.* (B) হলুদ hôlud, (PB) হলদে hɔlde

yes *adv.* হ্যাঁ hyæ̃ (hæ̃)

yesterday *adv.* গতকাল gɔtôkal; *n.* কালকে kalke *(Note: this also means tomorrow)*

yet *adv.* এখনও ækhônô

you *pr. (pl. pol.)* আপনারা apnara, *(sg. fam.)* তোমাকে tomake *see* তুমি tumi, *(sg. fam.)* তোমার tomar *see* তুমি tumi, *(sg. pol.)* আপনি apni

young *adj.* তরুণ tôruṇ

Z

zero *num.* শূন্য śūnyô (shunno)

zoo *n.* চিড়িয়াখানা ciṛiẏakhana

APPENDICES

Appendix 1: The inherent vowel

The inherent vowel poses two separate puzzles to the foreign learner: (1) its presence or absence, i.e., whether the inherent vowel is pronounced or not and (2) its pronunciation. There are few hard-and-fast rules for either but there are some patterns that can help us to develop some intuition.

Presence or absence of the inherent vowel

- We can generally assume that the inherent vowel is pronounced **between** consonants that have no other vowel attached to them: গরম = গ+র+ম = gɔrôm, কেবল = ক+এ+ব+ল = kebôl, বলা = ব+ল+আ = bɔla, etc.

  There are, however, some words where two consonants stand next to one another without forming a conjunct and without the inherent vowel pronounced between them, e.g., চাকরি cakri *job*, আজকে ajke *today*, সামনে samne *ahead*, দরকার dɔrkar *need*, আটকানো aṭkano *obstruct*, and in all conjugated verb forms করব kôrbô *I will do*, বসলেন bôslen *you* (hon.) *sat*, etc. These words contain distinct morphological units that resist the forming of conjuncts.

- We have three indicators that the inherent vowel is **not** pronounced:

  - ং অনুস্বর onusvor never has a vowel after it: বরং bɔrông, সুতরাং shutôrang, কিংবা kingba, সংবাদ shɔngbad

  - ঃ খণ্ড ৎ khɔṇḍô tɔ which appears at the end of words and syllables and stops the inherent vowel from being pronounced: পশ্চাৎ pɔshcat, অর্থাৎ ɔrthat, হঠাৎ hɔṭhat, উৎসব utshɔb
  - ্ হসন্ত hasanta. This symbol is optionally attached underneath consonants where the inherent vowel might otherwise be pronounced. It is not frequently used.

- The inherent vowel is normally **not** pronounced at the end of words after single consonants. Here are some examples:

  ডাক ḍak *call*, মেঘ megh *cloud*, রং rɔng *color*, মাছ mach *fish*, দুধ dudh *milk*, দিন din *day*, খুব khub *very*, প্রেম prem *love*, ঘর ghɔr *building*, লাল lal *red*, দশ dɔsh *ten*, শেষ shesh *end*, মাস ma:sh *month*

- The inherent vowel is pronounced:

  - when a word ends in a conjunct: পর্যন্ত pôrjôntô *until*, স্বপ্ন shɔpnô *dream*, শান্ত shantô *peaceful*. The only regular exception to this are foreign words like এয়ারপোর্ট eŷarpôrṭ *airport*, পার্ক park *park*, প্যান্ট pænṭ *trousers*.

- after a final হ h and after ঢ় ṛh:

  দেহ dehô *body*, স্নেহ snehô *affection*, সিংহ siṃhô (singho) *lion*,
  সন্দেহ sɔndehô *doubt*, গাঢ় gaṛhô *deep*, প্রৌঢ় prouṛhô *middle-aged*
  but আষাঢ় ashaṛh *Bengali month*

- after য় preceded by i or e, except in the verb forms দেয় dæŷ *he/she gives* and
  নেয় næŷ *he/she takes*:

  প্রিয় priŷô *dear*, জাতীয় jatīŷô *national*, প্রয়োজনীয় prôŷojɔnīŷô *necessary*

- when the final consonant is preceded by a combination with ঋ (ri) ṙ or by ং or
  ঃ: মৃত mṙtô (mrito) *dead*, মাংস maṃsô (mangsho) *meat*, দুঃখ duḥkhô (dukho)
  sadness

- in noun- or verb-derived adjectives or adverbs ending in ত :

  সম্ভবত sɔmbhɔbôtô *possibly*, নিশ্চিত niścitô *certain*, জীবিত jībitô *alive*,
  চিন্তিত cintitô *worried*

- in the following very common adjectives, quantifiers, conjunctions, and question
  words (this list is not exhaustive):

  ছোট choṭô *small*, বড় bɔṛô *big*, ভাল bhalô *good*, গত gɔtô *previous*,
  কত kɔtô *how much*, এত ætô *so much*, তত tɔtô *so much*, যেন jænô *so that*,
  অথচ ɔthôcô *but*, কেন kænô *why*

- Both মত and কাল have double interpretations:

  মত mɔtô is a postposition meaning *like*
  মত mɔt is a noun meaning *opinion*
  কাল kalô (also spelled কালো kalo) is an adjective meaning *black*
  কাল kal is a noun meaning *time, season*

- in the following verb forms (this applies to all verbs):

  1st person future tense, e.g.: যাব jabô *I will go*, দেব debô *I will give*,
  করব kôrbô *I will do*, লাগাব lagabô *I will plant*

  2nd person (fam.) simple present, present continuous, present perfect, e.g.:
  কর kɔro *you do*, লেখ lekho *you write*, থাক thako *you stay*, করছ korcho
  you are doing, করেছ korecho *you have done*, খেলছ khelcho *you are
  playing*, খেলেছ khelechô *you have played*, যাচ্ছ jacchô *you are going*,
  গিয়েছ giyechô *you have gone*, গেছ gechô *you have gone,* etc.

  3rd person (ord.) simple past, past continuous, past perfect, past habitual,
  e.g.: ছিল chilô *he was*, গেল gælô *he went*, দিল dilô *he gave*, খাচ্ছিল
  khacchilô *he was eating*, নামছিল namchilô *he was getting down*, করেছিল
  kôrechilô *he had done*, নেমেছিল nemechilô *he had got down*, বলত bôltô *he
  used to say*, ভাবত bhabtô *he used to think*

Pronunciation of the inherent vowel

The pronunciation of the inherent vowel fluctuates between open ɔ as in *hot* (British pronunciation) and closed o as in *Roma* (Italian pronunciation). You will see from these examples that the pronunciation of the inherent vowel depends on the environment it occurs in.

Some of the regular patterns are:

- In words of two syllables with two inherent vowels, the first inherent vowel is pronounced ɔ, the second o.

খবর khɔbôr *news*		শহর shɔhôr *town*	
গরম gɔrôm *hot*		সকল shɔkôl *all*	
অন্তর ɔntôr *inside*		কলম kɔlôm *pen*	
ভবন bhɔbôn *residence*		মত mɔtô *like*	
গত gɔtô *last*		নরম nɔrôm *soft*	
তখন tɔkhôn *then*		সরল shɔrôl *honest*	

The inherent vowel is pronounced as closed o:

- in **all** instances where the inherent vowel is the final sound in a word.

- when the following syllable contains an i or u:

    ছবি chôbi *picture*, মধু môdhu *honey*, বন্ধু bôndhu *friend*, কঠিন kôṭhin *difficult*

    This also affects the following prefixes:

    প্রতি- prôti, অতি- ôti-, অনু- ônu-, অভি- ôbhi-, পরি- pôri-

    Note however that the negative prefixes অ- and অন- are pronounced ɔ, irrespective of what follows them: অনিয়ম ɔ-niŷôm *disorder*, অনিশ্চিত ɔ-niścitô *uncertain*, অনিচ্ছা ɔn-iccha *reluctance*, অনুপযুক্ত ɔn-upôjuktô *unsuitable*, অনুপস্থিত ɔn-upôsthit *absent*

- when preceded by a conjunct with র r :

    প্র- prô (prefix), পরিশ্রম pôrisrôm *hard work*, আগ্রহ agrôhô *interest*, অগ্রগতি ɔgrôgôti *progress*

- when followed by ক্ষ :

    লক্ষ lôkkhô *one hundred thousand*, লক্ষ্য lôkkhô *aim, goal*, দক্ষ dôkkhô *expert*, অক্ষর ôkkhôr *letter*

- when followed by a conjunct with য jophola:

    বন্যা bônna *flood*, সত্য shôttô *true*, অবশ্য ɔbôsshô *of course*, রহস্য rɔhôsshô *mystery*

Appendix 2: Consonant conjuncts

ক + ক (k + k) = ক্ক (kk)   চক্কর cɔkkôr *wheel*

ক + ত (k + t) = ক্ত (kt)   শক্তি śôkti *strength*

ক + র (k + r) = ক্র (kr)   আক্রমণ akrômôṇ *attack*

ক + ষ (k + ṣ) = ক্ষ (kṣ)   পরীক্ষা pôrīkṣa (porikkha) *trial, examination*

গ + ধ (g + dh) = গ্ধ (gdh)   স্নিগ্ধ snigdhô *cordial, affectionate*

গ + র (g + r) = গ্র (gr)   সমগ্র sɔmôgrô *whole, entire*

ঙ + ক (ṅ + k) = ঙ্ক (ṅk)   অলঙ্কার ɔlôṅkar *decoration, ornament*

ঙ + গ (ṅ + g = ঙ্গ (ṅg)   জঙ্গল jɔṅgôl (jonggol) *jungle*

চ + চ (c + c) = চ্চ (cc)   উচ্চারণ uccarôṇ *pronunciation*

চ + ছ (c + ch) = চ্ছ (cch)   কচ্ছপ kɔcchôp *turtle*

জ + জ (j + j) = জ্জ (jj)   বিপজ্জনক bipɔjjônôk *dangerous*

জ + ঞ (j + ñ) = জ্ঞ (jñ)   অভিজ্ঞতা ôbhijñôta (obhiggota) *experience*

ঞ + চ (ñ + c) = ঞ্চ (ñc)   পঞ্চাশ pɔñcaś (poncash) *fifty*

ঞ + জ (ñ + j) = ঞ্জ (ñj)   গেঞ্জি geñji (genji) *vest*

ট + ট (ṭ + ṭ) = ট্ট (ṭṭ)   ঠাট্টা ṭhaṭṭa *mockery*

ণ + ট (ṇ + ṭ) = ণ্ট (ṇṭ)   ঘণ্টা ghɔṇṭa *hour*

ণ + ঠ (ṇ + ṭh) = ণ্ঠ (ṇṭh)   কণ্ঠ kɔṇṭhô *voice*

ণ + ড (ṇ + ḍ) = ণ্ড (ṇḍ)   ঠাণ্ডা ṭhaṇḍa *cold*

ত + ত (t + t) = ত্ত (tt)   উত্তর uttôr *north; answer*

ত + র (t + r) = ত্র (tr)   মাত্র matrô *only*

দ + দ (d + d) = দ্দ (dd)   উদ্দেশ্য uddesyô (uddessho) *purpose*

দ + ধ (d + dh) = দ্ধ (ddh)   যুদ্ধ yuddhô (juddho) *war*

দ + ব (d + v) = দ্ব (dv)   দ্বন্দ্ব dvɔndvô *conflict*

দ + ভ (d + bh) = দ্ভ (dbh)   অদ্ভুত ɔdbhut *strange*

ন + ত (n + t) = ন্ত (nt)   অন্তর ɔntôr *interior*

ন + ত + র (n + t + r) = ন্ত্র (ntr)   মন্ত্রী môntrī *minister*

ন + থ (n + th) = ন্থ (nth)   গ্রন্থ grônthô *book*

ন + দ (n+ d) = ন্দ nd   মন্দ mɔndô *bad*

ন + ধ (n + dh) = ন্ধ ndh   অন্ধ ɔndhô *blind*

ন + ন (n + n) = ন্ন (nn)   ভিন্ন bhinnô *different*

প + ত (p + t) = প্ত (pt)   গুপ্ত guptô *spy*

প + প (p + p) = প্প (pp)   গপ্প gɔppô *story*

প + র (p + r) = প্র (pr)   প্রাণ praṇ *life*

ব + দ (b + d) = ব্দ (bd)   শব্দ śɔbdô *word*

ব + ধ b + dh) = ব্ধ (bdh)   লুব্ধ lubdhô *greedy*

ম + প (m + p) = ম্প (mp)   কম্প kɔmpô *tremor*

ম + ভ (m + bh) = ম্ভ (mbh)   সম্ভব sɔmbhɔb *possible*

র + ক (r + k) = র্ক (rk)   তর্ক tɔrkô *argument (see Unit 1 #52)*

র + ত (r + t) = র্ত (rt)   মূর্তি mūrti *image*

শ + চ (ś + c) = শ্চ (śc)   পশ্চিম pôścim *west*

ষ + ট (ṣ + ṭ) = ষ্ট (ṣṭ)   মিষ্টি miṣṭi *sweet*

ষ + ঠ (ṣ + ṭh) = ষ্ঠ (ṣṭh)   শ্রেষ্ঠ śreṣṭhô *best*

ষ + ণ (ṣ + ṇ) = ষ্ণ (ṣṇ)   উষ্ণ uṣṇô (ushno) *warm*

স + ক (s + k) = স্ক (sk)   স্কুল skul *school*

স + ত (s + t) = স্ত (st)   রাস্তা rasta *road*

স + ত + র (s + t + r) = স্ত্র (str)   মিস্ত্রি mistri *carpenter*

স + থ (s + th) = স্থ (sth)   ব্যবস্থা bybôstha (bæbostha) *arrangement*

স + ব (s + v) = স্ব (sv)   স্বর্গ svɔrgô (shɔrgô) *heaven*

হ + ন (h + n) = হ্ন (hn)   চিহ্ন cihnô (cinhô) *sign*

হ + ম (h + m) = হ্ম (hm)   ব্রহ্ম brɔhmô (brɔmmhô) *Brahmin*

Consonant vowel combinations

গ + উ (g + u) = গু (gu)   গুহা guha *cave*

ত + র + উ (t + r + u) = ত্রু (tru)   ত্রুটি truṭi *fault*

ন + ত + উ (n + t + u) = ন্তু (ntu)   কিন্তু kintu *but*

র + উ (r + u) = রু (ru)   রুটি ruṭi *bread*

র + ঊ (r + ū) = রূ (rū)   রূপা rūpa *silver*

শ + উ (ś + u) = শু (śu)   শুক্রবার śukrôbar *Friday*

স + ত + উ (s + t + u) = স্তু (stu)   প্রস্তুত prôstut *ready*

হ + উ (h + u) = হু (hu)   বাহু bahu *arm*

হ + ঋ (h + ṙ) = হৃ (hṙ)   হৃদয় hṙdɔŷ (ridɔŷ) *heart*

Appendix 3: Verb charts

For explanations and abbreviations please see Unit 6 and the abbreviations chart. Where two alternative forms are given, the first is more formally correct, the second more colloquial.

Class 1 CVC (ɔ – ô)
বলা *say, speak*

tenses	আমি	তুমি	সে	আপনি, উনি
pr.s.	বলি bôli	বল bɔlô	বলে bɔle	বলেন bɔlen
pr.c.	বলছি	বলছ	বলছে	বলছেন
pr.perf.	বলেছি	বলেছ	বলেছে	বলেছেন
fut.	বলব	বলবে	বলবে	বলবেন
p.s.	বললাম	বললে	বলল	বললেন
p.c.	বলছিলাম	বলছিলে	বলছিল	বলছিলেন
p.perf.	বলেছিলাম	বলেছিলে	বলেছিল	বলেছিলেন
p.habit.	বলতাম	বলতে	বলত	বলতেন
imp.	---	বল bɔlô, বল bôlô	বলুক	বলেন, বলুন
non-finites	VN বলা	IP বলতে	CP বললে	PP বলে

Class 1 VC (o – u)
ওঠা *rise, get up*

tenses	আমি	তুমি	সে	আপনি, উনি
pr.s.	উঠি	ওঠ	ওঠে	ওঠেন
pr.c.	উঠছি	উঠছ	উঠছে	উঠছেন
pr.perf.	উঠেছি	উঠেছ	উঠেছে	উঠেছেন
fut.	উঠব	উঠবে	উঠবে	উঠবেন
p.s.	উঠলাম	উঠলে	উঠল	উঠলেন
p.c.	উঠছিলাম	উঠছিলে	উঠছিল	উঠছিলেন
p.perf.	উঠেছিলাম	উঠেছিলে	উঠেছিল	উঠেছিলেন
p.habit.	উঠতাম	উঠতে	উঠত	উঠতেন
imp.	---	ওঠো, ওঠো	উঠুক	ওঠেন, উঠুন
non-finites	VN ওঠা	IP উঠতে	CP উঠলে	PP উঠে

Class 2 CaC
থাকা *stay*

tenses	আমি	তুমি	সে	আপনি, উনি
pr.s.	থাকি	থাক	থাকে	থাকেন
pr.c.	থাকছি	থাকছ	থাকছে	থাকছেন
pr.perf.	থেকেছি	থেকেছ	থেকেছে	থেকেছেন
fut.	থাকব	থাকবে	থাকবে	থাকবেন
p.s.	থাকলাম	থাকলে	থাকল	থাকলেন
p.c.	থাকছিলাম	থাকছিলে	থাকছিল	থাকছিলেন
p.perf.	থেকেছিলাম	থেকেছিলে	থেকেছিল	থেকেছিলেন
p.habit.	থাকতাম	থাকতে	থাকত	থাকতেন
imp .	---	থাকো, থেকো	থাকুক, থাক	থাকেন, থাকুন
non-finites	VN থাকা	IP থাকতে	CP থাকলে	PP থেকে

Class 2 (1) aC
আনা *bring*

tenses	আমি	তুমি	সে	আপনি, উনি
pr.s.	আনি	আন	আনে	আনেন
pr.c.	আনছি	আনছ	আনছে	আনছেন
pr.perf.	এনেছি	এনেছ	এনেছে	এনেছেন
fut.	আনব	আনবে	আনবে	আনবেন
p.s.	আনলাম	আনলে	আনল	আনলেন
p.c.	আনছিলাম	আনছিলে	আনছিল	আনছিলেন
p.perf.	এনেছিলাম	এনেছিলে	এনেছিল	এনেছিলেন
p.habit.	আনতাম	আনতে	আনত	আনতেন
imp.	---	আনো	আনুক	আনেন, আনুন
non-finites	VN আনা	IP আনতে	CP আনলে	PP এনে

Class 2 (2) aC
আসা *come* (has some additional forms)

tenses	আমি	তুমি	সে	আপনি, উনি
pr.s.	আসি	আস	আসে	আসেন

pr.c.	আসছি	আসছ	আসছে	আসছেন
pr.perf.	এসেছি	এসেছ	এসেছে	এসেছেন
fut.	আসব	আসবে	আসবে	আসবেন
p.s.	এলাম / আসলাম	এলে / আসলে	এল / আসল	এলেন / আসলেন
p.c.	আসছিলাম	আসছিলে	আসছিল	আসছিলেন
p.perf.	এসেছিলাম	এসেছিলে	এসেছিল	এসেছিলেন
p.habit.	আসতাম	আসতে	আসত	আসতেন
imp.	---	আসো / এসো	আসুক	আসেন, আসুন
non-finites	VN আসা	IP আসতে	CP এলে	PP এসে

Class 3 CV

হওয়া *be, become*

tenses pr.s.	আমি হই	তুমি হও	সে হয়	আপনি, উনি হন
pr.c.	হচ্ছি	হচ্ছ	হচ্ছে	হচ্ছেন
pr.perf.	হয়েছি	হয়েছ	হয়েছে	হয়েছেন
fut.	হব	হবে	হবে	হবেন
p.s.	হলাম	হলে	হল	হলেন
p.c.	হচ্ছিলাম	হচ্ছিলে	হচ্ছিল	হচ্ছিলেন
p.perf.	হয়েছিলাম	হয়েছিলে	হয়েছিল	হয়েছিলেন
p.habit.	হতাম	হতে	হত	হতেন
imp.	---	হও	হোক	হন
non-finites	VN হওয়া	IP হতে	CP হলে	PP হয়ে

Class 3 CV

দেওয়া *give* (has some irregularities)
নেওয়া *take* (conjugates the same way)

tenses pr.s.	আমি দিই / দেই	তুমি দাও	সে দেয়	আপনি, উনি দেন
pr.c.	দিচ্ছি	দিচ্ছ	দিচ্ছে	দিচ্ছেন
pr.perf.	দিয়েছি	দিয়েছ	দিয়েছে	দিয়েছেন
fut.	দিব / দেব	দেবে	দেবে	দেবেন

p.s.	দিলাম	দিলে	দিল	দিলেন
p.c.	দিচ্ছিলাম	দিচ্ছিলে	দিচ্ছিল	দিচ্ছিলেন
p.perf.	দিয়েছিলাম	দিয়েছিলে	দিয়েছিল	দিয়েছিলেন
p.habit.	দিতাম	দিতে	দিত	দিতেন
imp.	---	দাও, দিও	দিক	দেন, দিন
non-finites	VN দেওয়া	IP দিতে	CP দিলে	PP দিয়ে

Class 3 CV
শোয়া *lie down*

tenses	আমি	তুমি	সে	আপনি, উনি
pr.s.	শুই	শোও	শোয়	শোন
pr.c.	শুচ্ছি	শুচ্ছ	শুচ্ছে	শুচ্ছেন
pr.perf.	শুয়েছি	শুয়েছ	শুয়েছে	শুয়েছেন
fut.	শুব	শুবে	শুবে	শুবেন
p.s.	শুলাম	শুলে	শুল	শুলেন
p.c.	শুচ্ছিলাম	শুচ্ছিলে	শুচ্ছিল	শুচ্ছিলেন
p.perf.	শুয়েছিলাম	শুয়েছিলে	শুয়েছিল	শুয়েছিলেন
p.habit.	শুতাম	শুতে	শুত	শুতেন
imp.	---	শোও	শুক	শোন
non-finites	VN শোয়া	IP শুতে	CP শুলে	PP শুয়ে

Class 3 Ca
যাওয়া *go* (has some irregularities)

tenses	আমি	তুমি	সে	আপনি, উনি
pr.s.	যাই	যাও	যায়	যান
pr.c.	যাচ্ছি	যাচ্ছ	যাচ্ছে	যাচ্ছেন
pr.perf.	গিয়েছি / গেছি	গিয়েছ / গেছ	গিয়েছে / গেছে	গিয়েছেন / গেছেন
fut.	যাব	যাবে	যাবে	যাবেন
p.s.	গেলাম	গেলে	গেল	গেলেন
p.c.	যাচ্ছিলাম	যাচ্ছিলে	যাচ্ছিল	যাচ্ছিলেন
p.perf.	গিয়েছিলাম / গেছিলাম	গিয়েছিলে / গেছিলে	গিয়েছিল / গেছিল	গিয়েছিলেন / গেছিলেন
p.habit.	যেতাম	যেতে	যেত	যেতেন

| imp. | --- | যাও, যেও | যাক | যান |
| non-finites | VN যাওয়া | IP যেতে | CP গেলে | PP গিয়ে |

Class 3 Ca
পাওয়া *get, receive*

tenses	আমি	তুমি	সে	আপনি, উনি
pr.s.	পাই	পাও	পায়	পান
pr.c.	পাচ্ছি	পাচ্ছ	পাচ্ছে	পাচ্ছেন
pr.perf.	পেয়েছি	পেয়েছ	পেয়েছে	পেয়েছেন
fut.	পাব	পাবে	পাবে	পাবেন
p.s.	পেলাম	পেলে	পেল	পেলেন
p.c.	পাচ্ছিলাম	পাচ্ছিলে	পাচ্ছিল	পাচ্ছিলেন
p.perf.	পেয়েছিলাম	পেয়েছিলে	পেয়েছিল	পেয়েছিলেন
p.habit.	পেতাম	পেতে	পেত	পেতেন
imp.	---	পাও	পাক	পান
non-finites	VN পাওয়া	IP পেতে	CP পেলে	PP পেয়ে

Class 3 Ca
চাওয়া *want, ask, look*

tenses	আমি	তুমি	সে	আপনি, উনি
pr.s.	চাই	চাও	চায়	চান
pr.c.	চাচ্ছি, চাইছি	চাচ্ছ, চাইছ	চাচ্ছে, চাইছে	ছাচ্ছেন, চাইছেন
pr.perf.	চেয়েছি	চেয়েছ	চেয়েছে	চেয়েছেন
fut.	চাইব	চাইবে	চাইবে	চাইবেন
p.s.	চাইলাম	চাইলে	চাইল	চাইলেন
p.c.	চাইছিলাম	চাইছিলে	চাইছিল	চাইছিলেন
p.perf.	চেয়েছিলাম	চেয়েছিলে	চেয়েছিল	চেয়েছিলেন
p.habit.	চাইতাম	চাইতে	চাইত	চাইতেন
imp.	---	চাও, চাইও	চাক	চান, চাইয়েন
non-finites	VN চাওয়া	IP চাইতে	CP চাইলে	PP চেয়ে

Class 4 CVCA
ঘুমানো *sleep*

tenses	আমি	তুমি	সে	আপনি, উনি
pr.s.	ঘুমাই	ঘুমাও	ঘুমায়	ঘুমান
pr.c.	ঘুমাচ্ছি	ঘুমাচ্ছ	ঘুমাচ্ছে	ঘুমাচ্ছেন
pr.perf.	ঘুমিয়েছি	ঘুমিয়েছ	ঘুমিয়েছে	ঘুমিয়েছেন
fut.	ঘুমাব	ঘুমাবে	ঘুমাবে	ঘুমাবেন
p.s.	ঘুমালাম	ঘুমালে	ঘুমাল	ঘুমালেন
p.c.	ঘুমাচ্ছিলাম	ঘুমাচ্ছিলে	ঘুমাচ্ছিল	ঘুমাচ্ছিলেন
p.perf.	ঘুমিয়েছিলাম	ঘুমিয়েছিলে	ঘুমিয়েছিল	ঘুমিয়েছিলেন
p.habit.	ঘুমাতাম	ঘুমাতে	ঘুমাত	ঘুমাতেন
imp.	---	ঘুমাও, ঘুমাইও	ঘুমাক	ঘুমান
non-finites	VN ঘুমানো	IP ঘুমাতে	CP ঘুমালে	PP ঘুমিয়ে

Incomplete verb আছ– *exist, be present*
(আছ– only has present simple and past simple forms. For the future tense, the past habitual and for non-finite verb forms the verb থাকা *stay* steps in.)

tenses	আমি	তুমি	সে	আপনি, উনি
pr.s.	আছি	আছ achô	আছে	আছেন
p.s.	ছিলাম	ছিলে	ছিল chilô	ছিলেন
imp.	---	থাকো, থেকো	থাকুক	থাকুন
non-finites	VN থাকা	IP থাকতে	CP থাকলে	PP থেকে

Appendix 4: Common verbs (grouped by their vowel mutation pattern)

ɔ – o stem

করা	*make, do*		পরা	*wear*
চলা	*move, go*		বলা	*speak, say*
ধরা	*catch, hold*		বসা	*sit*
পড়া	*read, fall*		মরা	*die*

o – u stem

ওঠা	*rise, get up*		বোঝা	*understand*
খোলা	*open*		ভোলা	*forget*
ঘোরা	*move, turn*		শোনা	*hear, listen*
তোলা	*lift*		শোয়া	*lie down*
ধোয়া	*wash*		হওয়া	*be, become*

e – i stem

কেনা	*buy*		লেখা	*write*
চেনা	*know, recognize*		শেখা	*learn*

æ – e stem

খেলা	*play*		দেখা	*see, look*
ঠেলা	*pull*		ফেলা	*throw*

irregular

দেওয়া	*give*		নেওয়া	*take*

a stem

আনা	*bring*		পাওয়া	*get, receive*
আসা	*come*		পারা	*be able to*
কাটা	*cut, spend*		বাঁচা	*survive*
খাওয়া	*eat*		ভাঙা	*break*
চাওয়া	*want, look*		ভালবাসা	*love*
ছাড়া	*leave*		যাওয়া	*go*
জাগা	*wake up*		রাখা	*keep, put*
জানা	*know*		লাগা	*be attached to*
ডাকা	*call*		হাঁটা	*walk*
থাকা	*stay, remain*		হারা	*be lost*
থামা	*stop*		হাসা	*laugh*

extended, causative

ঘুমানো	sleep		পাঠানো	send
জ্বালানো	ignite, irritate		পালানো	flee, escape
তাকানো	look at		বানানো	make, prepare
দাঁড়ানো	stand, wait		বোঝানো	explain
দেখানো	show		হারানো	lose

Appendix 5: Common compound verbs (Unit 9)

with যাওয়া *go*				
নিয়ে যাওয়া	*take*	from	নেওয়া	*take*
ফিরে যাওয়া	*return*	from	ফেরা	*return*
চলে যাওয়া	*arrive / go away*	from	চলা	*move, go*
ভুলে যাওয়া	*forget*	from	ভোলা	*forget*
পড়ে যাওয়া	*fall*	from	পড়া	*fall*
হয়ে যাওয়া	*occur, happen*	from	হওয়া	*be, become*
ভেঙে যাওয়া	*get broken*	from	ভাঙা	*break*
রেখে যাওয়া	*leave behind*	from	রাখা	*keep, put*
হারিয়ে যাওয়া	*lose*	from	হারানো	*lose*
উঠে যাওয়া	*come off*	from	ওঠা	*rise, get up*
ছেড়ে যাওয়া	*leave behind*	from	ছাড়া	*leave*
with আসা *come*				
হয়ে আসা	*become*	from	হওয়া	*be, become*
নিয়ে আসা	*bring*	from	নেওয়া	*take*
ফিরে আসা	*come back*	from	ফেরা	*return*
চলে আসা	*arrive*	from	চলা	*move*
with পড়া *fall*				
এসে পড়া	*come suddenly*	from	আসা	*come*
ভেঙে পড়া	*break down*	from	ভাঙা	*break*
ঘুমিয়ে পড়া	*fall asleep*	from	ঘুমানো	*sleep*
with ওঠা *rise*				
কেঁদে ওঠা	*burst out crying*	from	কাঁদা	*cry, weep*
হেসে ওঠা	*burst out laughing*	from	হাসা	*laugh, smile*
ফুলে ওঠা	*swell, blossom*	from	ফোলা	*blossom, swell*

with আছ– / থাকা *stay*				
বসে আছ– / থাকা	*stay seated*	from	বসা	*sit*
শুয়ে আছ– / থাকা	*stay lying down*	from	শোয়া	*lie down*
ঘুমিয়ে আছ– / থাকা	*stay asleep*	from	ঘুমানো	*sleep*
with দেওয়া *give*				
ফেলে দেওয়া	*throw away*	from	ফেলা	*throw*
বলে দেওয়া	*tell, inform*	from	বলা	*speak*
ছেড়ে দেওয়া	*give up*	from	ছাড়া	*leave*
বুঝিয়ে দেওয়া	*explain*	from	বোঝানো	*explain*
রেখে দেওয়া	*put down*	from	রাখা	*put*
পাঠিয়ে দেওয়া	*send off*	from	পাঠানো	*send*
লিখে দেওয়া	*write (for someone)*	from	লেখা	*write*
কেটে দেওয়া	*cut*	from	কাটা	*cut*
বুঝিয়ে দেওয়া	*explain*	from	বোঝানো	*explain*
with নেওয়া *take*				
লিখে নেওয়া	*write (for oneself)*	from	লেখা	*write*
খেয়ে নেওয়া	*eat up*	from	খাওয়া	*eat*
চেয়ে নেওয়া	*ask for*	from	চাওয়া	*want, ask*
with ফেলা *throw*				
বলে ফেলা	*blurt out*	from	বলা	*speak*
ভেঙে ফেলা	*break, damage*	from	ভাঙা	*break*
মেরে ফেলা	*kill*	from	মারা	*beat, hit*
খেয়ে ফেলা	*eat up*	from	খাওয়া	*eat*
ছিঁড়ে ফেলা	*tear up*	from	ছেঁড়া	*tear, rip*
চিনে ফেলা	*recognize*	from	চেনা	*recognize, know*
হেসে ফেলা	*burst out laughing*	from	হাসা	*laugh*
কেঁদে ফেলা	*burst out crying*	from	কাঁদা	*cry*

with রাখা *keep*				
ধরে রাখা	*hold, detain*	from	ধরা	*hold, catch*
লুকিয়ে রাখা	*keep hidden*	from	লুকানো	*hide*
খুলে রাখা	*keep open*	from	খোলা	*open*

lexicalized compound verbs				
খুঁজে পাওয়া	*find*	from	খোঁজা	*search*
ভেবে পাওয়া	*resolve, imagine*	from	ভাবা	*think*
ভেবে দেখা	*think about*	from	ভাবা	*think*
চেয়ে দেখা	*look at*	from	চাওয়া	*look at*
জড়িয়ে ধরা	*embrace*	from	জড়ানো	*entangle, embrace*
চেপে ধরা	*squeeze*	from	চাপা	*press, suppress*
কিনে আনা	*buy*	from	কেনা	*buy*

Appendix 6: Common conjunct verbs (Unit 10)

অংশ নেওয়া *take part*

অনুবাদ করা *translate*

অন্যায় করা *do wrong*

অনুভব করা *feel*

অনুরোধ করা *request*

অপমান করা *insult*

অপেক্ষা করা *wait*

অবহেলা করা *neglect*

অভ্যাস করা *practice*

আদর করা *caress*

আদেশ করা *order*

আন্দাজ করা *guess*

আপত্তি করা *object*

আবিষ্কার করা *discover, invent*

আরম্ভ করা *start*

আলাপ করা *talk, introduce*

আলোচনা করা *discuss*

আশা করা *hope*

আশীর্বাদ করা *bless*

ইচ্ছা করা *wish*

ইতস্ততঃ করা *hesitate*

উচ্চারণ করা *pronounce*

উত্তর দেওয়া *reply, answer*

উন্নতি করা *improve*

উপকার করা *help, do a favor*

কথা দেওয়া *promise*

কথা বল *speak*

কথা রাখা *keep promise*

কল্পনা করা *imagine, fancy*

কষ্ট পাওয়া *suffer*

ক্ষতি করা *harm*

ক্ষমা করা *forgive*

খরচ করা *spend (money)*

খিদা পাওয়া *feel hungry*

খোঁজ করা *search*

গল্প করা *gossip, chat*

টিকিট কাটা *buy a ticket*

টের পাওয়া *feel, perceive*

ঠিক করা *correct, repair*

তর্ক করা *argue*

তুলনা করা *compare*

দেরি করা *delay, be late*

নজর রাখা *keep watch, look out*

নষ্ট করা *spoil*

না করা *forbid, deny*

নাচ করা *dance*

নিঃশ্বাস নেওয়া *breathe*

নিমন্ত্রণ করা *invite*

পছন্দ করা *like, choose*

পরিষ্কার করা *clean*

পরীক্ষা করা *examine, test*

পার হওয়া *cross*

প্রকাশ করা *reveal, publish*

প্রমাণ করা *prove*

প্রশংসা করা *praise*

প্রশ্ন করা *ask*

বিক্রি করা *sell*

বিদায় করা *dismiss*

বিয়ে করা *marry*

বিশ্বাস করা *believe, trust*

ব্যবস্থা করা *arrange*

ব্যবহার করা *use, behave*

ভুল করা *make a mistake*

মন দেওয়া *concentrate*

মনোযোগ দেওয়া *concentrate*

রক্ষা করা *protect*

রাগ করা *be angry*

রান্না করা *cook*

লক্ষ্য করা *notice, observe*

লজ্জা করা *be embarrassed*

শাস্তি দেওয়া *punish*

শীত করা *feel cold*

গান করা *sing*

গ্রহণ করা *accept*

চিকিৎসা করা *treat*

চিৎকার করা *shout*

চিন্তা করা *think, worry*

চুপ করা *shut up, be quiet*

চেষ্টা করা *try*

ছবি তোলা *take picture*

জিজ্ঞাসা করা *ask*

ঝগড়া করা *quarrel*

শুরু করা *start, begin*

শেষ করা *finish*

সন্দেহ করা *doubt, suspect*

সময় কাটানো *spend (time)*

সাঁতার কাটা *swim*

সাহায্য করা *help*

হিসেব করা *calculate*

হাত দেওয়া *undertake*

হুকুম দেওয়া *order, command*

Appendix 7: Family relationships, Kinship terms

The vocabulary for family relationships is much more specific in Bangla than it is in English. An aunt is not just an aunt but your mother's sister, your father's sister, your father's brother's wife, or your mother's brother's wife. Bangla has separate terms for all of these. In addition to this, there are some differences between Muslim and Hindu relationship terms. In general, younger siblings, nephews and nieces, grandchildren, etc. are addressed by name although you may sometimes hear parents address their children affectionately as মা ma *mother* and বাবা baba *father*. Older members of the family are usually addressed by the relationship term.

	Muslim		**Hindu**	
younger brother	ভাই	bhai	ভাই	bhai
older brother	বড় ভাই	bɔṛo bhai	দাদা	dada
younger sister	বোন	bon	বোন	bon
older sister	আপা	apa	দিদি	didi
grandson	নাতি	nati	নাতি	nati
granddaughter	নাতনি	natni	নাতনি	natni

In-laws
These terms for in-laws are the same for Muslims and Hindus. They are on the whole not used in addressing people, except বউদি *older brother's wife* (Hindu), ভাবী *older brother's wife* (Muslim), and বউমা *younger brother's wife*.

husband	স্বামী shami
wife	স্ত্রী stri *or* বউ bou
father-in-law	শ্বশুর shoshur
mother-in-law	শাশুড়ি shashuṛi
daughter's husband	জামাই jamai
son's wife	বউ bou
older sister's husband	দুলাভাই dulabhai
older brother's wife	বউদি boudi *or* ভাবী bhabi
younger brother's wife	বউমা bouma
wife's older brother	সম্বন্ধী shɔmmondhi
wife's younger brother	শালা shala
wife's younger sister	শালি shali
husband's older brother	ভাশুর bhashur
husband's younger brother	দেবর / দেওর debor
husband's older sister	ননাস nɔnash
husband's younger sister	ননদ nɔnod

Paternal relatives

	Muslim	**Hindu**
father	আব্বা abba	বাবা baba
grandfather	দাদা dada	ঠাকুরদা, দাদু ṭhakurda
grandmother	দাদি dadi	ঠাকুরমা ṭhakurma
father's older brother	বড় চাচা bɔṛo caca	জেঠা jeṭha
father's older brother's wife	বড় চাচি bɔṛo caci	জেঠি jeṭha
father's younger brother	চাচা caca	কাকা kaka
father's younger brother's wife	চাচি caci	কাকি kaki
father's sister	ফুফু phuphu	পিসি pishi
father's sister's husband	ফুফা phupha	পিসা pisha
brother's son (nephew)	ভাতিজা bhatija	ভাইপো bhaipo *or* ভাইস্তা bhaista
brother's daughter (niece)	ভাতিজি bhatiji	ভাইঝি bhaijhi *or* ভাইস্তি bhaisti

Maternal relatives

	Muslim	**Hindu**
mother	আম্মা amma	মা ma
grandfather	নানা nana	দাদু dadu
grandmother	নানি nani	দিদিমা didima
mother's brother	মামা mama	মামা mama
mother's brother's wife	মামি mami	মামি mami
mother's sister	খালা khala	মাসি mashi
mother's sister's husband	খালু khalu	মেসো mesho
sister's son (nephew)	ভাগনে bhagne	ভাগনে bhagne
sister's daughter (niece)	ভাগ্নি bhagni	ভাগ্নি bhagni

Appendix 8: Months and seasons

The Bengali calendar is still in use with monolingual publishers and newspapers. The Bengali new century 1400 began on April 15, 1993. The second half of the year 2016 is therefore 1423 in Bengali counting. Bengalis count six seasons, lasting two months each.

Months	Seasons
বৈশাখ boiśakh (April – May)	গ্রীষ্ম grīṣmô (grissho) summer
জ্যৈষ্ঠ jyoiṣṭhô (May – June)	
আষাঢ় aṣaṛh (June –July)	বর্ষা bɔrṣa (bɔrsha) rainy season
শ্রাবণ śrabôṇ (July – August)	
ভাদ্র bhadrô (August – September)	শরৎ śɔrôṯ early autumn
আশ্বিন aśvin (September – October)	
কার্তিক kartik (October – November)	হেমন্ত hemôntô late autumn
অগ্রহায়ণ ɔgrôhaŷôṇ (November – December)	
পৌষ pouṣ (December – January)	শীত śīt winter
মাঘ magh (January – February)	
ফালগুন phalgun (February – March)	বসন্ত bɔsôntô spring
চৈত্র coitrô (March – April)	

Appendix 9: Numbers

Cardinal numbers

1 ১ এক æk
2 ২ দুই dui
3 ৩ তিন tin
4 ৪ চার car
5 ৫ পাঁচ pāc
6 ৬ ছয় chɔŷ
7 ৭ সাত sat
8 ৮ আট aṭ
9 ৯ নয় nɔŷ
10 ১০ দশ dɔś
11 ১১ এগারো ægaro
12 ১২ বারো baro
13 ১৩ তেরো tero
14 ১৪ চৌদ্দো couddo
15 ১৫ পনেরো pɔnero
16 ১৬ ষোলো ṣolo
17 ১৭ সতেরো sɔtero
18 ১৮ আঠারো aṭharo
19 ১৯ উনিশ uniś
20 ২০ বিশ biś / কুড়ি kuṛi
21 ২১ একুশ ekuś
22 ২২ বাইশ baiś
23 ২৩ তেইশ teiś
24 ২৪ চব্বিশ côbbiś
25 ২৫ পঁচিশ põ̃ciś
26 ২৬ ছাব্বিশ chabbiś
27 ২৭ সাতাশ sataś/ সাতাইশ sataiś
28 ২৮ আটাশ aṭaś/ আটাইশ aṭaiś
29 ২৯ উনত্রিশ unôtriś
30 ৩০ ত্রিশ triś
31 ৩১ একত্রিশ ektriś
32 ৩২ বত্রিশ bôtriś
33 ৩৩ তেত্রিশ tetriś
34 ৩৪ চৌত্রিশ coutriś
35 ৩৫ পঁয়ত্রিশ põŷtriś
36 ৩৬ ছত্রিশ chôtriś
37 ৩৭ সাঁইত্রিশ sãitriś
38 ৩৮ আটত্রিশ aṭtriś
39 ৩৯ উনচল্লিশ unôcôlliś
40 ৪০ চল্লিশ côlliś
41 ৪১ একচল্লিশ ækcôlliś

42 ৪২ বিয়াল্লিশ biŷalliś
43 ৪৩ তেতাল্লিশ tetalliś
44 ৪৪ চুয়াল্লিশ cuŷalliś
45 ৪৫ পঁয়তাল্লিশ põŷtalliś
46 ৪৬ ছেচল্লিশ checôlliś
47 ৪৭ সাতচল্লিশ satcôlliś
48 ৪৮ আটচল্লিশ aṭcôlliś
49 ৪৯ উনপঞ্চাশ unôpɔñcaś
50 ৫০ পঞ্চাশ pɔñcaś
51 ৫১ একান্ন ækannô
52 ৫২ বাহান্ন bahannô
53 ৫৩ তিপ্পান্ন tippannô
54 ৫৪ চুয়ান্ন cuŷannô
55 ৫৫ পঞ্চান্ন pɔñcannô
56 ৫৬ ছাপ্পান্ন chappannô
57 ৫৭ সাতান্ন satannô
58 ৫৮ আটান্ন aṭannô
59 ৫৯ উনষাট unôṣaṭ
60 ৬০ ষাট ṣaṭ
61 ৬১ একষট্টি ækṣôṭṭi
62 ৬২ বাষট্টি baṣôṭṭi
63 ৬৩ তেষট্টি teṣôṭṭi
64 ৬৪ চৌষট্টি couṣôṭṭi
65 ৬৫ পঁয়ষট্টি põŷṣôṭṭi
66 ৬৬ ছেষট্টি cheṣôṭṭi
67 ৬৭ সাতষট্টি satṣôṭṭi
68 ৬৮ আটষট্টি aṭṣôṭṭi
69 ৬৯ উনসত্তর unôsôttôr
70 ৭০ সত্তর sôttôr
71 ৭১ একাত্তর ækattôr
72 ৭২ বাহাত্তর bahattôr
73 ৭৩ তিয়াত্তর tiŷattôr
74 ৭৪ চুয়াত্তর cuŷattôr
75 ৭৫ পঁচাত্তর põcattôr
76 ৭৬ ছিয়াত্তর chiŷattôr
77 ৭৭ সাতাত্তর satattôr
78 ৭৮ আটাত্তর aṭattôr
79 ৭৯ উনআশি unôaśi
80 ৮০ আশি aśi
81 ৮১ একাশি ækaśi
82 ৮২ বিরাশি biraśi

83 ৮৩ তিরাশি tiraśi	96 ৯৬ ছিয়ানব্বই chiŷanɔbbôi
84 ৮৪ চুরাশি curaśi	97 ৯৭ সাতানব্বই satanɔbbôi
85 ৮৫ পঁচাশি pɔ̃caśi	98 ৯৮ আটানব্বই aṭanɔbbôi
86 ৮৬ ছিয়াশি chiŷaśi	99 ৯৯ নিরানব্বই niranɔbbôi
87 ৮৭ সাতাশি sataśi	100 ১০০ এক শ ek śô
88 ৮৮ আটাশি aṭaśi / অষ্টাশি ɔṣṭôaśi	200 ২০০ দু শ du śô
89 ৮৯ উননব্বই unônɔbbôi	1000 ১০০০ হাজার hajar
90 ৯০ নব্বই nɔbbôi	100.000 ১,০০,০০০ এক লাখ æk lakh
91 ৯১ একানব্বই ækanɔbbôi	one million ১০, ০০, ০০০ দশ লাখ dɔś lakh
92 ৯২ বিরানব্বই biranɔbbôi	ten million ১,০০,০০,০০০ এক কোটি æk koṭi
93 ৯৩ তিরানব্বই tiranɔbbôi	/ এক ক্রোড় æk kror
94 ৯৪ চুরানব্বই curanɔbbôi	zero ০ শূন্য śūnyô
95 ৯৫ পঁচানব্বই pɔ̃canɔbbôi	

one and a half দেড় deṛ   two and a half আড়াই aṛai

Fractions and time

কিলো kilo *kilometer* (the word মাইল mail *mile* is also in use)
কেজি keji *(kg) kilograms*

আধ adha / আধা adh *half*	আধ ঘণ্টা adh ghɔnṭa *half an hour*
	আধা কেজি adha keji *500 grams*
পোয়া poŷa *a quarter*	তিন পেওয়া tin poŷa *three quarters*
তেহাই tehai *a third*	
সাড়ে saṛe *plus one half*	সাড়ে ছয় মাইল saṛe chɔŷ mail *six and a half miles*
	সাড়ে তিন ঘণ্টা saṛe tin ghɔnṭa *three and a half hours*
	সাড়ে পাঁচটা saṛe pãcṭa *half past five*

পৌনে poune *minus one quarter, three quarters*
    পৌনে দুই কেজি poune dui keji *1,750 grams*
    পৌনে সাতটা poune satṭa *quarter to seven*

সওয়া sɔoŷa *(pron.* showa*) plus one quarter*
    সওয়া ঘণ্টা soŷa ghɔnṭa *an hour and a quarter*
    সওয়া চার মাইল soŷa car mail *four and a quarter miles*
    সওয়া দশটা soŷa doṣṭa *quarter past ten*

Ordinal numbers

প্রথম prothom *first*	ষষ্ঠ ṣɔṣṭhô *sixth*
দ্বিতীয় dvitīŷô *second*	সপ্তম sɔptôm *seventh*
তৃতীয় tr̥tīŷô *third*	অষ্টম ɔṣṭôm *eighth*
চতুর্থ côturthô *fourth*	নবম nɔbôm *ninth*
পঞ্চম pɔñcôm *fifth*	দশম dɔśôm *tenth*

From 11 onward we say এগারো নাম্বা, বারো নাম্বা, etc.

INDEX

CD TRACK LIST

R01 Alphabet

R02 Numbers

R03 Unit 2, Dialogue এটা কি, ও কে? eṭa ki, o ke? *What's this? Who is he? (Part 1)*

R04 Unit 3, Dialogue এইবার আমার পালা eibar amar pala *My turn now! (Part 2)*

R05 Unit 4, Dialogue সাঈদা কোথায়? saīda kothaŷ? *Where is Saida?*

R06 Unit 4, Narrative বিমলের বাড়ি bimɔler baṛi *Bimol's home*

R07 Unit 5, Dialogue চিড়িয়াখানায় ciṛiŷakhana *At the zoo*

R08 Unit 5, Narrative আমার পরিবার amar pôribar *My family*

R09 Unit 7, Dialogue প্রতিবেশী protibeshi *Neighbors*

R10 Unit 7, Narrative গ্রামের ছুটি gramer chuṭi *Village holiday*

R11 Unit 8, Dialogue নিমন্ত্রণের পরে nimontroner pɔre *After the invitation*

R12 Unit 8, Narrative বোকা চাকর boka cakor *Stupid servants*

R13 Unit 9, Dialogue পোস্টাপিসে posṭapise *At the post office*

R14 Unit 9, Narrative মেজাজ খারাপ mejaj kharap *Bad mood*

R15 Unit 10, Dialogue বাজারে bajare *At the market*

R16 Unit 10, Narrative সূর্যোদয় surjodoy *Sunrise*

R17 Unit 11, Dialogue হোটেলে hoṭele *At a hotel*

R18 Unit 11, Narrative অসময়ের শাসন ɔsɔmoyer shashon *Untimely punishment*

R19 Unit 12, Dialogue মাথা ব্যথা matha bætha *Headache*

R20 Unit 12, Narrative ভয় নেই bhɔy nei *No fear*

R21 Unit 13, Dialogue কোন দিকে? kon dike? *Which way?*

R22 Unit 13, Narrative ঋতু ritu *Seasons*

R23 Unit 14, Dialogue মজার ব্যাপার mojar bæpar *That's funny!*

R24 Unit 14, Narrative পদ্মা pɔdda *The Padma*

Also by Hanne-Ruth Thompson

Bengali-English/English-Bengali (Bangla) Dictionary & Phrasebook

This reference—perfect for business-people, foreign aid workers, and travelers—offers instant access to key words and phrases in a pocket-sized volume. The phrasebook covers topics like introductions, accommodations, shopping, and dining out and a concise grammar section provides an overview of the language.

- 4,000 dictionary entries
- Simple phonetics for all Bengali words
- An introduction to the Bengali alphabet
- A basic pronunciation guide

ISBN: 978-0-7818-1252-8· $14.95pb

Bengali-English/English-Bengali Practical Dictionary

With current vocabulary and usage, this is the most up-to-date and comprehensive two-way Bengali dictionary available on the market. Designed to facilitate translation and understanding for speakers of either Bengali (Bangla) or English, this dictionary is an ideal reference for learners of Bengali (Bangla) or English as a foreign language, business people, NGO workers, and travelers.

- More than 13,000 total entries
- Each entry includes a transliteration, word class information, and pronunciation aid
- Alphabet and pronunciation key
- Concise grammar of the language

ISBN 978-0-7818-1252-8 · $24.95pb

Prices subject to change without prior notice. **To purchase Hippocrene Books** contact your local bookstore or visit www.hippocrenebooks.com.